Y0-DOV-714

Third Sector Research

Rupert Taylor
Editor

Third Sector Research

Published in cooperation with the International Society
for Third Sector Research

 Springer

Editor
Rupert Taylor
Department of Political Studies
School of Social Sciences
University of Witwatersrand
WITS 2050
Johannesburg
Gauteng
South Africa
rupert_taylor@yahoo.com

ISBN 978-1-4419-5706-1   e-ISBN 978-1-4419-5707-8
DOI 10.1007/978-1-4419-5707-8
Springer New York Dordrecht Heidelberg London

Library of Congress Control Number: 2010921285

Printed on acid-free paper

Springer is part of Springer Science+Business Media (www.springer.com)

Contents

Contributors

Patrick Bond Centre for Civil Society, University of KwaZulu-Natal, Durban, South Africa

Jacqueline Butcher Centro Mexicano para la Filantropia (CEMEFI), Mexico City, Mexico

Ram A. Cnaan University of Pennsylvania, Philadelphia, USA

Olaf Corry University of Cambridge, UK

Freda Donoghue Trinity College Dublin, Ireland

Angela M. Eikenberry University of Nebraska at Omaha, Omaha, USA

Stephen Elstub University of West Scotland, Paisley, Scotland, UK

Alan Fowler Erasmus University, The Hague, The Netherlands and University of KwaZulu Natal, Durban, South Africa

Brenda Gainer York University, Toronto, Canada

Femida Handy University of Pennsylvania, Philadelphia, USA

Jenny Harrow City University London, UK

Bernd Helmig University of Mannheim, Germany

Lesley Hustinx Catholic University of Lueven, Lueven, Belgium

Ashwani Kumar Tata Institute of Social Sciences, Mumbai, India

Vicky Lambert University of Edinburgh, Scotland, UK

Irvine Lapsley University of Edinburgh, Scotland, UK

Håkon Lorentzen Institutt for Samfunnsforskning, Oslo, Norway

Laurie Mook University of Toronto, Canada

Ronaldo Munck Dublin City University, Ireland

Jonathan Murphy Cardiff University, Wales, UK

Patricia Mooney Nickel Victoria University of Wellington, New Zealand

Per Selle University of Bergen, Norway

Marilyn Taylor University of West England, Bristol, UK

Rupert Taylor University of the Witwatersrand, Johannesburg, South Africa

Julia Thaler University of Mannheim, Germany

Vanessa Timmer University of British Columbia, Vancouver, Canada

Isabel Vidal Centro de Investigacion de Economia y Sociedad (CIES), Barcelona, Spain

Dag Wollebæk Institutt for Sammenliknende Politikk, University of Bergen, Norway

Annette Zimmer Westfälische Wilhelms-Universität, Münster, Germany

Abbreviations

AMA	American Marketing Association
CAF	Charities Aid Foundation
CEO	Chief Executive Officer
CSI	Civil Society Index
CSO	Civil Society Organization
CRM	Cause-Related Marketing
CSR	Corporate Social Responsibility
DFID	Department for International Development (UK)
ENSAV	Encuesta Nacional de Solidaridad y Acción Voluntaria (Mexico)
ESS	European Social Survey
EU	European Union
EVAS	Expanded Value Added Statement
GCS	Global Civil Society
GRI	Global Reporting Initiative
ICNPO	International Classification of Nonprofit Organizations
ILO	International Labour Organization
IMF	International Monetary Fund
INGO	International Nongovernmental Organization
ISTR	International Society for Third Sector Research
JHCNP	The Johns Hopkins Comparative Nonprofit Sector Project
MDGs	Millennium Development Goals
NGO	Nongovernmental Organization

NPO   Nonprofit Organization

OECD   Organization for Economic Co-operation and Development

TI   Transparency International

TSO   Third Sector Organization

UN   United Nations

UNDP   United Nations Development Program

UNEP   United Nations Environment Program

WSF   World Social Forum

WTO   World Trade Organization

WWF   World Wildlife Fund for Nature

About the Authors

Patrick Bond is Director of the Centre for Civil Society at the University of KwaZulu-Natal, Durban, South Africa. His areas of research focus include political economy, environment (energy, water, and climate change), and social policy and geopolitics. His books include *Against Global Apartheid* (2003, Zed, 2nd edn) and *Looting Africa: The Economics of Exploitation* (2006, Zed).

Jacqueline Butcher is Adjunct Professor at the Universidad Iberoamericana, Sta. Fe, Mexico City, in the Department of Psychology and Human Development. She is an advisor on civil society issues to the First Lady of Mexico, Margarita Zavala, and is President of the Board of Directors of the Centro Mexicano para la Filantropía. She is editor of *Mexican Solidarity, Citizen Participation and Volunteering* (2009, Springer).

Ram A. Cnaan is a Professor and Associate Dean for Research and Doctoral Education at the University of Pennsylvania School of Social Policy and Practice. He is also the President of ARNOVA (Association for Research on Nonprofit Organizations and Voluntary Associations).

Olaf Corry is currently a post-doctoral scholar at The Centre of International Studies at Cambridge University and Research Associate at Jesus College, Cambridge. His Ph.D. from the University of Copenhagen was on the repercussions of protests at global summits and the emergence of a global polity. He is author of *Theory of Global Polity* (forthcoming, Palgrave).

Freda Donoghue is Senior Research Fellow, Centre for Nonprofit Management, School of Business, Trinity College Dublin, Ireland. Her research interests include quantifying the size and scope of Irish nonprofit organizations, philanthropy, volunteering, and the relationship between the state and nonprofit organizations.

Angela M. Eikenberry is an Assistant Professor in the School of Public Administration at the University of Nebraska at Omaha. Her research interests include voluntary associations, nonprofit organizations, and philanthropy and their role in democratic governance. She is author of *Giving Circles: Philanthropy, Voluntary Association, and Democracy* (2009, Indiana University Press).

Stephen Elstub is Lecturer in Politics at the University of the West of Scotland. His research interests relate to civil society, democratic governance, and particularly deliberative democracy. He is the author of *Towards a Deliberative and Associational Democracy* (2008, Edinburgh University Press).

Alan Fowler is an academic practitioner, holding professorial appointments at Erasmus University in The Netherlands and the University of KwaZulu-Natal in South Africa. He was an elected member and Chairman (2001–2007) of the program sub-committee of the Civicus Board and is a former President of the International Society for Third Sector Research.

Brenda Gainer is the Royal Bank Professor of Nonprofit Management at York University. Her research interests focus on nonprofit marketing and management; she teaches in the areas of marketing, resource development, and social entrepreneurship. She is President-Elect of the International Society for Third Sector Research.

Femida Handy is Professor at the School of Social Policy and Practice at the University of Pennsylvania, Philadelphia. Her research focuses on the economics of nonprofit organizations and volunteering. She is the co-author of *Grass-roots NGOs by Women for Women: The Driving Force of Development in India* (2006, Sage) and *From Sewa to Cyberspace: The Changing Face of Volunteering in India* (forthcoming, Sage).

Jenny Harrow is Professor of Voluntary Sector Management and Co-Director of the ESRC Research Centre for Charitable Giving and Philanthropy at Cass Business School, City University London, UK. Her research is focused on voluntary/public sector partnerships, sectoral management development, program evaluation, and trusteeship. She is an active trustee in the fields of disability and community action.

Bernd Helmig is Professor of Management and holds the Chair for Business Administration, Public and Nonprofit Management at the University of Mannheim, Germany. He is also Associate Dean for International Relations and Academic Director at Mannheim Business School.

Lesley Hustinx is a Postdoctoral Fellow of the Research Foundation, Flanders, at the Centre for Sociological Research, Katholieke Universiteit Leuven, Belgium. Her research focuses on the changing nature of civil society and civic engagement in late modernity and has appeared in *Nonprofit and Voluntary Sector Quarterly*, *Voluntas*, *Journal of Civil Society*, *Social Service Review*, and *British Journal of Sociology of Education*.

Ashwani Kumar is Associate Professor at the Tata Institute of Social Sciences, Mumbai. He is author of *Community Warriors: State, Peasants and Caste Armies in Bihar* (2008, Anthem Press) and co-editor of *Global Governance* (2009, Anthem Press). He has been a visiting fellow at the Centre for the Study of Global Governance at the London School of Economics and at the German Development Institute (Bonn).

Vicky Lambert is a doctoral student, researching Governance in Charities within the Institute of Public Sector Accounting Research (IPSAR), at the University of Edinburgh Business School, Scotland. She is also a research assistant at Queen Margaret University, Edinburgh, investigating leadership in community nursing.

Irvine Lapsley is Professor of Accounting and Director of IPSAR (Institute of Public Sector Accounting Research), University of Edinburgh Business School, Scotland. He is editor of *Financial Accountability and Management* and co-chair of the EIASM (European Institute for Advanced Studies in Management) Third Sector research workshop.

Håkon Lorentzen is Senior Researcher at the Institute for Social Research, Oslo, Norway, and Associate Professor at Norwegian School of Theology in Oslo. He has published in the area of civil society and modernization, most recently *Fellesskapets Fundament* (*The Foundation of Fellowship*, 2004, Pax) and *Moraldannende Kretsløp* (*Circuits of Morality*, 2007, Abstrakt).

Laurie Mook is Director of the Social Economy Centre at the University of Toronto, Canada. She is co-author of *What Counts: Social Accounting for Nonprofits and Cooperatives* (2007, 2nd edn, Sigel Press) and *Understanding the Social Economy: A Canadian Perspective* (2010, University of Toronto Press). Her research focuses on social and environmental accounting, social economy organizations, and volunteerism.

Ronaldo Munck is theme leader for internationalization, interculturalism, and social development in the President's Office of Dublin City University and Visiting Professor of Sociology at the University of Liverpool. He has written widely on globalization and social transformation, and his most recent book is *Globalization and Security: An Encyclopaedia* (2009, Praeger Security International).

Jonathan Murphy has spent 25 years as a third sector manager and international development consultant in Africa, Asia, and North America. He is author of *The World Bank and Global Managerialism* (2008, Routledge). He currently teaches international management at Cardiff University, Wales, UK.

Patricia Mooney Nickel is a Lecturer in the School of Social and Cultural Studies at Victoria University of Wellington, New Zealand. Her main research interests include critical social theory, the nonprofit sector and philanthropy, political economy of academic publishing, theories of the state and civil society, and globalization.

Per Selle is Professor of Political Science at the Department of Comparative Politics, University of Bergen, Norway. He is co-editor of *Government and Voluntary Organizations: A Relational Perspective* (1992, Avebury) and co-author of *Unique Environmentalism: A Comparative Perspective* (2006, Springer).

Marilyn Taylor is Emeritus Professor of Urban Governance and Regeneration at the University of the West of England, Bristol, and Visiting Research Fellow at the Institute of Voluntary Action Research, London. Her research interests include community participation and empowerment, democratic renewal, and neighborhood regeneration. She is author of *Public Policy in the Community* (2003, Palgrave Macmillan).

Rupert Taylor is Associate Professor of Politics at the University of the Witwatersrand, Johannesburg, South Africa. He is editor of *Creating a Better World: Interpreting Global Civil Society* (2004, Kumarian) and *Consociational Theory: McGarry and O'Leary and the Northern Ireland Conflict* (2009, Routledge) and was editor-in-chief of *Voluntas* from 2001 to 2009.

Julia Thaler is a doctoral student as well as teaching and research assistant at the Public and Nonprofit Management program at the University of Mannheim, Germany.

Vanessa Timmer is a Postdoctoral Research Fellow at the University of British Columbia, Vancouver, Canada. Her areas of research include sustainability, civil society, systems theory, and global environmental governance. She is Director of the One Earth Initiative, a nonprofit research and advocacy group focused on transforming unsustainable consumption and production patterns.

Isabel Vidal is Professor of the Department of Economic Theory at the University of Barcelona and President of CIES. Since 1994 she has been academic director of the master's program in social economy and nonprofit organizations at the University of Barcelona. Her fields of research interest are cooperatives, nonprofit organizations, and corporate social responsibility.

Dag Wollebæk is a researcher at the Rokkan Centre, University of Bergen, Norway. He is the author of many articles on voluntary associations, social capital, and organizational theory, publishing in such journals as *Journal of Civil Society*, *Nonprofit Management and Leadership*, *Nonprofit and Voluntary Sector Quarterly*, *Scandinavian Political Studies*, and *Voluntas*.

Annette Zimmer is Professor of Social Policy and Comparative Politics at the Institute for Political Science at the University of Münster, Germany. She is a member of the Board of the German Political Science Association (DVPW) and of the Executive Board of the International Society for Third Sector Research. She is co-author of *Strategy Mix for Nonprofit Organisations* (2004, Kluwer).

Chapter 1
Moving Beyond Empirical Theory

Rupert Taylor

The Rise of Third Sector Research

As *Voluntas: International Journal of Nonprofit and Voluntary Organizations* – a journal for which I have been the fifth and longest-serving editor – now enters its third decade of publication, the time seems good to assess the state of the field of third sector research and to ask how far it has come and where it is going. By now, it is generally accepted that the term "third sector" stands as a "catch-all" term for "the organizational universe that emerges in many societies between government and the market" (Wagner 2002, p. 51; Gidron 2002). More specifically, the third sector can – following Salamon and Anheier (1992a,b) – be defined with respect to five structural and operational features: it is organized, private (i.e., institutionally separate from government), self-governing, nonprofit distributing, and noncompulsory. To date, the central task for scholars working in the field has been to delineate the composition, scope, and structure of the third sector and to map the field, first nationally and then – with the impetus of *Voluntas*, The Johns Hopkins Comparative Nonprofit Sector Project, and the International Society for Third Sector Research (ISTR) – cross-nationally and globally. All told, it is incontrovertible that there has been a dramatic rise in research in this regard.

The rise of third sector research can be illustrated in a number of ways. Most prominent is the rapid global expansion in academic centers and graduate degree programs dedicated to nonprofit management, voluntary organizations, and philanthropy (Brudney and Herman 2004). In the United States the Yale Program on Nonprofit Organizations and Philanthropy, Indiana University's Center on Philanthropy, and the Center for the Study of Philanthropy at the City University of New York have all risen to gain international repute. Moreover, the number and stature of academic journals publishing in the field have grown; alongside *Voluntas* stand the *Annals for Public and Cooperative Economics*, *Nonprofit Management and Leadership*, *Journal for Nonprofit and Public Sector Marketing*, *Nonprofit*

R. Taylor (✉)
University of the Witwatersrand, Johannesburg, South Africa
e-mail: rupert_taylor@yahoo.com

R. Taylor (ed.), *Third Sector Research*, DOI 10.1007/978-1-4419-5707-8_1,
© Springer Science+Business Media, LLC 2010

Quarterly, and *Nonprofit and Voluntary Sector Quarterly* (*NVSQ*). In particular, the ever-increasing number of *Voluntas* paper downloads from the Internet is marked. Downloads to the journal have increased by almost 800% since 2002, the first year the journal was available online.

These developments not only are about sheer quantity, but also reflect the quality of third sector scholarship and the strength of its theoretical foundations as laid down in the field's formative years, the mid- to late 1970s. From modest beginnings, scholars working in the realms of neoclassical economic theory at a number of prestigious American universities applied demand- and supply-side theories pertaining, respectively, to the role and behavior of nonprofit organizations. Such studies, initially focused on the hospital industry (e.g., Newhouse 1970), have mushroomed into a wide range of empirically driven case studies, and the field now boasts a number of leading scholars with international reputations. Foremost, the publications of Burton Weisbrod, Henry Hansmann, Lester Salamon, and Helmut Anheier have largely defined the field.[1] Weisbrod's (1991) *The Nonprofit Economy*, Hansmann's (1980) paper on "The role of nonprofit enterprise," Salamon's (1999) primer on *America's Nonprofit Sector*, Salamon and Anheier's (1997) *Defining the Nonprofit Sector: A Cross-National Analysis*, and Salamon et al.'s two-volume (1999, 2004) *Global Civil Society* have attracted acclaim as key works and have between them accumulated more than 3,000 academic citations (Google "Advanced Scholar" search).

Theorizing the Third Sector

In *The Nonprofit Sector: A Research Handbook*, now in its second edition, the leading third sector scholars have contributed to what is a definitive text.[2] Here, nonprofit and voluntary organizations as providers of education, health, and social services are characterized as being "precluded, by external regulation or [their] own governance structure, from distributing [their] financial surplus to those who control the use of organizational assets" (Steinberg and Powell 2006, p. 1). And it is this "nondistributional constraint" that underpins theorizing as to why nonprofit organizations have emerged: they do so; it is maintained, in response to market or state failure. Consequently, the "public goods" theory (Weisbrod 1975, 1977) argues that nonprofits come into being to provide public goods and services for those areas that are less preferred or too contentious for public agencies. Complementary to this, the "contract failure" theory maintains that since the nondistributional constraint removes any incentive to maximize profits, consumers come to place greater "trustworthiness" in nonprofits that provide services in areas – such as health care – where

---

[1] See, in particular, Weisbrod (1975, 1977, 1991, 1998), Hansmann (1980, 1987), Salamon (1994, 1995, 1999), Salamon et al. (1999, 2004), and Salamon and Anheier (1996, 1997, 1998).

[2] The first edition was edited by Walter W. Powell and published in 1987; the second edition was edited by Walter W. Powell and Richard Steinberg and published in 2006.

they find it hard to reach rational judgment about quality or performance (Hansmann 1980). Not only have questions as to how the nondistribution constraint affects non-profit behavior been explored, tested, and developed in case-by-case studies, but from such starting points much concern has been directed to empirically mapping typologies in terms of such factors as income source and organizational structure.

While not disputing the high quality of such formative work and its relevance for governmental policy-making, it is true to say that by the late 1980s a growing sense of intellectual disquiet had begun to develop; concern being directed toward the limited amount of comparative research being conducted and the lack of more general theoretical advance. Anheier and Ben-Ner, for example, writing in 1997 (pp. 94–96) viewed the period since the mid-1980s as having been one of theoretical "refinements and elaborations" and go on to use the term "theoretical inertia." Precisely to reinvigorate third sector research, Helmut Anheier in his role as a founding editor of *Voluntas* sought to encourage the generation of cross-national data and concepts (Anheier 2002), and ISTR was expressly founded as a network organization "to encourage and expand high-quality comparative international research" (www.istr.org).

Leading the way in the endeavor to systematically study, map, and standardize cross-national and global patterns has been The Johns Hopkins Comparative Nonprofit Sector Project: a large-scale collaborative research undertaken in some 40 countries (Salamon et al. 1999, 2004). As this work progressed, it was found that the existing theoretical tools, formulated for the American context, did not travel well when set against the cross-national patterns that were uncovered. Finding established theories unable to explain cross-national variation in patterns of third sector development, Salamon and Anheier (1998) – in what is one of the most cited *Voluntas* papers – followed a form of inductive enumeration to connect the varying structure of the nonprofit sector to differing historical path-dependent patterns of nonprofit–government and nonprofit–society relations.[3] In this "social origins" theory, four "nonprofit regime types" are identified – liberal, social democratic, statist, and corporatist – and as with other third sector theorizing, this approach has led to many, and on the whole confirming, case studies.

While The Johns Hopkins Project has seen itself as being global in scope, it has nonetheless taken the nation-state as its unit of analysis. Given, however, what Lester Salamon (1994) has termed "the global associational revolution" and the fast-growing number of international NGOs working across and beyond borders, a truly post-national global perspective and process of mapping had to be initiated – as most notably with the London School of Economics (LSE) Global Civil Society initiative and their *Global Civil Society Yearbook*. Here, concern has primarily been directed to territorially map the domain of global civil society on the grounds that "the normative content is too contested to be able to form the basis for an operationalisation of the concept" (Anheier et al. 2001, p. 17). Also, alongside this comparative

---

[3]This paper, "Social origins of civil society: Explaining the nonprofit sector cross-nationally," according to Google "Advanced Scholar" has been cited over 250 times.

and internationally focused work, a stream of neo-Tocquevillian studies has arisen from political science scholars who have focused on how nonprofit and voluntary organizations, cast as "civil society," contribute to good citizenship through creating "social capital," a foundational text here being Putnam et al.'s (1993) *Making Democracy Work: Traditions in Modern Italy* (see also Putnam 2000).

Despite these most recent developments and a continuing plethora of case study research to test the breadth and consistency of third sector theory,[4] most scholars would still admit that the field remains comparatively under-theorized. Theory and analysis seem to lag behind what is happening on the ground, with middle-range theory-building – as with social origins theory – representing best practice. It is certainly true to say that *no* "single" or mono-causal theory has "come to dominate the field" (Anheier and Salamon 2006, p. 103). That said, the field *is* dominated by a particular understanding of what constitutes theorizing; third sector research is centered on the privileged set of American-based texts discussed herein, all of which are epistemologically tied to empirical theory – the consequences of which bear critical scrutiny.

Third Sector Research as Empirical Theory

In respecting the distinction between "facts" and "values" when it comes to framing analysis, in taking the social system – as it is – as the unit of investigation, and in shying away from engagement with substantive moral obligations and concerns, third sector research upholds and represents empirical theory. It is this very conception of "theory" that requires far more attention than it has hitherto been given – particularly with regard to how empirical enquiry stands in relation to political theory.

All the third sector studies cited above are committed to empirical theory, where, simply stated, theory-building is seen as a particular way of executing scientific inquiry concerned with the making of well-founded empirical generalizations within a hypothetical framework that holds both explanatory power and predictive capacity, set apart from philosophy and ideology (Jackson 1972; Ricci 1984). Here, empirical findings are incorporated into new conceptual and explanatory schemes, wherein social action is "objectified" and scientifically studied through rigorously constructed categories of instrumental rationality relating to the choice of means and selection of ends (Weber 1949). The focus is on explaining what *is* rather than considering what *ought* to be.

Outwardly, all this may appear all well and good, but the problem is that by adopting a value-neutral approach that sets out to provide an empirically based account of the third sector as it is, researchers commit a double error. One, it is pretense to believe that third sector research is itself free of normative commitment; the "third

---

[4]To date, the typical *Voluntas* paper has been of the empirically driven case study variety; see Hodgkinson and Painter (2003).

sector" is presented in neutral terms, but third sector research is actually laden with its own political values. Two, it is misguided to believe that social science can best progress through separating empirical understanding from explicit moral and political theorizing (Gerring and Yesnowitz 2006), for, in truth, any "adequate social and political theory must be *empirical, interpretative,* and *critical*" (Bernstein 1979, p. 235).

Whether one takes Powell and Steinberg's nonprofit *Research Handbook,* The Johns Hopkins Project, or the LSE global civil society initiative, the third sector is unequivocally seen in non-normative terms. And *yet* all these approaches, including those pertaining to social capital, actually rest on forms of empirical political theory that take the "good" principles of a market economy and liberal democracy as given. The market model of democracy (Buchanan and Tullock 1962; Olson 1965) underpins the mainstream economic theories of nonprofit and voluntary organizations, while those scholars who focus on how the associational life of the third sector promotes social capital to make "democracy work" do so within terms of a pluralist model of democracy (Dahl 1982; Putnam et al. 1993). Take, for instance, one of the key foundational texts for third sector theorizing, James Buchanan and Gordon Tullock's (1962) *The Calculus of Consent,* which from the starting premise that we "must take men as they are, not as [we] would like them to be" (p. 311) proceeds to apply the utilitarian, rational type of behavior and exchange processes underpinning a market economy to the political realm so as to explain when nonprofit and voluntary organizations occur to deal with externalities.[5]

The critique of market and pluralist models of democracy is that they rest upon a rather hollow image of "man" and society (Dallmayr 1970), project a limited horizon of political action and vision (Ricci 1984), and are intrinsically contained within the shell of a sovereign territorially defined economic community, the nation-state (Kuper 2004). And while it might be thought that the political imagery projected by third sector research is relatively benign, it is not. Transposed to the international level, the main motifs of individual rights, a market economy, and liberal pluralism, serve to rationalize the interests of the American nation. It is undoubtedly going too far to argue, as Roelofs (1995) does, that the US nonprofit sector "has attempted to create an entire world in its own image," but third sector research is semantically American and does advance a historicist understanding of its democratic designs as representing "civilized" progress to be emulated by developing and formerly socialist states (Clemens 2006; Vogel 2006).

What all this comes down to then is that the very context and meaning of the third sector cannot be described independently of normative considerations and those that mainstream research presume and infer are – due to epistemological predilections – intellectually weak. In consequence, third sector research has failed to give due consideration to how social injustice, economic inequality, and political exclusion are produced and reproduced by the way things *are*; to interpreting the subjective meaning of third sector organizations; and to probing how things could be *other*

---

[5]On the foundational importance of this text, see further Douglas (1987) and Clemens (2006).

than they are by analyzing "the possibilities of radical, innovative and normatively informed political change" (Stears 2005, p. 331). Beyond the blinkers of existing empirical theory, such possibilities are, though, already in view.

Beyond Empirical Theory

Contrary to the non-normative mantra, there is critical intent within the third sector to articulate and actualize a more emancipatory democratic politics (Edwards 2004; Najam 1996). Moreover, transformative possibilities with respect to the third sector are occurring in a number of ways: notably, with respect to its formal structure, with regard to new methods of governance, and with the rise of a global civil society. In each case, mainstream theorizing can be found wanting, precisely because its specific reading of the relation between empirical and normative political theory blocks comprehension as to how the dialectic of new organizational forms and social relations pushes the meaning of democracy beyond existing domain assumptions.

Even in its own terms, mainstream third sector research is – in the context of growing multidimensionality, hybridization, and complexity – beginning to unravel and thereby expose the limits of existing theory-building attempts.[6] In particular, the rise of market neoliberalism has seen an increasing reliance placed on third sector partnerships with government and business, and with the increasing convergence and blurring of boundaries between the state, market, and third sector, there is real reason to challenge the appropriateness both of a tri-sectoral model of society and of ever achieving international standardization of the field. All the more so, when due recognition is given to the "social economy" research tradition found in a number of European countries – France, Belgium, Italy, Spain, and Portugal – a tradition that has long emphasized sectoral convergence (Evers and Laville 2004).

More than this, a strict adherence to market and pluralist models of democracy, with their inherent acceptance of the centrality of the nation-state, no longer seems credible when set against the rise of new types of governance and a new globalized environment. In the last decade or so there has been a significant de-centering of the nation-state (Ellison 1997), such that its traditional status as *the* sovereign political unit has come under threat in two main regards: first, with a shift from government to governance, and second, with the rise of global civil society.

Governance has arisen as a "*new* method by which society is governed" (Rhodes 1996, pp. 652–653). Specifically, it is marked by "the development of governing styles in which [the] boundaries between and within public and private sectors" become increasingly interdependent and blurred (Stoker 1998, p. 17) and in which ideas of New Public Management, "joined-up" government, and partnership structures have taken hold. Governance represents a shift from formal hierarchically organized systems to more fragmented and horizontally organized networks of

---

[6] As also witnessed in the search for new theoretical insight from fields such as neo-institutionalism and systems theory, see Kramer (2000).

authority that operate above and below the level of the nation-state – all told, it has significantly broadened the scope for nongovernmental and philanthropic action (Beck 1997).

Much the same can be said for the rise of global civil society. Given that the very distinctiveness of global civil society is that it transcends the boundaries of the nation-state and is driven by explicit normative concerns, it is not perhaps surprising that there have been serious problems in trying to correctly theorize the phenomenon (Corry 2006; Taylor 2002). Global civil society has, though, to be interpreted in terms of its intrinsic meaning and critical intent, namely, that of promoting a cosmopolitan identity politics and ethics that centers on "the oneness of humanity," the equality of all people, and "the idea that we have obligations to others, obligations that stretch beyond those to whom we are related by the ties of kith and kind" (Appiah 2006, pp. xiv–xv; see also Nussbaum 1994). Progressive campaigns around such issues as human rights, environmentalism, and North–South economic inequality have emerged to further global justice (Khagram et al. 2002; Taylor 2004) – to some degree coming together and being further energized at meetings of the World Social Forum.

Taken together the transformative potential of these developments does lead to and require one to critically reinterpret the meaning of the third sector today. The configuration of new governance networks and disaggregation of national sovereignty signify the need for new post-empirical theorizing beyond the state, market, and third sector as traditionally understood.[7] In looking at the contemporary meaning of democracy, Alain Touraine is of the view that by and large "we now see ourselves as living in consumer societies" in which "the existence of social actors and the ability to think about society" have "been weakened" (Touraine 1997, p. 190). It is indisputable that third sector research as empirical theory has been and is implicated in the marketization of democracy, but appropriately reformulated through a turn to more explicit normative theorizing, it can be the source of new critique. This, fittingly, is the central theme conveyed in the chapters that follow.

References

Anheier, H. K. (2002). *Voluntas*: The early years. In ISTR *Celebrating ISTR's Tenth Anniversary* (pp. 25–33), International Society for Third-Sector Research.

Anheier, H. K., and Ben-Ner, A. (1997). Economic theories of non-profit organisations: A *Voluntas* symposium. *Voluntas*, 8(2), 93–96.

Anheier, H., Glasius, M., and Kaldor, M. (2001). Introducing global civil society. In H. Anheier, M. Glasius, and M. Kaldor (eds) *Global Civil Society Yearbook* (pp. 5–27), Oxford, Oxford University Press.

Anheier, H. K., and Salamon, L. M. (2006). The nonprofit sector in comparative perspective. In W. W. Powell and R. Steinberg (eds) *The Nonprofit Sector: A Research Handbook*, 2nd edn (pp. 89–114), New Haven, Yale University Press.

---

[7] See further, Sørensen and Torfing (2005); also consider the development of deliberative democratic theory (Dryzek 2000).

Appiah, K. A. (2006). *Cosmopolitanism: Ethics in a World of Strangers*, London, Penguin.

Beck, U. (1997). *The Reinvention of Politics: Rethinking Modernity in the Global Social Order*, Stanford, CA, Polity Press.

Bernstein, R. J. (1979). *The Restructuring of Social and Political Theory*, London, Methuen.

Brudney, J. L., and Herman, R. D. (2004). Readers' perceptions of philanthropy and nonprofit management journals. *American Review of Public Administration*, 34(3), 293–301.

Buchanan, J. M., and Tullock, G. (1962). *The Calculus of Consent: Logical Foundations of Constitutional Democracy*, Ann Arbor, University of Michigan Press.

Clemens, E. S. (2006). The constitution of citizens: Political theories of nonprofit organizations. In W. W. Powell and R. Steinberg (eds) *The Nonprofit Sector: A Research Handbook* (pp. 207–220), New Haven, Yale University Press.

Corry, T. O. (2006). Global civil society and its discontents. *Voluntas*, 17(4), 303–324.

Dahl, R. (1982). *Dilemmas of Pluralist Democracy*, New Haven, Yale University Press.

Dallmayr, F. R. (1970). Empirical political theory & the Image of Man. *Polity*, 2(4), 443–478.

Douglas, J. (1987). Political theories of nonprofit organizations. In W. W. Powell (ed.) *The Nonprofit Sector: A Research Handbook*, 1st edn (pp. 43–54), New Haven, Yale University Press.

Dryzek, J. S. (2000). *Deliberative Democracy and Beyond: Liberals, Critics, Contestations*, Oxford, Oxford University Press.

Edwards, M. (2004). *Civil Society*, Cambridge, Polity Press.

Ellison, N. (1997). Towards a new social politics: Citizenship and reflexivity in late modernity. *Sociology*, 31(4), 697–717.

Evers, A., and Laville, J. -L. (2004). *The Third Sector in Europe*, Cheltenham, Edward Elgar.

Gerring, J., and Yesnowitz, J. (2006). A normative turn in political science? *Polity*, 38(1), 101–133.

Gidron, B. B. (2002). Intellectual challenges during the first phase of ISTR's development. In ISTR *Celebrating ISTR's Tenth Anniversary* (pp. 43–46), International Society for Third-Sector Research.

Hansmann, H. (1980). The role of nonprofit enterprise. *Yale Law Journal*, 89, 835–901.

Hansmann, H. (1987). Economic theories of nonprofit organization. In W. W. Powell (ed.) *The Nonprofit Sector: A Research Handbook*, 1st edn (pp. 27–42), New Haven, Yale University Press.

Hodgkinson, V., and Painter, A. (2003). Third sector research in international perspective: The role of ISTR. *Voluntas*, 14(1), 1–14.

Jackson, M. W. (1972). The application of method in the construction of political science theory. *Canadian Journal of Political Science*, 5(3), 402–417.

Khagram, S., Riker, J. V., and Sikkink, K. (eds) (2002). *Restructuring World Politics: Transnational Social Movements, Networks, and Norms*, Minneapolis, University of Minnesota Press.

Kramer, R. M. (2000). A third sector in the Third Millennium. *Voluntas*, 11(1), 1–23.

Kuper, A. (2004). *Democracy Beyond Borders: Justice and Representation in Global Institutions*, Oxford, Oxford University Press.

Najam, A. (1996). Understanding the third sector: Revisiting the prince, the merchant, and the citizen. *Nonprofit Management & Leadership*, 7(2), 203–219.

Newhouse, J. P. (1970). Toward a theory on nonprofit institutions: An economic model of a hospital. *American Economic Review*, 60(1), 64–74.

Nussbaum, M. (1994). Patriotism and cosmopolitanism. *The Boston Review*, available online, www.soci.niu.edu/~phildept/Kapitan/nussbaum1.html

Olson, M. (1965). *The Logic of Collective Action*, Cambridge, MA, Harvard University Press.

Powell, W. W. (ed.) (1987). *The Nonprofit Sector: A Research Handbook*, 1st edn, New Haven, Yale University Press.

Powell, W. W., and Steinberg, R. (eds) (2006). *The Nonprofit Sector: A Research Handbook*, 2nd edn, New Haven, Yale University Press.

Putnam, R. D. (2000). *Bowling Alone: The Collapse and Revival of American Community*, New York, Simon and Schuster.

Putnam, R. D., Leonardi, R., and Nanetti, R. Y. (1993). *Making Democracy Work: Traditions in Modern Italy*, Princeton, NJ, Princeton University Press.

Rhodes, R. A. W. (1996). The new governance: Governing without government. *Political Studies*, 44(4), 652–667.

Ricci, D. M. (1984). *The Tragedy of Political Science: Politics, Scholarship, and Democracy*, New Haven, Yale University Press.

Roelofs, J. (1995). The third sector as a protective layer for capitalism. *Monthly Review*, 47(4), available online, www.monthlyreview.org

Salamon, L. M. (1994). The rise of the nonprofit sector. *Foreign Affairs*, 73(4), 109–122.

Salamon, L. M. (1995). *Partners in Public Service: Government–Nonprofit Relations in the Modern Welfare State*, Baltimore, MD, Johns Hopkins University Press.

Salamon, L. M. (1999). *America's Nonprofit Sector: A Primer*, 2nd edn, New York, The Foundation Center.

Salamon, L. M., and Anheier, H. K. (1992a). In search of the non-profit sector. I: The question of definitions. *Voluntas*, 3(2), 125–151.

Salamon, L. M., and Anheier, H. K. (1992b). In search of the non-profit sector. II: The international classification of non-profit organisations: A framework for analysis. *Voluntas*, 3(3), 267–309.

Salamon, L. M., and Anheier, H. K. (1996). *The Emerging Nonprofit Sector: An Overview*, Manchester, Manchester University Press.

Salamon, L. M., and Anheier, H. K. (1997). *Defining the Nonprofit Sector: A Cross-National Analysis*, Manchester, Manchester University Press.

Salamon, L. M., and Anheier, H. K. (1998). Social origins of civil society: Explaining the nonprofit sector cross-nationally. *Voluntas*, 9(3), 213–248.

Salamon, L. M., List, R., Sokolowski, S. W., Toepler, S., and Anheier, H. K. (1999). *Global Civil Society: Dimensions of the Nonprofit Sector*, vol. 1, Bloomfield, CT, Kumarian Press.

Salamon, L. M., Sokolowski, S. W., et al. (eds) (2004). *Global Civil Society: Dimensions of the Nonprofit Sector*, vol. 2, Bloomfield, CT, Kumarian Press.

Sørensen, E., and Torfing, J. (2005). Network governance and post-liberal democracy. *Administrative Theory & Praxis*, 27(2), 197–237.

Stears, M. (2005). The vocation of political theory: Principles, empirical inquiry and the politics of opportunity. *European Journal of Political Theory*, 4(4), 325–350.

Steinberg, R., and Powell, W. W. (2006). Introduction. In W. W. Powell and R. Steinberg (eds) *The Nonprofit Sector: A Research Handbook*, 2nd edn (pp. 1–10), New Haven, Yale University Press.

Stoker, G. (1998). Governance as theory: Five propositions. *International Social Science Journal*, 155, 17–28.

Taylor, R. (2002). Interpreting global civil society. *Voluntas*, 13(4), 339–347.

Taylor, R. (ed.) (2004). *Creating a Better World: Interpreting Global Civil Society*, Bloomfield, CT, Kumarian Press.

Touraine, A. (1997). *What is Democracy?* Boulder, CO, Westview Press.

Vogel, A. (2006). Who's making global civil society: Philanthropy and US empire in world society. *British Journal of Sociology*, 57(4), 635–655.

Wagner, A. (2002). Creating a platform to negotiate meaning. In ISTR *Celebrating ISTR's Tenth Anniversary* (pp. 47–54), International Society for Third-Sector Research.

Weber, M. (1949). *The Methodology of the Social Sciences*, New York, Free Press.

Weisbrod, B. A. (1975). Toward a theory of the voluntary sector in a three-sector economy. In E. Phelps (ed.) *Altruism, Morality, and Economic Theory* (pp. 171–195), New York, Russell Sage Foundation.

Weisbrod, B. A. (1977). *The Voluntary Nonprofit Sector: An Economic Analysis*, Lexington, MA, Lexington Books.

Weisbrod, B. A. (1991). *The Nonprofit Economy*, Cambridge, MA, Harvard University Press.

Weisbrod, B. A. (ed.) (1998). *To Profit or Not to Profit: The Commercial Transformation of the Nonprofit Sector*, New York, Cambridge University Press.

Chapter 2
Defining and Theorizing the Third Sector

Olaf Corry

Introduction

According to some, the third sector is by nature unsuited to singular definitions (Osborne 2008), and it has famously been deemed a "loose and baggy monster" (Knapp and Kendal 1995). There are reasons of both substance and terminology for this pessimism. First, the "third sector," often closely associated with the idea of civil society and voluntarism (see Chapter 3 by Håkon Lorentzen, this volume), is often thought of as having non-system qualities. Unlike the state and the market economy, it is something that can scarcely be subjected to detailed planning or regulated without it loosing some of its third sector qualities such as voluntary participation, value-based motivation, and independence from more institutionalized power structures. This naturally makes generalization about it trickier. Second, the term "third" itself betrays the idea of the third sector as a residual category for things that do not fit into two other "primary" and "secondary" categories – usually the state and the market. Residual categories are naturally prone to becoming loose and baggy. In practice "third sector" is used to refer to widely differing kinds of organization such as charities, nongovernmental organizations (NGOs), self-help groups, social enterprises, networks, and clubs, to name a few that do not fall into the state or market categories. In fact, a case could be made to refer to it as the "fourth sector" since communitarian groups such as clans and families and informal associations are also often excluded from the idea of a third sector (Priller and Zimmer 2001).

However, even if less rigorous theorizing makes the third sector look "loose and baggy," the reality of the monster is rarely denied. The idea of third *sector* suggests that these entities, however diverse, together make up a coherent whole – a sector with its own distinct type of social form and practical logic. But whereas the state has "state theory" and the academic subject of public administration and

O. Corry (✉)
University of Cambridge, UK
e-mail: oc239@cam.ac.uk

R. Taylor (ed.), *Third Sector Research*, DOI 10.1007/978-1-4419-5707-8_2,
© Springer Science+Business Media, LLC 2010

comparative politics to theorize it, and the study of markets has its own highly prestigious scientific discipline of economics, the "third sector" remains comparatively under-theorized despite some good efforts to the contrary.

This chapter aims to present a brief overview of existing definitions and theorizations of the third sector. It divides them into two main categories. The first puts the emphasis on definitions, while the second comprises approaches that theorize. First, those who aim to define the third sector seek to understand it as a certain kind of institution (or group of actors) with specific "third sector" characteristics. These "ontological" definitions of the third sector offer differing views on what it is made up of and what is excluded from this category. This category can be subdivided into an American and a European view (though no neat geographical division exists). The former sees the third sector as a discrete sector characterized by certain qualities such as civility, whereas European theorists tend to take "the hybrid view" that views third sector organizations essentially as mixtures of other kinds of social organization such as private and public, or hierarchic and anarchic.

The second approach conceives of the third sector not as an object out there waiting to be authoritatively defined but as a kind of societal process. These "epistemological" approaches (so-called because they look at the kinds of knowledge that they depend upon) include a variety of perspectives too. A systems theory view sees the third sector as a particular form of communication between different societal systems facilitating certain activities while obstructing others. Discourse-theoretical accounts view it as a form of ordering of people and ideas (e.g., a "governmentality"). Finally, a critical communicative civil society view of it as a zone of dialogue or struggle between diverse actors and holders of institutional power.

If the former ontological approaches are interested in defining what things "are," charting out their existence and finding methodology to uncover the truth of their being, epistemological ones tend to be concerned with how things (structures, organizations, or identities) come to be made real, defined, and authorized, and how different perspectives generate different understandings of them. Studying something epistemologically means interrogating the lenses, vocabulary, and practices it relies upon for coherence (Åkerstøm 2003). An ontological approach to the third sector assumes its existence as a singular and meaningful category, defines it as clearly as possible, and then gets on with the job of investigating what it is, how big it is, perhaps what the causal relations between it and other sectors are, and so on. This has the advantage of simplicity, facilitating the massing of empirical and statistical data. On the other hand, the risk is that one perspective among many possible is privileged. As Jenei and Kuti note, "different disciplines (economics, sociology, political sciences) have different foci on third sector organisations" (2008, p. 13). Economists focus on the non-redistribution of wealth generated, and sociologists on the value-driven motivation of the participants. We can add that different social and geographical settings tend to lead to different analytical perspectives. Laying down one definition necessarily excludes other ways in which the third sector is understood and treated. For the epistemologist the point is that all of the different takes on the third sector exist at the same time in the necessarily messy social construction of the field of the third sector. An epistemological approach would therefore focus on how the third sector is generated, the position of observations that identify a third sector in a particular way, and what makes it possible to see such a thing in different ways.

Defining the Third Sector

Most ontological accounts of the third sector place it in relation to the state and the market. For Etzioni, who coined the term "the third sector" in 1973, in his "The third sector and domestic missions," it was an alternative sector separate from and balancing the state and the market, themselves considered separate sectors. If something is ruled neither primarily by market logic nor via a bureaucratic chain of command, it must be part of the "third" sector. Many current operational definitions follow this basic schema. For the British government, for example, "The term is used to distinguish such organisations from the other two sectors of the economy: the public sector ('government') and the private sector ('businesses')" (NAO 2009). According to a new textbook on social enterprises, a national economy can be conceptualized as having three sectors: the public sector, a private economy, and a third sector "with organisations established by people on a voluntary basis to pursue social or community goals" (Ridley-Duff and Seanor 2008, p. 1). This view is not restricted geographically to the United States – even though it has been widely associated strongly with researchers at The Johns Hopkins University in Baltimore, Maryland (Salamon and Anheier 1997).

Theorizing the third sector in this way usually goes beyond negative stipulations of non-state and not-for-profit. Without further criteria, a purely residual category remains dependent for conceptual coherence on the primary categories they "tidy up" for. This has led people to look for defining characteristics, as in the above textbook definition which adopts the idea of voluntary recruitment and the pursuit of social or community goals. For Etzioni the third sector is characterized by value-driven action and commitment from individuals operating within it. If the state ultimately achieves compliance via coercion and sanctions (or the threat of them) and market organizations work through rewards or remuneration (or the threat of incurring costs), a "third sector" exists without either of those two mechanisms instead relying on "the manipulation of symbolic rewards and deprivations, the power of persuasion and on appeals to shared values and idealism" (Lewis 2003, p. 328). Normative appeals and communicative rationality are considered dominant. In extension of this, for Salamon and Anheier, third sector organizations share five common characteristics:

Firstly they are *organized*, i.e., they possess some institutional reality. They are *private*, i.e., institutionally separate from government. They are *non-profit-distributing*, i.e., not returning any profits generated to their owners or directors. They are *self-governing*, i.e., equipped to control their own activities. They are *voluntary*, at least in part, i.e., they involve some meaningful degree of voluntary participation, either in the actual conduct of the agency's activities or in the management of its affairs. (Salamon and Anheier 1997, p. 9)

The first of the above criteria distinguishes third sector organizations from private or informal ones such as family or friendships (the above-mentioned "fourth sector"). The second and third represent the earlier mentioned non-state and non-market criteria. In an "American" context, this tends to mean that the organization does not allow the generation of wealth for redistribution to those who run the organization, thus excluding cooperatives or "the people's economy" (see below). The fourth refers to independence, again implicitly from state or market actors.

The final stipulation of voluntary participation reflects the fact that the third sector has many of its roots in ideas about "civil society." Before modern times, civil society referred to the idea of a society ruled by law as opposed to patronage or tradition. These were termed "civil societies" also with reference to virtues of citizenship associated with the rule of law and political society. Civil society was therefore at one stage closely related to the idea of the state itself and political society that governed and ordered a society. However, today the bureaucratic logic of command and control of the state and the depersonalizing force of (global) markets are considered incompatible with a rejuvenated conception of civil society that has advanced since emerging as a key concept in Eastern Europe in the 1980s and in global protests and movements during the 1990s and after the turn of the millennium (Kaldor 2003). Some of the civic virtues central to earlier conceptions live on in modern definitions such as non-violence, the pursuit of shared public interests, adherence to value-based rationality, and strong reliance on communicative power.

One example of the civil view of the third sector is that chosen by the Centre for Civil Society at the London School of Economics:

> Civil society refers to the arena of uncoerced collective action around shared interests, purposes and values. In theory, its institutional forms are distinct from those of the state, family and market, though in practice, the boundaries between state, civil society, family and market are often complex, blurred and negotiated. Civil society commonly embraces a diversity of spaces, actors and institutional forms, varying in their degree of formality, autonomy and power. Civil societies are often populated by organisations such as registered charities, development non-governmental organisations, community groups, women's organisations, faith-based organisations, professional associations, trades unions, self-help groups, social movements, business associations, coalitions and advocacy group. (Centre for Civil Society 2009)

The "uncoerced" properties imputed into civil society are particularly interesting since this associates coercion with both the state and markets. It refers not to a free-floating power-free situation but to being outside a system of hierarchic state control and freedom from a market-driven imperative to generate or keep surplus value. Third sector organizations are therefore usually considered organizations that obey the "non-distribution constraint" that exclusively allows reinvestment of profits and not their distribution among the members and/or the employees (Jenei and Kuti 2008, p. 12). "Social enterprises" – key components of a third sector – are defined as organizations or associations that explicitly exist to benefit a wider community rather than private owners and whose pursuit of profits are limited to the purpose of reinvesting to further the social aims of the organization. A greater emphasis on economic risk-taking marks these out from other kinds of third sector organizations such as the charity or the pressure group. But the stipulation that profits must be reinvested or distributed to a wider social purpose remains.

In contrast, a "European" definition of the third sector does not envisage separate sectors. The third sector or third system is thus conceived not as a corrective add-on to the blind spots of a market economy, but as a hybrid form of various kinds of organizations such as firms, bureaucracies, and kinship associations that "act as hybrids, intermeshing different resources and connecting different areas, rather than setting clear demarcation lines around a sector and mapping its size" (Evers 1995, p. 160). The rejection of the notion of sectors "avoids creating the impression that there is a clear line of demarcation between, on the one hand, the market place, the political arena and the community and, on the other, the Third Sector" (Laville et al. 1999, p. 5). This leads among other things to an inclusion of cooperative firms and the so-called people's economy that may be profit-seeking but are guided above all by social purpose. Organizations with strong links to (welfare) states are also included. Leaning more on this tradition, the British government's Office of the Third Sector views it as comprising "non-governmental organisations which are value-driven and which principally reinvest their surpluses to further social, environmental or cultural objectives; it includes voluntary and community organizations, charities and social enterprises, cooperatives and mutuals" (NAO 2009, p. 5). Some European researchers define third sector organizations as "organisations with an explicit aim to benefit the community, initiated by a group of citizens and in which the material interests of capital investors is subject to limits" (Defourny and Nyssens 2006, p. 5, quoted in Nyssens 2008, p. 87).

These two definitions are the most common and seem to produce a large amount of agreement concerning the type of organizations that make up the third sector, and as such they form the main basis of third sector research. Nonetheless, they suffer from some weaknesses. As a residual category, the "third" sector is always one (or two) steps behind in terms of primacy. It implies that the third sector is parallel to the first two while not being their equal. Defining the third sector in relation to the market and the state (as separate or hybrid) points focus toward its functionality vis-à-vis those sectors: nongovernmental organizations fill a service gap for welfare states; the "social economy" covers for failings in the market economy. If the fourth "private" sector of family and community is included, the third sector is again conceived in terms of its functionality for "cohesion" or "the family." This is why the third sector, despite its potentially subversive effects, is accused of being a "tamed" sector subservient to other societal forces, in particular neoliberalism (Kaldor 2002).

Theorizing the Third Sector as Process

An alternative approach is to view the third sector as a particular kind of process of interaction or communication between different sectors, usually the public and private sectors. Rather than looking for another "sector," similar or somehow equal to the state or the economy, this approach looks at what communicative forms allow third sector organizations – be they social enterprises, partnerships, community organizations, or pressure groups – to form and function.

One strain works on organizational identity formation and emphasizes how identities such as "social enterprise" emerge out of interaction, negotiation, and shared processes of sense-making avoiding "the danger of making a particular organizational identity appear to be essential, to be the 'true self' of an organization" (Clegg et al. 2007, p. 498). Similarly, focusing on process, a public–private partnership is not like a contract that can be "had," but is a "promise to give further promises" – what Åkerstøm (2008, p. 4), using Luhmann-inspired systems theory, considers a "second order contract" designed to facilitate further forms of cooperation and interaction: "Partnerships provide an answer to the increasing differentiation of society. They link systems of communication in a way where new possible couplings are continually sought out ... Partnerships constitute a machine of possibilities on the perimeter of multiple different systems of communication" (ibid, p. 5). In this view, third sector organizations are essentially processes of negotiation between citizens and political or economic agents. Their third sector quality lies in their viewing the world not according to the market logic of investment for-profit or a hierarchical logic of formal super- and sub-ordination, but in their ability to transgress such logics and provide identities and action possibilities while closing off others.

In a similar vein, but an overtly critical theorization of the third sector, is what I will call the "governmental" view. It has a longer pedigree and in its contemporary form tends to draw heavily on the work of Michel Foucault, suggesting that civil society and the third sector are not free of power or coercion, nor essentially dialogical, but on the contrary forms of power that to a large degree condition and constrain which actors can exist and what they can do and say. The idea of a "governmentality" described by Foucault (1978) is an interconnected system of discourse and techniques or institutions that allows certain practices to flourish and others to appear impossible, wrong, or just ludicrous. Neoliberalism has – using this concept – been viewed not as a purely economic system allowing "free individuals" to operate voluntarily in "free markets," but as a mentality and technique of governing that creates a certain kind of individual who is self-disciplining, adapted to market competition and consumption, and subservient to the social order that this depends on (Barry et al. 1996).

In this light, the third sector is not to be taken at face value as a power-free zone of non-coerced realization of shared values where authentic human communication can take place, nor as a zone of contestation. For a governmental view, both would be naïve. Discourses and institutions of civil society such as partnerships, private associations, or guilds form part of the power technologies through which a certain kind of governance is achieved. Usually the third sector is seen as part of – or even a tool for – the dominant liberal order in Western countries and the global Western conglomerate of international organizations and global civil society. For example, Sending and Neumann (2006) have pointed out how states use NGOs to implement their policies on population control. Lipschutz (2005) argues that a global governmentality is arising, whereby the state system deploys civil society or third sector organizations to further its state aims, for example, in environmental politics.

This view is reductionist in its own way, reducing the third sector to being a tool in the hands of an impersonal discursive project that orders society. But it is an epistemological view insofar as the third sector is seen not as something time-less or generically known by a distinct logic (such as that suggested by the civil or communicative views), since social forms and logics of behavior are beasts of changing dominant discourses of society. Where the European view has the third sector as a hybrid of market and state forms of organization, and the civil view has the third sector as one of communicative rationality, the governmental view puts it under the auspices of the dominant form of power. In Western societies this is seen to be a form of neoliberal, capitalist order. Third sector organizations are recruited to implement neoliberal policies of downsizing the state, disciplining the individual and family, and oiling the wheels of the economy; but that would change as the hegemonic societal formation changed.

In a third kind of epistemological approach, the third sector can be seen as a zone of contestation. This tradition draws on the likes of the Italian theorist Antonio Gramsci, who theorized civil society as a zone in which social forces vie for dominance: hegemonic blocks sparking their own counter-hegemonic forces and vice versa (Gramsci 1971). This allows for the possible dominance of society from a particular segment of society, e.g., capital (the narrative of the governmentalists), but also theorizes how change happens when other forces manage to band together and assert themselves. The third sector would, seen in this way, be a process – one of potential cooperation or conflict, depending on the social forces at work.

In a similar vein, Mary Kaldor has pointed to civil society as a process of nego-tiation or communicative interaction (not necessarily harmonious) between rulers and ruled, formerly in city states, then in nation states, and now in a global dis-course between global governance and social movements: "Civil society could be described as those organisations, groups and movements who are engaged in this process of negotiation and debate about the character of the rules – it is the process of expressing 'voice'" (Kaldor 2002, p. 10). In an even wider sense, "civil soci-ety is a process not an end point. Moreover, it is a contested process ... the term offers a future direction which is not dictated" (Kaldor 2003, p. 14). Civil society becomes the dialogue (dialogical in the traditional sense of negotiating or in a more antagonistic sense of, for example, a strike or a protest) or struggle between bodies or systems in a society that otherwise operate on separate planes or according to mutually incomprehensible logics.

The "third sector," for Kaldor, denotes only one aspect of civil society, namely a relatively depoliticized part of it rather than such things as charities or NGOs that orient themselves wholly toward participation alongside state or market institutions. However, understood more broadly, a third sector process would be one in which communicative rationality – the force of the better argument – predominated over instrumental rationality and/or the force of tradition or coercion. This definition of the third sector would mean that social movements, anarchic eruptions, spon-taneous protest movements, formal NGOs, cooperatives, as well as the chaos and cacophony of (global) civil society would be included – as long as they all furthered a deliberative process (verbally or symbolically).

Conclusion

Distinctions are always problematic because they pick out certain features and ignore others. On the other hand, that is precisely what makes them useful, provided they are used consciously and with humility. The existence of borderline cases or hybrids is often used as a way of discrediting a distinction but could just as well justify it: without a definition or theorization, we would have no way of thinking about how something is borderline and between which two types of entities it lays. A statistician would need a formal definition to lean on. Someone exploring the emergence or functioning of a given actor would do well to leave the formal definition open to begin with and explore how the entity in question is made to work and made intelligible by the actors in and around it. It would seem that the aim behind much third sector research is to find new and better ways of organizing human life. Rather than ossify an existing conception of what building blocks society is supposedly made of, those who deploy the term "the third sector" should be attuned to the changing relations between social actors, the way different kinds of organizations and ways of looking at those organizations condition what and who has which possibilities of acting. A processual view should therefore always at least accompany a formal definition, acknowledging and questioning the lens that produces the distinctions it relies upon.

Furthermore, that processual view should be open to different logics – not just harmonizing or logics of domination. The Gramscian approach has strengths in this respect. Of course it shifts attention in third sector research naturally away from service provision and onto political processes, highlighting pressure groups, interest groups, social movements, and resistance movements rather than charities, NGOs, or public–private partnerships. All the same, many agents, even service providers, often identified as "third sector" like social enterprises or charities perform a similar function seen through a process lens. A social enterprise links an economic sector dynamic to a public or political world goal that might otherwise be seen separate or even antagonistic and will also challenge/buttress each of its adjacent sectors. Cooperatives or ethical businesses may exert pressure on authorities or other companies to change their ways (and vice versa) – or they may lend legitimacy to each other. Pressure groups communicate directly between agents of particularist interest such as trade unions or business associations and the political system of representation, hierarchy, and bureaucratic control.

An open processual approach would make third sector research more than just the study of certain organizations or a particular sector of society. It would also make it a way to analyze the balance of social forces in a society (e.g., Katz 2006). It would also prevent the writing-out of subversive or revolutionary elements – something third sector and civil society research is often accused of doing; the African National Congress (ANC) of South Africa would have qualified as a third sector organization (until it assumed the reins of the state). At the same time, the identity of the third sector would not be lost. Only those processes aimed at governing the whole – affecting discourse between incongruous societal sectors – would be included; mafias or clans would not be included in the third sector, since they would be governed by the drive for private gain rather than an ultimately political vision for society.

References

Åkerstøm, N. (2003). *Discursive Analytical Strategies: Understanding Foucault, Koselleck, Laclau, Luhmann*, Bristol, The Policy Press.

Åkerstøm, N. (2008). *Partnerships: Machines of Possibility*, Bristol, The Policy Press.

Barry, A., Osborne, T., and Rose, N. (1996). *Foucault and Political Reason: Liberalism, Neo-liberalism and Rationalities of Government*, Chicago, University of Chicago Press.

Centre for Civil Society. (2009). What is civil society? www.lse.ac.uk/collections/CCS/introduction/what_is_civil_society.htm

Clegg, S. R., Rhodes, C., and Kornberger, M. (2007). Desperately seeking legitimacy: Organizational identity and emerging industries. *Organization Studies*, 28, 495–513.

Defourny, J., and Nyssens, M. (2006). Defining social enterprise. In M. Nyssens (ed.) *Social Enterprise: At the Crossroads of Market, Public Policies and Civil Society* (pp. 29–49), London, Routledge.

Etzioni, A. (1973). The third sector and domestic missions. *Public Administration Review*, 33(4), 314–323.

Evers, A. (1995). Part of the welfare mix: The third sector as an intermediate area. *Voluntas*, 6(2), 159–182.

Foucault, M. ([1978] 2002). Governmentality. In M. Foucault, *Power: The Works of Michel Foucault*, London, Penguin.

Gramsci, A. (1971). *Selections from The Prison Notebooks*, New York, International Publishers.

Jenei, G., and Kuti, E. (2008). The third sector and civil society. In S. P. Osborne (ed.) *The Third Sector in Europe: Prospects and Challenges* (pp. 9–24), London, Routledge.

Kaldor, M. (2002). Civil society and accountability. Occasional background paper for HDR, UNDP.

Kaldor, M. (2003). *Global Civil Society: An Answer to War?* Cambridge, Polity Press.

Katz, H. (2006). Gramsci, hegemony, and global civil society networks. *Voluntas*, 17(4), 332–348.

Kendall, J., and Knapp, M. (1995). *Voluntary Means, Social Ends*, Canterbury, PSSRU.

Laville, J.-L, Borzaga, C., Defourny, J., Evers, A., Lewis, J., Nyssens, M., and Vestoff, P. (1999). Third system: A European definition. Paper prepared for the European Commission pilot action "Third system and employment" www.istr.org/networks/europe/laville.evers.etal.pdf

Lewis, D. (2003). Theorizing the organization and management of non-governmental development organizations: Towards a composite approach. *Public Management Review*, 5(3), 325–344.

Lipschutz, R. D. (2005). Global civil society and global governmentality: Resistance, reform or resignation? In G. Baker and D. Chandler (eds) *Global Civil Society: Contested Futures* (pp. 171–185), London, Routledge.

National Audit Office (NAO). (2009). *Building the Capacity of the Third Sector*, London, House of Commons, www.nao.org.uk/publications/0809/building_the_capacity_of_the_t.aspx

Nyssens, M. (2008). The third sector and the social inclusion agenda: The role of social enterprises in the field of work integration. In S. P. Osborne (ed.) *The Third Sector in Europe: Prospects and Challenges* (pp. 87–102), London, Routledge.

Osborne, S. P. (ed.) (2008). *The Third Sector in Europe: Prospects and Challenges*, London, Routledge.

Priller, E., and Zimmer, A. (eds) (2001). *Der Dritte Sektor international*. Berlin, Sigma.

Ridley-Duff, M. B., and Seanor, P. (2008). Understanding social enterprise: Theory and practice. Introduction to a new textbook, SERC Conference, www.lsbu.ac.uk/bcim-cgcm/conferences/serc/2008/speakers/theory-and-practice-paper.pdf

Salamon, L. M., and Anheier, H. K. (1997). The third world's third sector in comparative perspective. Working papers of The Johns Hopkins Comparative Nonprofit Sector Project, no. 24, The Johns Hopkins Institute for Policy Studies, Baltimore, MD.

Sending, O. J., and Neumann, I. B. (2006). Governance to governmentality: Analyzing NGOs, states, and power. *International Studies Quarterly*, 50(3), 651–672.

Chapter 3
Sector Labels

Håkon Lorentzen

Introduction

The aim of this chapter is to investigate the historical and normative roots behind four of the most dominant sector labels in use: "nonprofit," "civil," "voluntary," and "third sector."[1] Readers of *Voluntas* and books that deal with associations have probably noted that these sector labels are commonly used to encompass organizational units outside "state" and "market." What are the theoretical assumptions embedded in these sector labels? At times, the choice of a sector term seems to be more or less accidental. Authors may change between different sector concepts without any obvious reason, or several sector labels are combined (Gidron et al. 1992; Janoski 1998; Salamon et al. 1999). Most often, sector labels are handled as if they were value-free neutral terms which encompass a broad and unspecified number of associations which, in some way or another, stand forth as different from activities within "state" and "market."

Most sector labels encompass associations with reference to properties they have in common. Shared properties form lines of demarcation between the sector and its neighbors, most often "state" and "market," but sometimes also "family." Sector labels are founded upon schemes of classification which label, mark, or designate organizational units as state or public agencies, as for-profits, or as part of the family, the informal sphere. Classifications are mutually exclusive; no unit should belong to two sectors simultaneously. For the sake of simplicity, this chapter labels the multitude of organizational units "associations."

Sector labels first emerged in the 1970s, where they affected the well-established dichotomy of "private" and "public" sectors. Before that time, research literature clustered organizations and associations in groups according to their values or purposes rather than to a "sector" of its own. Before the Second World War, most

H. Lorentzen (✉)
Institutt for Samfunnsforskning, Oslo, Norway
e-mail: hakon.lorentzen@samfunnsforskning.no

[1]I am grateful for comments to earlier drafts of this chapter from Lars Svedberg and the Civil Society Research Group at the Institute for Social Research, Oslo, Norway.

associations were part of broader social movements where members and adherents were connected by shared ideals and values.

In what follows it is argued that sector labels should be regarded as social constructs. They have, without exception, emerged from normative (or "political") arguments, intended at making associations and their roles and properties more visible in the political landscape. Normative arguments depart from ideas of comparative advantages, political arguments, or empirical evidence for why we should keep up and fight for "our" sector as something different from and better than "state" and "market." They also fuel political demands for government support and public grants. Thus, sector labels and the arguments that legitimize them are more than academic tools; they lie behind political arguments, tax rules, and public support.

The Structure of Sector Concepts

Sector ideas emerge from ideas about why individuals connect to associations and why associations should band together to form a sector. Consequently, sector paradigms contain ideas about individual motives, as well as the common denominators that connect the universe of associations. Sector approaches are founded upon definitions, criteria that make it possible to identify units that belong here. Most sector definitions are formed around dichotomies: civil relates to state, independent to dependent, nonprofit to for-profit, nongovernmental to governmental, and voluntary to paid work or state action. The exception here is third sector, which simultaneously refers to a first, second, and, eventually, a fourth sector. All sector labels presuppose state and market as more or less friendly neighbors.

Sector ideas also include arguments, explicit statements about the comparative advantages of associations. Some arguments connect individuals to associations. In philanthropy, for example, one argues that each of us has moral obligations which cannot be delegated to the state by acts of taxpaying or voting. Associations outside state and market are needed to fulfill philanthropic obligations. Another set of arguments connects associations to each other. The nonprofit constraint argues that since associations have it in common that they do not distribute surplus to private owners, they should belong to a common sector.

Definitions, together with arguments, form sector paradigms: consistent ways of understanding relations between individual motives and associations framed by a sector. Paradigms create a lens through which we observe associations; their concepts and models make one see some details and overlook others. They also mold the forms of global academic efforts; they shape commonly accepted ways of perceiving associations and their relations to state and market. The question to be addressed here is: What are the founding elements of dominant sector paradigms?

The "Voluntary" Approach

In the United Kingdom, individual engagement and an interest in matters outside one's own family and daily life have for many centuries been embedded in the concept of charity. In its original form, charity describes an individual act of giving "as almsgiving or ... other benevolent actions of any sort for the needy with no expectation of material reward."[2] Acts of charity presuppose an individual disposition, a feeling of responsibility toward those worse off, and a willingness to share (Jordan 1986). Historically, charity is rooted in Christianity and norms of compassion and sympathy toward the sick and poor.

From the seventeenth century onward, the term charity also describes organizational units that mediate charitable acts and donations. Religious societies, monasteries, funds, and legacies and the like mediate the humane and sympathetic dispositions toward human beings. In 1604 the Charity Uses Act defined the state's rights to tax exemption for charities in England. This law reform marked the first line of demarcation between the state (the King) and civil efforts toward the sick and poor. Since the 1890s, several other societal goals were added to the original ones, for charitable purposes (Gladstone 1979). Acts of charity founded on feelings of responsibility are closely interwoven in the normative foundation of philanthropy as well. However, while charity gradually came to include a wider spectrum of purposes, philanthropy historically describes gifts and donations supported mainly through two channels: from the wealthy, with the foundation or the legacy as the legal frame (Anheier and Leat 2002; Walkenhorst 2001), and from "ordinary people," as donations for charitable purposes.

The voluntary tradition arose from the continuous ideological struggle between associations and the state in England in the nineteenth century. Industrialization created a new urban underclass marked by poverty and bad health, which became the object of the moral spirit of charity. Charity work of associations, congregations, and wealthy people was rooted in a conviction of individual responsibility for those worse off. During the years between 1830 and 1940, a continuous struggle between the state and associational life took place about the division of responsibility between charity and government (Hatch 1980; Luxton 1990; Mellor 1985; Wolfenden 1978). In the Charity Law of 1834, responsibilities were dichotomized, based on a division of labor between state and charity.[3]

Here, among the ideological arguments of charity associations, the idea of voluntary activity emerges. The defenders of individual charity argued that moral responsibilities for fellow human beings rest upon each and every one of us. State action for the underprivileged presupposes tax incomes, which again are based on state authority. In addition, the state's efforts are founded on positivist knowledge, verified by science and different from religious beliefs.[4] Based on this, and for other

---

[2] *Webster's Encyclopedic Unabridged Dictionary of the English Language*, 1996, p. 248.

[3] Here a distinction was made between "those whose failures might be attributed to ill luck (and they were the province of voluntary organizations) and those whose failure was due to character defects and for them there existed a Poor Law" (Mess 1948, p. 12).

[4] According to Mess (1948, p. 12), those who believed in charity work "were firmly convinced that state social services were based on a deterministic philosophy, based on that it is on the assumption that man was a victim of his environment and could do little to control it, whereas they at least paid

similar reasons, ideological borderlines were drawn, first between obligatory state action on one side, and voluntary acts of free will on the other. A second line was drawn between acts based on positivist (i.e., scientific) knowledge and on moral belief and conviction on the other. Voluntary acts were, in other words, founded upon free will and moral convictions, while state action presupposed legal frames, paid work, and scientific knowledge.

From the beginning of the twentieth century, the term also came to characterize not only acts but also associations that mediated charitable acts of free will, outside the continuously expanding welfare state. As labor and related collectivistic movements increased their influence, the term voluntary also denoted free will, opposed to the perceived totalitarianism of socialism and communism. As late as 1949, Beveridge and Wells confirmed the distinction between free and voluntary associations on the one hand, and coerced state intervention on the other (Beveridge and Wells 1949, p. 10).

During the years between 1945 and 1970, important structural changes took place in the landscape of associations in most countries in Europe. The relative proportion of classical charity associations diminished, as the number of interest and leisure associations increased. For many of these, the charity paradigm did not fit particularly well. For leisure associations, volunteering simply meant unpaid work by members for its own sake, pragmatically motivated: If things are to be done, we have to do them ourselves. Here one can trace the contours of an emerging challenge: How should one describe aims for the sector as a whole, in terms that will cover the motivations and self-understanding of all groups and associations?

In the United Kingdom, the report of the Wolfenden Committee (1978) promoted the idea of a distinct voluntary sector. The committee was appointed in 1974 to "review the roles and functions of voluntary organizations in the United Kingdom over the next twenty-five years" (Wolfenden 1978, p. 9). At this time, no public register of voluntary associations existed, and the committee faced the task of "building" what they named "the voluntary sector" (ibid, p. 15). The committee collected evidence and viewpoints from more than 400 associations. The sample was dominated by associations and other units within health and welfare, which consequently came to give birth to the committee's idea of purposes that constituted organizations inside the voluntary sector.[5] For this group, it was argued that voluntary efforts "are born because an inspired individual, or a group, of likeminded individuals sees a need or a shortcoming in our society and is determined to do

---

man the compliment of assuming that being above the animals and possessed of free will, he could largely mould the environment into his liking."

[5] The committee presented the challenges they faced as having to decide "what meaning we were to give the words 'voluntary organisations'" (p. 11). The conclusion was that "we would take as the centre or focus of our review voluntary organisations dealing with personal social services and what is generally known as the 'environment'" (pp. 11–12).

something about it" (ibid, p. 189). The sector idea was here dominated by "welfare" organizations and individual efforts that reflected the idealism of the charity tradition.[6]

The emergence of a voluntary sector, as it appeared in late 1970s, reveals that this concept was a response to expanding state welfare and the continuous integration of voluntary efforts into public services, a development that some saw as a threat. The empirical reference of the emerging sector was related to the somewhat diffuse term "welfare services," which limited the number of relevant associations. A normative intent was to protect the tradition of voluntary engagement in the welfare field against "colonization" from the state. A well-established "charity" paradigm was threatened by the expanding welfare state, and its adherents were searching for relevant strategies to meet new developments (Brenton 1985; Griffith 1988).

Third Sector

The third sector idea emerged in the United States in the first part of the 1970s. In 1973, Theodore Levitt, professor of business administration at Harvard University, published *The Third Sector: Tactics for a Responsive Society.* The same year the sociologist Amitai Etzioni published *The Third Sector and Domestic Missions.* Together, Levitt and Etzioni stand forth as the founding fathers of the third sector idea. However, in spite of a shared term, their analyses of the emerging sector(s) were quite different.

They both departed from a concern for the weak legitimacy of market as well as state as institutional welfare systems. Levitt expressed the New Left's skepticism toward bureaucracies, public as well as private ones, "bureaucracies are rigid and unresponsive to ordinary human and social problems," he stated (1973, p. 15). Levitt encompassed what he called the "Old Third Sector," which included "classical" associations: such as charity and community associations, sport clubs, societies, and unions – those well-established units, often with a single purpose, an "operating style" of persuasion, lobbying, education, and direct aid given by volunteers.

Levitt's main interest, however, was the emerging "New Third Sector," as something basically different from the old one. The New Third Sector was born on May 3, 1963, in a confrontation between Martin Luther King's nonviolent strategies and the police in Montgomery, Alabama. This incident laid the ground for new, confrontational strategies, which, according to Levitt (1973, p. 73), divided the old sector from the new: "The most obvious different tactics are the New Third Sector's intense pushiness, jarring, rhetoric, massed demonstrations, moral outrage, and sometimes outright violence." With no staff and little money, these associations were functionally autonomous from the society in which they worked and "uniquely manned

---

[6]According to Gladstone (1979, p. 3) volunteering includes "the work of volunteers, those generous spirits who devote their leisure to the benefit of others, whether it be to relieve the loneliness of isolated elderly people, the preservation of footpaths or any of a thousand and one other causes."

by people without the slightest aspiration to social position" (ibid, p. 76). Levitt described them as a "counterculture," having an "overall discontent with things and values as they are" (ibid, p. 73).

Etzioni's ideas were founded upon skepticism toward the expanding state, as well as market-based welfare. As a solution, he enthusiastically launched the idea of a "third sector," a sphere that combined "the best of two worlds, efficiency and expertise from the business world, with public interest, accountability and broader planning from government" (Etzioni 1973, p. 315). Etzioni focused on domestic service production and the emergence of what he observed as a third alternative between the state and the market sectors. Here, he found a mix of voluntary associations (like the Red Cross), nonprofit corporations (like the Ford Foundation), nonprofit universities, and similar entities. However, he also included what he labeled "government–private sector partnerships," which included for-profits merged with state action into one "system." The space program NASA, student loans, postal services, and health insurances were examples of "third sector bodies," as Etzioni coined them (1973, p. 316).

Levitt and Etzioni both placed their focus on emerging trends in the early 1970s – trends that challenged the traditional public–private dichotomy. Etzioni's original, but rather loose idea of a third sector was founded upon new types of partnerships between governmental agencies, for-profits, and voluntary units. His approach put into focus the borderline cases – hybrids situated between the state, the market, and the sphere of associations. Nothing indicates that Etzioni intended to encompass *all* associations in a sector of its own. Levitt's analysis captured the manifold of protest, anti-establishment, human rights, and grassroot groups that emerged after the 1968 student revolution. Levitt's key to the sector the idea of "responsiveness." As the Old Third Sector became institutionalized and unresponsive to new challenges, new associations confronting basic political structures emerged. Levitt's ideas are closely related to the concept of "empowerment" that was coined by Berger and Neuhaus (1977) some years later, which also focused on radicalization processes among ethnic minorities and marginalized groups.

Etzioni's ideas of the third sector as a new institution were followed up in the European welfare mixed approach some years later (Evers and Laville 2004; Evers and Wintersberger 1988). Levitt's focus on political activism as well as his ideas about the sector's responsiveness as a defining sector criterion has waned. Still, Levitt and Etzioni represent early birds of the emerging nongovernmental-ism that later became a dominant and influential ideology within public policy and international development (Lewis 2001, 2006).

The "Civil" Label

During the late 1980s, "civil society" gained ground as the dominant label of asso-ciations outside state and market. According to Cohen (1995, p. 37), civil society defines "a sphere of social interaction distinct from economy and state, composed above all of associations (including the family) and publics. Modern civil society is created and reproduced through forms of collective action, and it is institutionalized through laws, especially subjective rights that stabilize social differentiation." This definition does not look very different from other attempts to encompass a sector of associations. However, the revitalization of civil society offered a qualitatively new approach to the understanding of relations between state and associations.

Most authors identify the Polish Solidarity movement as the initial source of the rebirth of this tradition.[7] The former communist countries of Eastern Europe did not leave any space for non-state initiatives, and no associational space existed outside the state apparatus (Rupnik 1988). During the 1970s, small underground dissident groups were established, which brought new reform ideas from the West; some of these received public attention and influenced the thoughts of the ruling leaders (Ehrenberg 1999). From here, the idea of change from "below," outside the state apparatus, was articulated as a strategy against totalitarianism and state-controlled reforms. The idea was labeled the "new evolutionism" and was theoretically anchored in the civil society tradition and the need for an autonomous civil sphere outside the state. As the Solidarity movement confronted the Polish government in the early 1980s, they advanced the civil society argument to gain legitimacy and acceptance by the rulers (Cohen and Arato 1992; Ehrenberg 1999; Pelczynski 1988).

Why did the civil society tradition also gain influence in capitalist countries of the West, far away from totalitarian regimes? Basically, the tradition captured existing sentiments among those who worried about the continuous expansion of state welfare. As early as 1962, Jürgen Habermas described the ongoing transformation of the public sphere, which takes place as the state intervenes in private structures and transforms the arenas for public discourse (Habermas 1962). In the 1970s, the influential Finnish philosopher Georg Henrik von Wright worried about the expansion of the welfare state; as the individual is integrated in the state, the world becomes increasingly dehumanized, he argued (von Wright 1978). The Danish author Jørgen S. Dich (1974), who labeled the new welfare professions "the ruling class," was critical of how people lost control of their own problems since the professions, as the instrument of the Social Democratic parties, came to dominate society.

In several countries the inspiration from the emerging civil approach fueled a new wave of state welfare criticism. State welfare was taken to represent a form of social patronage where the individual is reduced to a client, unable to take care of themselves, and where moral obligations are transformed into welfare rights (Arvidsson et al. 1994). Wolfe (1989) investigated Nordic welfare models and concluded that close bonds of kinship, community, and family seemed to be replaced by distant obligations of state welfare. Zetterberg and Ljungberg (1997) argued that the slow disintegration of social bonds and the emerging individualism could be explained as a result of expanding welfare regimes. And the message of John Keane

---

[7]Cohen and Arato (1992) do mention other sources, notably the Second Left in France in the 1960s and the West German Greens in the 1970s.

(1988) was that welfare state intervention creates corporative structures that tend to blur the demarcation line between the state and civil society. Similar arguments were proposed by Norberto Bobbio (1987), who argued that the integration of civil groups in hierarchical systems threatens the uniqueness and the autonomy of civil structures. Criticism of a welfare state that provides too many rights and too few responsibilities is also traceable in Etzioni's works, with his worries about the disintegration of community networks and their inherent moral obligations (Etzioni 1988, 1993).

The message from these writers can be summarized as follows: social obligations represent norms supported by civil associations, the family, and the community sphere. The replacement of these by rights and public services erodes moral obligations and drains civil networks. Welfare states, in particular the Nordic ones, pose no inherent limits for their own expansion into the civil sphere. Like totalitarian regimes, they threaten the autonomy of civil structures, not by suppressing them, but by replacing them by rights, professionals, and welfare programs. Habermas's description of state colonization of the private sphere, followed by processes of disintegration and shifting "logics," formed the basic argument for many of these authors.

In Nordic countries with a tradition for "state friendliness" among social scientists, the elements of state skepticism embedded in the civil society approach have been hard to swallow. Trägårdh (2007, p. 21) showed that the concept, when it was introduced in Sweden, was met with considerable skepticism, perceived as politically suspect by some, and unusable by others, while Pestoff (1998) wanted to leave the civil society tradition to the philosophers.[8] A shared ground for many social scientists in the Nordic countries has been that no sharp line of demarcation between the state and the society exists there. It is maintained that the strong expansion of state welfare programs – stronger than in most other countries – has *not* erased civil associations and civil engagement. On the contrary, Norway and Sweden are among the highest ranking countries in the world when it comes to active membership in associations (Svedberg and Jeppson Grassmann 2007).

One reason for this seemingly paradoxical observation can be traced in the historical relations between the state and associations. For more than 50 years, social-democratic regimes have been founded upon close ties between interest groups and government. Networks and corporate channels have mediated the exchange of interests from below and governmental considerations from above. The result has been a unity that transcends the classical state–society antagonism, which again implies that the need for civil autonomy, as prescribed by many, is not a universal or inherent demand, but relative to the political regime in question.

---

[8] Victor Pestoff (1998, p. 38) concluded that for civil society, "There is ... every reason to keep in mind warnings about this concept and to reserve it for philosophical questions with a specific political character and critical potential, rather than treating it as a special sector, an economic or legal category or a sociological structuring principle."

Today, after having lived with a civil sector for almost three decades, one can observe that the elements of state criticism, influenced by Habermas's idea of colonization, have largely been answered by the defenders of state welfare. Cohen (2007, p. 45) is representative of the new sentiment:

> provisions such as social security, health and unemployment insurance, job training programs, family support such as day care or paid parental leave, and laws establishing collective bargaining and other procedures providing for participatory conflict resolution do not undermine civil society. Far from creating dependency and fragmentation, the procedural provisions help constitute economic society (civilizing the economy) and the substantive ones provide the basic preconditions for autonomy *and* solidarity within civil society.

Cohen later makes some reservations to this general and positive view, arguing that some types of welfare services may undermine civil society and democracy; "sorting out which state regulations, benefits, and protections foster or undermine civil society and democracy is a complex issue," she admits (2007, p. 45).

The issue of the welfare state and its effects on civil structures can also be traced to a quite different tradition: civil society as a revitalization of an interest in democracy's preconditions included the underlying formation of individual identities and social belonging. These issues were brought into the academic debate by Cohen and Arato and their view on civil society as a sphere with particular functions for democracy: "the rights to communication, assembly, and association, among others, constitute the public and associational spheres of civil society as spheres of *positive freedom* within which agents can collectively debate issues of common concern, act in concert, assert new rights, and exercise influence on political (and potentially economic) society" (Cohen and Arato 1992, p. 23). Here, the prime function of the civil sphere is to mediate discourses, debates, viewpoints, and opinions between civil actors and the state. In order to fulfill these functions, the civil sphere demands active participation from citizens in "*egalitarian* institutions and civil associations, as well as in politically relevant organizations" (ibid, p. 19).[9]

Another source of inspiration for the interest in democratic functions goes back to Robert Putnam (1993). Applying terms like "civic virtue" and "civic community," like MacIntyre (1981), Putnam focused on virtues like honesty, trust, and law-abidingness, properties he assumed were embedded in civil associations:

> The norms and values of the civic community are embodied in, and reinforced by, distinctive social structures and practices ... Civil associations contribute to the effectiveness and stability of democratic government, it is argued, both because of their 'internal' effects on individual members and because of their 'external' effects on the wider polity. (Putnam 1993, p. 89)

Putnam's core argument was that democracy does not function in a vacuum; its success depends on well-functioning social structures and networks: "The practical

---

[9]Cohen and Arato (ibid) add that "Without active participation on the part of citizens in egalitarian institutions and civil associations, as well as in politically relevant organizations, there will be no way to maintain the democratic character of the political culture or of social and political institutions."

performance of institutions ... is shaped by the context within which they operate," he argued (ibid, p. 8). Civic virtues capture activities that are essential preconditions for democracy: the reading of newspapers, membership in voluntary associations, and a general "interest in public issues and devotion to public causes" (ibid, p. 87). Putnam identified social structures upon which social interaction and, more generally, trust depended. Among these, vigorous associations and civic networks stand forth as the most important elements.

Anchoring associations as democratic actors, as mediators of active participation based on civic virtues, networks, and social capital, connects civil society to processes of political "input" rather than to the production of welfare services and related worries about state colonization. The civil society tradition renewed interest in public life and the democratic functions of associations in modern societies (Walzer 1984).

The Nonprofit Label

Before 1980, few writers talked about "nonprofit" as a sector in its own right. One exception was Weisbrod (1975), who used the term "voluntary nonprofit sector," which he sorted into three categories.[10] Weisbrod, however, seems to be an exception; early writers analyzed nonprofit firms, economy, services, and organizations, and they underlined the extreme heterogeneity among these. James (1989) and Weisbrod (1988) also underlined the hybrid character of many nonprofits. Attaching the "independence" label to nonprofits hindered a better understanding of their hybrid character, Hall argued (1992).[11]

In fact, the political climate that led to the birth of the nonprofit sector label can be traced back to the 1970s. According to Hansmann (1987), nonprofit service providers, such as schools, hospitals, museums, day-care centers, and similar entities, were threatened by lack of funding, expansion of for-profit services, and an increase in dependence on public funding and public control. The Program on Non-Profit Organizations that was launched in 1977 at Yale University formed a response to these challenges. Over the following decade more than 175 journal articles and book chapters as well as 32 books were produced (Brewster 1989). A united academic effort, based on economic models and theoretical assumptions, laid the ground for the nonprofit approach which came into increasing use over the 1980s.

James (1989) best explained why it was necessary to mark lines of demarcation between the state, market, and nonprofit sectors. First, a boundary line with

---

[10]Namely, a private type consisting of commercial or proprietary units and two public ones. First, collective units which produce services not paid for by those who benefit; these are "virtually indistinguishable from those of governmental agencies," Weisbrod argued. Second, those producing trust goods "of the kind about which consumers are often poorly informed" (Weisbrod 1988, p. 60).

[11]"The pervasive characterization of the nonprofit sector as an independent one is not only misleading but also destructive" (Hall 1992, p. 106).

for-profits was needed, since these were the major institutional competitors for non-profits. Second, a line had to be drawn with the public sector. In many countries, nonprofits compete with services provided by national and local governments, and a line of demarcation makes it easier to prevent further integration of state and nonprofits.

Two basic arguments were used to legitimize the two boundary lines. In its simplest form, the thesis of the "non-distribution constraint" articulated the higher trustworthiness of nonprofit welfare services, compared to for-profit ones. In James's words (1989, p. 4), "Consumers may be more willing to trust non-profit organizations, where, because of the non-profit constraint, managers do not have the same monetary incentive to downgrade quality that profit-making managers would have." Second, the thesis of "differentiated demand" formed a line of arguments toward the state. The demand for private services forms a market response to situations where the government does not produce as much, or the precise kind of, service that people want. Where tastes in welfare services are differentiated, one should expect a wider range of nonprofit welfare services.

The nonprofit approach, as the idea that encompassed the sector in the late 1980s, was, according to Weisbrod (1988, p. 60), tied to the tax-law classification scheme that gave associations a tax-exempt status in the United States. Here, a "perfect fit" was established between nonprofit theories and their empirical universe, clearing the ground for the idea of a nonprofit sector, different from state and market. This classification scheme also formed the point of departure for The Johns Hopkins Comparative Nonprofit Sector Project (Salamon et al. 1999). An important premise for the success of this approach was the political breakthrough for neoliberalism that followed the Reagan presidency in the United States and the Thatcher era in the United Kingdom. The arguments for nonprofit welfare laid the groundwork for the division between public financing and "private" (for-profit and nonprofit) production of welfare and strengthened the view on voluntary associations as welfare providers.

In many ways, the nonprofit approach stands forth as radically different from the civil one. Based on economists' models, the approach perceives individuals as consumers demanding welfare services or goods (Hansmann 1987). This is a model that is almost in diametrical opposition to the civil one that is driven by political participants demanding justice within the political system.

Conclusion: Integration and Autonomy

Comparing different sector approaches reveals that their basic paradigmatic hallmarks vary quite a lot. They all depart from broader political tensions between state and society and emerged during the 1970s, a period of strong state welfare expansion, but there was also skepticism toward growing bureaucracies and expanding professions in the fields of welfare. Forming a sector of its own, with a boundary line opposed to expanding state welfare, these approaches came into use as counter-strategies. A shared frontier demanded arguments that could distinguish the comparative advantages of the sector, compared to those of the state. First, the voluntary sector term flagged individual moral obligations as opposed to bureaucratic state welfare. The double meaning of charity and philanthropy, as moral acts as well as organizational units, marked the common ground for welfare providers outside the state.

Second, the nonprofit approach was founded upon rational-driven economic models. The nonprofit approach did not, interestingly enough, address state, but market welfare as the main competitor. The nonprofit approach turned out to be a success, for several reasons. The emergence of the approach coincided with the new welfare liberalism of the 1980s and the strategy of contracting out public welfare services to market or nonprofit providers. Within the American context, accentuating nonprofit welfare providers as advantageous to for-profit ones seems like a sensible strategy. In other countries, like the Nordic ones, the nonprofit arguments had little meaning, since for-profit welfare was almost totally absent in the early 1980s. Still, the nonprofit term gradually came into use there as well.

A common denominator behind the voluntary, the third sector (Etzioni's version), and the nonprofit sector approaches is their focus on the need for welfare services different from those of state and market. These sector ideas share their interest in the output side of the state: welfare provisions and services. As such, they contrast sector approaches which depart from an interest in political participation or the input side of democratic governance. The civil and third sector (Levitt's version) approaches both accentuate associations as parts of the opinion-making structures of society. Here, participation, engagement, and influence become essential keywords. Associations promote interests, balance state power, and are essential in the democratic circuit between the people, the state, and public policies.

Between the output (service) and input (democracy) aspects of associations, an inherent contradiction seems to exist. Most often, service roles call for integration and cooperation between service providers from different sectors. From a governmental point of view, public funding of non-state service provisions raises a need for improved coordination. As a result, public funding of non-state welfare activities seems to go hand in hand with integrative processes which tend to make welfare services within a field more like each other. The democracy approach, on the other hand, underlines the need for autonomy of associations. In order to honor their democratic functions, associations need independent roles where they feel free to criticize authorities and politicians. The main function of the state is to guarantee the legal frames and institutional conditions that are needed for associations to fulfill their democratic functions.

How do the social sciences handle this inherent tension between integration and autonomy? One way forward is to focus on "governance," as a regulative ideology for the state and associations that might transcend the historical tensions between service and democracy functions. The governance approach connects the state and associations in basically three ways: first, by negotiations which (hopefully) give associations opportunities to articulate their views and forward their interests; second, by partnership agreements, where associations undertake the task of implementing public programs (Kooiman 1993; Majone 1997); third, the governance approach offers a set of common norms for civil and state agencies, where the need for efficiency, accountability, ethical standards, strategic planning, good leadership, and professional competence is the focus (Newman 2001; Rhodes 2001). Partnership strategies are, by some, described as a form of democratic renewal; they give associations political influence and improve their roles as welfare providers (Alcock and Scott 2002; Rhodes 2001). The need for autonomy and independence seems to wither, as the state and organizations agree on goals as well as ends.

Governance integration will also undermine the classical comparative arguments for an independent sector with qualities different from those of the state. A reasonable scenario is that we are now beginning to see the end of the idea of a sector with qualities different from those of the state and market. As sharp lines of demarcation between sectors increasingly become blurred, as integration and cooperation between sectors increase, ideas of a sector as an independent entity outside the state and market will gradually vanish.

References

Alcock, P., and Scott, D. (2002). Partnership with the voluntary sector: Can compacts work? In C. Glendinning, M. Powell, and K. Rummery (eds) *Partnerships New Labour and the Governance of Welfare* (pp. 113–130), London, The Policy Press.

Anheier, H. K., and Leat, D. (2002). *From Charity to Creativity: Philanthropic Foundations in the 21st Century*, London, Comedia.

Arvidsson, H., Berntson, L., and Dencik, L. (1994). *Modernisering och välfärd – om stat, individ og civil samhälle i Sverige*, Stockholm, City University Press.

Berger, P. L., and Neuhaus, R. J. (1977). *To Empower People: The Role of Mediating Structures in Public Policy*, Washington, DC, The AEI Press.

Beveridge, Lord, and Wells, A. F. (1949). *The Evidence for Voluntary Action*, London, George Allen and Unwin.

Bobbio, N. (1987). *The Future of Democracy*, Cambridge, Polity Press.

Brenton M. (1985). *The Voluntary Sector in British Social Services*, London, Longman.

Brewster, K. (1989). Series foreword. In E. James (ed.) *The Nonprofit Sector in International Perspective* (pp. v–viii), New York, Oxford University Press.

Cohen, J. (1995). Interpreting the notion of civil society. In M. Walzer (ed.) *Toward a Global Civil Society* (pp. 35–40), New York, Berghahn Books.

Cohen, J. (2007). Civil society and globalization: Rethinking the categories. In L. Trädhgård (ed.) *State and Civil Society in Northern Europe: The Swedish Model Reconsidered* (pp. 37–66), New York, Berghahn Books.

Cohen, J. L., and Arato, A. (1992). *Civil Society and Political Theory*, Cambridge, MA, The MIT Press.

Dich, J. S. (1974). *Den herskende klasse*, Copenhagen, Borgen.

Ehrenberg, J. (1999). *Civil Society: The Critical History of an Idea*, New York, New York University Press.

Etzioni, A. (1973). The third sector and domestic missions. *Public Administration Review*, 33(4), 314–323.

Etzioni, A. (1988). *The Moral Dimension: Towards a New Economics*, New York, The Free Press.

Etzioni, A. (1993). *The Spirit of Community: Rights, Responsibilities and the Communitarian Agenda*, New York, Crown Publishers.

Evers, A., and Wintersberger, H. (1988). *Shifts in the Welfare Mix*, Wien, Europäisches Zentrum für Ausbildung und Forschung.

Evers, A., and Laville, J. L. (2004). *The Third Sector in Europe*, Cheltenham, Edgar Elgar.

Gidron, B., Kramer, R. M., and Salamon, L. M. (1992). *Government and the Third Sector: Emerging Relationships in Welfare States*, New York, Jossey Bass.

Gladstone, F. J. (1979). *Voluntary Action in a Changing World*, London, Bedford Square Press.

Griffith, R. (1988). *Community Care: Agenda for Action. A Report to the Secretary of State for Social Services*, London, Her Majesty's Stationery Office.

Habermas, J. (1962). *Strukturwandel der Öffentlichkeit. Untersuchungen zu eine kategorie der Bürgerlichen Gesellschaft*, Berlin, Luchterhand Verlag.

Hall, P. D. (1992). *Inventing the Nonprofit Sector and Other Essays*, Baltimore, MD, The Johns Hopkins University Press.

Hansmann, H. (1987). Economic theories of nonprofit organization. In W. W. Powell (ed.) *The Nonprofit Sector* (pp. 27–41), New Haven, Yale University Press.

Hatch, S. (1980). *Outside the State: Voluntary Organisations in Three English Towns*, London, Croom Helm.

James, E. (1989). *The Nonprofit Sector in International Perspective*, New York, Oxford University Press.

Janoski, T. (1998). *Citizens and Civil Society*, Cambridge, Cambridge University Press.

Jordan, W. K. (1986). *The Charities of London 1480–1660*, London, George Allen & Unwin.

Keane, J. (1998). *Civil Society: Old Images, New Visions*, London, Polity Press.

Kooiman, J. (ed.) (1993). *Modern Governance: New Government Society Interactions*, London, Sage.

Levitt, T. (1973). *The Third Sector: New Tactics for a Responsive Society*, New York, Amacom.

Lewis, D. (2001). *The Management of Non-Governmental Development Organizations*, London, Routledge.

Lewis, D. (2006). Elusive spaces and organisational forms: A partial recovery of the history of the "third sector idea." Paper for the ESCR seminar series on Rethinking Economies, University of Manchester, UK.

Luxton, P. (1990). *Charity Fund-Raising and the Public Interest*, Aldershot, UK, Gower.

MacIntyre, A. (1981). *After Virtue: A Study in Moral Theory*, Indiana, Notre Dame Press.

Majone, G. (1997). From the positive to the regulatory state: Causes and consequences of change in the mode of governance. *Journal of Public Policy,* 17(2), 139–167.

Mellor, H. W. (1985). *The Role of Voluntary Organisations in Social Welfare*, London, Croom Helm.

Mess, H. A. (1948). *Voluntary Social Services Since 1918*, London, Kegan Paul.

Newman, J. (2001). *Modernising Governance: New Labour, Policy and Society*, London, Sage.

Pelczynski, Z. A. (1988). Solidarity and the rebirth of civil society in Poland, 1976–81. In J. Keane (ed.) *Civil Society and the State* (pp. 361–380), London, Verso.

Pestoff, V. (1998). *Beyond the Market and State: Social Enterprises and Civil Democracy in a Welfare Society*, Aldershot, Ashgate.

Putnam, R. D. (1993). *Making Democracy Work*, Princeton, NJ, Princeton University Press.

Rhodes, R. A. W. (2001). *Understanding Governance: Policy Networks, Governance, Reflexivity and Accountability*, Philadelphia, Open University Press.

Rupnik, J. (1988). Totalitarianism revisited. In J. Keane (ed.) *Civil Society and the State* (pp. 263–290), London, Verso.

Salamon, L., Anheier, H. K., List, R., Toepler, S., Sokolowski, S. W., and Associates (1999). *Global Civil Society: Dimensions of the Nonprofit Sector*, Baltimore, MD, The Johns Hopkins Center for Civil Society Studies.

Svedberg, L., and Jeppson Grassmann, E. (2007). Voluntary association involvement in comparative perspective. In L. Trägårdh (ed.) *State and Civil Society in Northern Europe: The Swedish Model Reconsidered* (pp. 126–164), New York, Berghahn.

Trägårdh, L. (2007). *State and Civil Society in Northern Europe: The Swedish Model Reconsidered*, New York, Berghahn.

von Wright, G. (1978). *Humanismen som livshållning*, Stockholm, Rabén & Sjögren.

Walkenhorst, P. (2001). *Building Philanthropic and Social Capital: The Works of Community Foundations*, Bielefeld, Germany, Bertelsmann Foundation Publishers.

Walzer, M. (1984). Civility and civic virtue in contemporary America. In M. Walzer, *Radical Principles* (pp. 54–72), New York, Basic Books.

Weisbrod, B. A. (1975). Toward a theory of the voluntary nonprofit sector in a three-sector economy. In E. S. Phelps (ed.) *Altruism, Morality and Economic Theory* (pp. 171–195), New York, Russell Sage.

Weisbrod, B. A. (1988). *The Nonprofit Economy*, Cambridge, MA, Harvard University Press.

Wolfe, A. (1989). *Whose Keeper? Social Science and Moral Obligation*, Berkeley, University of California Press.

Wolfenden, L. (1978). *The Future of Voluntary Organisations: Report of the Wolfenden Committee*, London, Croom Helm.

Zetterberg, H. L., and Ljungberg, C. J. (1997). *Vårt land–den svenska socialstaten*, Stockholm, City University Press.

Chapter 4
Social Origins

Freda Donoghue

Introduction

Social origins theory marked a major development in nonprofit scholarship and is one of the most important theories on nonprofit organizations to emerge in the past decade. Drawing on the fruits of the largest-ever comparative study of nonprofit organizations internationally, Lester Salamon and Helmut Anheier sought to understand and explain differences emerging in data collected by the project's associates. This chapter will examine the social origins debate, that is, the theory and the main critiques that have emerged. It will then go on to apply the theory to the case of Ireland, and it will argue that the theory, while a major step in nonprofit scholarship, deserves a more qualitative approach, as recommended by critics such as Charles Ragin (1998).

Social Origins Theory

Neoclassical theories in economics seeking to explain why the nonprofit sector exists were important antecedents to social origins theory and helped set its foundations. Such neoclassical theories based their explanations for the nonprofit sector's existence on state failure (Weisbrod 1977) and market failure (Hansmann 1987). Salamon entered this fray with his theory of voluntary failure and the interdependence of governmental and nonprofit sectors (Salamon 1987). All of these theories were to play a part in the formulation by Salamon and Anheier of social origins theory in the late 1990s. During that decade they started what was to become the largest international comparative study of the nonprofit sector (The Johns Hopkins Comparative Nonprofit Sector Project or JHCNP), which reported on eight countries in its first phase (Salamon and Anheier 1994) and 22 countries in its second phase (Salamon et al. 1998). The project used a standardized definition of nonprofit

F. Donoghue (✉)
Trinity College Dublin, Ireland
e-mail: fredadonoghue@gmail.com

R. Taylor (ed.), *Third Sector Research*, DOI 10.1007/978-1-4419-5707-8_4,
© Springer Science+Business Media, LLC 2010

organizations, which they called the structural-operational definition, according to which nonprofit organizations were said to be private, formal, separate from government, autonomous, and involving some degree of voluntary input (Salamon and Anheier 1996). A classification system was devised (the International Classification of Nonprofit Organisations or ICNPO), which adapted standard industrial classification systems such as ISIC and NACE so that comparisons could be made with other economic and industrial sectors and which has more recently been adopted by the United Nations for using in satellite accounts (United Nations 2003).

The first published paper on social origins theory (Salamon and Anheier 1998a) used the data from phase I of JHCNP to test existing nonprofit theories. Discarding such theories as unsuitable for the data in hand, Salamon and Anheier looked elsewhere to try to explain the diversity and variation they were seeing in the international comparative data that their international partners had collected (Britain, France, Germany, Hungary, Italy, Japan, Sweden, and the United States). Drawing on Esping-Andersen's welfare regimes model (Esping-Andersen 1990) and Barrington Moore's work on the social origins of fascism and democracy (Moore 1966), they argued that the shape and character of nonprofit sectors internationally were influenced by the specific historical and political developments of those countries. In order to understand the diversity of nonprofit sectors worldwide, therefore, they argued, it was necessary to take into account the specific social origins of the countries in question. Accordingly, they suggested there were two key variables to consider in seeking to explain national variances in nonprofit sectors; these were government spending on social welfare and the size of the nonprofit sector measured in terms of full-time equivalent employment. On this basis, following Esping-Andersen's terminology, they posited four routes to a particular kind of nonprofit regime. These four regimes also took cognizance of certain social origins which were influential such as the presence of societal elites, the strength of working class mobilization, or the dominance of the middle class (what Steinberg and Young would call the "ascendancy of various social classes," 1998, p. 258).

Briefly, these four nonprofit regimes are liberal, corporatist, social-democratic, and statist. The liberal nonprofit regime is characterized by low government spending on social welfare and the presence of a large nonprofit sector. The corporatist nonprofit regime, by contrast, involves high government spending on social welfare alongside a large nonprofit sector. High government spending on social welfare is typical of a social-democratic nonprofit regime, but coupled with a small nonprofit sector, while the statist regime comprises both low government spending on social welfare and a small nonprofit sector.

While Salamon and Anheier's first paper (1998b) assigned countries to these regimes, they later asserted, on foot of critiques of these in *Voluntas*, that rarely were countries to be considered as pure types and that these regimes were heuristic devices.

Several years later, using the data from the second phase of JHCNP and prompted by critiques of the paper published in the same volume of *Voluntas* (Ragin 1998; Steinberg and Young 1998), the number of cases was expanded to include data from the countries involved in phase II of JHCNP (which had been reported since 1998; Salamon et al. 1998). Placing data from these countries along a quadrant where the "*x*"-axis was government social spending as a percentage of GDP and the "*y*"-axis was nonprofit employment as a percentage of non-agricultural employment, 22 countries were plotted in this model, again using the monikers liberal, corporatist, social-democratic, and statist as assignations (Salamon et al. 2000, p. 18). Although the four regimes were maintained, this analysis allowed them to account for the "impure" types which they had found in the international data. Several years later, another paper increased the number of variables (Anheier and Salamon 2006) and volunteering and membership were included in calculating the size of the sector. The inclusion of these was an attempt to explain nonprofit sectors which were not welfare dominated but which were still large. Anheier and Salamon pointed to the example of Sweden in this paper and noted that its sector was large in terms of membership and volunteering, although its employment data were low.

Despite the eventual increase in the number of variables, the two key variables of nonprofit employment and government social expenditure were maintained. These had prompted a lengthy critique by Wagner (2000), but his voice was not alone in critiquing or commenting on social origins theory. Our attention now turns to those commentators.

Critiques of Social Origins Theory

The development of social origins theory marked a major step along the road in nonprofit theory and received praise for that (Appleton 2003; Evers and Laville 2004; Lee 2005; Mullins 2000; Ragin 1998; Steinberg and Young 1998; Wagner 2000), in particular its recognition of the embedding of nonprofit organizations in societal, economic, and political structures. There have been a number of important critiques, however. Steinberg and Young (1998), for example, drew attention to methodological discrepancies such as the paucity of cases on which social origins theory was originally built; they also critiqued the theoretical validity of the underpinnings of the route taken by Salamon and Anheier in their own testing of extant neoclassical economic theories. Steinberg and Young stated, furthermore, that nonprofit-distributing organizations that do not fit the structural-operational definition "may be substantially more important in some countries than others, causing measurement error biases" (1998, p. 250).

Similarly, several years later, Evers and Laville (2004) noted that the structural-operational definition did not make allowances for certain kinds of organizations which were historically important in many European countries. They pointed to the examples of mutuals, co-operatives, and social economy organizations and stated, "the theoretical concepts underlining US contributions to the debate mirror a history that does not correspond to contemporary European reality" (2004, p. 1). Just 4 years earlier, Wagner (2000) had also argued for an understanding of different European situations, proposing different variables, and claiming that it was risky to generalize about public and private choices "beyond a particular institutional context and a particular field of service provision" (Wagner, 2000, p. 549).

Steinberg and Young (1998) made a number of recommendations for further theory testing such as geographical, demographic, and technological factors; they also suggested the need to think about sub-sector or the field of activity. Mullins (2000), who adopted this line of enquiry and looked at nonprofit housing, concluded that the effects of time on different policy fields are important to consider. Steinberg and Young (1998) also noted the importance of cultural factors, a point, which was later reiterated by Lee (2005) who found that while Hong Kong's nonprofit sector was statist-corporatist, cultural values could have an influence on shaping a particular policy field. Ragin (1998) in his critique favored the development of theory in a more historical and qualitative direction, while also noting the small number of cases on which social origins theory rested and what he termed were "crude indicators." Ragin advocated broadening the number of variables to "construct historically-nuanced comparative analyses" (p. 269) so that what he termed "a different beast in every country" (p. 265) is given deeper understanding and explanation.

Salamon and Anheier in their response (1998b) and in later papers sought to address some of the issues highlighted by Steinberg and Young, and Ragin. They acknowledged the small number of cases and several years later increased these substantially (Salamon et al. 2000), but still relied on the two key indicators of size and FTE employment. Six years later they increased the numbers of variables included in measuring the size of the sector, but did not then use these to plot against regime types. In so doing, they were seeking to offset some of the criticisms of their model for being perhaps American biased, yet important critiques have not been significantly addressed to date, and it is those critiques which help inform analysis of the Irish situation which features in the next section.

Applying Social Origins Theory to Ireland

Ireland, included under Phase II of JHCNP, was classified as liberal in social origins theory (Salamon et al. 2000, p. 17; also see Appleton's, 2003, application of social origins modeling to 12 EU countries). Since those JHCNP data were collected (Donoghue et al. 1999) and building on the experience of data collection for that study, we conducted the largest-ever survey of Irish nonprofit organizations in 2005 (Donoghue et al. 2006), which significantly updated the earlier data. Several years later, we further updated the data on government spending on the nonprofit sector (Donoghue 2008). What follows draws on both those data sets to reassess the application of social origins theory to Ireland.

Possibly the best place to start is with the two key variables used in modeling the empirical data, namely, the size of the sector and government social spending. In 2005 Irish government social spending as a proportion of GNI came to 19.6%, lower than the OECD 26-country average of 20.9%.[1] While lower than the average, social expenditure was higher than in the United States (15.8%), Canada (16.7%), Iceland (17.5%), Australia (17.8%), Japan (18.1%), and Switzerland (18.5%) (www.oecd.org). Using employment data collected as part of the 2005 survey on nonprofit organizations (Donoghue et al. 2006), full-time equivalent employment can be calculated as ranging between 9.9% and 15.1% of non-agricultural employment.[2] The JHCNP had earlier found that Ireland had a large sector based on an estimated 11.5% of non-agricultural employment (Salamon et al. 1998, p. 5). Using those two variables only, therefore, Ireland has a large nonprofit sector coupled with below-average social spending, which would suggest that according to social origins modeling, Ireland's nonprofit regime is liberal. Is this the full picture, however?

A liberal nonprofit regime is one where there is "a strong commercial middle class that has effectively neutralized both landed elites and the working class, and that is consequently able to resist demands for expanded government social-welfare benefits" (Anheier and Salamon 2006, p. 106). A quick trawl through Ireland's history does not indicate the predominance of such characteristics, however. Ireland was colonized by Britain up to 1921, when after the Easter Rising in 1916, the War of Independence 1919–1920, protracted negotiations over a treaty led to the division of the island into two jurisdictions; six counties in the northern part of the island remaining under British rule, the remaining 26 counties constituting the newly formed Free State of Ireland (since 1949, the Republic of Ireland). The national identity movement, comprising sporting, language, and cultural voluntary organizations, was very important in challenging the British elite, and many of those prominent in that movement entered national politics after the establishment of the Free State. At the same time, because national identity was closely bound up with religious identity, for historical and cultural reasons, the Catholic Church was to hold a powerful position in Irish society, a position which only waned in the past two decades.

Ireland was a peasant country, where voluntary action was integral to social and societal relationships. There was a strong culture of co-operation and self-sufficiency, which began to be institutionalized in the Co-Operative Movement from the late nineteenth century and in rural community development from the 1930s. Middle class and working class elements were small in number, although this changed from the 1960s when education provision opened up and industrial development occurred through foreign direct investment.

The religious orders had been delivering health and social services since the mid-eighteenth century, and provision by the religious had continued in the Free State, mainly because of subsidiarity, which was an important guiding principle. From the 1930s in education and hospitals, and the 1950s in social services, increasing

---

[1] In line with usage in Ireland, gross national income rather than gross domestic product is taken because of the high profits repatriated to foreign-owned multinationals. The use of GDP gives a distorted picture.

[2] These data are grossed up from survey returns, applied to the estimated size of the Irish sector, and are based on applying the median (9.9%) and the mean (15.1%).

formalization occurred and state funding began to be provided for voluntary or non-profit delivery. State provision of welfare began to increase itself, although this was not significant until the 1970s. Ireland did not develop a sizeable welfare state unlike other European countries, and a mixed economy of welfare characterizes the health and welfare system in Ireland. Indeed, Wagner (2000) argues that this is found in many Western European states.

There is also a strong urban community development strand with an ideology of co-operation and self-sufficiency similar to that of the Co-Operative Movement. Principles of inclusion, empowerment, participation, and sustainability are important influences, and European Union as well as national government funding has been significant in this area. The increasing importance of the community sector, as it is called, can be seen in policy documents, which began to refer to the community and voluntary sector (rather than the voluntary sector), and its participation with other prominent voluntary organizations since the mid-1990s on the Community and Voluntary pillar in the social partnership process. This process, referred to as a neo-corporatist arrangement (O'Donnell and Larragy 1998), has played a very important role in developing socioeconomic policy over the past two decades.

From this brief synopsis, the use of two variables to categorize the nonprofit regime in Ireland already seems limiting. In the field of welfare service provision, a corporatist-type arrangement exists, which has been underpinned by the principle of subsidiarity. Evers and Laville (2004) outline the characteristics of a corporatist regime which is not dissimilar to that found in Ireland where there is "a significant role to the third sector ... services are considered as an integral part of social policy based on taxes or social security resources" (Evers and Laville 2004, p. 28), although in Ireland the provenance of such an arrangement may be a little different. In the corporatist regime outlined under social origins theory, nonprofits are "one of several pre-modern mechanisms that are deliberately preserved by the state in its efforts to retain the support of key social elites while pre-empting more radical demands for social welfare protections" (ibid, p. 17). It can be suggested, therefore, that despite Ireland's ranking as liberal, the predominance of the Catholic Church (a pre-modern mechanism) in service provision up until recent decades is one signal of corporatist arrangements, but also the neo-corporatist structure of social partnership deserves recognition (Appleton 2003).

Wagner (2000) noted that the intermeshing of public and private organizations is a feature in welfare delivery in Ireland. Recent events might serve as an example. In 2008 the state won a High Court case taken by a survivor of sex abuse which had occurred when she was a pupil in national (primary) school on the basis that there was no "employer/employee relationship, formal or substantive" (*Irish Times* 2009, p. 4) between the state and the school.[3] From March 2009, all public servants were subjected to a new levy to cover the future costs of rising pensions. The teachers in that same national school, therefore, pay this state levy as public servants and

---

[3] National schools were established, on a denominational basis, in the eighteenth century. Although regarded as part of the state apparatus, these schools receive charitable recognition via their diocese. The teachers' salaries are paid by the state, but the state denies proprietary interest, as seen in this recent legal case.

because they are legally (in certain circumstances at least) part of the public sector. These two examples neatly exemplify the anomalies of the Irish situation, which arise out of the interdependence between public and private organizations (Wagner 2000).

In 2004, the government provided 60% of the nonprofit sector's income (Donoghue et al. 2006, p. 47). A later detailed examination of state funding (2007 data) revealed that the welfare service areas received the majority (83%) (see Table 4.1). A similar profile of welfare dominance appears in the income, expenditure, and employment data on nonprofit organizations (Donoghue et al. 2006) (see Table 4.2).

Table 4.1 State funding of nonprofit sector by field of activity (2007)

ICNPO field	Percentage of state funding 2007
Health	48.60
Social services	21.29
Education and research	13.22
Community development and housing	6.15
Civil rights, advocacy, and legal	2.63
Arts, culture, and heritage	2.53
Sports and recreation	2.29
International development	2.28
Trade unions, representative, and professional	0.41
Environment	0.41
Philanthropy and promotion of volunteering	0.34
Religious and faith based	0.05
Total	100.00

Source: Donoghue (2008, p. 3).

Table 4.2 Breakdown of nonprofit organizations' income, expenditure, and employment

ICNPO field	Percentage of total income	Percentage of total expenditure	Percentage of total employment
Health	24.2	24.9	21.5
Education and research	15.8	13.4	27.8
Social services	16.4	17.8	18.5
Community development and housing	14.9	14.2	13.4
International development	9.2	9.9	6.0
Arts, culture, and heritage	4.5	5.9	2.6
Civil rights, advocacy, and legal	3.6	3.2	2.9
Religious and faith based	3.5	3.8	1.3
Sports and recreation	2.5	2.2	2.4
Trade unions, representative, and professional	2.3	1.9	1.1
Philanthropy and promotion of volunteering	1.9	1.3	1.7
Environment	0.9	1.6	0.7

Source: Donoghue et al. (2006).

Social origins theory, influenced by neoclassical economic theory, emphasized the importance of variables such as size, income, expenditure, and employment. Focusing on these variables, therefore, a picture of state funding and welfare dominance emerges. Might the sector be envisaged differently, however? Given that the Irish state provides funding for service delivery; data on income, expenditure, and paid employment distribution in the sector reflect that pattern of funding. In other words, social origins theory points to the significance of state funding and the role of nonprofits in service delivery, but might not one be a function of the other and vice versa?

Anheier and Salamon in their later paper (2006) included volunteering and membership in their size data, and when we look at Irish findings on volunteering, a different profile from that presented above emerges (see Table 4.3). In their critique of social origins theory, Evers and Laville (2004) noted the important juncture between voluntary work and political and social participation. They said that the role played by social movements changed the perspective of the third sector from being "no longer the mere delivery of services and jobs" (Evers and Laville 2004, p. 29). We might agree and add that "modeling" of this space must include a wider view of the roles played by nonprofit organizations and not just service delivery, a point also made in Anheier and Salamon (2006) but which deserved greater development.

Table 4.3 Proportion of volunteers in Irish nonprofit organizations

ICNPO	Volunteers (%)
Sports and recreation	44.4
Community development and housing	29.0
Social services	14.5
Civil rights, advocacy, and legal	2.8
Arts, culture, and heritage	2.6
International development	2.5
Health	1.0
Religious and faith based	0.9
Environment	0.7
Philanthropy and promotion of volunteering	0.7
Education and research	0.4
Trade unions, representative, and professional	0.4
Total	100.0

Source: Donoghue and Prizeman (2006).

As part of the nationwide survey of Irish organizations in 2005, respondents were asked to indicate the importance of a variety of different roles performed by their organization. Table 4.4 shows how these are ranked (along a scale from 0 = not applicable to 6 = most important). Despite the predominance of service provision in neoclassical economic theory and in social origins theory, respondents from nonprofits do not regard this as their main role, nor even among their top roles, because as shown, this role was ranked sixth out of seven.

Table 4.4 Roles performed by Irish nonprofit organizations (in order of importance)

Roles (ranked)	Mean score for importance (0–6)
1. Providing a route for interaction with the community	4.7
2. Offering space for individual expression	4.3
3. Maintaining and/or changing societal values	4.1
4. Identifying and/or addressing social needs	4.1
5. Influencing or involvement in national policy development	2.9
6. Delivering welfare services	2.6
7. Developing the social economy	2.2

Source: Donoghue et al. (2006, p. 73).

Furthermore, while organizations involved in welfare services, community development, housing, advocacy, and legal services gave welfare service delivery a higher average score than arts, sports, and environmental organizations, all organizations, regardless of their field of activity, ranked the other roles more highly. It might also be worth noting that the role "Identifying and/or addressing social needs" may include some service delivery, but it is not concerned with mere service provision. This might lead to the conjecture that service delivery is regarded as a means to an end, and not an end in itself. Evers and Laville noted that the legitimacy of service delivery by organizations "strongly depends on their ability to give users a voice" (Evers and Laville 2004, p. 33); advocacy and other roles, therefore, are important ingredients to throw into the social origins debate.

Discussion and Conclusions

This chapter has examined the debate surrounding social origins theory and has applied the theory to Ireland, using key variables identified in social origins theory and in critiques of the theory. A number of salient points arising from that exercise can be noted.

First of all, if organization size is a concern, multivariate analysis comprising variables other than employment (and its comparison with service sector employment) could be more useful. The profile of Ireland's nonprofit sector is very different when compared from the perspective of volunteering numbers than when examined from the perspective of paid employment. A case could be made for the inclusion of volunteering in social origins theorizing because of that theory's use of the structural-operational definition (Salamon and Anheier 1996). Volunteering is one of the five key defining characteristics of nonprofit organizations (rather than employment), and so it would appear to make sense to use that as one indicator. Multivariate analysis using a number of dependent variables (Steinberg and Young 1998) would be more beneficial, particularly as the nonprofit sector differs depending on specific cultural, demographic, political, economic, and social factors.

Second, we need to be wary of discussing the "sector" as if its boundaries were fixed and immutable, and social origins, by adopting a historical approach, allows us to include the temporal aspect and therefore the notion of development over time (Mullins 2000). Ireland's civil society space is populated by a variety of organizations which define themselves differently and can make common cause with each other depending on the issue under consideration (Evers and Laville 2004; Kramer 2000; Smith and Grønbjerg 2006; Wagner 2000). In other words, the "sector" does not always act as a "sector," leaving us to ponder with Kramer (2004) whether "sector" matters.

Third, nonprofit sectors cannot just be compared to welfare service employment (Smith and Grønbjerg 2006), for a variety of reasons as the data presented above would suggest. For a start, while paid employment may be highest in welfare service fields, volunteering numbers are not, and the nonprofit sector does not just exist to provide welfare services. As seen above, service delivery was regarded as among the least important of nonprofits' roles. It can be advanced that a theory attempting to understand the social origins of civil society should also include the voices of those organizations occupying that space, rather than, or at very least alongside, the roles assigned by neoclassical economic theory. This inclusion can be particularly suggested in an area of activity noted for its value expression (Frumkin 2002) upon which its distinctiveness is claimed.

If the nonprofit "problem" is approached from the point of view of government financing, then understandably service provision will be more important and a particular perspective on and profile of nonprofit will result. If the focus is on nonprofits themselves, a different profile may emerge, which can also lead to different theorizing, as Wagner (2000) has suggested. If the economic contribution of the sector is the guide, then it is probably understandable that income and expenditure are dependent variables. If state funding is a guide, then the service role as a dependent variable probably makes sense. If civil society's importance is the rationale (and its social origins), however, advocacy, community, and self-expression are important roles and contribute to a different sense of the space that these organizations occupy than economic significance would suggest.

As Steinberg and Young (1998), Ragin (1998), Kramer (2000), Wagner (2000), Evers and Laville (2004), and Smith and Grønbjerg (2006) have argued, therefore, the choice of lens through which we view an object must itself be carefully considered and open to critique, otherwise that which is hidden from view may never come to light. In these straitened economic times where major questions are being raised about national economies within the context of the global economy and what roles states can and do play in these, it is right to ask where the nonprofit sector fits into this debate. It may be the case – just as Evers and Laville (2004) argue for "economies" in their bid to move the focus from nonprofit to civil society – that we can develop theory which allows for framing built on multiple perspectives. As Anheier (2007) has written elsewhere, if this territory which we are concerned with is a "zoo," the adoption of multiple perspectives on that "zoo" allows for its "zooness" to be explored, assessed, and ultimately appreciated. The use of a historical approach comprising political ideology, philosophy, demographic changes, culture, as well as economics is very important in the social origins approach. The theory itself is not done justice by the constraints of the measurement variables used at present, which the examination of Ireland above would suggest. The variables used in the measurement are too limiting for the analysis, and it is in the qualitative, historical picture that more depth is obtained. Ragin (1998), Steinberg and Young (1998), and Wagner (2000) among others raise serious questions about the choice of variables used in social origins theory. One might ask, furthermore, how a nonprofit "regime" can mainly be measured by employment size and government social expenditure. Different variables as well as a qualitative approach (Ragin 1998) deepen the analysis and mean that the exercise is not overly constrained by quantitative measurement.

References

Anheier, H. (2007). Reflections on the concept and measurement of global civil society. *Voluntas*, 18(1), 1–15.

Anheier, H., and Salamon, L. (2006). The nonprofit sector in comparative perspective. In W. W. Powell and R. Steinberg (eds) *The Nonprofit Sector: A Research Handbook*, 2nd edn (pp. 89–114), New Haven, Yale University Press.

Appleton, L. (2003). The contribution of NPOs to family policy formulation in EU member and applicant states. *Voluntas*, 14(1), 79–103.

Donoghue, F. (2008). *Quantifying the Economic Value of the Nonprofit Sector in Ireland*, unpublished report to Irish Government.

Donoghue, F., Salamon, L., and Anheier, H. (1999). *Uncovering the Nonprofit Sector in Ireland*, Dublin, National College of Ireland/The Johns Hopkins University.

Donoghue, F., and Prizeman, G. (2006). *Third Sector Mapping Project*, Dublin, Centre for Nonprofit Management, Trinity College Dublin.

Donoghue, F., Prizeman, G., O'Regan, A., and Noël, V. (2006). *The Hidden Landscape: First Forays into Mapping Nonprofit Organisations in Ireland*, Dublin, Centre for Nonprofit Management, Trinity College Dublin.

Esping-Andersen, G. (1990). *The Three Worlds of Welfare Capitalism*, Cambridge, Polity Press.

Evers, A., and Laville, J.-L. (2004). *The Third Sector in Europe*, Cheltenham, Edward Elgar.

Frumkin, P. (2002). *On Being Nonprofit: A Conceptual and Policy Primer*, Cambridge, MA, Harvard University Press.

Hansmann, H. (1987). Economic theories of nonprofit organizations. In W. W. Powell (ed.) *The Nonprofit Sector: A Research Handbook*, 1st edn (pp. 27–42), New Haven, Yale University Press.

Irish Times. (2009). State pursues abuse victim for legal costs. 24 February, p. 4.

Kramer, R. M. (2000). A third sector in the third millennium? *Voluntas*, 11(1), 1–23.

Kramer, R. M. (2004). Alternative paradigms for the mixed economy: Will sector matter? In A. Evers and J.-L. Laville (eds) *The Third Sector in Europe* (pp. 219–236), Cheltenham, Edward Elgar.

Lee, E. W. Y. (2005). Nonprofit development in Hong Kong: The case of a statist-corporatist regime. *Voluntas*, 16(1), 51–68.

Moore, Barrington, Jr. (1966). *Social Origins of Dictatorship and Democracy: Lord and Peasant in the Making of the Modern World*, Boston, Beacon Press.

Mullins, D. (2000). Social origins and transformations: The changing role of English Housing Associations. *Voluntas*, 11(3), 255–275.

O'Donnell, R., and Larragy, J. (1998). Social partnership in Ireland: Principles and interactions. In R. O'Donnell and J. Larragy (eds) *Negotiated Social and Economic Governance and European*

Integration: Proceedings of the COST A7 Workshop (pp. 84–107), Luxembourg, European Commission.

Ragin, C. (1998). Comments on "Social origins of civil society." *Voluntas*, 9(10), 261–270.

Salamon, L. (1987). Partners in public service: The scope and theory of government–nonprofit relations. In W. W. Powell (ed.) *The Nonprofit Sector: A Research Handbook*, 1st edn (pp. 99–117), New Haven, Yale University Press.

Salamon, L., and Anheier, H. (1994). *The Emerging Sector: An Overview*, Manchester, Manchester University Press.

Salamon, L., and Anheier, H. (1996). The international classification of nonprofit organizations – revision 1. Working papers of The Johns Hopkins Comparative Nonprofit Sector Project, no. 19, The Johns Hopkins Institute for Policy Studies, Baltimore, MD.

Salamon, L., and Anheier, H. (1998a). Social origins of civil society: Explaining the nonprofit sector cross-nationally. *Voluntas*, 9(3), 213–248.

Salamon, L., and Anheier, H. (1998b). On developing comparative nonprofit-sector theory: A reply to Steinberg and Young, and Ragin. *Voluntas*, 9(3), 271–281.

Salamon, L., Sokolowski, W., and Anheier, H. (2000). Social origins of civil society: An overview. Working papers of The Johns Hopkins Comparative Nonprofit Sector Project, no. 38, The Johns Hopkins Center for Civil Society Studies, Baltimore, MD.

Salamon, L., Anheier, H., and Associates (1998). *The Emerging Sector Revisited: A Summary*, Baltimore, MD, The Johns Hopkins Center for Civil Society Studies.

Smith, S. R., and Grønbjerg, K. A. (2006). Scope and theory of government-nonprofit relations. In W. W. Powell and R. Steinberg (eds) *The Nonprofit Sector: A Research Handbook*, 2nd edn (pp. 221–242), New Haven, Yale University Press.

Steinberg, R., and Young, D. (1998). A comment on Salamon and Anheier's "Social origins of civil society," *Voluntas*, 9(12), 249–260.

United Nations. (2003). *Handbook on Non-Profit Institutions in the System of National Accounts*, New York, United Nations.

Weisbrod, B. (1977). *The Voluntary Nonprofit Sector*, Lexington, MA, Lexington Books.

Wagner, A. (2000). Reframing "social origins" theory: The structural transformation of the public sphere. *Nonprofit and Voluntary Sector Quarterly*, 29(4), 541–553.

Chapter 5
The Civil Society Index

Alan Fowler

Introduction

In third sector research which (now) relies on concepts associated with civil society, whatever happened to the politics? This chapter argues that, in common with other major international research initiatives in this field, the Civil Society Index (CSI) exhibits a political "gap." At best, the CSI and similar macro-comparative approaches to understanding and investigating civil society provide only oblique views into an essentially political phenomenon. Findings from secondary analysis of CSI country studies successfully tease out interesting political perspectives, but are more tentative than robust in reaching conclusions or causations. But civil society was and remains an essentially political concept in need of robust, multi-country, comparative political enquiry in its own right. So why was politics not central to research theory and method and what might be done to move in this direction?

Answers to these questions are explored in relation to a compound hypothesis combining a particular historical moment and geo-academic predispositions, allied to Western normativism and funders' sensitivity to a sovereignty imperative. This confluence of factors led to scholastic containment and epistemic elision in favor of pre-existing economic, socio-institutional "sector" or "arena" analytic frameworks. These preferences were linked to interests in creating international "indexes" as a stimulus to public policy discourses and to test a particular, liberal theory of democratization. Allied to utilitarian agendas and biases in the funding of international research, framing of enquiries occurred at the cost of an explicit application of debates central to political theory, namely the acquisition, (re)distribution, and reproduction of power and authority in, by, and over a polity.

A. Fowler (✉)
Erasmus University, The Hague, The Netherlands and University of KwaZulu-Natal, Durban, South Africa
e-mail: alanfowler@compuserve.com

R. Taylor (ed.), *Third Sector Research*, DOI 10.1007/978-1-4419-5707-8_5,

This chapter offers a critical reflection on each aspect of such a hypothesis, leading to suggestions about how the politics of civil society could be more directly approached, perhaps as an analytic priority for the recently revised and currently implemented CSI and similar initiatives.[1]

Civil Society as an "Apolitical" Field of Enquiry

Some 20 years ago, emboldened by assertions of analysts such as Francis Fukuyama (1992), the West was seen to have "won" the battle of political-economic ideologies. Liberal democracy, allied to market capitalism, is "conclusively" proven better than alternatives at optimizing critical trade-offs between human freedoms, social stability, and adequate (material) well-being for a polity.[2] Notwithstanding many counter-arguments and subsequent revisionisms, this achievement had an important subtext, namely, that what had emerged unplanned from the histories of North America, England, and continental Europe is, with modest variation (Coates 2000), a superior model of how economic growth is attained with a lessening cost to society. This self-propelled trajectory of socioeconomic success was codetermined by political arrangements through which popular compliance is achieved with minimal need for (expensive) coercion and unnecessary restraint on human potential. In other words, over time this political system reduces the transaction costs required for gaining well-being, maintaining social order, managing the risks, and producing the "predictability" and "certainties" that efficient market capitalism requires. Regimes and policies in the post-Soviet states should therefore be supported along these "winning" lines. The task then was to propagate into Russia and Eastern and Central Europe the values, norms, and distributions of institutional functions and power relationships between rulers and the ruled that became embedded within Western institutional configurations. Geopolitically, as was already the case for some 40 years toward developing countries, international aid was a malleable device for implementing this agenda.

Explaining Soviet implosion and subsequent struggles of previously subordinated countries to find and embed a new political dispensation spawned a re-emergence of civil society as a concept inviting active scholarly enquiry. For example, the cases of Hungary, Poland, and Czechoslovakia reinvigorated interest in the role of activist citizens and self-organization of civic actors in the political evolution of nation-states. As a result, pre-existing and contending conceptualizations of civil society were dusted off and brought into the "overseas development,"

---

[1] For this chapter, the CSI is divided into two phases after the design, testing, and independent evaluation of the methodology. Phase I is the substantive application of the method in some 60 countries with subsequent analysis and dissemination of findings (2003–2008). Phase II (2008– ongoing) involves evaluation of and revisions to the CSI. At the time of writing, implementation is taking place in some 20 countries – some for the first time, and in others, as repeats.

[2] Exemplified in the words of Jeremy Bentham as "the greatest good to the greatest number."

rather than the mainstream domestic, discourse of major aid donors. And, given the context of "victory" described above, first among equals in this (theoretical) rediscovery of civil society was the liberal, "associational" explanation of democratization advanced some 100 years before in Alexis de Tocqueville's sociopolitical analysis of the United States of America.

Hence, the historical moment of the 1990s generated interest in the poorly understood but seemingly attractive concept and democratizing potential of civil society. As an instrument in foreign relations, this interest permeated into policy frameworks and discourse of and beyond government development agencies (e.g., Bernhard et al. 1998). In terms of the latter, a cluster of US philanthropies dedicated themselves to establishing entities which would enhance knowledge about and the profile of civil society through an international infrastructure for civil society research and activism. Their investments in the early 1990s established the International Society for Third Sector Research (ISTR) and Civicus – The World Alliance for Citizen Participation. The titles of these organizations reflected the contending language and thinking of the time – an (economically) institutionalized nonprofit "sector" on the one hand and citizenship as a sociopolitical identity on the other.

Another feature of this era was a plethora of conferences, seminars, and (overview type) books about civil society (e.g., Cohen and Arato 1992; Edwards 2004; Hodgkinson and Foley 2003). But, as many critics noted (e.g., Chambers and Kymlicka 2002; Hanna and Dunn 1996), these contributions drew on little evidence outside of Western contexts and experiences over relatively short historical time frames. Publications like the World Assembly edition *Citizens Strengthening Global Civil Society* (Oliviera and Tandon 1994) presenting the results of reviews in seven regions of the world and the *Civicus Atlas* (1997) covering some 60 countries were early attempts to remedy this situation. However, they demonstrated extreme difficulties in moving beyond the positive impressionism of the time to achieve a robust, empirical grounding. Recognition of this shortcoming translated into proposals and availability of funds to "define," "map," and "landscape" this phenomenon more accurately. Motives for doing so were mixed across funders and applicants. Objectives spanned academic entrepreneurialism, civic advancement, and utilitarian development agendas of, for example, diversified service delivery and better popular participation in state/donor projects and planning (Fowler 2008).

Nevertheless, a common feature was a framing of research questions and methods in associational terms by, first, establishing quantitatively and/or qualitatively what the universe of civil society "contains" and looks like. With this data, causal explanations for the configurations and behaviors of civil society could be elucidated. This logic was also practical. Despite contentions about labels, epistemologies, categories, criteria, measures, and indicators – articulated for example through articles in Volume 1 of the *Journal of Civil Society* (Heinrich 2005; Sokolowski and Salamon 2005) – from an international comparative research point of view, it is "easier" to populate sectors or terrains or arenas than to substantively investigate civic agency in political processes that span and connect institutional types and power arrangements over time.[3] Yet, for Civicus, the latter was clearly understood to be the real challenge:

> Underlying the notion of civil society is the understanding that it is fundamentally a political concept, which distinguishes it from other terms much in use today, including the voluntary, independent, third, philanthropic, nonprofit, or nongovernmental organizations (NGO) sector. Each of these terms describes a characteristic of civil society, but none of them provide the defining feature. In short, civil society is a political concept because it is concerned with exercising power to advance and defend the economic, social and political interests of citizens. (Civicus 1999, p. 8)

Consequently, political power should be central in such a research undertaking. However, this empirical imperative was confronted by two circumscribing factors: one geopolitical, the other epistemological. The political dimension was seen in donors' sensitivity to a potentially overt "intrusion" into the sovereignty of countries. Signs that "civil society" was not being universally positively received within the community of nation-states were already signaled in contentious debates about civic participation attached to lending conditions imposed by Multilateral Development Banks (Mohamed 1997). Similarly, millennium-inspired discussions about reform of global governance with a more prominent role for civil society heightened a backlash against the "unaccountable power" and questionable legitimacy of NGOs (Bond 2000; Kapur and Webb 2000; Van Rooy 2004). Consequently, an explicit political framing of the intended enquiry was best avoided. This research dimension was better approached indirectly by, for example, employing benign labels such as participation and values. Explicit questions about power, and the word itself, were not included in the CSI research categories and indicators. However, the factor of power was implicit in the formulation of many statements against which qualitative perceptions, translated into ordinal scores, would be made. It was also implicit in the action-oriented methodology which was intended to underpin and help catalyze civic action which could have political outcomes.[4]

A second constraint on adopting methods required for direct political analysis stemmed from a predisposition to the construction of a ranking index. Such an endeavor would create a simple and compelling way of presenting comparisons to the aid community, media, and public in participating counties akin to that pioneered by, for example, Transparency International. However, such an enumerated "static" measure was not methodologically amenable to investigation of dynamic political processes. Further, it was also recognized that constructing a country-based ranked index was technically not possible based on the "diamond" research categories (Anheier 2005; Heinrich and Naidoo 1999). However, once publicized, the index label stuck. One interpretation for this decision is that – in the political moment of the late 1990s alluded to above – an international index captured the imagination.

---

[3] An exception was a series of country studies led by James Manor of the Institute of Development Studies, University of Sussex, to investigate the interface between citizens and government in relation to public policy. However, the results of this endeavor do not appear in many references.

[4] Results of an impact study of Phase I – not available at the time of writing – will determine the extent to which this has occurred.

It drew attention to a new field of enquiry and emerging international debates that would be advanced by creating new knowledge and drivers for local action communicated through a familiar comparative, ranking "product." While the latter was not attempted, the former has been achieved.[5]

Finally, the CSI definition of civil society was explicitly non-normative. Yet the CSI approach, reflecting the mission and values of Civicus, introduced normative assumptions and inferences about "preferred" outcomes of sociopolitical processes that influenced statement specifications for scores (Heinrich and Fioramonti 2007). This methodological orientation created difficulties for arriving at unambiguous interpretations of findings and causal relations as well as attaining a full breadth and values diversity of local collaborators (as explained later).

In summary, the geopolitical moment, Western triumphalism, existing theoretical predispositions and institutional drivers, donor utilitarianism, and sovereign sensitivities as well as epistemological choices and communication imperatives interacted in ways that created an ostensibly apolitical, functional research agenda as a precursor to subsequent political analysis discussed below.

Bringing Politics Back In

In common with other studies about civil society, the CSI relied on a nation-state to delineate the borders for comparative study. Research mobilization, financing, methods, and subsequent analysis provided the country-based data sets from which, among others, political dimensions and explanations could be elucidated. And in keeping with similar enquiries, interpretation of national-level CSI data relied on a search for patterns of similarity and difference as pointers toward causal explanations of the configurations found (e.g., Heinrich and Fioramonti 2008; Salamon et al. 2004). In other words, there was a move from preoccupations with civil society composition and functions toward analytic concern for relationships and processes. It is beyond the scope of this chapter to compare the results of these various studies (particularly of the same countries) as a form of third-order analysis. Nor is it the place to delve into the technical problems of ordinal score aggregation and questionable elision between nonprofit and civil society epistemologies. Such a valuable investment could both deepen understanding and offer directions for critical "confirmatory" enquiry. Nevertheless, public availability of detailed CSI data and the very comprehensive comparative review of country-based findings provided in the second volume of the CSI publication offer a significant advance in our understanding of civil society and its limits.

For our purposes it is worth noting that the CSI method paid particular attention to the notion of the "environment" or context for civil society, albeit in ways that

---

[5] I am grateful to Finn Heinrich for this and other observations on drafts of this chapter. Civicus has not produced an international index of civil society. And, as Anheier (2005) points out, the methods of The Johns Hopkins team would not produce an empirically valid index either.

called for improvement in the methodology and analytic categories of CSI Phase II. Experience of Phase I showed that the "environment" permeated many indicators and could not be isolated from them. Consequently, distinguishing contextual features for all indicator categories was required. Hence, in the current phase, the environment is treated as an independent variable (socioeconomic, political, and cultural) within which civil society operates (illustrated as a circle straddling them all).[6]

This type of methodological revision was itself a product of difficulties in reaching robust conclusions with respect, for example, to the dynamics of political influences on the relative "strength" of civil society (Bailer et al. 2008).[7] An illustration of interesting findings meeting interpretative limits is the impossibility to explain why a positive correlation found between socioeconomic heterogeneity and the strength of civil society does not manifest itself in settings where heterogeneity stems from ethnicity (ibid, p. 246). Similarly, CSI results argue against a historical-deterministic explanation for civil society's configurations and comparative vibrancy. This finding relies on a direction of causality for civil society strength that runs from political and economic systems toward civil society rather than vice versa or iteratively. Yet this interpretation suffers from normative "blindness" to uncivil society and to forms of democracy which rely on corrupted or polarizing politics or contribute to state "failure." It also precludes a more complex interpretation of political codetermination between state and non-state actors as a positive-sum outcome seen, for example, in the mass-driven political transformations in Eastern Europe or ousting of presidents through civic action in The Philippines. Moving toward a more political enquiry can help remedy such limitations.

While not inherent to the definition of civil society used by the CSI, the country respondents were typically NGOs and activists sympathetic to Civicus's values, often introducing pro-civility biases to the scoring (Malena 2008, p. 186). In other words, as noted previously, a non-normative definition did not necessarily produce a non-normative enquiry. However, a critical review of the Values dimensions of the CSI results undertaken by Kopecký and Mudde (2008, p. 316) is particularly helpful in highlighting the need for interpretive caution. These authors call into question implicit assumptions about positive correlations between (the scale and strength of) civil society and democratic processes. They demonstrate that civic–political relations are more uncertainly complex than rationally linear, as is the nature of democracies as a range of systems. For example, identity-based mobilization and campaigning strategies that demonize the opposition, exemplified in the "fundamentalist" party politics of the United States (Boyte 2008), are quite pervasive. A recent expression is seen in the appeal of political xenophobia in elections to the European parliament. These, and other "frailties" of (mature) democracy in decline,

---

[6] I am grateful to Federico Silva of Civicus for comments on the draft information about the current version of the index. See also http://civilsocietyindex.wordpress.com/

[7] Strength is understood as "the capacity to contribute to democracy and development" (Bailer et al. 2008, p. 238).

signal the need for a re-reading of CSI findings that question the nature of Western democracy as practiced set against its idealized external projection.

The more general point is that comparing the political essence of civil society and of civic agency across the world calls for a more direct, less utilitarian, and aid-framed research agenda and forms of enquiry (e.g., Ottoway and Carothers 2000, on democratization). This type of conclusion was also arrived at by leaders of the CSI project:

> Stressing the importance of the relationship between civil society and the state inevitably leads us to an actor that is often alluded to in this book, but has probably not received the attention it deserves: the political party. According to the CSI's operational definition, political parties are civil society actors in their own right, since they operate in the public sphere to advance the interests of their constituencies. However, a large number of CSI country teams did not include political parties in their studies because of the closeness of these organisations to state institutions, but also because mainstream civil society stakeholders did not accept that political parties can perform roles similar to CSOs. In a way, this attests to the crisis of political parties in performing their key role of aggregating social interests and representing them in the political process. (Heinrich and Fioramonti 2008, p. 386)

This ending to CSI Volume 2, reflects a growing concern that party-based "democracy" – understood as a fair and transparent system that makes operational a reasonable citizen mandate for and control over political authority – is possibly past its sell–by date. Virtually across the global board, politicians do not enjoy much public trust. Notwithstanding important recent exceptions – India, Indonesia, Iran, and the United States – electoral engagement shows a general decline. Democracies that were consolidated and mature are being hollowed out, as is the public realm of open debate (Marquand 2004). Media spin and intentional mis-communication is rife (O'Shea 2007). Political access is increasingly privileging a "netocracy" (Bard and Söderqvist 2002). And choices between substantively alternative economic or political projects for society to pursue are difficult to find in the manifestos of major political parties, the 2009 election in India being a recent example.[8] These experiences invite a more direct enquiry about the interface between civil society and political processes, with power as a critical dimension of analysis. What this could mean for strengthening the CSI project forms the concluding section of this chapter.

Third Sector Research: The CSI as a Political Enquiry

Embarking on a more clearly political research perspective in the CSI can be undertaken in a number of ways as well as at different depths and refinements. Risks for those involved are associated with such choices. However, while the issue of sovereign sensitivity and regime "backlash" has not abated, action research conducted by the Institute of Development Studies (IDS) on claiming the rights of

---

[8] An observation by Arundhati Roy on the BBC World Service Forum, July 4, 2008.

citizenship demonstrates the scope for a more unambiguous approach.[9] More crucially, this body of work is important in terms of substance in that the CSI assumes that citizenship is more or less a given, without critically testing its meaning in different country contexts. A more political and power-oriented enquiry would require explicit attention to the nature of citizenship as a precondition for robust interpretation. From here, what might a layered and deepening political CSI engage with?

A straightforward starting point would be to investigate and test findings of CSI Phase I in terms of factors underpinning the transmission of civil society into political processes. These are popular grassroots support, the capacity to exert influence on authorities, and the ability to mobilize resources (Malena 2008, p. 195).[10] However, exploring these pathways and deeper research questions requires a firm analytic grounding in the theory, typology, and practical analysis of power. Again, the IDS project provides one type of categorization and useful analytic framework:

> Power 'within' often refers to gaining the sense of self-identity, confidence and awareness that is a pre-condition for action. Power 'with' refers to the synergy which can emerge through partnerships and collaboration with others, or through processes of collective action and alliance building. Power 'over' refers to the ability of the powerful to affect the actions and thought of the powerless. The power 'to' is important for the exercise of civic agency and to realise the potential of rights, citizenship or voice. (Gaventa 2007, p. 2)

An important complementary lens draws on the work of other analysts that interrogate power as individually socialized and embedded as well as actively constructed by interaction. They also move from covert or hidden to more overt, institutionalized, and transactional dimensions of power. For example, Bourdieu exposes power deeply hidden with acculturated worldviews and resulting predispositions toward and interpretations of identity and life's experiences (Navarro 2007). The work of Lukes (2005) and others point to additional, progressively overt, expressions of power. One is the function of language to define the parameters of thought and nature of knowledge. Language also dictates public and private discussion, communications, and messages, typically favoring existing systems of dominance. A further influence of language is to label "reality" in ways that manipulate or mislead peoples' predispositions or cause them to misrecognize their "objective" interests (Lukes 2005, p. 149; Moncrieffe and Eyben 2007). Further, Haugaard (1997) demonstrates how, following Giddens (1986), the structuration of power codetermines processes of (political) inclusion and exclusion and the rules of the game in sociopolitical arrangements and engagement. Finally, many authors treat physical coercion and force as, often, the most visible manifestation of power upon which – in the Weberian sense – states enjoy a defining monopoly.

---

[9] Visit www.drc-citizenship.org

[10] This triad bears similarity to the analysis provided by Michael Bratton (1992) drawing on theories associated with Marx (the material base), de Tocqueville (associational forms), and Gramsci (values that drive interests and direction of influence).

Effectiveness in this capability is argued to still be a critical factor in contemporary classifications of countries (Harris et al. 2009).

These complementary views of power as expressions and processes are not mutually exclusive. In fact, they offer a rich interpretive repertoire called for when probing the complexity of political processes. By way of illustration, Table 5.1 combines both ways of appreciating the qualities of power as an individual, collective, and transactional phenomenon that can be empirically investigated, often in terms of civic agency capabilities and outcomes (Fowler 2009).

Beyond investigating the three sources of civil society influence identified from Phase I, CSI Phase II could, through its participatory methods and planned country case studies, seek better understanding of how citizens "navigate" politics – that is, how and why they interact with the political system from the perspective of making it more (equitably) beholden to their influence. What is the political culture, why does it matter, and how (far) does it correspond to the formally constituted political system? For example, does the nature of political construction – bi-party with constituencies, proportional representation with party lists, and so on – make any difference to civil society's impact on the quality of governance? How far is it more robust to treat state–civil society relations as an iterative action–reaction from both sides, rather than dependent process? These are simply illustrations of what could be considered. In fact, in CSI a participatory process would be needed to come to a contextually meaningful political research agenda.

Table 5.1 Power from citizenship perspectives

Power expressions/ power substance	Power *within*	Power *with*	Power *to*	Power *over*
Psychosocial conditioning	Empowering acculturation and socialization	Self-selection of co-actors and collaboration for public action	Gain civic rights; choose and live a self-determined identity and livelihood	Assertion in and over society as a personal and joint political project
Control of language and thought	Applying critical thinking and interpretations	Creating a shared vocabulary	Impose or challenge discourses and what is publicly debated	Diversify types and sources and gain access to information
Control of rules and conventions	Knowing and asserting rights and interests	Negotiating collective outcomes	Fulfilling civic obligations; challenging exclusion	(Co-)determining society's values, norms, laws, and policies
Applying coercion	Questioning expectations of self-compliance	Adopting protective collaboration	Opposing unaccountable authority	Just use of public instruments of force

CSI Phase II is recommitted to action-research methods and the pursuit of follow-up activities. It is therefore imperative for the CSI process to actively include debate among local partners about the most important issues that appear across the civic–political interface. In particular, what can be done to regenerate politics as a source of active concern and engagement for citizens in all walks of life, not just in their roles within civil society? For citizenship is a socio-political category. This type of identity does not inhabit a sector, or arena. While problems of incorporating power analysis into the diamond remain, the Civicus Civil Society Index is well placed to include this broader perspective in its fieldwork and interpretation of results.

References

Anheier, H. (2005). Measure for measure: A commentary on Heinrich and the state of civil society indicators research. *Journal of Civil Society*, 1(3), 241–246.

Bailer, S., Bodenstein, T., and Heinrich, F. (2008). What makes civil society strong? Testing bottom-up and top-down theories of a vibrant civil society. In F. Heinrich and L. Fioramonti (eds) *Global Survey of the State of Civil Society, Vol. 2* (pp. 217–234), Bloomfield, CT, Kumarian Press.

Bard, A., and Söderqvist, J. (2002). *Netocracy: The New Power Elite and Life After Capitalism*, Harlow, Pearson Educational.

Bernard, A., Helmich, H., and Lehning, P. (1998). *Civil Society and International Development*, Paris, OECD, Development Centre.

Bond, M. (2000). Special report: The backlash against NGOs. *Prospect*, pp. 1–5.

Boyte, H. (2008). Civic driven change and developmental democracy. In A. Fowler and K. Biekart (eds) *Civic Driven Change: Citizen's Imagination in Action* (pp. 119–138), The Hague, Institute of Social Studies.

Bratton, M. (1992). Civil society and political transitions in Africa. In J. W. Harbeson, D. Rothchild, and N. Chazan (eds) *Civil Society and the State in Africa* (pp. 51–81), Boulder, CO, Lynne Rienner.

Chambers, S., and Kymlicka, W. (eds) (2002). *Alternative Conceptions of Civil Society*, Princeton, NJ, Princeton University Press.

Civicus. (1997). *The New Civic Atlas: Profiles of Civil Society in 60 Countries*, Washington, DC, Civicus.

Civicus. (1999). *Civil Society at the Millennium*, Washington, DC, Civicus.

Coates, D. (2000). *Models of Capitalism: Growth and Stagnation in the Modern Era*, London, Polity Press.

Cohen, J., and Arato, A. (1992). *Civil Society and Political Theory*, Cambridge, MA, The MIT Press.

Edwards, M. (2004). *Civil Society*, Cambridge, Polity Press.

Fowler, A. (2009). Civic agency. In H. Anheier and S. Toepler (eds) *International Encyclopaedia of Civil Society* (pp. 150–155), New York, Springer.

Fowler, A. (2008). Donors and civil society strengthening the CSI experience. In F. Heinrich and L. Fioramonti (eds) *Global Survey of the State of Civil Society, Vol. 2* (pp. 55–72), Bloomfield, CT, Kumarian Press.

Fukuyama, F. (1992). *The End of History and the Last Man*, New York, Free Press.

Gaventa, J. (2007). Finding the spaces for change: A power analysis. *IDS Bulletin*, 37(6), 23–33.

Giddens, A. (1986). *The Constitution of Society: Outline of the Theory of Structuration*, Berkeley, University of California Press.

Hann, C., and Dunn, E. (eds) (1996). *Civil Society: Challenging Western Models*, London, Routledge.

Harris, D., Moore, M., and Schmitz, H. (2009). Country classifications for a changing world. Working paper, no. 326, Institute of Development Studies, University of Sussex, Brighton.

Haugaard, M. (1997). *The Constitution of Power: A Theoretical Analysis of Power, Knowledge and Structure*, Manchester, Manchester University Press.

Heinrich, F. (2005). Studying civil society: Exploring the thorny issue of conceptualisation and measurement. *Journal of Civil Society*, 1(3), 211–228.

Heinrich, F., and Fioramonti, L. (eds) (2007). *Global Survey of the State of Civil Society, Vol. 1*, Bloomfield, CT, Kumarian Press.

Heinrich, F., and Fioramonti, L. (eds) (2008). *Global Survey of the State of Civil Society, Vol. 2*, Bloomfield, CT, Kumarian Press.

Heinrich, V., and Naidoo, K. (1999). From impossibility to reality: A reflection and position paper on the CIVICUS Index on Civil Society project. Civicus Index project occasional paper series, vol. 1, no. 1, Civicus, Johannesburg.

Hodgkinson, V., and Foley, M. (eds) (2003). *The Civil Society Reader*, Medford, MA, Tufts University Press.

Kapur, D., and Webb, R. (2000). Governance-related conditionalities of international financial institutions. G-24 Discussion paper series, no. 6, United Nations, New York.

Kopecký, P., and Mudde. C. (2008). Civil or uncivil? Civil society's role in promoting values, norms and rights. In F. Heinrich and L. Fioramonti (eds) *Global Survey of the State of Civil Society, Vol. 2* (pp. 307–323), Bloomfield, CT, Kumarian Press.

Lukes, S. (2005). *Power: A Radical View*, 2nd edn, Basingstoke, Palgrave.

Malena, C. (2008). Does civil society exist? In F. Heinrich and L. Fioramonti (eds) *Global Survey of the State of Civil Society, Vol. 2* (pp. 183–200), Bloomfield, CT, Kumarian Press.

Marquand, D. (2004). *The Decline of the Public: The Hollowing-Out of Citizenship*, London, Polity Press.

Mohammed, A. (1997). Notes on MDB conditionality on governance. In *International Monetary and Financial Issues for the 1990s* (pp. 139–145), Research papers for the Group of 24, vol. III, United Nations, New York and Geneva.

Moncrieffe, J., and Eyben, R. (2007). *The Power of Labelling: How People are Categorized and Why It Matters*, London, Earthscan.

Navarro, Z. (2007). In search of a cultural interpretation of power: The contribution of Pierre Bourdieu. *IDS Bulletin*, 37(6), 11–22.

Oliveira, A., and Tandon, R. (eds) (1994). *Citizens: Strengthening Global Civil Society*, Washington, DC, Civicus.

O'Shea, T. (2007). The doors of perception and the language of spin: Why Americans will believe almost anything. www.thetruthseeker.co.uk/article.asp?ID=185

Ottaway, M., and Carothers, T. (eds) (2000). *Funding Virtue: Civil Society Aid and Democracy Promotion*, Washington, DC, Carnegie Endowment for International Peace.

Salamon, L., Sokolowski, A., and Associates (2004). *Global Civil Society: Dimensions of the Nonprofit Sector – Volume Two*, Bloomfield, CT, Kumarian Press.

Sokolowski, S., and Salamon, L. (2005). Mirror, mirror on the wall? Commentary on Heinrich. *Journal of Civil Society*, 1(3), 235–240.

Van Rooy, A. (2004). *The Global Legitimacy Game: Civil Society, Globalization and Protest*, Basingstoke, Palgrave.

Chapter 6
Social Economy

Isabel Vidal

Introduction

Economic theory characterizes businesses as instruments to maximize the financial profitability of invested capital. This important supposition does not explain what drives a large number of initiatives within the production network. A field analysis shows that many organizations exist for reasons very different than the mere maximization of profits. In a market economy, private and autonomous organizations that deal in financial resources must cover their costs with their income. And they must report their profits. But they should not necessarily be governed or run by the objective of maximizing profits for private distribution.

In early twentieth century Europe, the label that was coined to identify this cohort of "other businesses" was the social economy. In academic circles, Charles Gidé, a French economist and the main representative of the historical school of economics, was one of the first scholars to use the term social economy (1905a,b) and to consider it a key element of social progress.[1]

I. Vidal (✉)
Centro de Investigacion de Economia y Sociedad (CIES), Barcelona, Spain
e-mail: ividal@grupcies.com

[1] For a more in-depth look at Charles Gidé (1847–1932), see Marc Penin (2006). The historical school of economics was an approach to academic economics and to public administration that emerged in nineteenth-century Germany and held sway there until well into the twentieth century. This school held that history was the key source of knowledge about human action and economic matters, since economics was culture specific and hence not generalizable over space and time. In English-speaking countries, the historical school is perhaps the least known and least understood approach to the study of economics, yet it forms the basis – both in theory and in practice – of the social market economy, for many decades the dominant economic paradigm in most countries of continental Europe.

R. Taylor (ed.), *Third Sector Research*, DOI 10.1007/978-1-4419-5707-8_6,
© Springer Science+Business Media, LLC 2010

The Rise of Not-For-Profit Organizations

In the mid-nineteenth century, the European market was far from developed and it still lacked a welfare state; as a result, a number of collectives were organized voluntarily, forming businesses to deliver services. The first manifestations were consumer cooperatives started by workers from the factories that emerged during the Industrial Revolution. The most prominent consumer cooperative was that of Rochdale, near Manchester, England, which had a lasting impact for having created and imposed the International Cooperative Principles around the world. These workers banded together to make purchases for their "market basket" at lower prices than those offered by retailers at the time. Following the consumer cooperatives were agricultural cooperatives, worker cooperatives, housing cooperatives, social security mutualism, and associations.

This group of socioeconomic initiatives seeks to improve the well-being of each member. It is the concept of mutual aid. These citizen initiatives were not limited to financial pursuits. In parallel, they promoted intense social endeavors: the members of these organizations dedicated their free time to training and to the collective sharing of their leisure. These mid-nineteenth-century socioeconomic organizations in Europe developed as a vehicle for business activities. But fundamentally they were schools of democracy promotion, local identity, and a primary source of social capital.

After the two world wars, a path of economic growth was forged that gave way to the development of more competitive markets in Western Europe and the construction of welfare states characterized by the growing capacity of production and public service provision. The result was a new institutional environment where mutualism and nonprofit entities emerged as economic actors geared not only toward their members but also to the public market. When public administrations began to establish strategic alliances with private organizations, they started adjusting their action plans and directing them toward the market, preferentially the public. The solid development of mutual benefit societies and associations in France and Belgium throughout the course of the second half of the twentieth century is largely due to the contracting of public services to nonprofits.

Currently, the growing demand for relational goods in industrialized countries opens new market doors for businesses specializing in the delivery of handmade and custom relational goods. These new markets foster the expression of the new social economy combining the economic rationality of wealth generation with the political rationale of promoting cohesion and social welfare. During 2002–2003, in 25 European Union countries, the social economy provided more than 11 million jobs, equivalent to 6.7% of salaried employment in the European Union (CIRIEC 2007).

The Concept of Social Economy

It is commonplace among many continental European scholars to distinguish between two main research traditions, which are "Anglo-Saxon" and "Francophone" or "Latin." Social economy is a term that forms part of the "Francophone" or "Latin" tradition. In the mid-1980s, major strides were made to define the concept of social economy.[2] In this chapter, we present two definitions. The first employs a normative perspective and the second a legal or institutional perspective.

A Normative Perspective

From a normative standpoint, organizations that form part of the social economy can be categorized as private, autonomous organizations with the following characteristics: they are formed by a group of citizens; political power within such organizations is not based on capital ownership; there is dedication to the production and delivery of goods and services on a continual basis; there is partial or no distribution of profits; and there is an explicit objective of mutual assistance or community benefit.

Social economy organizations are part of the private sector and do not rely on third parties. The characteristic of "being autonomous organizations" is very important. It means that their members are the ones who actually make vital decisions such as to close the organization. These organizations are created voluntarily by a group of citizens who – by their association, subsequent creation of an enterprise, and their becoming principal actors in the organization – hope to reach a goal which would be difficult to attain on their own and which the conventional private sector or the public sector does not adequately serve in the present time and place. This interpretation often depicts the social economy as being driven by a demand that is unmet or in need: citizens come together, decide to create a productive entity, and become principal actors in the organization by necessity.

The definition of social economy emphasizes that the organizations are democratic in nature. This is the principle of "one person, one vote"; political power is not a function of the capital invested. The legal restriction on profit distribution plays a minor role in relation to being an organization governed by democratic principles. In the age of Charles Gidé, the factor of mutual aid was the main driver for these organizations. It bears mention that at that time, Europe was undergoing a significant economic and organizational transformation without having created a welfare state. As a result, the nascent social class comprised of workers from the new factories tapped into the social economy as a tool to defend their interests. Social economy organizations are also typically commercial organizations. Once again, primary emphasis is on who runs the organization and who the organization serves. Businesses and organizations that share the label of social economy indeed form part of the market.

---

[2] Among the first contributions relating to social economy and the third sector is the book by Defourny and Monzón (1992), written in French. Monzón and Chaves (2008) published an article in English, compiling the primary institutional definitions of the concept of social economy.

A Legal/Institutional Perspective

From a legal or institutional standpoint, the three major components of the social economy concept, both in the age of Gidé (early twentieth century) and 100 years later, are cooperatives, mutual societies, and associations. These three structural forms fall under the same formal definition of being an association of people. This formal definition spans the legal obligation of democratic governance based on the inspiring principle of "one person, one vote." As Defourny points out (2001, p. 5),

> The third component, association, includes a lot of advocacy organizations which may also be seen as providers of services to their members, to other people ... or to the whole community ... More generally, it includes all other forms of free associations of persons for the production of goods or services where making a profit is not the essential purpose. Obviously, these organizations have a wide variety of names, such as: associations, non-profit organizations, voluntary organizations, non-governmental organizations, and so on. Foundations and some other country-specific organizations (such as charities in the United Kingdom) are also often considered under this heading.

The influence of territory in the social economy's profile is understood in terms of its specific strongly defined historical identity. The context is not therefore a fabric compatible with any type of print; history, culture, and relationships among public administrations and private organizations determine, or rather select, the forms of development taken by the social economy. For this reason, it is important to recognize territory as a space populated by people, institutions, and businesses that are interrelated; understanding the way in which these people, institutions, and businesses interact is crucial to understanding the dynamic of the social economy in each time and place. Consequently, although the social economy is considered to be composed of three major legal structures, every country has a group of related businesses that bear a different legal structure yet still comply with the normative definition proposed above. In Monzón and Chaves (2008), the different forms of these related businesses are detailed for each country within the European Union.

Terminological Debate

In Europe, social economy was the prominent term to designate a group of business initiatives whose objective is not to earn profits for subsequent distribution to private shareholders. Following the mid-1980s, new labels began to emerge that partially eclipsed the term social economy, which had dominated until then. Third sector is a term originating in the United States. In Europe, many scholars are gradually replacing social economy with third sector. As Hodgkinson and Painter point out (2003, p. 4), on an international level, it has not been easy to arrive at a universally accepted definition of third sector: "Part of the problem stems from the role of the sector in different societies and economies. Some countries want to include the social economy and cooperatives, whereas others see these types of organizations as part of the market sector." In Europe, the result of this tension is that third sector has two meanings, depending on the scholar's focus. Researchers of the Anglo-Saxon tradition identify the third sector with nonprofit organizations. For those of the Francophone or Latin tradition, the third sector is synonymous with social economy. In Europe there are two definitions of third sector: one that identifies the third component of the social economy and another that spans the three major components of the social economy in addition to related businesses.

In 1992, Laville claims the existence of "another economy," which is more plural, for Europe. He identifies new nonprofit organizations that are emerging under the term "solidarity-based economy." Little by little, this term is being used to identify a group of small, local businesses that offer custom services in which the worker establishes a direct relationship with the user.

The institutional recognition of the social economy rose dramatically during Jacques Delors's presidency of the European Commission (1985–1995). In this period, a general director of social economy was instituted within the Commission. In the cascading effect typical of Commission decisions, countries then created their own directors of social economy in different levels of public administration. This institutional recognition resulted in greater visibility and led to the exploration of a new field of research by young economic scholars.[3] This period also coincided with a wave of high unemployment rates throughout the member countries of the European Union. At the time, the cooperative movement reflected a more favorable job rate than did public or private businesses. This led the public heads of labor to promote the cooperative movement as a vehicle of active labor politics. In the year 2000, the general director of Labor and Social Affairs of the European Commission ordered a study to evaluate the overall contribution of these organizations in terms of jobs. In order to identify this cohort of organizations and eschew the polemical issue brewing of that time building between those who favored the use of the term social economy and those who favored third sector, the Commission created a new category name: "third system."[4]

Having defined the key terms, it bears mention that some scholars consider social economy, third sector, solidarity-based economy, and third system to be labels that aim to categorize different forms of people-serving business and economy without regard to legal structures. The term "social enterprise" refers to a subgroup from any of the four terms mentioned. Of course, when emphasis is placed on the words "business" and "economy," it refers to a group of market-oriented organizations, public or private, including other organizations whose mission is carried out on a completely voluntary basis, outside the market.

---

[3] The doctoral theses of Demoustier (1981), Vidal (1987), and Defourny (1990) emerged in this period.

[4] According to the European Commission (2000), organizations that belong to third system are private, autonomous groups with the following characteristics: the aim is not profit; limit profit distribution; paid work; an explicit aim to benefit the community or a specific group of people; a participatory nature, which involves the persons affected by the activity; multi-stakeholder organization.

Researching the Social Economy

The academic community is probably wider than what is commonly thought, but as Perri 6 and Vidal (1994) pointed out, it is highly fragmented, and many individuals in it are working in very isolated settings. It is larger than is sometimes recognized because there are so many scholars working in the sector who would not think of themselves as doing so. This fragmentation is amplified when a term is used that spans several legal structures within a single realm of structures; for example, in the cooperative movement there are different types of cooperatives – agricultural, consumer based, and worker – and as such, scholars focus on a single legal structure (such as mutual benefit societies) or on concrete types of cooperatives (such as worker cooperatives) or on a concrete sector of activity (such as production and delivery of relational goods in a particular geographic area).

Another element that deepens division and fragmentation among European researchers is the distinction between the two major research traditions in the social sciences: the Anglo-Saxon and the Francophone or Latin. The broad concept of social economy is accepted in academic circles of Francophone or Latin tradition; this tradition also includes French Canada, the province of Québec, which boasts a group of researchers who are very active in the study of different social economy organizations (see the websites of Louis Favreau, Bénoit Lévesque, and Marie Claire Malo, three professors affiliated with the University of Québec).[5] Social economy is a term used in academia in Belgium, France, Italy, and Spain on the European continent. As a result of human migrations springing from mutual and cooperative experiences in the early twentieth century, the term social economy is also known in some academic circles of Latin America, such as the case of Venezuela (for example, the title of the journal CIRIEC-Venezuela is *Cayapa: Revista Venezola de Economía Social*).

That said, even though the social economy from a research perspective is supported by a broad community of researchers from different fields within the social sciences, from the viewpoint of academic legitimacy, there is still a long way to go to reach full recognition and become a prominent focal point in social science research. Social economy is not at the core of any theoretical or empirical work of research in any social science discipline. It may appear to be a core area of interest, but it is not. It always plays a secondary role in the interest of the academic community, as understood as a whole.

A review of three leading international journals covering third sector issues confirms this perception. Taking the *Revue International de l'Économie Sociale (Revue des études coopératives, mutualistes et associatives) (RECMA), Annals of Public and Cooperative Economics,* and *Voluntas*, it is clear that only the first – *RECMA* – features the social economy label and specifies the three principal components of

---

[5]The University of Québec has campuses throughout Québec Province. Louis Favreau is part of the Université du Québec in Outaouais (www.uqo.ca). Bênoit Lévesque and Marie Claire Malo are part of the Université du Québec in Montréal (www.uqam.ca).

social economy. This journal was founded in 1921 by Charles Gidé and Bernard Lavergne.[6] Its social base is in Paris, its language of communication is French, and in October 2008 the journal published its 310th edition, representing 87 years of publication. *RECMA*'s articles contain studies and reflections surrounding the three components of the social economy, and recently they have featured other legal business structures, such as foundations. The journal is not well known in academic circles, however, where English remains the primary language of communication.

A second journal of greater international impact, which in December 2008 published its centennial-year issue, has since 1974 been titled the *Annals of Public and Cooperative Economics* in English and *Annales de l'economie publique, sociale et coopérative* in French. It is a review journal published on behalf of the International Centre of Research and Information on the Public Social and Cooperative Economy (CIRIEC), based in Liège, Belgium.[7] Edgard Milhaud was the journal's founder and its first editor.[8] As noted by Fecher and Lévesque (2008), this journal incorporates the term social economy in its French title. Geerkens (2008), in an evaluation of the journal, cites that one-quarter of its articles reference topics related to the public sector economy, cooperation, and economy organization. Among the articles that address the third sector, as understood from a wide viewpoint of social economy and nonprofits, Fecher and Lévesque (2008) demonstrate that from 1975 to 2007 articles related to the third sector grew in relative importance, reaching 56% of the total published in the 100-year-old journal (see Table 6.1).

Table 6.1 Third sector articles published by the *Annals* journal, 1975–2007	Year	Percentage
	1975–1985	24.6
	1986–1996	44.1
	1997–2007	55.9

Source: Fecher and Lévesque (2008)

Fecher and Lévesque (2008) recognize that one of the main drivers of the academic community's current interest in third sector organizations is the generalized practice of public administrations contracting out certain services in countries with welfare states. Regarding the growing interest of scholars, Fecher and Lévesque (2008, p. 679) begin an article highlighting that "The social economy did not yet constitute a recognized 'third sector,' despite the fact that mutual societies, cooperatives and associations had existed for over a hundred years."

The third journal referenced to illustrate academic interest in third sector organizations is *Voluntas*, published by the International Society for Third Sector

---

[6]Bernard Lavergne (1884–1975) was a law professor in Lille, France, an influential member of the cooperative movement in France, and a member of the Political Economy Society. In 1938, he published a book entitled *Grandeur et déclin du Capitalisme*.

[7]This journal's history, from its inception as the *Annales de la Regie Directe* to the present, is outlined in Geerkens (2008).

[8]To understand the importance of Milhaud in *Annales*, see Geerkens (2008).

Research. An analysis of published article titles reveals that the dominant approach is to identify the third sector with the third component of the social economy: associations, foundations, nonprofit organizations, voluntary organizations, and NGOs. For the period spanning 2003–2008, following the analysis of Hodgkinson and Painter (2003), the concept of social economy and cooperatives is used preferentially by authors from Italy and France, as seen in the papers of Thomas (2004) and Lindsay and Hems (2004). Nevertheless, it has also been observed that the Anglo-Saxon community has begun to express interest in the wider definition of third sector, as noted in Kerlin (2006) and also by the fact that this book has a dedicated chapter on social economy.

Social economy is an identification label; it is not an academic concept. The academy has opted for the disciplinary division of social science and stringent specialization – a state of affairs that make things difficult for researchers who consciously or not contribute to the study of social economy organizations, for much research is widely dispersed within the academy and often rather instrumental in approach, with a corresponding lack of visibility. This is a situation that does not facilitate the advance of sector studies, attract new scholars to the field of research, or provide incentive for the funding of empirical work. Furthermore, such diversification and lack of visibility results in a paucity of basic social statistics.

Final Considerations

In summary, this chapter presents two main reflections: first, it flags the risk of not knowing how to properly grasp the potential of a particular term, and second, not unrelated, it highlights how the credibility of social economy/third sector studies has been compromised – especially among social economy researchers.

As pointed out, the term "social economy" has existed in Europe since 1905 when introduced by economist Charles Gidé. The three major components of social economy in Europe are cooperatives, mutual societies, and associations. All three share a formal meaning of being associations of persons; as a result of this formal meaning their main characteristic lies in their governance, which is based on the democratic principle of one person one vote. All three emerged primarily as tools to serve the new social class which arose in the Industrial Revolution. At that time, workers decided voluntarily to come together and face new social challenges in a coordinated fashion; even today, they use organizations as a tool to meet their ever-changing demands.

As the socioeconomic environment has evolved, these organizations, in turn, adjust their objectives to the new institutional context, and as European countries began to build welfare state models, the mutual societies and associations in countries such as Belgium, France, Italy, and Spain evolved into primary stakeholders in public administration. Hence, the social origins of the three components of social economy remain, while organizations' management and operations are adjusted. Over the past 50 years, social economy organizations have not ceased to grow in economic, social, and political importance (CIRIEC 2007); there have been no exclusion on behalf of governments responsible for managing the welfare model in each region (see Vidal 2008, for the case of Spain). Associations, mutual societies, and cooperatives complement the duties fulfilled by conventional businesses and government. Evidently, regional considerations play a key role in how the social economy is structured in any given place. Relations based on cooperation and collaboration among the private conventional sector, government, and social economy organizations are crucial to understanding the profile of the social economy.

The term social economy is not an academic concept. As Lorentzen argues in his contribution to this volume (Chapter 3), terms may be an academic tool, but they are fundamentally a tool that these organizations use to identify themselves and gain the support of citizens – public support. That said, we must avoid the risk of failing to preserve the potentiality of a term that facilitates the identification of a group of organizations that share the same formal traits. The proliferation of terms in the past 40 years to refer to organizations of the same structure has caused the misperception among the general population that each term is referring to a distinct and separate group of organizations. As Lorentzen further states, the formal meaning and, therefore its style of governance, is what is vital for knowing if one is referring to very different or similar organizations. After having reviewed some of the terms that have emerged, this chapter maintains that social economy, third sector, third system, and solidarity economy refer to the same type of organizations – cooperatives, mutual societies, and associations – in addition to other related types that have come about in each specific area.

Perhaps the main obstacle dividing those who study the social economy and/or third sector organizations in their broadest definition is the uncertain or debated status of these terms in academia. Among economists, businesses are disproportionately portrayed as producers of goods and services, whose objective in a market economy is to generate profits for subsequent distribution to private shareholders. Far too often, organizations are classified as private and public only. And in the realm of the private sector, no differentiation is made. This gives the impression that all businesses are geared toward the same single purpose and that all organizations in the private sector act solely based on economic rationale. Another major obstacle impeding the social economy from becoming a more popular research area is the widespread shortage of information specifically related to these organizations in a great number of national statistics systems. As such, the research methodology that prevails far too often is that of the case study. This method is valid for an initial approach to research analysis and in particular to track innovations occurring in organizations, but in the middle- and long term case studies fall short, and, in the end, researchers seeking quantitative results end up making generalizations without distinguishing the behavior of different organizations across disparate industries.

In light of all the aforementioned difficulties, there is clearly a long way to go in this research field, including a need to evolve from descriptive analyses to more theoretical analyses. All the same, social scientists – especially economists – should make an effort to think more often in terms of plurality. Social economy organizations have existed since the Industrial Revolution; they will not disappear from productive networks – on the contrary, their presence is growing. These organizations are rooted in solidarity, in the appreciation of social, cultural, human, and environmental resources. Such values are the basis of all sustainable development. Any society that hopes to achieve sustainable growth must have a very efficient public sector, a lucrative innovative private sector that is competitive and socially responsible, and a strong and visible third sector. All three sectors are necessary. With unique strategies or action plans, each one meets different, occasionally divergent, objectives, but they all work together toward sustainable development. All three depend on each other and all three should act in coordination. They should not be studied as though they were three streams of water flowing side by side; on the contrary, they are three organizational forces whose action and coordinated work efforts guarantee the sustainability of a welfare society.

References

6, Perri, and Vidal, I. (eds) (1994). *Delivering Welfare: Repositioning Non-Profit and Co-Operative Action in Western European Welfare States*, Barcelona, CIES.

CIRIEC. (2007). *The Social Economy in the European Union*, Brussels, European Economic and Social Committee.

Commission Européenne. (2000). Troisième système et emploi: rapport à mi-parcours. Dossier pour la Conference au Parlament Européen, Bruxelles, June 29–30.

Defourny, J. (1990). *Démocratie cooperative et efficacité économique. La performance comparée des SCOP françaises*, Bruxelles, De Boeck.

Deforny, J. (2001). Introduction: From third sector to social enterprise. In C. Borzaga and J. Defourny (eds) *The Emergence of Social Enterprise* (pp. 1–29), London, Routledge.

Defourny, J., and Monzón, J. L. (eds) (1992). *Economie sociale – The third sector*, Bruxelles, De Boeck.

Demoustier, D. (1981). *Entre l'efficacité et la démocratie: les coopératives de production*, Paris, Entente.

Fecher, F., and Lévesque, B. (2008). The public sector and the social economy in the *Annals* (1975–2007): Towards a new paradigm. *Annals of Public and Cooperative Economics*, 79(3/4), 679–727.

Gidé, C. (1905a). *Économie sociale. Les institutions du progress social au début du XXe siècle*, Paris, Larose.

Gidé, C. (1905b). *Cooperation et économie sociale*, Paris, Larose.

Geerkens, E. (2008). *Des Annales de la Regie Directe aux Annales de l'Economie Publique, Socialee et Cooperative*: un siecle de metamorphoses d'une revue economique international. *Annals of Public and Cooperative Economics*, 79(3/4), 373–416.

Hodgkinson, V., and Painter, A. (2003). Third sector research in international perspective: The role of ISTR. *Voluntas*, 14(1), 1–14.

Kerlin, J. A. (2006). Social enterprise in the United States and Europe: Understanding and learning from differences. *Voluntas*, 17(3), 247–264.

Laville, J.-L. (ed.) (1992). *Les services de proximité en Europe. Pour une economie solidaire*, Paris, Syros.

Lindsay, G., and Hems, L. (2004). Sociétés cooperatives d'intérêt collectif: The arrival of social enterprise within the French social economy. *Voluntas*, 15(3), 266–287.

Monzón, J. L., and Chaves, R. (2008). The European social economy: Concept and dimensions of the third sector. *Annals of Public and Cooperative Economics*, 79(3/4), 549–577.

Pénin, M. (2006). Charles Gidé est-il toujours d'actualité? *RECMA*, 301, 65–81.

Thomas, A. (2004). The rise of social cooperatives in Italy. *Voluntas*, 15(3), 243–265.

Vidal, I. (1987). *Crisis económica y transformaciones en el mercado de trabajo. El asociacionismo económico en Cataluña*, Barcelona, Diputación de Barcelona.

Vidal, I. (2008). Beyond the welfare state: New trends in social welfare policies in Spain: Implications for nonprofit organizations. Working paper, no. 52, Facolta'Di Economia, Universita' di Bologna, Sede Forli, www.aiccon.it/working_paper.cfm

Chapter 7
Volunteering

Lesley Hustinx, Femida Handy, and Ram A. Cnaan

Introduction: The State of the Art and Beyond

In recent decades, there has been a burgeoning interest in the study of volunteering, and the number of publications devoted to volunteering has grown exponentially. The study of volunteering is inherently interdisciplinary and represents a rich diversity of questions and perspectives. At the basis is a common fascination with the phenomenon, which appears as a paradox in certain disciplines, while others see it as a natural part of social life or a matter of personality. For example, given the underlying assumptions of the self-interested rational *Homo sapiens* in economics, why would any rational individual make an effort and undertake to bear the costs of an activity that provides no material gains to him or her? Thus, economists set out to do a cost–benefit analysis of volunteering for individuals, paying attention to material and nonmaterial benefits that may compensate for the cost of volunteering to resolve this otherwise irrational behavior (Handy et al. 2000). Sociologists and political scientists, on the contrary, view volunteering as an expression of core societal principles such as solidarity, social cohesion, and democracy (Putnam 2000; Wuthnow 1998). And psychologists have identified a prosocial personality type, that is, a durable set of predispositions that distinguish volunteers from non-volunteers (Musick and Wilson 2008).

Volunteering is a complex phenomenon that is not clearly delineated, and it often spans a wide variety of types of activities, organizations, and sectors. Studies of

L. Hustinx (✉)
Catholic University of Lueven, Belgium
e-mail: lesley.hustinx@soc.kuleuven.be

F. Handy (✉)
University of Pennsylvania, Philadelphia, USA
e-mail: fhandy@sp2.upenn.edu

R.A. Cnaan (✉)
University of Pennsylvania, Philadelphia, USA
e-mail: cnaan@sp2.upenn.edu

R. Taylor (ed.), *Third Sector Research*, DOI 10.1007/978-1-4419-5707-8_7,
© Springer Science+Business Media, LLC 2010

volunteering typically focus on unique and discrete subsets of volunteers who perform diverse tasks ranging from sitting on governance boards to stuffing envelopes (Cnaan et al. 1996). In addition, volunteering continues to be a social construct with multiple definitions; and what is understood as volunteering is a matter of public perception (Handy et al. 2000; Meijs et al. 2003). As a consequence, the boundaries between what definitely constitutes volunteering and what does not are permeable. Thus, the very definition of volunteering is elusive, and there are limits to the ability to generalize the findings of many excellent studies. At the same time, the diversity of perspectives and approaches demonstrates the richness and versatility of the scholarship on volunteering.

The study of volunteering has resulted in a number of established frameworks. For example, one of the most agreed-upon aspects of volunteer research is that people with higher social and economic status tend to volunteer more (Wilson 2000). David Horton Smith (1994) conceptualized this phenomenon as the "dominant status model." Those with high socioeconomic statuses have higher rates of volunteering and they also tend to occupy more prestigious positions and fulfill more meaningful tasks in the organization. Sociologists Wilson and Musick (1997) have advanced an "integrated theory of volunteering" based on three assumptions: that volunteering is productive work that requires human capital; it is done collectively and as such needs social capital; and finally, it is "ethically" guided and hence requires cultural capital. Using data from the Americans' Changing Lives panel study, they indeed found evidence for this "resource model." In a recent publication, Musick and Wilson (2008) offer advanced discussions of key resources for volunteer participation based on an extensive review of scholarship in the field.

While our understanding of volunteerism is greatly indebted to these seminal frameworks, it should be recognized that there are a number of important limitations. First, existing research is biased toward explaining the supply of volunteers. The core interest is to predict *who* volunteers – the determinants of volunteering, and *why* people volunteer – the motivations to volunteer and benefits of volunteering (Handy and Hustinx 2009). Thus, the focus lies essentially on micro-structural theories and models, viewing volunteering primarily as an individual behavior, explainable by individual structural and cultural features (Penner and Finkelstein 1998; Sokolowski 1996; Wilson 2000). As yet, the organizational and institutional context of volunteering remains ill-understood.

Second, prevailing explanations of volunteering are directed toward uniformity and stability. Because of the core interest in explaining participation in volunteering (yes/no), the complex reality of volunteering is commonly studied by means of a unidimensional measure, as if it were a uniform and robust entity (Cnaan and Amrofell 1994; Cnaan et al. 1996). In addition, the phenomenon is treated as a stable factor, not taking into account how the nature of involvement may change through the different phases of organizational socialization (Haski-Leventhal and Bargal 2008; Lois 1999) and over time (Hustinx and Lammertyn 2003; Lorentzen and Hustinx 2007; Wuthnow 1998). Prevailing frameworks developed when the dominant trends were the more traditional types of volunteering and may fail to capture the newer trend of episodic volunteering (Cnaan and Handy 2005; MacDuff

2004) with more short-term and individualized types of involvement, for instance where individuals do all their volunteering over the Internet or take trips to foreign lands and incur substantial costs to volunteer in exotic locations.

Recently, an increasing number of scholars have been broadening the scope of their observations to include contextual determinants of volunteering and to focus more on the dynamics and changes in volunteering. For example, Omoto and Snyder (2002) have advanced a conceptual model of the "context and process of volunteerism." It characterizes volunteering "as a phenomenon that is situated at, and builds bridges between, many levels of analysis and that unfolds over time" (Omoto and Snyder 2002, p. 847). Thus, we need to consider multiple levels of analysis (individual, interpersonal, organizational, and broader societal level) for different stages in the life course of volunteers (i.e., antecedents, experiences, and consequences).

In this chapter, we examine emerging theories and new directions in volunteering research, to account for the multilayered and dynamic nature of volunteering. First, micro-structural explanations of volunteering – the antecedents – have been supplemented with macro-structural theories and analyses. Second, recent research has provided more insight into the actual process and experiences of volunteering beyond the conventional unidimensional understanding. Third, we note that the profile of the volunteer and the nature of volunteering are undergoing radical changes because of broader social changes, and we observe new trends with concomitant innovations in volunteer management. Next, the third sector itself is changing as a result of a changing public policy, raising the question, what will be the influence of sector-wide changes on the experience of volunteering? Finally, in the light of these sector changes, new methods of social accounting have emerged that expand traditional financial statements of nonprofits to account for volunteer labor. These address the question of the value of volunteering – that is, what volunteerism is worth.

Antecedents of Volunteering: Toward a Macro-Structural Theory

Until recently, the complex question of how the larger sociocultural context, or the macro-system, impacts individual volunteering has received little attention among scholars in the field (Hodgkinson 2003; Wilson 2000). It however is imperative to situate these micro-level attributes in the broader social, structural, and cultural context of volunteering. Volunteer activities are embedded in interpersonal relationships with other volunteers, paid staff, and recipients of the services, as well as in specific organizational programs and settings and broader societal characteristics and dynamics. Kulik (2007a,b), in an attempt to understand volunteering across different service organizations in Israel, uses an "ecological systems model" (Bronfenbrenner 1979), which explains human behavior as influenced by a continuing process of "mutual interactions" between individuals and their environment. It represents a multilayered system of ecological variables at different levels, from the "ontogenic" system including variables related to the individual (sociodemographic variables and personality traits), over the micro-system (family and volunteer context) to the macro-system (social norms and values, and institutions).

Recently, the comparative study of volunteerism at the macro-level has gained momentum. An increasing number of studies are devoted to explaining cross-national differences in volunteer participation above and beyond individual-level determinants. Such macro-structural theories concentrate on the opportunity structures or social conditions that facilitate or impede volunteering (Salamon and Sokolowski 2003). It is assumed that the three types of capital (i.e., human, social, and cultural) that predict volunteering at the individual level (Wilson and Musick 1997) are also important resources at the country level (Parboteeah et al. 2004). Key context variables that have been identified as relevant in explaining differences in the amount and type of volunteering between countries are economic (national economic development), political (stability and level of democracy, and welfare state regimes), and cultural (values and religion) factors (Curtis et al. 1992; Hodgkinson 2003; Ruiter and De Graaf 2006; Schofer and Fourcade-Gourinchas 2001; Salamon and Sokolowski 2003).

One of the most systematic contributions to the development of a macro-structural theory of volunteering is based on the social origins theory put forward by Salamon and Anheier (1998) and Salamon, Sokolowski, and Anheier (2000). This theory explains the size and development of the nonprofit sector as an outcome of broadly defined power relations among social classes and social institutions (see also Chapter 4). It differentiates among four different regimes – liberal, social-democratic, corporatist, and statist – with corresponding levels of government social welfare spending and nonprofit sector size ranging from high to low. At one end, in the liberal model or regime, low government spending on social welfare services is associated with a relatively large nonprofit sector mainly focused on service provision. At the opposite end is the social-democratic model in which high government spending on social welfare results in a limited role for nonprofit service provision, but a larger role for the expression of political, social, or recreational interests. In addition, corporatist and statist models also exist, both characterized by strong states, with the state and nonprofits partnering in the corporatist model, while the state retains the upper hand in many social policies in the statist model.

Using the social origins theory for understanding cross-national variation, more recent work by Salamon and Sokolowski (2001, 2003) argued that the amount and type of volunteering in a country would also depend on the nature of the regime, that is, the larger the size of the nonprofit sector, the greater the volunteer participation. Thus, they hypothesized that "the amount of volunteering in countries with strong liberal or corporatist traditions is generally larger than in those with statist and social-democratic traditions" (Salamon and Sokolowski 2001, p. 14). However, the authors observed that the relationship between nonprofit regime and the structure of volunteering is more complex. For example, they noted that some Scandinavian countries with strong government involvement in social welfare have a smaller nonprofit sector but relatively higher rates of volunteering. Hence, there is a need to examine whether volunteers play service or expressive roles in different regimes to understand their effect on volunteering. Yet, in general, these authors expect the nonprofit regime model to help explain cross-country variation in the amount of volunteering.

The Process of Volunteering: Styles, Stages, and Transitions

While the bulk of volunteering research has focused on the determinants of participation in volunteering, a more in-depth and dynamic understanding of the volunteer process is lacking. Here we explore the two new frameworks that seek to provide more complexity and dynamism. First, it should be recognized that volunteering is an inherently multidimensional phenomenon. Existing research has focused on manifold aspects of volunteering: length of service, intensity of involvement, organizational commitment, motivation to volunteer, and so on. Although there is a sense of complexity, few studies have explored the interplay among these separate variables. For example, Pearce (1993) coined a basic distinction between "core" and "peripheral" volunteers and described their differential organizational experiences on the basis of a number of structural (e.g., formal office and intensity of involvement) and cultural (e.g., dedication to the organization) features. Although no formal role distinctions between both groups existed, Pearce found that core volunteers took an interest in the organization and usually, but not always, held a formal office. They provided the time and commitment that was necessary for the coordination of the organization and were considered "the leadership." In contrast, members of the periphery were less involved. They spent less time on the organization's activities and were less informed about them.

A more recent account of the multidimensional nature of volunteering was offered by Hustinx and Lammertyn (2003). These authors advanced a new analytical framework of "styles of volunteering" (the SOV construct) based on three criteria. First, the nature of volunteering is essentially multidimensional (motivations, frequency of volunteering, types of activities, etc.). Second, volunteering is a multilayered phenomenon that requires multiple levels of analysis (structural and cultural, but also the level of the individual volunteer, the organization, and the broader context). Finally, volunteering is a multiform reality. Various volunteer characteristics intertwine in systematic and multiple ways. In an empirical study of Red Cross volunteers in Flanders (Belgium), Hustinx (2005) found five distinct styles of volunteering that reflected complex and distinct interactions among multiple structural and cultural indicators of volunteering. Volunteers with similar levels of participation could perform highly diverging volunteer roles and embrace heterogeneous motivational and attitudinal dispositions. Hustinx, for instance, identified two completely different categories of board members, both of which were significantly more involved in a number of vital volunteer activities (e.g., coordination of meetings, decision making, organization of activities, administrative tasks, training, and lecturing), but despite their comparable job responsibilities, they differed greatly in their intensity of involvement (episodic and limited hours versus unrestricted) and motivational-attitudinal dispositions (formal and distant versus unconditional but also critical toward the organization).

While these frameworks consider the multifaceted and multidimensional nature of volunteering, other frameworks have focused on the dynamic nature of the volunteer experience. Omoto and Snyder (2002) conceptualized the volunteer process or "life cycle of volunteers" in terms of three broad stages – antecedents, experiences, and consequences – thereby treating the complex stages and transitions involved in the volunteer experience itself as a single category. A new differentiated and more complex model of the process of volunteering, called the Volunteer Stages and Transitions Model (VSTM), was advanced by Haski-Leventhal and Bargal (2008). The VSTM identifies five distinct phases (nominee, newcomer, emotional involvement, established volunteering, and retiring), four transitions (entrance, accommodation, affiliation, and renewal), and two kinds of turnover (early ejection and exit at the end) within the process of organizational socialization. The authors explain transitions between the phases and detail the process, experiences, and emotions involved in each phase as they are reflected in different aspects of volunteer work: "On the one hand, VSTM binds together motivation, satisfaction, rewards, and costs that until now have been studied separately. On the other, it differentiates these aspects according to the phases of volunteering and does not just categorize them generally" (Haski-Leventhal and Bargal 2008, p. 97).

Haski-Leventhal and Bargal conducted an ethnographic study of volunteers working for at-risk youth in Israel and indeed found that all volunteers went through several phases, involving deep changes and shifts in their activity, perceptions, attitudes, emotions, and relationships with others. Furthermore, different aspects of volunteering (activity and training, emotions, relationships with other players, motivation and commitment, attitudes and perceptions, and costs and benefits) were differently described by each of the groups of volunteers (newcomers, active volunteers, and established volunteers), suggesting the transitions predicted in their model (Haski-Leventhal and Bargal 2008).

Volunteering and Social Change: Emergence of the Reflexive Volunteer

A recent and more narrative stream of theorizing deals with the consequences of broader social changes on the nature of volunteering (Eckstein 2001; Jakob 1993; Hustinx and Lammertyn 2003; Lorentzen and Hustinx 2007; Wuthnow 1998). Such theories combine the analysis of context and process of volunteering, reflecting upon the apparent shift in the way in which people participate in volunteering as a result of broader processes of modernization, secularization, and individualization. These changes are commonly grasped in terms of a transition from "traditional" or "collective" to "modern" or "individualized" types of involvement. Important dimensions along which the face of volunteering is assumed to be changing are the shift from habitual and dedicated involvement toward more episodic or one-off volunteer efforts, more self-interested motivations, and weaker organizational attachments (for a discussion, see, among others, Cnaan and Handy 2005; Gaskin 1998; Handy et al. 2006; Hustinx 2001, 2008; MacDuff 2004; Rehberg 2005; Wollebæk and Selle 2003; Wuthnow 1998).

From a sociological point of view, recent changes in volunteering could be framed in a broader process of "human development" (Inglehart and Welzel 2005) that breeds self-expressive values at the expense of traditional authorities and collective frames of reference. Today's volunteers are more autonomous and self-conscious actors articulating their own views and preferences, thereby challenging traditional organizational structures. Hustinx and Lammertyn (2003) coined the notion of "reflexive volunteering" to conceptualize the shift from former heteronymous or collective monitoring of agents to the autonomous, active, and permanent self-monitoring of individual life courses and lifestyles. Reflexive volunteering is fundamentally entrenched in the active (re-)design of individualized biographies and lifestyles (Hustinx 2008). The notion of a "biographical match" refers to the idea that individualized conditions and volunteer experiences have to be reconciled in an active way: motivation, occasion, and opportunity have to match in a particular biographical stage or situation (Kühnlein and Mutz 1999). The biographical match can be analytically decomposed in a subjective-cultural willingness and an objective-structural availability to volunteer (Hustinx and Lammertyn 2003; Meijs et al. 2006).

Trends in Volunteering

Recent literature has reflected upon the ways in which the volunteer labor supply shifts in response to these biographical changes. Modern volunteers often prefer short-term volunteering assignments or discrete task-specific volunteering projects, which commit them to particular tasks or times rather than traditional long-term assignments, which involve a greater commitment to the organization itself. Such volunteering, termed "episodic volunteering" (MacDuff 2004), has been rising significantly in recent years, and an increasing number of studies are devoted to understanding the phenomenon (Cnaan and Handy 2005; Handy et al. 2006; Hustinx et al. 2008).

One of the new and more episodic types of volunteering is "virtual volunteering." Rapid changes in technology have enabled many individuals, in particular technologically savvy youth, to assist organizations without being physically present. The opportunity to "volunteer in your pajamas" significantly widens the scope of volunteer opportunities available. Indeed, nonprofits across the globe are now increasingly relying on virtual volunteers for tasks such as translating, managing online website content, organizing campaigns, fundraising, sending out information and communications to members, conducting online research, and providing online mentoring. The Internet thus changes the way both organizations and their volunteer programs operate in a radical way.

According to Cravens (2006), the Internet is used to effectively reach out to volunteers and targets a variety of audiences. For many organizations, the Internet has been a successful way of attracting volunteers who have not responded to the usual recruitment methods of volunteering. This applies in particular to those introverted individuals who may hesitate to get involved because of social anxiety about going to new places and working among strangers (Handy and Cnaan 2007), to the disabled, or to those who lack transportation. Thus, virtual volunteering has presented many opportunities to those who want to volunteer without having to leave the comfort of their homes and to those who want flexibility in their volunteer hours.

Another successful type of episodic volunteering involves traveling outside of one's country to volunteer in foreign locations. Such volunteering, which often combines volunteering with tourism, is called "voluntourism." It brings volunteers to foreign countries for a period of anywhere between a week to a few years. Volunteer assignments vary depending on the interests of the volunteer and the needs of the host organization, but commonly include projects related to ecological preservation or social and economic development (Sherraden et al. 2006, 2008).

In the past, travel to volunteer typically meant a significant investment of time – generally requiring people to spend several months or even years supporting a project – and often took the form of missionary work through one's religious congregation or outreach programs through government-supported initiatives such as the Peace Corps (United States) and CUSO (Canada). The new trend of voluntourism reflects many of the same concerns that have led to episodic volunteering, allowing individuals to combine their vacation time with service activities while still holding full-time employment in their countries of residence. This new trend again reflects the responses to lifestyle changes and diminished long-term loyalty to any one organization or cause.

This sort of volunteer project has an appeal that resonates with tourists of all ages who are seeking a deeper understanding of the places they visit and the opportunity to experience life in less widely traveled regions. In a recent study of individuals who had participated in a volunteer vacation, participants were asked their main motive for participating in each of their volunteer tourism trips. Although respondents gave more than one motive for going on their trip, the primary and most often quoted motive was that participants "desired a new experience" (Carter 2008, p. 71).

A third new trend is that of volunteering by employees of large corporations, where the employer provides support and often initiates projects. Such volunteering often arises as part of corporate initiatives aimed at meeting their social responsibilities to the communities in which they exist and which support their businesses. One of the ways many corporate social responsibility (CSR) initiatives are carried out is through employer-supported volunteering (ESV) programs. Sometimes ESV programs are supported by employers by giving incentives to recruit employees to company-sponsored projects, and at other times, the company simply provides approval and support, tangible or otherwise, for employee-initiated community projects (Meinhard et al. 2009).

In a study of Canadian ESV programs, Easwaramoorthy et al. (2006, p. iii) note that "the most common forms of [volunteer] support are adjusting work schedules (78%), providing time-off without pay (71%), and allowing access to company facilities and equipment (70%)." Other forms of ESV initiatives mentioned in the literature include corporate sponsorship of events such as fundraising runs/walks, where employees' participation is encouraged through corporate teams (Hall et al. 2007; Rog et al. 2004); forming partnerships or liaising with local volunteer centers (Easwaramoorthy et al. 2006); forming long-term partnerships with community agencies to share expertise through the volunteering of their employees (Rog et al. 2004); providing resources and allowing volunteers to use company equipment or facilities for their programs (Hall et al. 2006); modifying work hours or giving time-off for employee volunteers (Easwaramoorthy et al. 2006); and honoring volunteers for exemplary community work and rewarding them by donating to their organization of choice (Graff 2004).

Innovations in Volunteer Management

Innovations in volunteer management are often very specific to the kinds of organization. Certain well-tried and true volunteer management techniques are ubiquitous and form the backbone of all volunteer programs and are no doubt impacted by what volunteers do in the organization, why they come to volunteer, and the intensity of their participation. Two recent books by Liao-Troth (2008) and Gazley and Dignam (2008) are practitioner-based volumes, with innovations in volunteer management. They pay close attention to the perennial "what's in it for my work?"-demands from busy practitioners.

Liao-Troth's (2008) edited volume, *Challenges in Volunteer Management*, presents many examples of managing volunteers in different contexts and underscores the well-founded argument that there exists no one way that is best to manage volunteers, a point we agree with given the increasingly diverse and individualized nature of volunteering. Meijs and Ten Hoorn (2008) point out that volunteers often have conflicting goals: volunteers prefer to have efficiently run, successful organizations with clear inputs and effective task assignments. At the same time, they want flexibility, fun, and respect for what they are willing to accomplish in their leisure time. How to balance these needs? They offer varying management styles that help with this question that is dependent on whether the organization is run by volunteers versus paid staff and that is dependent on whether the nonprofit is organized for mutual support, service delivery, and campaigning.

In their book *The Decision to Volunteer*, Gazley and Dignam (2008) direct their response management of volunteers based on their findings of the "why" people volunteer – and "who" volunteers. This suggests that innovative management practices need to be preceded with a thorough understanding of not only the organizational goals but also the volunteers (Liao-Troth and Dunn 1999). Furthermore, volunteer participation rates can be used to calculate the value of volunteering to the organization; this would give managers insights into the resources being invested in its volunteer programs and the return on that investment – a topic we return to later in this chapter. Gazley and Dignam (2008) also suggest that information from those who do *not* volunteer or who *quit* volunteering is useful to isolate management practices that may be unfriendly to volunteering and may create new ways that allow non-volunteers to volunteer.

In a recent article, Meijs and Brudney (2007) approach volunteer management using the metaphor based on a "slot machine." They define a volunteer scenario as a combination of the "Assets" of a volunteer, the "Availability" of volunteers, and a particular volunteer "Assignment" offered by the organization. Their management techniques seek to optimize "winning" volunteer scenarios – that is equivalent to getting AAA on the slot machine and winning the prize. The focus on the three A's is useful in designing strategies in the changing world of volunteers (as described above). The model offers flexibility of adaptation in a variety of organizational contexts and from multiple perspectives.

Volunteering and Third Sector Change

The previous section looked at changes in volunteering through the sociological lens of broad social transformations and how these processes affect the availability and willingness of volunteers. A different stream of recent research has focused on another dimension of macro-changes, namely, at the level of the third sector and its relation to the other sectors. As we have discussed above, macro-structural theories of volunteering have demonstrated that the amount and type of volunteering vary across the different nonprofit regimes. However, little is understood so far about how changes in these regimes affect settings, practices, and experiences of present-day volunteers.

Lie and Baines (2007) highlight the importance of understanding the impact of reforms in the voluntary sector on organizations and individuals who participate in them. The authors note that the role of the voluntary sector has been increasingly mainstreamed, particularly in English-speaking countries, "where governments aim to harness the energies of voluntary agencies and charitable bodies to supplement the state and the private sector" (Lie and Baines 2007, p. 227). Indeed, international scholarship has been pointing to a historically new process of institutional hybridization in the classical mixed welfare provision (Bode 2006; Brandsen et al. 2005). A basic observation relates to the increasing privatization of the public–private mix. There is a fundamental openness toward the market as a social service deliverer, and the state is more frequently involved in buying and regulating commercial services. Market principles also intrude the public sector, and nonprofit organizations are increasingly confronted with a new contract culture based on competitive tendering, outsourcing, and output performance (Bode 2003; Evers and Laville 2004; Freise et al. 2006; Lewis 2004).

A second rationale behind the intensifying relationships between the statutory sector and the voluntary sector has to do with public policy geared toward promoting civic renewal and reinvigorating civic life (Lie and Baines 2007; Milligan and Fyfe 2005; Musick and Wilson 2008). Volunteering is increasingly seen as a means through which citizenship and civic responsibility can be resuscitated. Indeed, recently there has been an increasing involvement of "third parties" (Haski-Leventhal et al. 2010), such as governments, corporations, and institutions of higher education, in the promotion of volunteerism, the mobilization of volunteers, and the organization of their activities.

As yet, the consequences of these sector-wide changes for the nature and experience of volunteering are ill-understood, and little is written about how these changes are likely to be perceived by volunteers. In their study of older volunteers in the north of England, Lie and Baines (2007) found that the changing organizational strategies can be disempowering and that there is an increasing misfit between the volunteering role and the essential nature of what volunteering means to the volunteers. Bloom and Kilgore (2003), in a case study of American middle-class volunteers providing social support to families in poverty (as part of the US administration's neoliberal agenda), concluded that while these services may bring meaning to lives of the volunteers, the problems and needs of families in poverty are too complex and rooted in society-wide structural inequalities, hence cannot be addressed by volunteers, who risk frustration and disappointment. Recent ethnographic study on volunteering in hybrid organizational settings in the United States revealed that the growing emphasis on short-term contracting, competition, and output orientation results in a stronger formalization and top-down steering of volunteer activities (Eliasoph 2009). As a result, the emphasis shifts to the measurement of activities and results and to organizing short-term projects with a predictable success rate. Volunteers are approached in a more instrumental way and lose their authentic and spontaneous character. Within hybrid organizations, volunteers develop weak ties and, in some cases, their efforts are useless and even destructive.

The Value of Volunteering: What is it Worth?

Given the ubiquitous nature of volunteering, it is easy to assume that it must have some social or personal value. However, more complex is the question of what that value is and of who derives it. In this section, we discuss the recent methods for addressing the question of what volunteerism is worth. This question becomes all the more important given nonprofit's increasing role and responsibility in the delivery of public services.

Scholars of social accounting have made many cogent arguments suggesting that nonprofits that do not make visible the invisible contribution of volunteers are in fact doing their organizations a disservice in the long run (Mook et al. 2007a,b; see also Chapter 13 by Mook in this volume). Such scholars have attempted to promote a method of social accounting that expands the traditional financial statements of organizations to take account of volunteer labor. If volunteers create value, then it must be made visible to the volunteers, to the organization, to the funders, and, finally, to the general public. As part of a growing pressure for accountability and transparency in the voluntary sector, and reflecting the increasing demands on its limited resources, more and more volunteer program coordinators are being asked to explain their program expenditures and justify their program budget requests.

Ideally speaking, nonprofits should seek to input volunteer labor until the marginal benefits to the NGO are equal to the marginal costs of volunteer labor. However, many real-world factors complicate the achievement of this idealistic equilibrium. For example, calculations are hard to make in the absence of some accounting methods that allow nonprofits to measure all of the costs and benefit entailed in the use of volunteer labor. Furthermore, organizational constraints may limit the use of volunteers even when they may be cost-effective (e.g., union regulations, which prevent volunteers from encroaching upon work done by paid labor). Other benefits of the use of volunteer labor, such as spillover benefits to the community (e.g., volunteers act as goodwill ambassadors for the organization in the community), may be difficult, if not impossible, to accurately measure.

The Expanded Value Added Statement (EVAS) developed by Laurie Mook and her colleagues (Mook et al. 2007a,b) is one recent tool available to capture the value created by nonprofits, which captures the contribution of its multiple stakeholders. It recognizes the uniqueness of the nonprofit contribution by focusing on both economic and social impacts, instead of just the "bottom line" of financial surpluses or deficits. The EVAS is able to identify key aspects of a nonprofit's functioning that is not apparent from conventional financial statements alone. Although acknowledging the debate on how to value the volunteer hour, the authors suggest that volunteer labor is valued at what it would cost the organization to replace its volunteers with paid staff and continue the services currently provided by a volunteer.

The EVAS builds on the Value Added Statement. For example, the value-added created by an ice-cream-making company is calculated by taking the difference between the price the ice cream is sold for and the cost of the materials that went into making the ice cream (milk, cream, sugar, nuts, fruits, flavors, etc.). However, the Value Added Statement concentrates on only those items that have established market values and does not include other items such as social and environmental services. Organizations have social as well as economic impacts. Thus the EVAS adapts the Value Added Statement. For example, in the case of nonprofits, the EVAS will include the non-market value of using volunteers. The EVAS is not intended to replace existing financial statements but rather to be presented alongside them. By synthesizing traditional financial data with other data, the EVAS is another instrument for integrating the dynamics of an organization and one that shows great potential for focusing attention on value creation and use.

The adoption of new accounting models such as the EVAS is a complex process and may represent a challenge, in part because it requires detailed information on volunteer hours and tasks and of the low availability published values of volunteer time, which could potentially be used as replacement values. However, simply accounting for volunteer hours in the financial statements as an important asset and value-added will go a long way in producing accurate statements for those nonprofits that rely on volunteers and toward acknowledging and honoring the volunteer role as a valuable resource in the production of services.

Conclusion: A Kaleidoscopic View

In this chapter, we have examined emerging theories and new directions in volunteering research. These theories and studies represent, on the one hand, multi-level perspectives that try to understand volunteering in complex interaction with the organizational and institutional context. On the other hand, they embody more process-oriented approaches that focus on the experience of volunteering, as it changes through different stages of organizational socialization and as a consequence of broader societal and sector-wide transformations. These frameworks offer an indispensable and complementary angle to the more unidimensional and static approaches of established research on determinants of, and reasons for, volunteering.

This review demonstrates that, as research on volunteering further expands, it tends to grow in its diversity of questions and viewpoints and to reflect the complex and dynamic nature of volunteering more precisely. Indeed, rather than one clear image, the study of volunteers and volunteering represents a multifaceted and brilliant kaleidoscopic picture. Whether examined under a microscope – for micro-level studies – or with a telescope – for macro-level studies – we find that the instrument really is a kaleidoscope, which gives us different pictures each time the field of vision shifts, and in each, there is color, clarity, and coherence.

The metaphor of the kaleidoscope is powerful and inspiring. The kaleidoscopic nature of volunteering makes it difficult to pin down the phenomenon as it takes a myriad of forms, its colors reflected by the mirrors that are the organizations in which volunteering takes place, the varying management approaches and degrees of support volunteers receive, and the cultural and institutional contexts in which volunteering occurs. At the same time, a kaleidoscopic view of volunteering recognizes that the answer to central questions like who is a volunteer, why they volunteer, and how best to manage volunteers remains elusive as it is meant to be. Just as the images and colors change in the kaleidoscope, by a mere movement of the instrument, so do the changing nature of our societies impacts the trends, issues, and challenges that arise and affect volunteers in all sectors and all settings (Merrill 2006). These "movements" are further impacting the nature of volunteering as seen in the kaleidoscope. With new trends in volunteering, such as episodic volunteering, virtual volunteering, and tourism volunteering, we find new colors in the evolving kaleidoscope, and the journey for researchers and practitioners continues to be fascinating with many new perspectives to be revealed and innovative managerial approaches to be offered.

References

Bloom, L. R., and Kilgore, D. (2003). The volunteer citizen after welfare reform in the United States: An ethnographic study of volunteerism in action. *Voluntas*, 14(4), 431–454.

Bode, I. (2003). A new agenda for European charity: Catholic welfare and organizational change in France and Germany. *Voluntas*, 14(2), 205–225.

Bode, I. (2006). Disorganized welfare mixes: Voluntary agencies and new governance regimes in Western Europe. *Journal of European Social Policy*, 16(4), 346–359.

Brandsen, T., van de Donk, W., and Putters, K. (2005). Griffins or chameleons? Hybridity as a permanent and inevitable characteristic of the third sector. *International Journal of Public Administration*, 28(9), 749–765.

Bronfenbrenner, U. (1979). *The Ecology of Human Development: Experiments by Nature and Design*, Cambridge, MA, Harvard University Press.

Carter K. A. (2008). Volunteer tourism: An exploration of the perceptions and experiences of volunteer tourists and the role of authenticity in those experiences. Unpublished Masters dissertation, Lincoln University, New Zealand, http://researcharchive.lincoln.ac.nz/dspace/bitstream/10182/526/3/carter_mapplsc.pdf

Cnaan, R. A., and Amrofell, L. M. (1994). Mapping volunteer activity. *Nonprofit and Voluntary Sector Quarterly*, 23(4), 335–351.

Cnaan, R. A., and Handy, F. (2005). Towards understanding episodic volunteering. *VIO – Vrijwillige Inzet Onderzocht*, 2(1), 29–35.

Cnaan, R. A., Handy, F., and Wadsworth, M. (1996). Defining who is a volunteer: Conceptual and empirical considerations. *Nonprofit and Voluntary Sector Quarterly*, 25(3), 364–383.

Cravens, J. (2006). Involving international online volunteers: Factors for success, organizational benefits, and new views of community. *Journal of Volunteer Administration*, 24(1), 1–23.

Curtis, J. E., Baer, D. E., and Grabb, E. G. (2001). Nations of joiners: Explaining voluntary association membership in democratic societies. *American Sociological Review*, 66(6), 783–805.

Easwaramoorthy, M., Barr, C., Runte, M., and Basil, D. (2006). *Business Support for Employee Volunteers in Canada: Results of a National Survey*, Toronto, Imagine Canada.

Eckstein, S. (2001). Community as gift-giving: Collectivistic roots of volunteerism. *American Sociological Review*, 66(6), 829–851.

Eliasoph, N. (2009). Top-down civic projects are not grassroots associations: How the differences matter in everyday life. *Voluntas*, 20(3), 291–308.

Evers, A., and Laville, J.-L. (2004). Social services by social enterprises: On the possible contribution of hybrid organizations and a civil society. In A. Evers and J.-L. Laville (eds) *The Third Sector in Europe* (pp. 237–255), Cheltenham, Edward Elgar.

Freise, M., Hallmann, T., and Zimmer, A. (2006). Dritter Sektor als Hoffnungsträger? Bürgerengagement und New Public Management. (Third sector as a refuge? Civic engagement and New Public Management.) In H. Voesgen (ed.) *Brückenschläge – Neue Partnerschaften zwischen Institutioneller Erwachsenenbildung und Bürgerschaftlichem Engagement*, (*Building Bridges – New Partnerships Between Adult Education and Civic Engagement*), Bielefeld, Bertelsmann Verlag.

Gaskin, K. (1998). Vanishing volunteers: Are young people losing interest in volunteering? *Voluntary Action*, 1(1), 33–43.

Gazley, B., and Dignam, M. (2008). *The Decision to Volunteer: Why People Give their Time and How you can Engage Them*, Washington, DC, ASAE and the Center for Association Leadership.

Graff, L. (2004). *Making a Business Case for Employer-Supported Volunteerism*, Ottawa, Volunteer Canada.

Hall, M., Easwaramoorthy, M., and Sandler, W. (2007). *Business Contributions to Canadian Communities: Findings from a Qualitative Study of Current Practices*, Toronto, Imagine Canada.

Hall, M., Lasby, D., Gumulka, G., and Tryon, C. (2006). Caring Canadians, involved Canadians: Highlights from the 2004 Canada Survey of Giving, Volunteering and Participating. Ottawa, Ontario, Statistics Canada.

Handy, F., Brodeur, N., and Cnaan, R. A. (2006). Summer in the island: Episodic volunteering. *Voluntary Action*, 7(3), 31–46.

Handy, F., and Cnaan, R. A. (2007). The role of social anxiety in volunteering. *Nonprofit Management and Leadership*, 18(1), 41–58.

Handy, F., Cnaan, R. A., Brudney, J. L., Ascoli, U., Meijs, L. C. M. P., and Ranade, S. (2000). Public perception of "Who is a volunteer": An examination of the net-cost approach from a cross-cultural perspective. *Voluntas*, 11(1), 45–65.

Handy, F., and Hustinx, L. (2009). Review essay. The why and how of volunteering. *Nonprofit Management & Leadership*, 19(4), 549–558.

Haski-Leventhal, D., and Bargal, D. (2008). The volunteer stages and transitions model: Organizational socialization of volunteers. *Human Relations*, 61(1), 67–102.

Haski-Leventhal, D., Meijs, L., and Hustinx, L. (2010). The third party model: Enhancing volunteering through governments, corporations and educational institutes. *Journal of Social Policy*, 39(1), 139–158.

Hustinx, L. (2001). Individualisation and new styles of youth volunteering: An empirical exploration. *Voluntary Action*, 3(2), 57–76.

Hustinx, L. (2005). Weakening organizational ties? A classification of styles of volunteering in the Flemish Red Cross. *Social Service Review*, 79(4), 624–652.

Hustinx, L. (2008). I quit, therefore I am? Volunteer turnover and the politics of self-actualization. *Nonprofit and Voluntary Sector Quarterly*, Online First 16 December 2008.

Hustinx, L., Haski-Leventhal, D., and Handy, F. (2008). One of a kind? Comparing episodic and regular volunteers at the Philadelphia Ronald McDonald House. *International Journal of Volunteer Administration*, 25(3), 50–66.

Hustinx, L., and Lammertyn, F. (2003). Collective and reflexive styles of volunteering: A sociological modernization perspective. *Voluntas*, 14(2), 167–187.

Hodgkinson, V. A. (2003). Volunteering in global perspective. In P. Dekker and L. Halman (eds) *The Values of Volunteering* (pp. 35–53), New York, Kluwer Academic/Plenum Publishers.

Inglehart, R., and Welzel, C. (2005). *Modernization, Cultural Change and Democracy: The Human Development Sequence*, Cambridge, Cambridge University Press.

Jakob, G. (1993). *Zwischen Dienst und Zelbstbezug, (Between Service and Self-Centeredness: A Biographical-Analytical Study)*, Opladen, Leske + Budrich.

Kühnlein, I., and Mutz, G. (1999). Individualisierung und Bürgerschaftliches Engagement in der Tätigkeitsgesellschaft. (Individualization and civic engagement in the work society.) In E. Kistler, H.-H. Noll, and E. Priller (eds) *Perspektiven Gesellschaftlichen Zusammenhalts. Empirische Befunde, Praxiserfahrungen, Messkonzepte, (Perspectives on Social Integration. Empirical Findings, Practical Experiences, and Measurement Concepts)*, (pp. 291–306), Berlin, Sigma.

Kulik, L. (2007a). Predicting responses to volunteering among adolescents in Israel: The contribution of personal and situational variables. *Voluntas*, 18(1), 35–54.

Kulik, L. (2007b). Explaining responses to volunteering: An ecological model. *Nonprofit and Voluntary Sector Quarterly*, 36(2), 239–255.

Lewis, J. (2004). The state and the third sector in modern welfare states: Independence, instrumentality, partnership. In A. Evers and J.-L. Laville (eds) *The Third Sector in Europe* (pp. 169–187), Cheltenham, Edward Elgar.

Liao-Troth, M. (ed.) (2008). *Challenges in Volunteer Management*, Charlotte, NC, Information Age.

Liao-Troth, M. A., and Dunn, C. P. (1999). Social constructs and human service: Managerial sensemaking of volunteer motivation. *Voluntas*, 10(4), 345–361.

Lie, M., and Baines, S. (2007). Making sense of organizational change: Voices of older volunteers. *Voluntas*, 18(3), 225–240.

Lois, J. (1999). Socialization to heroism: Individualism and collectivism in a voluntary search and rescue group. *Social Psychology Quarterly*, 62(2), 117–135.

Lorentzen, H., and Hustinx, L. (2007). Civic involvement and modernization. *Journal of Civil Society*, 3(2), 101–118.

MacDuff, N. (2004). *Episodic Volunteering: Organizing and Managing the Short-Term Volunteer Program*, Walla Walla, WA, MBA Publishing.

Meijs, L. C. P. M., and Brudney, J. L. (2007). Winning volunteer scenarios: The soul of a new machine. *International Journal of Volunteer Administration*, 24(6), 68–79.

Meijs, L. C. P. M., Handy, F., Cnaan, R. A., Brudney, J. L., Ascoli, U., Ranade, S., Hustinx, L., Weber, S., and Weiss, I. (2003). All in the eyes of the beholder? Perceptions of volunteering across eight countries. In P. Dekker and L. Halman (eds) *The Values of Volunteering: Cross Cultural Perspectives* (pp. 19–34), New York, Kluwer Academic/Plenum Books.

Meijs, L. C. P. M., and Ten Hoorn, E. (2008). No "one best" volunteer management and organizing: Two fundamentally different approaches. In M. Liao-Troth (ed.) *Challenges in Volunteer Management* (pp. 29–50), Charlotte, NC, Information Age.

Meijs, L. C. P. M., Ten Hoorn, E. M., and Brudney, J. L. (2006). Improving societal use of human resources: From employability to volunteerability. *Voluntary Action*, 8(2), 36–54.

Meinhard, A., Handy, F., and Greenspan, I. (2009). Corporate participation in the social economy: Employer-supported volunteering programs. In L. Mook, J. Quarter, and S. Ryan (eds) *Why the Social Economy Matters* (pp. 291–318). Toronto, University of Toronto Press.

Merrill, M. V. (2006). Global trends and the challenges for volunteering. *The International Journal of Volunteer Administration*, 24(1), 9–14.

Milligan, C., and Fyfe, N. F. (2005). Preserving space for volunteers: Exploring the links between voluntary welfare organizations, volunteering and citizenship. *Urban Studies*, 42(3), 417–433.

Mook, L., Handy, F., and Quarter, J. (2007a). Reporting volunteer labour at the organizational level: A study of Canadian nonprofits. *Voluntas*, 18(1), 1–17.

Mook, L., Quarter, J., and Richmond, B. J. (2007b). *What Counts: Social Accounting for Nonprofits and Cooperatives*, London, Sigel Press.

Musick, M. A., and Wilson, J. (2008). *Volunteers: A Social Profile*, Bloomington, Indiana University Press.

Omoto, A. M., and Snyder, M. (2002). Considerations of community: The context and process of volunteerism. *American Behavioral Scientist*, 45(5), 846–867.

Parboteeah, K. P., Cullen, J. B., and Lim, L. (2004). Formal volunteering: A cross-national test. *Journal of World Business*, 39(4), 431–441.

Pearce, J. L. (1993). *Volunteering: The Organizational Behavior of Unpaid Workers*, New York, Routledge.

Penner, L. A., and Finkelstein, M. A. (1998). Dispositional and structural determinants of volunteerism. *Journal of Personality and Social Psychology*, 74(2), 525–537.

Putnam, R. D. (2000). *Bowling Alone: The Collapse and Revival of American Community*, New York, Simon & Schuster.

Rehberg, W. (2005). Altruistic individualists: Motivations for international volunteering among young adults in Switzerland. *Voluntas*, 16(2), 109–122.

Rog, E., Pancer, S. M., and Baetz, M. C. (2004). *Corporate Volunteer Programs: Maximizing Employee Motivation and Minimizing Barriers to Program Participation*, Toronto, Canadian Centre for Philanthropy.

Ruiter, S., and De Graaf, N. D. (2006). National context, religiosity, and volunteering: Results from 53 countries. *American Sociological Review*, 71(2), 191–210.

Salamon, L. M., and Anheier, H. K. (1998). Social origins of civil society: Explaining the nonprofit sector cross-nationally. *Voluntas*, 9(3), 213–248.

Salamon, L. M., and Sokolowski, S. W. (2001). *Volunteering in Cross-National Perspective: Evidence from 24 Countries*. Online: www.jhu.edu/~ccss/Publications/pdf/cnpwp401.pdf

Salamon, L. W., and Sokolowski, S. W. (2003). Institutional roots of volunteering: Toward a macro-structural theory of individual voluntary action. In P. Dekker and L. Halman (eds) *The Values of Volunteering* (pp. 71–90), New York, Kluwer Academic/Plenum Publishers.

Salamon, L. M., Sokolowski, S. W., and Anheier, H. K. (2000). *Social Origins of Civil Society: An Overview.* Online: www.jhu.edu/~ccss/Publications/pdf/cnpwp38.pdf

Schofer, E., and Fourcade-Gourinchas, M. (2001). The structural contexts of civic engagement: Voluntary association membership in comparative perspective. *American Sociological Review*, 66(6), 806–828.

Sherraden, M. S., Lough, B., and McBride, A. M. (2008). Effects of international volunteering and service: Individual and institutional predictors. *Voluntas*, 19(4), 395–421.

Sherraden, M. S., Stringham, J., Sow, S. C., and McBride, A. M. (2006). The forms and structure of international voluntary service. *Voluntas*, 17(2), 163–180.

Smith, D. H. (1994). Determinants of voluntary association participation and volunteering: A literature review. *Nonprofit and Voluntary Sector Quarterly*, 23(3), 243–263.

Sokolowski, S. W. (1996). Show me the way to the next worthy deed: Towards a microstructural theory of volunteering and giving. *Voluntas*, 7(3), 259–278.

Wilson, J. (2000). Volunteering. *Annual Review of Sociology*, 26, 215–240.

Wilson, J., and Musick, M. A. (1997). Who cares? Toward an integrated theory of volunteer work. *American Sociological Review*, 62(5), 694–713.

Wollebæk, D., and Selle, P. (2003). Generations and organizational change. In P. Dekker and L. Halman (eds) *The Values of Volunteering* (pp. 161–178), New York, Kluwer Academic/Plenum Publishers.

Wuthnow, R. (1998). *Loose Connections: Joining Together in America's Fragmented Communities*, Cambridge, MA, Harvard University Press.

Chapter 8
Volunteering in Developing Countries

Jacqueline Butcher

Introduction

This chapter points toward the need to seriously interrogate the forms of volunteer participation in developing nations and to recognize that the meaning of volunteering is far more contextually determined than is commonly assumed. Whether volunteering may be a path to democratic civic engagement (Halman 2003) or a path to community development, we find that volunteer activity itself is embedded in many religious practices, civic attitudes, signs of service, expressions of solidarity toward others, as well as in a myriad of daily activities that many a time go unnoticed. There has been much effort in comparability and understanding the values, participation, and activities of volunteers around the world – as in The Johns Hopkins Comparative Study, the World Values Survey (WVS), European Values Survey (EVS), and the work done by Civicus – their Civil Society Index (see Chapter 5). There is, however, also a need here to address "local" customs and cultures – since we are aware that culture is important in understanding how individuals set the pace for their own activities, including voluntarism (Harrison and Huntington 2000).

Key on the volunteer research agenda are issues such as motivation, self-interest, altruism, giving in time and in kind, philanthropy, organizational life, volunteer versus non-volunteer relationships, transnational and international volunteer activity, and impact studies of volunteer work. Descriptions of volunteering have been advanced and revised by many researchers (Dekker and Halman 2003; Govaart et al. 2001; Hustinx and Lammertyn 2003; Schervish 1993; Wilson 2000; Chapter 7 by Lesley Hustinx et al., this volume), and lately, volunteering has also become the focus of interest of governments, since it contributes to the services they provide and contributes to creating a stable and cohesive social order.

There are important common attributes of volunteering since there is a broad consensus on what this activity represents. Virginia Hodgkinson puts it bluntly:

J. Butcher (✉)
Centro Mexicano para la Filantropia (CEMEFI), Mexico City, Mexico
e-mail: rivasjb@prodigy.net.mx

R. Taylor (ed.), *Third Sector Research*, DOI 10.1007/978-1-4419-5707-8_8,
© Springer Science+Business Media, LLC 2010

"Volunteering means conducting work with no pay" (Hodgkinson 2003, p. 38), and it could be said that although non-remuneration has been widely discussed, three other factors of volunteering also prevail: that of choice and free will, to go beyond one's normal responsibilities of family obligations, and to contribute to society at large – even though individuals may benefit internally from its practice. Another consideration is the context of volunteering: as it can be unmanaged, as in sporadic help that takes place between neighbors and friends; or managed volunteering, which takes place through organizations in the nonprofit, private, and public sectors. The commonly accepted toolkit designed to measure volunteer participation around the world gives advice on how to conduct a volunteer survey and provides the "building blocks for a definition of volunteering," while also warning us that "it is up to users to add the details that are specific to the volunteering culture of that setting" (Independent Sector and Voluntarios de las Naciones Unidas 2001, p. 10).

What we discover beyond these specific factors is that there is variation in the meaning of volunteering in different contexts, and that many individuals that could, in essence, be considered volunteers (especially in informal environments) do not consider themselves as such (Butcher 2008). The research focus then becomes one of grasping the role of voluntary activities in developing nations that exhibit more informal, less-organized patterns of involvement: How do we best interpret and account for individual and informal volunteering in such settings?

Studies have demonstrated that there is a definite role for volunteering in society and in development – not only to add to the creation of social capital (Putnam 2000) or to promote social cohesion and the strengthening of democracy (Olvera 2001), but also as a mechanism to channel differences and dissent among the population. Today, we are witnessing, right around the world, more and more volunteers individually acting outside of formal structures and organizations, and even creating new forms of activism that are more flexible in nature. This may, of course, be caused by generational differences and does not mean that people are volunteering less, just that they are doing it differently (Wollebæk and Selle 2003; and their Chapter 16 in this volume). The role of volunteering in social development was enhanced by the United Nations in its Commission for Social Development of the UN Economic and Social Council (2000):

> Volunteering constitutes an enormous reservoir of skills, energy and local knowledge which can assist governments in carrying out more targeted, efficient, participatory and transparent public programs and policies. However, it is unusual for volunteering to be recognized as a strategic resource that can be positively influenced by public policy and even rarer for it to be factored into national and international development strategies. The International Year of the Volunteer (2001) offers a unique opportunity in bridging the gap between the acknowledgement of a long-standing tradition on the one hand, and a recognition of its potential as a major asset for promoting social development on the other. (Annex, pp. 3–4)

The year 2001 was declared the International Year of the Volunteer by the United Nations precisely to encourage more governments to conduct surveys and focus on volunteering activities. In the past, few governments actually collected data on various forms of volunteering. The engagement of social movements and citizen participation has worked to change this attitude, and in recent years several moves to close the information gap have been made, such as the *UN Handbook on Satellite Accounts* that covers nonprofit institutions as well as the *Volunteer Manual* developed under the auspices of the International Labour Organization (ILO) that sets out to promote the collection of data on volunteer work from labor surveys around the globe.[1]

Case Studies: Mexico and South Africa

Due to a growing body of research on giving and volunteering, Mexico and South Africa were chosen to illustrate the contrasts these countries exhibit when compared to patterns of organized volunteering in the Western world. The results of the studies cited below do not reflect the total universe of what are called countries of the South or developing nations, but we consider them illustrative enough to give an idea of what occurs where civil society is not so formalized or where local community service organizations (CSOs) are not fully or "officially" registered.

The questions to be asked here include: How does development affect volunteering? How are these two countries similar in how they understand the meaning of volunteering and its practice? What can be concluded from these cases as to guidelines for development and the fostering of volunteer activity in these and other parts of the world?

The South African Context for Volunteering: History and Background

Recent research in South Africa such as *The Poor Philanthropist, I and II* (Wilkinson-Maposa et al. 2005; Wilkinson-Maposa and Fowler 2009) gives us insight into where service to others and volunteer activity is not looked upon as philanthropy, but is considered "help." This study excluded the wealthy and looks into activities of a less-favored group of individuals in this region of the world.[2] South Africa has a long-standing tradition of ideas of solidarity among the community, plus it promotes the tradition and philosophy of *Ubuntu* – "oneness" or "I am because you are" (Wilkinson-Maposa et al. 2005, p. 53).

Ubuntu is the recognition of oneself through others, and in honor of this tradition people share and give off the little that they have. In a way, altruism as a "selfless" act does not occur, because to deny helping if one can do so is to deny one's sense of self. Offering services to others could be seen as work with no pay and would normally be considered volunteer work in the current literature, although in what is

---

[1] The ILO commissioned The Johns Hopkins University to create a *Volunteer Manual* that would add more questions to existing labor surveys.

[2] The results of *The Poor Philanthropist II* go beyond the 2005 description and point to new and practical approaches to sustainable development.

called here, "horizontal philanthropy," people help each other in time of need so that they receive the help they themselves will require when difficult times come upon them. These nuances partially explain that not all is altruism and generosity and that it is not always easy to find volunteers in the pure sense of the word. It reinforces the notion that volunteering takes on different meaning in various contexts and in varying cultures (Patel and Wilson 2004).

A more recent report by the Volunteer and Service Enquiry Southern Africa, VOSESA (Patel et al. 2007), presents a cross-national, five-country (Botswana, Malawi, South Africa, Zambia, and Zimbabwe) study that reviews international, national, and local community-based civic service programs.[3] The report also indicates that there seems to be a greater move toward civic service activity as a result of new governmental endeavors to establish civic participatory programs, so as to promote and consolidate democratization. These programs cater more to the young so as to fill a gap created by educational systems that are unable to provide the skills needed for employment and increase the options of young people for career choices. Importantly, this research makes a clear distinction between civic service and volunteering, since the first refers broadly to "citizen's action to promote the public good, which extends beyond the family to benefit local communities" (Perold et al. 2006, p. 6). This activity is sometimes paid, but mostly is not. It has both formal and informal dimensions and it is facilitated by the government in partnership with both civil society and business. For South Africa, the volunteering concept is taken to be the same as established for other countries and it contains elements of free will and choice, as well as not receiving compensation or reward. It may have religious motivation as well and is often seen as "charity" from the "haves" to the "have nots" (Perold 2003) as well as constituting informal support systems of care among the needy (Everatt and Solanki 2005).

A national survey, the "State of Giving" survey undertaken in late 2003 by the Centre for Civil Society, the Southern African Grantmakers' Association, and the National Development Agency, focused on the extent and nature of social giving among South Africans (Everatt and Solanki 2005) and is a vital source of information. The findings of the survey suggest that 17% of the South African population volunteer their time (that is, approximately 8 million people in relation to a total population of 47.4 million; Stats SA 2006). This contrasts with the 1.5 million people who actively volunteered their time to nonprofit organizations in 1999 where their contribution was equivalent to 316,991 full-time jobs and volunteer labor accounted for 49% of the nonprofit workforce (Swilling and Russell 2002).

In the State of Giving survey it was found that each individual, on average, gave 11 h of volunteer time. Given the extent of participation, this totals nearly 6,000 h per month. Women volunteered slightly more time than men; African volunteers

---

[3] VOSESA reports: there is a June 2007 report which is a five country report as well as the South Africa country report 2006.

gave the most time, followed by Coloured, Indian, and then White respondents.[4] The average time that is volunteered is constant among youth and adults (between 10 and 11 h) and only rises among those over 60 years of age (rising to an average of 12 h). Poor respondents (23%) were more likely to have volunteered than non-poor (17%). The study established that volunteering in South Africa is not simply the preserve of the middle class (Everatt and Solanki 2005, pp. 10–11).

The long history and tradition of giving and generosity in South Africa tells us about the varied ways voluntary activity promotes the public good beyond the family and outward to the community. Strong social networks created by kinship and mutual aid have promoted a sense of mutual help and reciprocity which reflects mostly as informal volunteer activity. There is plentiful research from the beginning of the twentieth century, the pre-apartheid era, the apartheid era, and since 1990 (the end of statutory apartheid) (McKendrick 1998; Potgieter 1998; Sewpual and Hölcher 2004), and in what is the most recent study, Habib and Maharaj (2008) focus on resource allocation and poverty alleviation and describe the variety of possibilities and ways of giving that include corporate giving, government spending, religious influences on giving, participation, and giving of time (volunteering) and resources. Habib and Maharaj specifically stress how philanthropy – volunteering included – cannot by itself address the problem of poverty alleviation and development; here, it is underlined that much more needs to be done to address the concerns of the socially marginalized. Modernization is having an impact on African societies and the way giving plays itself out and is interpreted is changing.

In other sources of information on how individuals give and relate to each other, such as *The Poor Philanthropist, I*, we find that South Africa stands out for having more of an associational life in informal associations at 35% representation, as compared to Mozambique with 2%, Namibia 2%, and Zimbabwe 4%.[5] Zimbabwe, at 16%, ranked the highest in formal group representation (Wilkinson-Maposa et al. 2005, pp. 64–65). Statistics indicate that this informality of volunteer activity may have an economic side, given increasing poverty and unemployment, especially in the case of South Africa where the HIV/Aids pandemic has hit.[6] It is, however, more likely that South Africa will turn to further formalize its giving and volunteer activities as a result of increasing market penetration and the growing market economy.

---

[4]This is to use the apartheid-inscribed racial categories; as such, these categories do not represent an accurate sociological reading of people's identity.

[5]Associational life includes membership or involvement in the following: street committee, *stokvel* (a kind of savings society), exchange club, cooking club, funeral group/burial society, family society/parent society, initiation society, dishes society, working society, blanket society, hoeing society, planting society, and women's league/guild.

[6]The estimated overall HIV-prevalence rate is approximately 11%. The HIV-positive population is estimated at approximately 5.2 million (Avert.org 2008).

The Mexican Context for Volunteering: History and Background

The sources of information for contextualizing Mexican volunteer activity are varied and many. The primary reference for data in this chapter is a recent study on Mexican solidarity and volunteer activity that included a national survey on solidarity and volunteer participation for Mexicans aged 18 and above (ENSAV), and a qualitative inquiry that drew on 15 case studies of Mexican CSOs which included 66 in-depth interviews with volunteers and CSO workers.[7] The study also included a review of the history of voluntary activity throughout the country (Butcher 2008).

The main findings of the ENSAV survey were that a surprisingly large number of individuals participate in acts of solidarity toward others. Some 66% of the adult population have "done something for someone else" outside of the family in their lifetime and have undertaken such activities with a certain regularity. In absolute terms this percentage represents some 41.4 million individuals. One of the other major findings of the research was that people from all socioeconomic sectors in the country contribute in equal measure to acts of solidarity; neither high-nor low-income individuals engage in more acts of solidarity, neither do those with lower educational levels contribute more or less time and effort than those who are more educated. Another significant finding was with regard to the question of gender equality: at national level there was only a slight preponderance of women engaged in voluntary activities. In the qualitative analysis, however, there was a 3:1 ratio of women to men participating in formal volunteer organizations.

The order of preference for where this kind of work and activity occurs is as follows: first, the Church (around 83% of Mexicans declare themselves Catholic); second, the school; and third, the neighborhood. And the degree of dedication to solidarity in these three areas is basically much the same in all regions of the country. Moreover, it was found that the majority of voluntary action plays itself out in informal settings – something that, in part, helps to explain the small size of the Mexican third sector (discussed below).

Overall the research revealed that, in volunteer time, the average number of days per solidarity actor was 27 days a year, which is equivalent to 2.2 days a month – a figure that was found to apply to 40% of the Mexican population above 18 (some 23 million people). In terms of labor power, this is equivalent to around 2.6 million full-time jobs, or viewed another way, it is equivalent to 11.3% of the employed population outside the agricultural sector. This number is in fact equivalent to 1.14% of the GNP for 2004 and 4.7% of the GNP if we consider GNP for community, social, and personal services.

It was also found in the qualitative analysis of the in-depth interviews that Mexican women mostly view volunteering as a personal duty which is based on family and religious traditions, while men mostly see it as a social responsibility. These findings highlight the religious and value-laden nature of volunteering in Mexico, as

---

[7]ENSAV, Encuesta Nacional de Solidaridad y Acción Voluntaria (National Survey on Solidarity and Volunteer Action).

well as the altruistic motivations that are at its base. Family certainly plays a pivotal role in the nurturing of volunteers as well as the promotion of solidarity with others, including one's community.

The size and scope of the third sector is a clear indication of the possibilities of organized volunteer participation. Looking at The Johns Hopkins Comparative Study, Mexico comes out as the smallest provider of employment at 0.2%, compared to Sweden's 8.2% and 4.6% for the United States (with the international average being 2.5%). These results come from a 24-country study where the levels of volunteering were expressed as a proportion of total nonagricultural employment (Salamon et al. 1999; Salamon and Sokolowski 2003). This international study took into account only formal volunteering and originally took into account syndicates which are not considered volunteer organizations in Mexico – thus it was concluded that:

> Mexico is an example of a 'statist' society where volunteering nevertheless takes a mainly expressive form according to our data, contrary to what the social origins theory would predict. The reason for this, however is that 40% of all volunteering in Mexico is for trade unions, which have been an extension of the state bureaucracy and the former ruling party (PRI). Because of this it is probably appropriate to exclude such volunteering as not wholly voluntary. Once this is done, the remaining expressive component of volunteering is quite small, only 20% of the total, which is more in line with the statist pattern predicted by the social origins theory. (Salamon and Sokolowski 2003, p. 87)

Other research also reveals information on participation. In particular, the Mexican government through the Ministry of State[8] has taken it upon itself to conduct several consecutive surveys on citizen participation: ENCUP 2001, 2003, 2005, and 2008.[9] Basically, this research was designed to further the understanding of Mexican attitudes and behavior in relation to politics, voting patterns, and citizen participation. Several questions had to do with associative practices, which are pertinent to understanding volunteer activity. These surveys reveal that in general in Mexico there is low institutional trust but high trust in family. The lowest grade of trust on a scale of 1–10 was given to the police (6.2) and political parties, the highest to the Church (7.2) and to the army. People in general do feel they are co-responsible with government in solving public issues (71%), but only 6% of those interviewed ever tried to ask their representatives in government for help in the solution of a public problem. Only 4 out of every 10 people have tried to get organized to solve a community problem and have volunteered in some shape or form in some community activity, although most people (85%) have donated either money or goods to charity. One out of every four declared having belonged to religious organizations as against only one out of every twenty who declared having belonged to a philanthropic or benefic organization. This data supports what was found in the ENSAV and taken together they present significant findings on volunteer participation in

---

[8] SEGOB, Secretaría de Gobernación (State Secretariat).
[9] ENCUP, Encuesta Nacional Sobre Cultura Política y Prácticas Ciudadanas (National Survey on Political Culture and Citizen Practices).

Mexico. Also, for 2008, the Mexican Center for Philanthropy (CEMEFI)[10] found that 33,212 associations exist, including civil, social, political, and religious ones, a figure that seems rather small for a country with a total population of over 110 million people. Of these associations, only around 6,000 CSOs were found to be able to give tax deductible receipts (CEMEFI 2009, p. 16).

Historically, there are good reasons to explain these numbers. For years, the relationship between government and CSOs in Mexico has been one of mutual mistrust (Butcher 2002, 2003, 2004; Verduzco 2003). A number of scholars have provided insight into patterns of civil participation by looking back into the customs and traditions of Mexico's indigenous population – reflecting on the influence of the Spanish culture from the sixteenth century until the present (Aguilar Valenzuela 1997; Méndez 1998; Olvera 2001; Reygadas 1998). Indeed, one must go all the way back to pre-colonial times to understand the culture of the indigenous population and their organizational structures of cooperation and mutual support.

In Aztec times, the social unit was the *calpulli*, made up of people of the same social background, owners of land where individual and collective action took place. Another important phenomenon was the *tequio*, where when one member of the community had received support, they had the obligation to reciprocate in equal amounts providing the same quality of the service rendered. *Tequio* also referred to relationships with government or religious authorities, and in the colonial period the Spaniards imposed this activity as tribute. In modern times it could be translated into a form of taxation. Other forms of associations, imported from Europe at that time, the co-fraternities (*cofradías*), were the only allowed form of lay participation, but always under some vigilance from the Catholic Church. During the colonial era, these forms of organization played an important role for forms of solidarity, evangelization, social integration, and subordination (Bechtloff 1989). Later on, there was a strong presence of the state in the area of social welfare – beginning with the victory of the liberals in 1860 and with the increasing secularization of Church property, right up until 1960 when civil society began to appear as an active partner in attending societal needs.

In recent Mexican history, civil participation gathered increasing momentum. Poverty and social differences became more and more apparent during the 1960s and 1970s, and many new groups formed as NGOs dedicated to addressing the concerns of a growing marginalized population. In the past 20 years, poverty has accelerated even further, and the capacity of the state has been increasingly questioned as the economy has worsened. Some authors argue that organized civil society emerged in the 1960s when NGOs generally proliferated around the globe (Miraftab 1997, pp. 361–375), while others point to the new sense of civic activism that emerged in the wake of the 1985 earthquake in Mexico City (Méndez 1998; Reygadas 1998).

Traditionally, voluntary work had to do with religious and moral obligation, or was looked upon as a social welfare issue. In rural areas, community participation, a form of voluntarism, has never been considered volunteering, and many groups

---

[10]CEMEFI, Centro Mexicano para la Filantropía.

outside of cities have not become, in a strict sense, legally formal organizations or voluntary associations. What becomes evident in the numbers shown in both the ENSAV and the ENCUP surveys is that both voluntary action and extensive expressions of solidarity have been ever present in Mexico, but they do not appear in the Tocquevillian tradition.

Changes have come about as of 2004, with a new law in place: the Federal Law for the Promotion of Activities undertaken by Civil Society Organizations.[11] There are expectations that the government will support old and new organizations as well as all forms of associational life throughout the country. There is, however, still a long way to go in its implementation due to the work that must be done as far as the rules and regulations for the proper functionality of this law are concerned – as well as with respect to its dissemination to the public and the CSOs that must abide by it.

Comparative Analysis

Surveys to analyze attitudes and themes on giving, volunteering, and solidarity were conducted in 2003 in South Africa and in 2005 in Mexico. The questionnaires employed were different, so precise comparability is not really possible. However, in both countries there was an interest in knowing who, why, and what people give in terms of time, money, and other types of resources. Both studies included surveys that were followed by qualitative work using interviews and focus groups, on the one hand, and in-depth interviews of members of CSOs, on the other, to allow trends and themes to emerge. Teams of researchers were trying to paint a coherent reality within their respective societies (Butcher 2008; Habib and Maharaj 2008). The results of this research can help portray what these two countries have in common and where they differ, but more than this they can point to what the patterns on the giving of volunteer time and other resources are likely to be within other developing nations.

What becomes very clear in both countries is that tradition, culture (Harrison and Huntington 2000), history, and environment play an enormous role in how societies are shaped and in how their citizens participate in solidarity toward others. In both countries, contrary to local belief, the myth of only women participating in volunteer efforts and acts of solidarity was shattered by the research findings; men and women give almost equally, although they distribute it a bit differently and their interests also vary. Moreover, one very interesting finding in both surveys was the overall configuration of educational background and socioeconomic levels in giving. In both countries, across the board, people's educational level had nothing to do with their giving status; all give equally. The South African study reported that "'giving' is not the domain of the wealthy, it is a part of everyday life for all South Africans,

---

[11] Ley Federal de Fomento a las Actividades Realizadas por las Organizaciones de la Sociedad Civil (Spanish).

rich and poor alike" (Habib and Maharaj 2008, p. 50), and the Mexican study concluded that "we can categorically affirm that participation in acts of solidarity by the Mexican population occurs more or less equally throughout the entire population, independently of their educational and socioeconomic situation" (Butcher 2008, p. 68).

Both studies found that there was more participation in voluntary action in the rural areas than in urban areas; solidarity in Mexico and volunteering in South Africa were found to happen more in the poorer areas of the respective countries. In Mexico, the south is less industrialized, and there is more participation in this area; some 78% of respondents answered "yes" to the question – "Have you ever done something for others without being paid?" – as compared to 59% in the Federal District. In South Africa the poorer provinces tended to have the highest levels of volunteering – respondents in both the Eastern Cape and Limpopo give more time than money.

An important factor in the giving of both time and money is religion; however, although both countries are highly religious and most of the volunteering and acts of solidarity are for the churches, curiously, people's main motivation for giving is not simply a religious one. The primary motivation for South Africans to give is to "alleviate poverty," and the main motivation in the survey for giving time and money in Mexico is to "help those in need." In both societies, social needs are great and their populations have been accustomed to make do with very little. There seems, then, to be a widely shared sense of responsibility toward others in countries that confront the stark reality of inequity and poverty.

In terms of percentages, the numbers are – by international standards – similarly high: some 17% of South Africans give volunteer time of 11 h per week, while 18% of Mexicans give more than 6 h a week to voluntary activity. This expression of generosity with time may well be linked to the fact that both countries have in recent years come out of dark eras of authoritarian political rule: South Africa with the end of 42 years of statutory apartheid and Mexico with the end of 72 years of hegemonic one-party rule. What it also indicates is that people have been willing to continue to uphold their traditional commitment to generosity and giving toward others. In Mexico, the ENSAV tells us that tradition and mistrust of governments have worked to keep volunteer activity as being more individualistic in form – with it happening outside of groups, more in informal settings. For around 21% of adults said they had participated in "acts of solidarity" on their own, with less than one-third (29%) having participated within organized structures or formal groups (moreover, it was found that only 24% of all respondents belong to a structured group or formal association). In the South African setting, there seems to be a broad understanding of "associational life," with more informality here (35%) than in the other countries of the five-country study cited earlier (Patel et al. 2007).

In both countries these studies cast a wide net of respondents and were very careful to obtain a representative sample of the population so as to be able to extrapolate to the national arena. In all, the data demonstrates that both societies in the cases presented participate, give, and volunteer more than had been reported in other research such as The Johns Hopkins Comparative Study (Salamon et al. 1999). This may very well have to do with how the questions were asked, since surveys are designed to answer specific questions. In both instances, the qualitative research provided a depth of understanding that revealed forms of expression of generosity and volunteer participation are ever present and the level of giving in general is quite high in informal settings, much higher than expected – especially if we consider not only volunteer time but money and other goods. This may be a logical expectation for countries with large informal economies, but more extensive and definitive research is required to differentiate exactly how associations and organizations are to be accounted for, as well as how the concept of "formality" is to be understood, in both contexts. To pinpoint what is happening in various forms of participation at both local and national levels is crucial for public policy decision-making.

To answer the questions posed at the beginning of this chapter, it could be argued that development exerts an influence on the degree of institutionalization of organizational life of a country, but not on the generosity of its population. It becomes evident that in developing nations, an effort has to be made to enhance, understand, and foster local customs and traditional forms of volunteer participation. As consciousness arises on the importance of diverse forms of associational life, there is a better chance to discover activities that will impact and enhance local and national development (UNDP Human Development Report 2005).

Such an effort requires increasing recognition from governments, corporations, and the public at large as to the nature and value of volunteering and to the awareness of what volunteers can positively contribute to the economy and the general well-being of society. In these shrinking philanthropic times, it is at the country level where the solutions to poverty alleviation and development must increasingly be found. Individually, participation and volunteer activity should be fostered and encouraged. At the same time, in developing countries, there is an all around need to create sufficient infrastructure, wealth of information, and institutionalization for volunteer groups to become formalized, transparent, and efficient – so that they are best able to participate in the market economy, receive more government subsidies, and have better access to international funding.

References

Aguilar Valenzuela, R. (1997). Apuntes para una historia de las organizaciones de la sociedad civil en México. *Sociedad Civil: Análisis y Debates*, 2(1), 9–32.

Avert.org. (2008). South Africa HIV and AIDS statistics. www.avert.org/safricastats.htm

Bechtloff, D. (1989). *Las cofradías de españoles en la ciudad de México (1526–1860)*, México, Universidad Autónoma Metropolitana, serie Humanidades.

Butcher, J. (2002). A new perspective in voluntarism and citizen participation in Mexico: Recreating civil society–government relationships. Working paper, 5th ISTR International Conference, University of Cape Town.

Butcher, J. (2003). A humanistic perspective on the volunteer–recipient relationship. In P. Dekker and L. Halman (eds) *The Values of Volunteering: Cross-Cultural Perspectives* (pp. 111–125), New York, Kluwer Academic/Plenum Publishers.

Butcher, J. (2004). Building citizenship and voluntary participation in Mexico: Social and economic implications from a national study. Working paper, 6th ISTR International Conference, University of Toronto.

Butcher, J. (ed.) (2008). *México Solidario: Participación ciudadana y voluntariado*, México, LIMUSA/CEMEFI.

CEMEFI. (2009). Compendio Estadístico del Sector No Lucrativo. México.

Dekker, P., and Halman, L. (eds) (2003). *The Values of Volunteering: Cross-Cultural Perspectives*, New York, Kluwer Academic/Plenum Publishers.

Everatt, D., and Solanki, G. (2005). The state of social giving in South Africa – Report series: Research report 1 – A nation of givers? Social giving among South Africans. Centre for Civil Society, University of KwaZulu-Natal, Durban.

Govaart, M.-M., Jan van Daal, J., Münz, A., and Keesom, J. (eds) (2001). *Volunteering Worldwide*, The Netherlands, Netherlands Institute of Care and Welfare.

Halman, L. (2003). Volunteering, democracy and democratic attitudes. In P. Dekker and L. Halman (eds) *The Values of Volunteering: Cross Cultural Perspectives* (pp. 179–198), New York, Kluwer Academic/Plenum Publishers.

Harrison, L., and Huntington, S. (eds) (2000). *Culture Matters*, New York, Basic Books.

Habib, A., and Maharaj, B. (eds) (2008). *Giving and Solidarity: Resource Flows for Poverty Alleviation and Development in South Africa*, Pretoria, HSRC Press.

Hodgkinson, V. (2003). Volunteering in global perspective. In P. Dekker and L. Halman (eds) *The Values of Volunteering: Cross-Cultural Perspectives* (pp. 35–53), New York, Kluwer Academic/Plenum Publishers.

Hustinx, L., and Lammertyn, F. (2003). Collective and reflexive styles of volunteering: A sociological modernization perspective. *Voluntas*, 14(2), 167–187.

Independent Sector and Voluntarios de las Naciones Unidas. (2001). *La Medición del Servicio Voluntario: Una guía práctica*.

McKendrick, B. W. (1998). *Introduction to Social Work in South Africa*, Pinetown, Owen Burgess.

Méndez, J. (Coordinador) (1998). *Organizaciones Civiles y Políticas Públicas en México y Centroamérica*, México, Miguel Ángel Porrúa.

Miraftab, F. (1997). Flirting with the enemy: Challenges faced by NGOs in development and empowerment. *Habitat International*, 21(4), 361–375.

Olvera, A. (2001). *Sociedad Civil, Gobernabilidad Democrática, Espacios Públicos y Democratización: Los contornos de un proyecto*, Cuadernos de la Sociedad Civil, Universidad Veracruzana, México.

Patel, L., and Wilson, T. (2004). Civic service and sub-Saharan Africa. *Nonprofit and Voluntary Quarterly*, 33(4, supplement), 22S–39S.

Patel, L., Perold, H., Mohamed, S. E., and Carapinha, R. (2007). *Five Country Study on Service and Volunteering in Southern Africa*. Unpublished research report, VOSESA/Centre for Social Development in Africa, Johannesburg.

Perold, H. (2003). *Soul City Literature Review on Service in South Africa*, Johannesburg, Helene Perold & Associates.

Perold, H., Carapinha, R., and Muhamed, S. E. (2006). *Five Country Study on Service and Volunteering in Southern Africa. Unpublished Research Report/ South Africa Country Report.* Johannesburg, VOSESA/Centre for Social Development in Africa.

Potgieter, M. C. (1998). *The Social Work Process: Development to Empower People*, South Africa, Prentice Hall.

Putnam, R. (2000). *Bowling Alone*, New York, Simon & Schuster.

Report on the Commission for Social Development. (2000). United Nations publication, Sales No E/CN 5/32001/6 Annex.

Reygadas, R. (1998). *Abriendo Veredas,Iniciativas Públicas y Sociales de las Redes de Organizaciones Civiles*, México, Convergencia de Organismos Civiles por la Democracia.

Salamon, L., Anheier, H., List R., Toepler, S., Sokolowski, W., and Associates (1999). *Global Civil Society Dimensions of the Nonprofit Sector*, Baltimore, MD, The Johns Hopkins Comparative Nonprofit Sector Project.

Salamon, L., and Sokolowski, W. (2003). Institutional roots of volunteering. In P. Dekker and L. Halman (eds) *The Values of Volunteering: Cross-Cultural Perspectives* (pp. 71–89), New York, Kluwer Academic/Plenum Publishers.

Schervish, P. (1993). The dependent variable of the independent sector: The definition and measurement of giving and volunteering. *Voluntas*, 4(2), 223–232.

Sewpaul, V., and Hölcher, D. (2004). *Social Work in Times of Neoliberalism: A Postmodern Discourse*, Pretoria, Van Schaik.

Swilling, M., and Russell, B. (2002). *The Size and Scope of the Non-Profit Sector in South Africa*, P&DM, University of the Witwatersrand, Johannesburg, and CCS, University of KwaZulu-Natal.

United Nations, Report on the Commission for Social Development. (2000). Sales No E/CN 5/32001/6 Annex.

UNDP Human Development Report. (2005). International cooperation at a crossroads: Aid, trade and security in an unequal world. Human Development Indicators, http://hdr.undp.org/reports/global/2005/pdf/HDR05_HDI.pdf

Verduzco, G. (2003). *Organizaciones del Sector No Lucrativo: Visión de su Trayectoria en México*, México, CEMEFI & COLMEX.

Wilkinson-Maposa, S., et al. (2005). *The Poor Philanthropist*, www.gsb.uct.ac.za/gsbwebb/userfiles/poor_philanthropist_screen.pdf

Wilkinson-Maposa, S., and Fowler, A. (2009). *The Poor Philanthropist II: New Approaches to Sustainable Development*, Graduate School of Business, University of Cape Town.

Wilson, J. (2000). Volunteering. *Annual Review of Sociology*, 26, 215–240.

Wollebæk, D., and Selle, P. (2003). Generations and organizational change. In P. Dekker and L. Halman (eds) *The Values of Volunteering: Cross-Cultural Perspectives* (pp. 161–178), New York, Kluwer Academic/Plenum Publishers.

Chapter 9
Participation

Stephen Elstub

Introduction

Participation of citizens in the third sector is an issue of perennial importance. Ever since Alexis de Tocqueville's (1835–1840) famous study, associations in civil society have been strongly related to the development of democracy: both externally, within the political system as whole, and internally, within the associations themselves. De Tocqueville considered participation of associational members in the decision-making structure of voluntary associations as central to the fulfilment of both these aims, but especially the latter: "The original argument for voluntary associations, from de Tocqueville onwards, has been in terms of their value in promoting democratic participation" (Lansley 1996, p. 224). Moreover, participation in decision-making has always had an essential relationship with democracy per se (Barber 1984; Macpherson 1977; Pateman 1970). Indeed, Beetham (1993, p. 40) suggests that the more equally people participate directly in a decision that effects them, the more democratic the arrangement is. It is also an issue of international importance. To quote from the United Nations Development Programme, "people's participation [*in the community*] is becoming the central issue of our time ... [*Participation*] can become a source of tremendous vitality and innovation for the creation of new and more just societies" (cited in Xu 2007, p. 622). However, the necessity of participation within third sector associations is a deeply contested issue. It is in this context that this chapter sets out to present a survey of debates in relation to the participation of associational members, users, and staff in the governance of third sector organizations.

The chapter is divided into two broad sections. The first section considers arguments for the need of members, users, and staff to participate in third sector associations' governance structures that derive from the "participatory" or "voluntary spirit" models of the third sector. These arguments revolve around the need for participation to enable the third sector to fulfil its attributed functions of being

S. Elstub (✉)
University of West Scotland, Paisley, Scotland, UK
e-mail: stephen.elstub@uws.ac.uk

R. Taylor (ed.), *Third Sector Research*, DOI 10.1007/978-1-4419-5707-8_9,   105
© Springer Science+Business Media, LLC 2010

schools of democracy and developing social capital and political skills, delivering services and representing people in policy-making, in a manner compatible with accountability and legitimacy. In particular participation in public deliberation is seen to enhance these aspects to the greatest extent. The second section reviews arguments against participation in the decision-making processes of the third sector, which derive from the "pluralist" or "economic" models of the third sector. Here it is suggested that exit is sufficient to ensure legitimacy and accountability; that requiring associations to ensure participation of members, users, and staff compromises freedom of association; and that participation levels are low in the third sector because people do not want to participate or are unable to do so.

Arguments for Participation in the Third Sector

The Fulfilment of Functions

The argument from the "participatory" (Stears 1999) or "voluntary spirit" (Brainard and Siplon 2004) normative models of the third sector is that if third sector associations are to fulfil the various functions attributed to them effectively, then the internal structure of the associations must be democratic and allow member, user, and staff participation in decision-making. Associations orientated to this model see participation of members as crucial, highlight the solidary and purposive benefits of participation, consider associational members to be citizens and not simply consumers, and expertise, although valued, requires justification and is not seen as necessarily superior to experiential feelings (Brainard and Siplon 2004). The third sector fulfils numerous functions, but three of these in particular are thought to require democratic and participatory structures. These are being schools of democracy where political skills are learnt and social capital is developed, the delivery of essential services to citizens, and the provision of information and representation of citizens' interests, views, and identities in policy-making.

The conditions required to generate social capital is one of the most contested issues in the study of the third sector and is an issue considered in depth in Chapter 16. Nevertheless, it is worth briefly considering here the extent participation in the association is necessary for social capital to be generated – especially as there is evidence that disputes this connection exists at all, some of which Wollebæk and Selle outline in Chapter 16 in this volume (see also Wollebæk and Selle 2003). They distinguish between institutional and socialization approaches to social capital and the third sector. In the institutional approach, social capital is related to scope of associational membership. In the socialization approach this membership needs to be active. Maloney (1999), an institutionalist, suggests that passive or "chequebook" membership requirements, where members are required and expected to provide only a membership fee, allows more people to be members and that such membership can still lead to the development of a sense of community, even if these members never meet each other. However, "chequebook membership" is also thought to leave members susceptible to manipulation by elites within the organization (Brainard and Siplon 2004; Day 1999). In a comparison of the Scottish city of Aberdeen and the German city of Mannheim, the size of the association and levels of member participation appeared to have little effect on the generation of political interest, trust, and tolerance. If, however, members are engaged in the "right" types of participation, then political interest is enhanced. Overall, the argument is that "it is affiliation per se" that is important to generate social capital, rather than participation in the association (Maloney et al. 2008, pp. 278–279).

In accordance with the socialization approach, theoretical and empirical evidence suggests it will be more likely that associations will produce social capital in their members if they are horizontally and democratically organized with opportunities for participation in the decision-making processes of the association (Mansbridge 1980; Putnam 1993; Skocpol 2003). Torpe's (2003) empirical evidence from Scandinavia reveals that third sector associational participation can stimulate feelings of efficacy and an inclination to participate more, but does not enhance political tolerance. Howard and Gilbert (2008) draw on data from Europe and the United States, to compare levels of participation in third sector associations. Their analysis of this data suggests that those who do participate in associations are indeed more likely to participate politically and have greater levels of trust. They further claim that this is dependent on active participation in the association itself, arguing that "nominal membership" is not sufficient. Other evidence from Hooghe (2003) implies that it is the amount someone has participated in third sector associations throughout their life that is decisive to the development of social capital, rather than the amount someone is participating at any one moment in their life. For Hooghe this accounts for why so many studies indicate that there is little connection between participation in an association and the presence of social capital. This criticism could be levelled at Wollebæk and Selle's study presented in Chapter 16, as its data source is the European Social Survey, which measures only associational participation over a 12-month period.

Warren astutely identifies a number of factors that affect a third sector association's ability to develop civic and participatory skills. First, they will be enhanced by an association that deals with collective action (Rosenblum 1998; Warren 2001), as associations involved in conflicts, regardless of whether these conflicts are internal or external, will provide increased opportunity for such skills to be used. Similarly, associations that are politically orientated will also present more opportunities for participants to develop these skills. Furthermore, the fewer the opportunities for easy and low cost exit from the association like neighborhood associations and housing associations, the greater the chance of developing political skills as this encourages them to internalize political conflict, which again will provide opportunities to develop their members' political skills. Groups with high opportunities for exit can still develop member's political skills, providing their focus is the development of public material goods, and inclusive social goods, as these can be achieved only through cooperation. These factors are strengthened if the association is embedded in social media, as this focuses the association on commonalities rather than conflict, which in turn is concentrated if opportunity for exit is high (Elstub 2008; Warren 2001).

The participatory model further contends that if associations are devolved powers, to fulfil key public activities and deliver important services, they must be accountable to those it serves, which suggests the need for an internal democratic structure within the association, with participation required from staff and service users in determining the nature, form, and extent of the welfare that is to be delivered (Elstub 2006; Hadley and Hatch 1981). Similarly, if associations are to provide authentic information, and representation in policy-making, these must be linked to the participation of all those who are said to be represented, if it is to be authentic. In fact those within the participatory model "assume that members should not only be expected, but actively encouraged to participate in the running of the organisations" (Lansley, cited in Powell and Guerin 1997, p. 166). Indeed, one of the key justifications for an increased role for the third sector in terms of delivering services and participating in policy-making has been their potential to enable participation of members, meaning that they can be "democratically self-governing." They operate at "accessible decentralised levels," which offer opportunities for inclusive participation, with greater knowledge of the affairs being discussed (Martell 1992, p. 166; also see Elstub 2008; Warren 2001).

Without internal democratic arrangements within the association, Cohen and Rogers (1995, p. 65) argue that the third sector will represent and provide services, in the interests of group oligarchs, but not their membership. Chaskin (2003, p. 175) informs us of third sector associations in the United States, where this occurred, with the leadership becoming "entrenched and disconnected from constituencies." For Hadley and Hatch (1981, p. 147) the participation of service users and staff in third sector associations is "indispensable if available resources are to be maximised and variations in need/demand are to be recognised" (see also Burns et al. 1995; Chaskin 2003; Clapham et al. 1996). Stears (1999) rejects the argument that individuals will know how to fulfil their own welfare needs, because these issues are so complicated; participants will focus on immediate rather than future goods; and will make claims to wants rather than needs. Here, as these can be objectively identified, the process should be left to experts.

Despite this criticism, empirical research supports the argument that participatory third sector organizations that encourage "active involvement of users" in the service that they receive result in staff developing much better personal relationships with the users (Hadley and Hatch 1981). Further evidence from the UK and the United States indicates that third sector organizations are more innovative if they are participatory, as change tends to be more easily introduced and implemented if those required to implement the changes – that is, staff and users – have participated in making those decisions (Burns et al. 1995; Chaskin 2003; Hadley and Hatch 1981). In addition, having staff participate with users in decision-making produces a more critical view of the current services and can also generate more ideas for change. Participatory third sector organizations are also more likely to take users' views as performance indicators, alongside the more "objective" and "concrete" targets of performance set by the state or experts (Hadley and Hatch 1981, p. 148).

An illuminating example comes from Drake's (2002) evidence from disabled self-advocacy third sector associations. Disabled people have historically been excluded from participating in the third sector advocacy associations that "represent" them or deliver key services to them, due to undemocratic methods employed within these organizations. In response they have formed associations *of* disabled people. These organizations tend to be more democratic, with high levels of participation and "an opportunity for every member to contribute to policy decisions" (Drake 2002, p. 380). In many developing countries, user participation in the third sector is becoming an increasingly important issue, as these associations' role in delivering key services grows. For example, in China participation in determining and delivering social services is seen as essential in making associations more efficient, sustainable, and better equipped to meet user needs (Xu 2007).

Accountability, Legitimacy, and Deliberative Participation

The need for democratic participation in the governance structures of third sector associations, if they are to fulfil these three key functions effectively, is completely tied in with accountability and legitimacy.

Different types of organizations have different processes of accountability. Chaskin defines accountability in terms of the third sector as "the extent to which organisations that speak for or act on behalf of a community are fulfilling their stated goals and can be held responsible for their actions" (Chaskin 2003, p. 182). Third sector associations have variable forms of regulation to achieve accountability and are accountable to a number of different agents, for example, governors, members, service users, staff, government, and taxpayers (Leat 1996; Powell and Guerin 1997). In Chaskin's research (2003) in the United States, accountability to the members was seen as the most important, and moreover, this required participation from these members. Despite these arguments, Leat (1996) believes that participation can act against the construction of accountability, as it means that all members are accountable for the decisions being made, which ultimately means that nobody is.

Participation of members, staff, and users is also considered to be integral to the development of political legitimacy, defined as "democratic representativeness, participation, transparency and accountability to constituencies for which third sector organisations speak and act" (Brown, cited in Taylor and Warburton 2003, p. 324). As Taylor and Warburton argue, if the third sector wants to promote legitimacy, inclusion, equality, justice, and democracy in society, then it must include these principles within its own organizations. Consequently, participation from members and staff should be institutionalized within the third sector (Taylor and Warburton 2003), if the decisions made in the associations themselves are to be legitimate. Chaskin (2003) offers specific criteria for legitimacy in third sector associations. The first of these is the nature and amount of participation; the second is diversity of those who are participating; the third is the resulting action. Here the more members that participate, and the more they get to participate in the formation of decisions within the association, the more legitimate the resulting decisions will be.

In developing countries, like Bangladesh and Nepal, the lack of participatory opportunities in third sector organizations, such as development nongovernmental organizations (NGOs), has seriously compromised the legitimacy of these organizations and indicated that they are removed from popular political movements. In turn this has fundamentally undermined the ability of NGOs operating in these countries to alleviate structural causes of poverty and cultivate political participation. Ulvila and Hossain argue that without these participatory opportunities, NGOs have established "nongovernmental bureaucracies favourable to elite interests" (Ulvila and Hossain 2002, p. 161).

Legitimacy of organizations and their decision-making processes is important not only for normative reasons, but instrumentally too. For example Bryman et al.'s (1992) research into community transport associations highlights the importance of trust within the organization for effective operation. They relate the absence of trust to a lack of legitimacy. In the more democratic organizations studied, where users and staff participated in the decision-making processes, there were higher levels of trust and an absence of conflict.

In line with the recent rise of public deliberation as the most normatively justifiable form of participation in democracy per se, I have argued (2006) that not all forms of participation in the third sector are equally desirable or suitable for generating accountability and legitimacy. In particular I argue that if the decision-making structures of third sector associations were compatible with the norms of deliberative democracy and allowed staff, users, and members to participate in public deliberation, the resulting decisions would be more legitimate. Moreover, if associations are to deliver services, such deliberatively democratic decision-making structures, which included the participation of service users, would ensure the needs of these users were more effectively met, ultimately making the delivery of welfare services more socially inclusive. This is because deliberative democracy aims to include all affected by a decision in public debate. This encourages participants to consider the common good and the interests and preferences of others when forming their own preferences and when offering reasons to justify these. Ultimately, selfish arguments will be unpersuasive to those whom the decisions will affect. In addition, public deliberation facilitates the dispersion of information, through debate, and enables participants to revise their preferences in light of the reasons offered and information provided. These arguments are employed to counter Stears's (1999) critique of the participatory model. To quote Brainard and Siplon, associations in the voluntary spirit model "would reorient their organisations to be important forums for the debate and enactment of democratic values and ideas by, for example, opening up lines of continuous two-way communication and interaction between staff, members, supporters, and service beneficiaries" (Brainard and Siplon 2004, pp. 441–442; see also Chaskin 2003; Roberts 1996; Taylor and Warburton 2003).

There are different forms of accountability identified by Leat (1988). Nevertheless, varying forms of participation can contribute to all of them, and in particular participation in public deliberation. The first type is "explanatory accountability," or holding to account. This is more likely to occur if there are opportunities to debate and criticize. The second type of accountability is "accountability with sanctions" and involves giving account. This requires decision-makers to justify their actions to affected agents. This is more likely to occur if these elites are elected, as this provides a clear incentive to explain one's decisions to the electorate. Moreover, if decisions are being made through a process of public deliberation, then preferences and proposals have to be justified to those affected by the decision, if the other agents are to be convinced to consent to the proposal. Finally, there is "responsive accountability," or taking into account, where decision-makers respond to the interests and views of relevant actors. Again participation of associational members, users, and staff in pubic deliberation is important to this aspect of accountability, as "qualitative feedback, debate, and dialogue" are vital (Taylor and Warburton 2003, p. 325). If one is required to justify one's preferences to others, then the reasons offered are likely to be "public" in orientation and consider the interests of the other associational constituents.

Arguments Against Participation in the Third Sector

Exit and Voice

The normative credentials of participation in third sector organizations are disputed by the pluralist (Stears 1999) or economic (Brainard and Siplon 2004) model. In this model, third sector associations "are effectively economic actors seeking to efficiently and effectively raise funds and produce and deliver goods and services" (Brainard and Siplon 2004, p. 436). Here it is thought that the third sector organizations should learn from and follow the organizational structure of private sector organizations, which means adopting hierarchical, leadership, managerial, and top-down processes. Associations compete against each other for finite resources, including members who are seen as rational utility maximizers that will only participate if they are materially rewarded. Hence, associations characterized by the economic model tend to accentuate material and purposive incentives. Experts are seen as vital, and their input is privileged above that of lay members. Hirst is one of the leading advocates of the pluralist model arguing that the manner in which the third sector approximates the market enables individuals to "craft the packages they need … because of the high levels of choice in the type and mode of services on offer, due to the fact that service providers are voluntary organisations in competition and that their provision is mainly demand led" (Hirst 1994, p. 169). Third sector associations in the pluralist and economic models therefore rely on exit to achieve accountability and legitimacy, rather than participation and voice in decision-making.

There are varying degrees of opportunity for exit and voice in an association. Hirschman (1970) thought that if an association has high costs of exit then it is more important for it to have a democratic structure that gives members voice, but this correspondingly means that associations that have low exit costs will not have the incentive, or need, to incorporate the voice of dissenting members. The logic is therefore that opportunities for voice, through participation, are not required where associational members can exit instead (Elstub 2008; Hirschman 1970; Warren 2001). Furthermore, the nature of third sector associations means that the membership will be fairly homogenous in terms of the members' purposes, which, according to Warren (2001), will lead to a general consensus over goals and means of the association. Consequently, he feels voice will not be encouraged and that those who disagree with the leadership will be encouraged to remain silent or leave the association rather than threaten "the solidarity, mission or purpose of the group" (Warren 2001, p. 104). Johnson's (1990) research indicates that those in the minority on decisions in third sector organizations often exit the association.

Day (1999) remains unconvinced by these arguments, stating that homogeneity of members' preferences can be established only through some level of participation from the members. If it is presumed a consensus already exists within an association, it will not be sensitive to new problems and information, differing types of need, or interpretations of needs, and the effectiveness of the association in delivering services and providing representation in policy-making will be compromised. It is apparent that there will be shared interests, beliefs, preferences, needs, or identities that will motivate people to join, or form, an association, so there will be a certain degree of homogeneity, but this may be as general as being blind, an asylum seeker, or a school teacher. There is nothing to suggest that because one shares these common factors, there will be exact agreement on the purposes or methods of the association (see also Elstub 2008).

Day also argues that apathetic membership can result in leaders pursuing their own interests. Empirical evidence indicates that associations do not passively represent the interests of their members, as these interests and preferences are revised and transformed through interaction of the membership (Streek and Schmitter 1986). Without opportunities for participation, associational elites will not be fully aware of the interests and preferences of their membership, and consequently these can be distorted (Mansbridge 1980). DeVall and Harry's (1975) research signals that in associations where participation levels are low, the members are often poorly informed about the options available to the association and lack firm opinions. As a consequence, there is likely to be a "communication gap" between leaders and members, and a gap between the interests of the leaders and ordinary members can develop. It therefore seems apparent that undemocratic associations, which provide important services, can be agents of social control, even where opportunities for exit exist (Elstub 2006). Day (1999) further contends that opportunities for exit are often restricted or involve high levels of cost, and ultimately without democratic and participatory decision-making mechanisms, the group lacks legitimacy and can misrepresent their members. In contradiction of the pluralist model, Day's research also reveals that where there are competing associations, opportunities for member participation will be increased, as the association strives to stop them exiting.

The Threat to Freedom of Association

A further criticism of the participatory model, presented effectively by political theorists Amy Gutmann (1998) and Brian Barry (2001), is that by failing to recognize associations that are internally undemocratic, with limited opportunities for member participation in decision-making, the right to freedom of association, which sustains the third sector in the first place, is not respected. Although, Gutmann accepts that associational membership requires informed ongoing consent, she thinks that this consent can be tacitly expressed through continued membership. Barry concurs, maintaining that it is not part of liberalism to "insist that every group must conform to liberal principles in its internal structure" (Barry 2001, pp. 147–148). Barry therefore suggests that associations should not have to conform to the same liberal democratic principles that are used to regulate public bodies. However, the argument from the participatory model is that, because third sector associations throughout the world are increasingly becoming a primary tool for representation, policy formation, and service delivery, they become quasi-public bodies and should consequently be regulated by the same principles as public bodies if they wish to gain this level of political recognition (Elstub 2008). As Moyser and Parry state (1997, p. 44), "in democracy the healthy 'private life' of associations is a matter of public concern."

Levels of Participation

It is also contended that it is pointless ensuring that there are opportunities for participation in third sector associations, because most members do not want to participate in them (Lansley 1996). Chaskin argues (2003, p. 178) that any legitimate process must recognize and adjust for this, while still ensuring that it is "accessible to participation for those who wish to participate." There is also research that indicates that members, users, and staff of third sector associations are interested in participating in the governance of their associations (Beyer and Nutzinger 1993; Moyser and Parry 1997; Parkes et al. 2004; Taylor and Warburton 2003; Torpe 2003).

However, participation in associations is generally low (Lansley 1996; Moyser and Parry 1997). The trend in third sector associations, at least in the United States and in Europe, seems to be toward professionalized, centralized, hierarchical, and action-orientated associations, based on private sector techniques for internal governance, where opportunities for participation and democracy are limited, with members contributing little less than membership fees (Bush 1992; Selle and Strømsnes 1998; Skocpol 2003; Torpe 2003). Other empirical studies indicate that most associations in the world do not have a democratic structure and have low levels of membership participation (Harrison 1980; Norton 1994; Roßteutscher 2000), whether in the UK (Moyser and Parry 1997; Taylor 1996), Ireland (Powell and Guerin 1997), the United States (Fukuyama 1995), or Scandinavia, where membership is quite extensive (Roßteutscher 2000). This is damming evidence as in

Scandinavia these organizations have traditionally been relatively democratic (Selle and Strømsnes 1998).

However, low levels of member participation can be explained by scarce opportunities to meaningfully influence decisions. Downs's seminal rational choice theory demonstrated that the more chance participation can affect outcomes, the more likely people are to participate, and vice versa (Downs 1957). Therefore, as the third sector continues to gain powers in service delivery and policy-making, in many countries throughout the world, participation in these associations' governance could make a real difference to members' lives. According to research in Switzerland and France, it is local political-opportunity structures – that is, degree of decentralization – that are the most decisive factor in determining levels of participation in third sector associations (Joye and Laurent 1997). Evidence from China indicates that when third sector organizations have a more decentralized structure, and provide genuine opportunities for participants to influence decisions, the motivation to participate is higher and more sustainable (Xu 2007). Nevertheless, if levels of participation are to be established and maintained in the third sector, then participatory demands must not be too excessive, both in the number and the duration of meetings. If meetings are too frequent, or too long, then this will put off some people from participating regularly, or even at all. Furthermore, the more time required to participate the less equal participation would be (Elstub 2008).

Variables of Participation

The final critique of the participatory model is that it is simply not possible to ensure that all third sector associations have democratic, and participatory, decision-making processes, due to the number of phenomena and variables that determine levels of participation. These include the goals, ideology, amount and source of funding of the association and size, geographical dispersion, and socioeconomic status of the membership.

Levels of participation in third sector associations depend on the type of association, and the differing incentives that exist to be a member of the association. Associations with material rewards for membership tend to be less democratic, with lower levels of participation, while associations that produce solidary and purposive rewards tend to have members who want to participate (Day 1999; DeVall and Harry 1975; Warren 2001). Opportunities for participation are also influenced by the purpose of the association. For example, religious and sports associations provide good opportunities for meaningful participation, while motorist, disease control, purchasing, trade unions, humanitarian, disability/patient, and environmental associations do not (Torpe 2003). A further participatory variable is the level of ideological commitment. The greater this is, the more likely members will want to and demand to participate in the formation of the association's policies and goals. This factor is accentuated if members do not personally, or exclusively, benefit from the association's actions (Lansley 1996). Associations with large financial resources surprisingly have less participatory opportunities, and the source of the resources also has an effect. The more reliant an association is on money from the membership, the more it needs to give decision-making influence to the membership (Day 1999). Alternatively, the more an association is reliant on state funding, the more likely it will be held accountable by the state, meaning fewer opportunities for participation in decision-making will be made available to staff, users, and members (Bryman et al. 1992; Chaskin 2003; Taylor and Warburton 2003).

There are many practical exigencies present within third sector associations that form significant barriers to achieving participation in decision-making. These include the number and geographical disparity of members. The larger the association, the less influence an individual member can have on the decision-making of that association, which reduces the incentive to participate (Elstub 2008). Torpe argues (2003, p. 339) that "passive membership is first and foremost connected with the big, corporation-like national organisations with hired staff." Furthermore, as the size of an association increases, levels of participation decrease, as it is harder to be a free rider in a small association (Olson 1965). Similarly, groups that demand high levels of participation tend to recruit fewer members, as people with the time to participate a lot are in the minority (Day 1999).

If the association is geographically dispersed, this can lead to ever greater inequality as decision-making power is concentrated in the hands of a few members, who will have authority to make more decisions and have greater influence over other members, due to their "central location in the communication network" (Gastill 1993, p. 131). Much relies on having democratic procedures, and participatory structures such as elections, meetings, forums, and caucuses to constrain the power of the representatives and hold the associational elites accountable to the members, but the ability of the members to do this is hindered by the fact the association's elites are geographically removed. Processes of globalization have led to increasing global interdependence and the need for international third sector associations (see Chapter 22). Issues of complexity like distance, language, cultural, and economic barriers to participation are intensified in associations that are international in scope and membership. A federal system, with semi-autonomous divisions, coordinated through "hierarchical and participative mechanisms," is seen as a potential solution, as it has "the flexibility to accommodate the twin demands for national diversity and international coordinated action" (Young 1992, p. 9). The more decentralized an association, the more opportunities to participate and vice versa. If large organizations have decentralized "chapters" then democratic decision-making and reasonable levels of participation can still be maintained (Day 1999). Furthermore, geographical dispersion of membership and globalization problems could be reduced through developments in communication technologies.

Brainard and Siplon (2004) have recently researched the effects communication technology can have on levels of participation in decision-making in the third sector. They revealed that technological development, particularly the Internet, can lower the opportunity costs of participation and enable people to participate in accordance with their own schedule. Cyber-organizations, which exist primarily on the Internet, tend to be "member driven, horizontal and organic" (Brainard and Siplon 2004, p. 444). In particular, two-way and deliberative communication between group members becomes much more attainable with the use of the Internet (Dahlgren 2005; Torpe 2006). This can be time consuming, but it does ensure that the norms, goals, activities, and strategy of the association reflect the ideas of the membership. However, the Internet does not have an entirely positive role within democratizing associations as it can also be used as a top-down tool to increase elite control over members. In this manner Day (1999) reports how the development of communications technologies has meant that more third sector associations are centrally organized, without "local chapters" where members can engage in face-to-face participation in decision-making.

The most significant participatory variable, however, is the socioeconomic standing of the individual themselves. Those with higher socioeconomic status are more likely to be members of associations and to participate in them (Chaskin 2003; Joye and Laurent 1997; Moyser and Parry 1997; Salamon and Anheier 1996; Schattsneider 1975; Skocpol 1999; Van Deth 1997; Verba et al. 1995; Xu 2007). The most salient barriers to participation include the lack of income and education and the presence of discrimination (Verba et al. 1995). Consequently, those who do participate tend not to be representative of their populations.

Warren (2001) is optimistic that the undemocratic effects of inequality will be softened by pluralism. If citizens have multiple and fluid membership in associations, some of the inequalities from each sphere can be contained (Warren 2001, p. 215). For example, those with low-status occupations can still receive high levels of respect and prestige in an association if they have certain attributes and skills that are useful to the association. However, this equalizing effect of associations decreases, or can be completely eliminated, in hierarchical associations (Rosenblum 1998), which further indicates the need for associations to be democratized. Ultimately, participation and inequality operate in a "vicious circle" (Macpherson 1977, p. 100). As Powell and Guerin argue (1997, p. 63), "the exclusion of the underclass should be addressed by the development of participatory democratic structures at grass-roots community level, which empower the poor. Unless there is a sense of involvement in decision-making, the alienation of the underclass will continue to fester." However, as long as socioeconomic inequalities are present, the current levels of low participation, particularly in the most marginalized socioeconomic groups, will be perpetuated.

Conclusion

The normative arguments from the participatory and voluntary spirit models of the third sector, based around accountability and legitimacy, are powerful. It is maintained that, if the third sector is to deliver essential services and represent people in policy-making, participation of members, users, and staff in the governance of the association is essential. This participation can also develop participant's political skills and generate social capital. In defense of the criticisms from the pluralist and economic models, it is contended that exit is not always sufficient to ensure legitimacy and accountability and undemocratic associations cannot appeal to freedom of association if they want to fulfil public functions. Participation levels are very low, but few third sector associations have participatory decision-making structures. If they did then the ability to influence these decisions might well encourage more people to participate. Nevertheless, the substantial barriers to participation that exist within the third sector should not be underestimated. The goals, ideology, amount and source of resources, also affect levels of participation, as do the size and geographical dispersion of the membership. However, it is socioeconomic inequalities that most influence people's ability to participate in third sector associations. The irony is that it is the participation of the marginalized groups in decisions that will affect them that will most effectively alleviate these inequalities. Whatever one's position on the need and possibility of participatory decision-making within the third sector, it seems apparent that it will be a recurring and global third sector issue. Moreover, the more the third sector fulfils key public functions, the more intense these debates will become.

References

Barber, B. (1984). *Strong Democracy*, Berkeley, University of California Press.

Barry, B. (2001). *Culture and Equality*, Oxford, Polity Press.

Beetham, D. (1993). Liberal democracy and the limits of democratisation. In D. Held (ed.) *Prospects for Democracy: North, South, East, West* (pp. 55–73), Cambridge, Polity Press.

Beyer, H., and Nutzinger, H. G. (1993). Hierarchy or co-operation: Labour–management relations in church institutions. *Voluntas*, 4(1), 55–72.

Brainard, L. A., and Siplon, P. D. (2004). Toward nonprofit organization reform in the voluntary spirit: Lessons from the Internet. *Nonprofit and Voluntary Sector Quarterly*, 33(3), 435–457.

Bryman, A., Gillingwater, D., and McGuiness, I. (1992). Decision-making processes in community transport organisations: A comparative case study of service providers. *Voluntas* 3(1), 71–87.

Burns, D., Hambleton, R., and Hoggett, P. (1995). *The Politics of Decentralisation: Revitalising Local Democracy*, London, Macmillan.

Bush, R. (1992). Survival of the nonprofit spirit in a for-profit world. *Nonprofit and Voluntary Sector Quarterly*, 21(4), 391–410.

Chaskin, R. J. (2003). Fostering neighborhood democracy: Legitimacy and accountability within loosely coupled systems. *Nonprofit and Voluntary Sector Quarterly*, 32(2), 329–343.

Clapham, D., Kintrea, K., and Kay, H. (1996). Direct democracy in practice: The case of "community ownership" housing associations. *Policy and Politics*, 24(4), 359–374.

Cohen, J., and Rogers, J. (1995). Secondary associations and democratic governance. In E. O. Wright (ed.) *Associations and Democracy* (pp. 7–98), New York, Verso.

Dahlgren, P. (2005). The Internet, public spheres, and political communication: Dispersion and deliberation. *Political Communication*, 22(2), 147–162.

Day, C. L. (1999). Grassroots involvement in interest group decision making. *American Politics Quarterly*, 27(2), 216–235.

DeVall, W. B., and Harry, J. (1975). Associational politics and internal democracy. *Nonprofit and Voluntary Sector Quarterly*, 4(1-2), 90–97.

Downs, A. (1957). *An Economic Theory of Democracy*, New York, Harper and Brothers.

Drake, R. F. (2002). Disabled people, voluntary organisations and participation in policy making. *Policy & Politics*, 3(3), 161–189.

Elstub, S. (2006). Towards an inclusive social policy in the UK: The need for democratic deliberation in voluntary and community associations. *Voluntas*, 17(1), 17–39.

Elstub, S. (2008). *Towards a Deliberative and Associational Democracy*, Edinburgh, Edinburgh University Press.

Fukuyama, F. (1995). *Trust: The Social Virtues and the Creation of Prosperity*, London, Penguin.

Gastill, J. (1993). *Democracy in Small Groups: Participation, Decision-making and Communication*, Philadelphia, New Society Publishers.

Gutmann, A. (1998). Freedom of association: An introductory essay. In A. Gutmann (ed.) *Freedom of Association* (pp. 3–31), Princeton, NJ, Princeton University Press.

Hadley, R., and Hatch, S. (1981). *Social Welfare and the Future of the State*, London, Allen & Unwin.

Harrison, R. J. (1980). *Pluralism and Corporatism: The Political Evolution of Modern Democracies*, London, Allen & Unwin.

Hirschman, A. (1970). *Exit, Voice and Loyalty: Responses to Decline in Firms, Organizations and States*, Cambridge, MA, Harvard University Press.

Hirst, P. (1994). *Associative Democracy: New Forms of Economic and Social Governance*, Cambridge, Polity Press.

Hooghe, M. (2003). Participation in voluntary associations and value indicators: The effect of current and previous participation experiences. *Nonprofit and Voluntary Sector Quarterly*, 32(1), 47–69.

Howard, M. M., and Gilbert, L. (2008). A cross-national comparison of the internal effects of participation in voluntary organizations. *Political Studies*, 56(1), 12–32.

Johnson, P. E. (1990). Unravelling in democratically governed groups. *Rationality and Society*, 2(1), 4–34.

Joye, D., and Laurent, A. (1997). Associative and political participation in Switzerland and France. In J. Van Deth (ed.) *Private Groups and Public Life: Social Participation, Voluntary Associations and Political Involvement in Representative Democracies* (pp. 163–182), London, Routledge.

Lansley, J. (1996). Membership participation and ideology in large voluntary organisations: The case of the National Trust. *Voluntas*, 7(3), 221–240.

Leat, D. (1988). *Voluntary Organisations and Accountability*, London, NCVO.

Leat, D. (1996). Are voluntary organisations accountable? In D. Billis and M. Harris (eds) *Voluntary Agencies* (pp. 61–79), London, Macmillan.

Macpherson, C. B. (1977). *The Life and Times of Liberal Democracy*, Oxford, Oxford University Press.

Maloney, W. A. (1999). Contracting out the participation function: Social capital and cheque-book participation. In J. van Deth, M. K. Newton, and P. F. Whiteley (eds) *Social Capital and European Democracy* (pp. 108–119), London, Routledge.

Maloney, W. A., van Deth, J. W., and Roßteutscher, S. (2008). Civic orientations: Does associational type matter? *Political Studies*, 56(2), 261–287.

Mansbridge, J. (1980). *Beyond Adversary Democracy*, Chicago, University of Chicago Press.

Martell, L. (1992). New ideas of socialism. *Economy and Society*, 21(2), 52–72.

Moyser, G., and Parry, G. (1997). Voluntary associations and democratic participation in Britain. In J. Van Deth (ed.) *Private Groups and Public Life: Social Participation, Voluntary Associations and Political Involvement in Representative Democracies* (pp. 24–46), London, Routledge.

Norton, P. (1994). *The British Polity*, New York, Longman.

Olson, M. (1965). *The Logic of Collective Action*, Cambridge, MA, Harvard University Press.

Parkes, T., Taylor, M., and Wilkinson, M. (2004). From protest to partnership? Voluntary and community organisations in the democratic process. In M. J. Todd and G. Taylor (eds) *Democracy and Participation: Popular Protest and New Social Movements* (pp. 307–325), London, Merlin.

Pateman, C. (1970). *Participation and Democratic Theory*, Cambridge, Cambridge University Press.

Powell, F., and Guerin, D. (1997). *Civil Society and Social Policy: Voluntarism in Ireland*, Dublin, A & A Farmar.

Putnam, R. D. (1993). *Making Democracy Work: Civic Traditions in Modern Italy*, Princeton, NJ, Princeton University Press.

Roberts, J. (1996). From discipline to dialogue. In R. Munro and J. Mouritsen (eds) *Accountability: Power, Ethos and the Technologies of Managing* (pp. 40–61), London, International Thompson Business Press.

Roßteutscher, S. (2000). Associative democracy: Fashionable slogan or constructive innovation. In M. Saward (ed.) *Democratic Innovation: Deliberation, Representation and Association* (pp. 173–183), London, Routledge.

Rosenblum, N. (1998). *Membership and Morals: The Personal Uses of Pluralism in America*, Princeton, NJ, Princeton University Press.

Salamon, L., and Anheier, H. (1996). *The Emerging Nonprofit Sector*, Manchester, Manchester University Press.

Schattsneider, E. E. (1975). *The Semi-Sovereign People: A Realists View of Democracy in America*, Orlando, Holt, Rinehart and Winston.

Selle, P., and Strømsnes K. (1998). Organized environmentalists: Democracy as a key value. *Nonprofit and Voluntary Sector Quarterly*, 9(4), 319–343.

Skocpol, T. (1999). Associations without members. *American Prospect*, 45(10), 66–73.

Skocpol, T. (2003). *Diminished Democracy: From Membership to Management in American Civic Life*, Norman, OK, University of Oklahoma Press.

Stears, M. (1999). Needs, welfare and the limits of associationalism. *Economy and Society*, 28(4), 570–589.

Streek, W., and Schmitter, P. C. (1986). *Private Interest Government: Beyond Market and State*, London, Sage.

Taylor, M. (1996). Between public and private: Accountability in voluntary organisations. *Policy and Politics*, 24(1), 57–72.

Taylor, M., and Warburton, D. (2003). Legitimacy and the role of UK third sector organizations in the policy process. *Voluntas*, 14(3), 321–338.

Tocqueville, A. de (1945 [1835–40]). *Democracy in America*, New York, Vintage.

Torpe, L. (2003). Democracy and associations in Denmark: Changing relationship between individuals and associations? *Nonprofit and Voluntary Sector Quarterly*, 32(3), 329–343.

Torpe, L. (2006). Online citizens: Does the net add something new to the local public and local politics? *Tidsskriftet Politik*, 9(2), 35–44.

Ulvila, M., and Hossain, F. (2002). Development NGOs and political participation of the poor in Bangladesh and Nepal. *Voluntas*, 13(2), 149–163.

Van Deth, J. (1997). Social involvement and democratic practice. In J. Van Deth (ed.) *Private Groups and Public Life: Social Participation, Voluntary Associations and Political Involvement in Representative Democracies* (pp. 1–21), London, Routledge.

Verba, S., Schlozman, K., and Brady, H. (1995). *Voice and Equality: Civic Voluntarism in American Politics*, Cambridge, MA, Harvard University Press.

Warren, M. (2001). *Democracy and Association*, Princeton, NJ, Princeton University Press.

Wollebæk, D., and Selle, P. (2003). Participation and social capital formation: Norway in a comparative perspective. *Scandinavian Political Studies*, 26(1), 67–91.

Xu, Q. (2007). Community participation in urban China: Identifying mobilization factors. *Nonprofit and Voluntary Sector Quarterly*, 36(4), 622–642.

Young, D. R. (1992). Organising principles for international advocacy associations. *Voluntas*, 3(1), 1–28.

Chapter 10
Philanthropy

Jenny Harrow

Introduction

The claims and challenges of philanthropy research exemplify the complexities and constraints facing philanthropic endeavor, globally and locally. Whether as a study field and discourse, a human attribute translated into powerful institutional structures, or an independent social problem-solving means, philanthropy's aims, reach, and impact are under increasing scrutiny. Heightened expectations of what philanthropy may achieve have arisen as growing but unequal global wealth over the past three decades has provided the backdrop for a resurgence of philanthropy. These expectations have produced pressures on donors at all levels, organizations acting philanthropically, the beneficiaries of philanthropic action, and governments enabling, regulating, or challenging philanthropy. As theoretical, ethical, and philosophical arguments for "why philanthropy" take on new urgency, the case for innovation and creativity, rather than indulgence and sameness within philanthropic action has also grown. The question as to what might philanthropy do next – prompted by expected continuing global growth in wealth – is now overtaken in a period of global downturn. Instead, priority-driven questions arise, regarding where and how philanthropy might best act and what philanthropy should now do.

Simultaneously a part of and an enabler of civil society, philanthropic action as a study field offers researchers a continuing set of contrasts. It reflects both uniformity and diversity, high degrees of personalization or highly institutionalized relationships. It may be embedded or transitory, choose soft or hard goals, work in secure or risky settings, attract praise for the generosity it expresses, or blame for the controlling power it accrues. The scholarship of philanthropy offers multiple insights into its nature, motivation, strategy, values, locations and institutions, human capital, expertise, regulation, and impact. Broadly speaking though, research interest in this field can be grouped around four main areas, namely the creation and

J. Harrow (✉)
Cass Business School, City University London, UK
e-mail: j.harrow@city.ac.uk

R. Taylor (ed.), *Third Sector Research*, DOI 10.1007/978-1-4419-5707-8_10,

sustenance of the philanthropic *impulse*, among groups and individuals; the organizational choices, formal or informal, permanent or limited-life, for the *expression* of philanthropy; the recognition of and response to philanthropy's *location*, its degree of interconnectedness, its geographies, and networks; and the alignment of and effects of philanthropic *values* on its range of achievements and inter-organizational relations. This chapter follows such an overall framework, exploring first the philanthropic impulse, asking who are the agents of and actors in philanthropy; second, the expressions of philanthropy, considering how philanthropy is modeled and organized; third, the location of philanthropy, reviewing where philanthropy is found; and fourth, the values of philanthropy and their effects on its form and direction. This is preceded by consideration of the nature of philanthropy, as expressed from a variety of research perspectives.

The Nature of Philanthropy

None of the four clusters of research interest have clear boundaries and a number have multiple linkages. Many draw from shared streams of empirically led research in which philanthropy's expressed goals – effectiveness, power, and influence; social problem-solving leadership and policy change – are the focus. Nor has the development of a shared definition of philanthropy within an extensive conceptual framework been marked. From the historians' standpoint, the broadest sense of the nature of philanthropy pertains, for example, to "a collective form of charitable giving," in which philanthropists tend to "impose their vision of the good society ... through collective ventures" (Friedman 2003, p. 2). Adam (2004, p. 4), exploring interrelations between European and North American philanthropy, notes that "on both sides of the Atlantic, scholars have failed to develop a united theoretical concept of philanthropy," with those from varying backgrounds using terms such as philanthropy, charity, NGOs, giving, donation, and benevolence interchangeably and without explanation. Adam defines philanthropy by its overarching goal, the "advancement of society," through services "not provided by the state or market, for political or economic reasons" or "which are provided by the state but not in a way that satisfies philanthropists" (ibid).

From such a perspective, philanthropy may be benign or malign, depending on the shape of the society envisaged. The latter case is linked particularly with "the increasing tendency within governments to view the third sector as a source of insecurity and uncivil society in the wake of terrorist attacks" (Sidel 2006, p. 199). This chapter, following the main direction of the literature, emphasizes a "positive" and pro-social view of philanthropy (Wright 2001). Philanthropy in much literature represents a scaled-up form of charitable giving, distinct from charity by being based on "humanitarian considerations ... concerned for bettering human conditions" (Checkland 1980, p. 2).

Philanthropy can be seen to represent a supply-side response in societies to welfare needs, operating on voluntarist principles: a view confirmed by Salamon's

(1992, p. 10) widely quoted understanding as "the private giving of time or valuables for public purposes." Payton and Moody (2008, p. 35), in contrast, seek a widened "affirmative concept of philanthropy," as "voluntary action that advances a vision of the public good." The action component is "moral action that intervenes in the lives of others, so as to make the world better through human effort" (ibid). This raises the question as to whose morality predominates, with possibility philanthropic moralities being competitive as well as collaborative. An action-oriented approach leads philanthropy to seek new ideas in the face of changing social needs as expounded in Anheier and Leat's (2002) work, *From Charity to Creativity*, which argues for philanthropy to move more toward social innovation.

Finding expression primarily through institutions, philanthropy is equated in Western cultures of giving, and globally, through the institutional form of the foundation, so creating a sub-sector of nonprofits or civil society. Though "notoriously individualistic" (Leat 2007a, p. 207), the foundation sector provides opportunities for leadership in social problem-solving, for example, the Gates Foundation which is "the subject of intense interest by the global health community" (Black et al. 2009, p. 1584). Defining or equating philanthropy with the world of foundations offers research challenges in as much that historical research points to a range of "foundation" forms across cultures (see, e.g., Toroman et al. 2007) and the fact that there is much differentiation within the foundation world; as Gijselinckx (2008, p. 6) puts it, "foundations cannot be analysed as if they were all look-alikes, forming a monolithic bloc." In the main, however, the foundation of the research literature is largely the Western (European and US) privately formed but publicly regulated model. Philanthropy as expressed through foundation-style work has been subject to the critique that they serve as "prime constructors of hegemony, by promoting consent and discouraging dissent against capitalist democracy" (Roelofs 2007, p. 479), while others stress the importance of seeing foundations engaged in a "permanent project" of achieving a social vision (Wang'ombe 1995).

Philanthropy is clearly a clustered concept capable of being multiply defined by multiple stakeholders, so that parallel understandings of its nature and purpose coexist in research. Its characteristically private nature guarantees a degree of pluralism in response, but also a fragmentation of effort. Philanthropic individuals and institutions variously link, share, and collaborate, so that philanthropy may also be understood by drawing on the conceptual literature of networks and network organization. Ball's work (2008) exemplifies this approach, exploring and mapping the "new philanthropy, new networks and new governance" in the context of research into the privatization of education in the UK, whereas using the Canadian National Survey of Giving, Volunteering and Participating, Apinunmahakul and Devlin (2008, p. 309) investigate "the link between networks and private philanthropy," reporting "strong evidence that networks promote donations of time and money." More generally, the extent of multi-purpose and multi-layered understandings of philanthropy is well brought together by Sulek (2009), who surveys "prominent instances of usage and definitions of philanthropy" and synthesizes "them into an overall framework" (p. 1) that succinctly presents differing modes of modern-day philanthropy.

The Philanthropic Impulse

With multiple usage of the notion of philanthropy come multiple actors, institution builders and supporters, donors, activists, role models, and even tax payers. Here research illustrates a wide range of impulses toward philanthropy, including those of religion, race, gender, entrepreneurialism, corporate interest, and cultural outreach. In contrast, there is a marked lack of research attention given to the beneficiaries of philanthropic action, though important work exists at the overview level. For example, Ostrander (2007) argues for a social relations conceptualization of philanthropy as a two-way, mutual, interactive relationship between donors and recipient groups. In some areas of philanthropic interest, the emphasis on the receivers of support may become more crucial, as Scaife (2006) explores and illustrates in focus group research concerning philanthropy for Australia's indigenous people.

Much of the research on the philanthropic impulse in terms of the salience of religion, gender, and race tends to elide with that on the predictability and sources of individual donor behavior and preferences. A key example is that of Van Slyke et al. (2007), whose research responds to growing findings on African American philanthropy, where "African Americans are found to be an untapped philanthropic resource who have yet to be leveraged" (p. 278). The donor and donor intent literature with its emphasis on resource acquisition, retention, and sustainability also conforms to many of the conceptual underpinnings of scholarship on individual giving and organization philanthropy, especially with respect to motivation and impulsion (Halfpenny 1999).

A number of studies take a wider "collective action and behaviour" perspective on philanthropy. Berger (2006), for example, uses data from Statistics Canada to contrast the voluntary and philanthropic behavior of the Canadian population across religious groups, articulating a model that traces the influence of religion on voluntary and philanthropic behavior in Canada's multicultural society. Monsma (2007) examines the social network and religious belief theories for explaining the conjunction between religion and philanthropic giving and volunteering and concludes that both help to explain this conjunction, but that social network theory is the stronger explanatory theory. The joint effects of concepts of local philanthropy together with "brotherhood and volunteer services" are examined by Kaleem and Ahmed (2009) in the development of a theoretical model for charity-based Islamic microfinance institutions. From a gender perspective, McCarthy's (1996) editorship of a *Voluntas* special issue on women in philanthropy explored the "public niche" which philanthropy has consistently offered women. The focus on gender is quite broad: ranging from Clift's (2005) edited work on women, philanthropy, and social change to single case study research on a Los Angeles–based women's donor group with "its democratic voting system, lack of hierarchy and flexibility" (Caster 2008, p. 353). Far less evident, though, is work which explores the impact of philanthropy *on* women's issues (Goss 2007).

That the philanthropic actor is enduringly "rich" or "very rich" is an inevitable research finding in philanthropic studies concerned with foundation sustainability and growth. Viewing philanthropic actors' roles through the lens of elite theory provides important insights into philanthropic directions and choices (notably in the arts), but also more elusively, philanthropy's activities (especially risk-taking) as a kind of luxury good. Yet cross-sectoral elites may not operate as strongly as the fiercer critics of philanthropy assert. In studying the extent of "elite interlock in three US sectors," business, nonprofit, and government advisory groups, Moore et al. (2002, p. 740) expected to find that "non profit organizations and their trustees would be important players in national elite networks," but this received "only partial support" in their findings; major charities in the research sample of 109 organizations did not have high-profile trustees on their boards, a finding which the authors argue is "somewhat less surprising for foundations ... [since they] dispense grants from their endowments and earnings and may thus be less concerned with forging external connections" (ibid, p. 741). Moreover, Ostrower's study of cultural elites (2003, p. xvii) found that board members "develop a bifurcation in their outlook and actions," organizationally supporting openness and change, while retaining board members as "an exclusive elitist enclave." This, Ostrower argues, demonstrates "the limitations of class control perspectives for understanding elite boards" (ibid). For Silver, however, the study of "alternative foundations in comparison to their more traditional counterparts reveals just how deeply class lies at the very core of philanthropy" (2007, p. 537).

In response to, or perhaps a factor in, the spread of foundation structures, research reveals that the professionalization of the foundation sector workforce is occurring. Schuyt (2009, p. 6), for example, has drawn attention to the role of the Giving Research Europe project in stimulating and supporting "the philanthropic sector, in its efforts to raise professional standards and quality." Professionalization heightens the importance of foundation employees (and boards) in decision-making. Yet research on the workforce is not extensively pursued. Where it is, it relates to specific aspects, as for example in Morris's (2007) exploration of the ethical problems encountered by foundation officers in their evaluation-related work.

That philanthropy emanates too from the poor is becoming more evident in research. Wiepking (2007), for example, in researching the relative generosity of lower income households with data from The Netherlands Giving Panel Study 2003 found "evidence in favor of a giving standard, norms concerning the level of donations in specific situations that people in different income groups share, leading lower income groups to donate a higher proportion of their income" (p. 339). Everatt et al. (2005, p. 33) confirm, from quantitative work on giving in South Africa, that "the spectrum of giving behaviors is so diverse in shape and form that it contradicts many of the basic assumptions of the philanthropic literature [locating] the act of giving primarily in the domain of the wealthy and powerful" (see also Centre for Leadership and Public Values 2009; Wilkinson-Maposa et al. 2008; and Chapter 8 of this volume). Similarly, Healy (2009, p. 3), in looking at Irish philanthropy, challenges philanthropy's "capture" by those who disburse large sums of money and asserts that "we can all be philanthropists," thus advocating a "democratization" of philanthropy.

A wealth-oriented and vertical trickle-down discourse is, though, central to the growth of research interest in "entrepreneurial philanthropy," where the philanthropic actor deploys special business skills. Acs and Phillips (2002) see the entrepreneurship–philanthropy nexus as an emerging research area and focus on how personal biography, the nature of wealthy entrepreneurs' philanthropic contributions, motivations around self-interest or altruism, and managerial operating style come together to impact on philanthropic behavior. Links between philanthropy and social entrepreneurship are also established by Oppedisano (2004) in relation to women's philanthropy and by Taylor et al.'s (2008) case study of how a major US foundation with a "unique entrepreneurship focus" resourced from an innovative business operation. Moreover, Shaw and Carter (2007, p. 434) have also sought to develop "a more nuanced understanding of social entrepreneurship" by emphasizing the role of "personal local credibility and reputation."

Further conceptual rebranding of philanthropy has occurred with the invocation of "venture philanthropy" (Van Slyke and Newman 2006), an emergent term reflecting both the relative worthiness of investment models generally and discontent with familiar foundation-based models (Frumkin 2003). As Cobb argues (2002, p. 125), in the context of arts philanthropy, while "venture philanthropy is neither as innovative nor as revolutionary as its proponents have claimed, some influential funders now look at philanthropic giving ... with a changed set of priorities," that is, with an expectation of investment-style resource distribution and a closer attention to promised outcomes and gains – a point at which philanthropic action becomes less about the impulse for philanthropy and more about its expression.

The Expressions of Philanthropy

The best institutional form for philanthropic action incontrovertibly seems to be that of the foundation. Even where an apparent reinvigoration through presenting philanthropic giving as investing and an overall business orientation occurs, the foundation structure is retained. Moreover, while the contemporary trend for rebranding philanthropy has created a series of demarcations among foundations and their operating styles, such developments are more apparent than real. Katz (2005, p. 124), for instance, has characterized such terms as "venture philanthropy" and "strategic philanthropy" as mere "catchwords." It is one thing to argue, following Grant (2006), that philanthropic grantmaking "should recognise its kinship with business" or that business prediction systems may have value in aiding grantmaking choices (Harrow et al. 2006), but quite another to argue that business models – with their emphasis on "performance" – are uniquely appropriate for where "a love of mankind" is the spur for action. As Anheier and Leat (2006, p. 2) have put it, "social change [the purpose of philanthropy] is a negotiated, contested political process, not simply a matter of better management."

Notwithstanding such reservations, it is the continuing linkage with business as the resource base of philanthropy that causes wariness about foundations' place in the wider sphere of civil society, with its non-market rationale. What is described in portmanteau terms as corporate philanthropy exemplifies this concern. Scholars such as Petrovits (2006) and Yermack (2009) demonstrate the potential for a direct gain in business when foundation giving is undertaken, while Koehn and Ueng (2009, p. 1) present findings that "paint a mixed picture of the morality of corporate philanthropy." Critiques of corporate philanthropy as forms of advertising run parallel to those that advocate its practice, while the wider issue of the public policy implications of philanthropy and product "success" is less often examined. Here, the work of King et al. (2007) investigating African Americans' opinions about the philanthropic contributions of the tobacco industry to black organizations is striking, not least their conclusion that "despite the perceived benefits to these communities, tobacco industry contributions could mitigate community concerns about tobacco-related diseases, mask their significance, and undermine tobacco control strategies and policies" (p. 464).

Research from differing national contexts points to the importance of understanding firms' histories. For example, Sanchez's (2000, p. 363) work on corporate philanthropy in El Salvador suggests that "philanthropic acts by Salvadoran firms are driven by altruistic and politically strategic motives, and reflect individualistic and paternalistic attitudes." And Foster et al. (2009) in reviewing Canadian-based firm research present an "emerging typology of the role of the corporation in civil society," from donor ("reacting when asked"), through sponsor ("creating goodwill, investing in community"), to partner ("fully engaged in community") (p. 450) – concluding that "only a select few" firms have corporate philanthropy fully embedded in their organizational culture. In no institutional model of philanthropic activity is this more in evidence than in the area of family business-based philanthropy (Uhlaner et al. 2004) and the "family foundation," an organizational type that runs across but often goes beyond formal notions of corporate-sourced philanthropic action.

As Pharoah (2009a, p. 1) shows, "family foundation philanthropy has evolved and persisted through very different political contexts, sometimes a response to these" and in a manner in which their extent of giving can be readily monitored due to regular formal annual reporting mechanisms. Indeed, Pharoah estimates that family foundations account for around 38% of all charitable foundation spending in the UK and 17% in the United States. Further comparative research into family foundation philanthropy in Italy, Germany, the UK, and the United States is ongoing (Pharoah 2009b), but challenging in as much that there is as yet no common typology of foundations that can embrace the differing legal and fiscal environments – even within Europe (European Foundation Centre 1995). It is the case, moreover, that while in the main British and American foundations are principally grantmaking organizations, many European foundations are operating organizations, with funding and assets from a mixture of sources (Anheier 2001). There is no doubt, as Pharoah contends, that systematic international comparison on family foundations would provide a valuable seam of research – especially as one of the striking points that has emerged from existing research is the capacity of family foundations to tie personal and family concerns to ethical, social, or corporate motivations. From here, research can be developed in multiple directions: from, for instance, under-taking community-based studies of small family business responsiveness to needs in particular localities (Litz and Stewart 2000) to assessing the argument of Breeze (2009, p. 49) that family business people are "natural philanthropists."

As the line between the personal imperative to give and the models most able to deliver organized giving become blurred, models that incorporate a more flex-ible, open, and community-locale orientation are being advanced by researchers. Eikenberry (2006), for instance, shows – in the American context – the importance of "giving circles," that is, informal groupings of givers who choose collaboratively (while expressing dissatisfaction with "mainstream" philanthropy). The worldwide growth of "community foundations" – operating in localities and seeking funding (and where feasible endowments) from within their communities – also marks new prospects for "community-based social change," despite increasing competition for resources (Graddy and Wang 2009). The Global Fund for Community Foundations (2008) best describes such foundations as "indigenous philanthropic grantmaking institutions, which accumulate financial resources from a variety of donors, includ-ing local individuals and companies, diaspora populations, government bodies and international funders . . . [illustrating] the idea that local people and groups are best placed to respond to local challenges" (see also Graddy and Morgan 2006). Daly (2008) has assessed the role of community foundation-based philanthropy in the civic renewal of Britain's communities and reviewed efforts to promote the com-munity foundation form worldwide, as it "highlights the challenges of transferring philanthropic forms from one context to another" (p. 219). An implied competi-tive development between community foundations and more traditional foundation models is thus seen to exist, not least in relation to understandings of effectiveness employed – a comparison critically examined by Ostrower (2007) in research on "the relativity of foundation effectiveness." This increasing interest in philanthropic models which help deliver a "philanthropy of place" (Delfin and Tang 2006; Irvin 2007) moves attention to the question of philanthropy's location.

The Location of Philanthropy

Geographically led notions of philanthropy enable striking contrasts to be made, across macro-, meso-, and micro-levels of activity. Thus, for example, Karlstrom et al. (2009) stress the role of locally "embedded funders," whose characteristics include making "community relationships and partnerships a primary vehicle of their philanthropic operation." In contrast there is a growing body of literature on diaspora philanthropy that draws attention to the global separation of commu-nities, groups, and individual philanthropists operating at physical distance but underpinned by shared values within recipient communities. Werbner's analysis of the diaspora concept (2002, p. 119) emphasizes "the shared sense of moral co-responsibility, embodied in material gestures and extended through and across space," but also stresses that "ultimately, there is no guiding hand, no command structure, organising the politics, the protests, the philanthropic drives." In illustration of this important but patchwork philanthropic form, research ranges from detailed considerations of diaspora philanthropy in relation to individual households in at-risk societies (Brinkerhoff 2008) to comprehensive reviews of its nature and multiple forms (Johnson 2007).

An interlinking of the disciplines of geography and history underpins much of this work. A further layer of discourse is added by scholars studying the geographies of colonial philanthropy. For example Lambert and Lester (2004, p. 320) examining eighteenth- to mid-nineteenth-century British Empire developments argue for "colonial philanthropy as an object of inquiry that has relevance for contemporary globalized humanitarianism." And Peterson (2005) in studying overseas Chinese merchants' activities from the mid-nineteenth to the early twentieth century identifies the practice of "merchant philanthropy," with ideological underpinnings drawn from such sources as Confucian culturalism and modern nationalism.

This dual disciplinary theme also follows through in the extensive literature on philanthropic growth and change in particular continental and regional contexts. Thus, for example, Sidel (2001, p. 171) sees developments in South Asia in general and India in particular as "one of the most exciting nonprofit and philanthropic research environments today" (see also Lyons and Hasan 2002). Also, Ibrahim and Sherif (2009) examine and reflect on Arab philanthropy "in transition" to show an increasing number of individuals seeking to formalize their giving, while Landim and Thomson (1997) review NGOs and philanthropy in Latin America to reveal their often ambiguous roles across public and private realms. Individual nation-based studies again draw on the specifics of national, sub-national, and local cultures in their portrayal and analysis of philanthropy's expressions, growth, strategies, and tactics. For instance, Imada (2003) considers the effects on philanthropy of the voluntary response to the Hanshin Awadi earthquake in Japan, and Leat (2004) focuses on the pressures for, and expectations of, governance and accountability operations in Australian foundations. In Nordic countries, scholarship on philanthropic action is predominantly set in the wider context of voluntary sector–governmental relations and the changing context of diminished or elevated philanthropic initiatives (Acs and Braunerhjelm 2005; Henriksen and Bundesen 2004).

With growing discussion on "global philanthropy" as a significant phenomenon, Leat (2007a) has drawn an important distinction between global philanthropy in the sense of cross-border giving and the globalization *of* philanthropy – that is, the process of spreading philanthropic institutions and practices globally. This latter trend has been spurred by foundations moving away from funding local NGOs and more toward funding local philanthropic infrastructures. While Desai and Kharas (2008, p. 155) see such global philanthropy as "remaking the relationship between the world's rich and poor," Barnes (2005, p. 352) views international firms' philanthropy in Africa as being more about "their own kind of community development" so as to protect markets against major external threats. The rise of virtual philanthropy, as Internet and other new technology communication sources are increasingly being used, is beginning to be researched in earnest – although "e-philanthropy" is generally seen in terms of offering a new vehicle for income generation (Austin 2002) rather than as about changing approaches to philanthropic achievement. Whether the current period of economic downturn works to reframe patterns of global philanthropy in line with changes in global business size, direction, and aims, or extends it as global need becomes more manifest, is an open question.

The Values of Philanthropy

To draw together the multiple threads of research on values in philanthropy requires focusing on the theory-driven literature rather than the mainly empirically led and problem-led research discussed above. Among the leading studies here is that of Rudich (2007), who identifies three key strands of relevant theory to describe and explain philanthropy: those of altruism, social exchange theory, and identification theory, with corresponding values of non-rewarding seeking, seeking and receiving gains as a giver, and creating mutually rewarding relationships. Nickel and Eikenberry (2009, and their Chapter 19 in this volume), on the other hand, point to how the values of the marketplace have shifted the discourse on philanthropy to the point where its potential for bringing about social change is increasingly lost. This is a stance inevitably challenged by those arguing that only market-based solutions are sufficient to finance philanthropy (Wood and Martin 2007). Here, the "philanthrocapitalism" debate, its pros (Bishop and Green 2008) and cons (Edwards 2008) as preserver or as impairer of philanthropy, has come to the fore, as yet predominantly at the level of exchange of ideas rather than very extensive research agendas. The cultural "copying" of philanthropic institutions – with the foundation-as-model as a predominantly US export – offers a further perspective into the underlying values informing the choice of best structures for implanting and sustaining philanthropy. This in turn raises questions as to the status of isomorphism as it impacts on philanthropy and as philanthropic institutions become made and remade in the context of shared governance debates (Harrow, forthcoming) and legitimacy challenges (Prewitt et al. 2006).

The complexities of demonstrating and articulating the social justice dimensions of philanthropy, as an aim and as a working philosophy, are demonstrated through the attempts at theory-building from fieldwork findings. For example, McCarthy (2004, p. 250) examines grantee–grantmaker relations in the environmental justice field, where her analysis "builds on, but also goes beyond, the channeling and co-optation literatures that emphasize the potentially negative influence of foundation funding on grantees" and also "contributes to the newly developing social relations perspective which conceptualizes social movement philanthropy as a relationship that is mediated by many factors (for instance, the political orientation of the funder and grantee, among others)." In contrast, Delfin and Tang (2008, p. 603) provide a perspective "different from the view of elitist critics that foundations co-opt their grant recipients," reporting NGO grantee respondents' view of foundations "as mildly constructive across several organizational domains." Attainment of social justice goals in relation to corporate philanthropy (as opposed to rhetorical claims) remain to be extensively researched (Newall and Frynas 2007), though empirical studies such as that of Wadham and Williams (2009) examining collaborative business support for advancing Millennium Goals in the context of the Africa Progress Panel is a striking, if small-scale, example of such work.

The extent to which values in and of philanthropy relate to those of welfare state or post-welfare-state perceptions of public need and public good represents another ongoing research field. Philanthropy is to be found to underpin a number of governmental policy initiatives – particularly in the field of education (Ball 2009; Minstrom and Vergari 2003; Scott 2009). Philanthropy also acts as a fallback resource for where governmental intervention has promoted voluntary agency "responsibilization" to act as community service providers (Ilcan and Basok 2004).

More generally, inter-governmental and philanthropic collaboration is posited as essential to ensuring that "a durable peace can be established in the post-9/11 era" (Greenberg 2006, p. 163). Weber (2008), however, notes that charitable activity may serve as a means for terrorist groups to advertise their ideals among potential sympathizers (citing Ly 2007), that philanthropy is essentially ambiguous in that its values can underscore anti-state as well as pro-state action. Weber's scrutiny of the outcomes of governmental counter-terrorism finance regimes, including "its negative impact on cross border giving" (p. 4), highlights a role for research in the political debate over regulating philanthropy – whether enabling or restrictive. Interestingly, a study by Aksartova (2003, p. 25) on peace grantmaking by US foundations, guided by neo-institutional organizational theory, found that overriding values around legitimacy concerns in the context of "normative pressure from the 'national security state'" adversely affected foundation grantmaking from the mid-1980s to the mid-1990s. Advancing the case for research on such sources of external influence on foundations would inevitably serve to highlight the extent to which philanthropic values are derived from *within* a circle of institutions, individual givers, and beneficiaries. A circle that is well shown in studies into proving philanthropy's "effectiveness" and "impact" as a legitimizer, an engine for sustaining resources, and a convenor on social issues (Cutler 2009; Leat 2007b).

On another theme, it is difficult to assess the value of privacy in philanthropy: although relinquished in part in return for tax advantages, it does seem to be a value in its own right as philanthropic donors choose to direct their funding as they wish, with the responses and experiences of beneficiaries going largely unresearched. The experience and the value of privacy appear coterminous with the rise of welfare states – in contrast to those periods in Europe when public organizations such as guilds and benevolent societies cared for impoverished members and "the church took care of the most poor" (Muukkonen 2009, p. 689). With privacy comes a further characteristic – or value – that of responsiveness to particular social problems or issues, which can engender a "choosiness" or uncoordinated approach to social problems. It is precisely this kind of particularistic response from philanthropy that can bring its values into disrepute. Thus, Dowler and Caraher (2003, p. 57), in relation to public policy on food poverty in the UK, accuse the state of "adopting the role

of philanthropist and tackling food poverty on a piecemeal basis through encourage-
ment of local food projects." More strongly and across a wider field, Levy (2002)
examines the case "against philanthropy, individual and corporate" through showing
how in the face of philanthropy governments relinquish their responsibilities.

The tendency for philanthropy to fund "its own" is a common critique of philanthropic action, a clear disvalue for some. For corporate philanthropy, for example,
Saiia et al. (2003, p. 169) report findings which highlight a rise in "strategic philanthropy" (that is, beneficial to the giver as well as to the receiver) and thereby "lend
support to the belief that the nature of corporate philanthropy is evolving to fit a
more competitive marketplace." Support for beneficiaries in the same work group
or social class, or for co-religionists or political sympathizers, has been a hallmark
of some kinds of philanthropy, but research is also beginning to explore those areas
where philanthropists' expected values may seem to run counter to their giving practices. Thus, Haklai (2008) has asked as to "Why transnational Jewish philanthropic
foundations donate to Palestinian NGOs in Israel?" and answered that "having
internalised liberal values of minority rights and pluralism in their countries of
residence ... donating foundations believe that the development of [these organi-
zations] is both normatively desirable and strengthens Israel as a whole." Haklai
stresses that the theoretical significance of this work is that it "demonstrate[s] how
the interpretation of communal interest is strongly related to the normative social
environment in which transnational activists operate" (p. 581).

Conclusion

This research review confirms Frumkin's (2006, p. 11) account of philanthropy as "a
complex and sprawling concept," while emphasizing the primary understanding of
the concept as "the ability of donors to use private funds to create social and political
change." Ilchman et al. (2007, p. 19) maintain that "philanthropy does not simply
reflect a culture but the struggles and contexts in which a culture finds itself and
of struggles between cultures. Like many other arenas, it becomes a location where
cultural norms are contested. The way philanthropy is done, the way it is structured,
and its preferred objects become battlegrounds for other issues." Correspondingly,
in times of economic downturn, the effects of declining asset bases, together with
local and global reflection on and revisiting of sociopolitical and economic priorities, will invigorate some forms of philanthropy and ossify others – as well as
challenging long-held operating assumptions (such as longevity in philanthropy as
some foundations explore "spending out" options and rationales).

As the wider nonprofit organization field faces increased demand, philanthropy
as the supply side of civil society may be increasingly driven by new and unusual
decision-making forces, including that of rationing. Rationing as a concept is
more readily rooted in public administration than philanthropy literatures, linked
to notions of equity and to public virtue. As some philanthropic institutions face
pressure for increased openness in their decisions and inability (as opposed to

unwillingness) to meet demand, so the overt rationing of philanthropic resources – if only in the form of "waiting in line" – may become more marked. Awareness of the risk in viewing philanthropy as possessing a "magic wand" for social problems may also grow. Research on, in, and for philanthropy will, then, continue to display a wide array of directions and goals, meeting up with or returning to the core notion of philanthropy not as a buy-off or alibi, as culturally expected, or as fiscally sensible – but as sacrifice.

References

Acs, Z. J., and Braunerhjelm, P. (2005). The entrepreneurship–philanthropy nexus: Implication for internationalisation. *Management International Review*, 45(3), 111–144.

Acs, Z. J., and Phillips, R. J. (2002). Entrepreneurship and philanthropy in American capitalism. *Small Business Economics*, 19(3), 189–204.

Adam, T. (2004). *Philanthropy, Charity and Civil Society: Experiences from Germany, Great Britain and North America*, Bloomington, Indiana University Press

Aksartova, S. (2003). In search of legitimacy: Peace grant making of U.S. philanthropic foundations, 1988–1996. *Nonprofit and Voluntary Sector Quarterly*, 32(1), 25–46.

Anheier, H. K. (2001). Foundations in Europe: A comparative perspective. Civil Society working paper 18, London School of Economics, www.lse.ac.uk/collections/CCS/pdf/CSWP18-revised_july_2001.pdf

Anheier, H. K., and Leat, D. (2002). *From Charity to Creativity: Philanthropic Foundations in the Twenty First Century*, Stroud, UK, Comedia in association with the Joseph Rowntree Reform Trust.

Anheier, H. K., and Leat, D. (2006). *Creative Philanthropy: Towards a New Philanthropy for the Twenty-First Century*, London, Routledge.

Apinunmahakul, A., and Devlin, R. A. (2008). Social networks and private philanthropy. *Journal of Public Economics*, 92(1/2), 309–328.

Austin, J. E. (2002). Marketing's role in cross-sector collaboration. *Journal of Nonprofit and Public Sector Marketing*, 11(1), 23–40.

Ball, S. J. (2008). New philanthropy, new networks and new governance in education. *Political Studies*, 56(4), 747–765.

Ball, S. J. (2009). Academies in context: Politics, business and philanthropy and heterarchical governance. *Management in Education*, 23(3), 100–103.

Barnes, S. T. (2005). Global flows: Terror, oil & strategic philanthropy. *Review of African Political Economy*, 32, Issue 104/105, 235–252.

Berger, I. E. (2006). The influence of religion on philanthropy in Canada. *Voluntas*, 17(2), 110–127.

Bishop, M., and Green, M. (2008). *Philanthrocapitalism: How the Rich Can Save the World*, London, Bloomsbury Press.

Black, R. E., Bhan, M. K., Chopra, M., Rudan, I., and Victora, C. G. (2009). Accelerating the health impact of the Gates Foundation. *The Lancet*, 373, Issue 9675, 1584–1585.

Breeze, B. (2009). *Natural Philanthropists: Findings of the Family Business Philanthropy and Social Responsibility Inquiry*, London, Institute for Family Business.

Brinkerhoff, J. M. (2008). Diaspora philanthropy in an at-risk society: The case of Coptic orphans in Egypt. *Nonprofit and Voluntary Sector Quarterly*, 37(3), 411–433.

Caster, J. J. (2008). A new direction in women's philanthropy. *Nonprofit and Voluntary Sector Quarterly*, 37(2), 353–361.

Centre for Leadership and Public Values. (2009). *The Southern Africa and United States Building Community Philanthropy Project*, University of Cape Town, South Africa, www.gsb.uct.ac.za/clpv/

Checkland, O. (1980). *Philanthropy in Victorian Scotland: Social Welfare and the Voluntary Principle*, Edinburgh, John Donald.

Clift, E. (eds) (2005). *Women, Philanthropy and Social Change: Visions of a Just Society*, Lebanon, NH, Tufts University Press and University Press of New England.

Cobb, N. K. (2002). The new philanthropy: Its impact on funding arts and culture. *The Journal of Arts Management, Law, and Society*, 32(2), 125–143.

Cutler, D. (2009). *The Effective Foundation: A Literature Review*, London, The Baring Foundation.

Daly, S. (2008). Institutional innovation in philanthropy: Community foundations in the UK. *Voluntas*, 19(3), 219–241.

Delfin, F., Jr., and Tang, S.-Y. (2006). Philanthropic strategies in place-based, collaborative land conservation: The Packard Foundation's conserving California landscape initiative. *Nonprofit and Voluntary Sector Quarterly*, 35(3), 405–429.

Delfin, F. G., Jr., and Tang, S.-Y. (2008). Foundation impact on environmental nongovernmental organizations: The grantees' perspective. *Nonprofit and Voluntary Sector Quarterly*, 37(4), 603–625.

Desai, R., and Kharas, H. (2008). The California consensus: Can private aid end global poverty? *Survival*, 50(4), 155–168.

Dowler, E., and Caraher, M. (2003). Local food projects: The new philanthropy? *The Political Quarterly*, 74(1), 57–65.

Edwards, M. (2008). *Just Another Emperor? The Myths and Realities of Philanthrocapitalism*, London, The Young Foundation.

Eikenberry, A. M. (2006). Giving circles: Growing grassroots philanthropy. *Nonprofit and Voluntary Sector Quarterly*, 35(3), 517–532.

European Foundation Centre. (1995). *Typology of Foundations in Europe*, www.efc.be/ftp/public/EU/EURweb/EFCtypology.pdf

Everatt, D., Habib, A., Maharaj, B., and Nyar, A. (2005). Patterns of giving in South Africa. *Voluntas*, 16(3), 275–291.

Foster, M. K., Meinhard, A. G., Berger, I. E., and Krpan, P. (2009). Corporate philanthropy in the Canadian context: From damage control to improving society. *Nonprofit and Voluntary Sector Quarterly*, 38(3), 441–466.

Friedman, L. J. (2003). Philanthropy in America: Historicism and its discontents. In L. J. Friedman and M. McGarvie (eds) *Charity, Philanthropy and Civility in American History* (pp. 1–22), Cambridge, Cambridge University Press.

Frumkin, P. (2003). Inside venture philanthropy. *Society*, 40(4), 7–15.

Frumkin, P. (2006). *Strategic Giving: The Art and Science of Philanthropy*, Chicago, University of Chicago Press.

Gijselinckx, C. (2008). Foundations: Catalysts of social change, innovation and civic action. ISTR Conference working papers, www.istr.org/conferences/barcelona/WPVolume/index.htm

Global Fund for Community Foundations. (2008). *Community Foundations and Local Philanthropy*, www.wings-globalfund.org/our-work-foundations.php

Goss, K. A. (2007). Foundations of feminism: How philanthropic patrons shaped gender politics. *Social Science Quarterly*, 88(5), 1174–1191.

Graddy, E. A., and Morgan, D. L. (2006). Community foundations, organizational strategy, and public policy. *Nonprofit and Voluntary Sector Quarterly*, 35(4), 605–630.

Graddy, E., and Wang, L. (2009). Community foundation development and social capital. *Nonprofit and Voluntary Sector Quarterly*, 38(3), 392–412.

Grant, P. (2006). The business of giving. *Alliance Magazine*, www.alliancemagazine.org/en/content/the-business-giving

Greenberg, M. (2006). Coordinating philanthropy for peace. *International Negotiation*, 11(1), 163–183.

Haklai, O. (2008). Helping the enemy? Why transnational Jewish philanthropic foundations donate to Palestinian NGOs in Israel. *Nations and Nationalism*, 14(3), 581–599.

Halfpenny, P. (1999). Economic and sociological theories of individual charitable giving: Complementary or contradictory? *Voluntas*, 10(3), 197–215.

Harrow, J., Harris, I., Mainelli, M., and Grant, P. (2006). Predicting the effectiveness of grant-making. *Strategic Change*, 15(2), 53–66.

Harrow, J. (forthcoming). Governance and isomorphism in local philanthropy: The interplay of issues among foundations in Japan and the UK. *Public Management Review*.

Healy, J. (2009). Irish philanthropy: Love or money? Fourth Annual Nonprofit Summer School, Centre for Nonprofit Management, Trinity College Dublin, www.cnm.tcd.ie/dialogue/summer-schools/

Henricksen, L. S., and Bundesen, P. (2004). The moving frontier in Denmark: Voluntary–state relationships since 1850. *Journal of Social Policy*, 33(4), 605–625.

Ibrahim, B. L., and Sherif, D. (eds) (2009). *From Charity to Social Change: Trends in Arab Philanthropy*, Cairo, The American University Press in Cairo.

Ilcan, S., and Basok, T. (2004). Community government: Voluntary agencies, social justice, and the responsibilization of citizens. *Citizenship Studies*, 8(2), 129–144.

Ilchman, W. F., Katz, S. N., and Queen II, E. L. (2007). Different traditions of philanthropy. In J. Mordaunt and R. Paton (eds) *Thoughtful Fundraising* (pp. 19–28), London, Routledge.

Imada, M. (2003). The voluntary response to the Hanshin Awadi earthquake: A trigger for the development of the voluntary and nonprofit sector in Japan. In S. P. Osborne (ed.) *The Voluntary and Non-Profit Sector in Japan: The Challenge of Change* (pp. 40–50), London, Routledge.

Irvin, R. A. (2007). Regional wealth and philanthropic capacity mapping. *Nonprofit and Voluntary Sector Quarterly*, 36(1), 165–172.

Johnson, P. D. (2007). Diaspora philanthropy: Influences, initiatives and issues. The Philanthropic Initiative and the Global Enquiry Initiative, Harvard University, www.tpi.org/downloads/pdfs/Diaspora_Philanthropy_Final.pdf

Katz, S. N. (2005). What does it mean to say that philanthropy is "effective"? The philanthropists' new clothes. *Proceedings of the American Philosophical Society*, 149(2), 123–131.

Kaleem, A., and Ahmed, S. (2009). The Quran and poverty alleviation: A theoretical model for charity-based Islamic microfinance institutions. *Nonprofit and Voluntary Sector Quarterly*, published OnlineFirst.

Karlström, M., Brown, P., Chaskin, R., and Richman, H. (2009). Embedded philanthropy and the pursuit of civic engagement. *The Foundation Review*, 1(2), 51–64.

King, G., Gebreselassie, T., Mallett, R. K., Kozlowski, L., and Bendel, R. B. (2007). Opinions of African Americans about tobacco industry philanthropy. *Preventive Medicine*, 45(6), 464–470.

Koehn, D., and Ueng, J. (2009). Is philanthropy being used by corporate wrongdoers to buy good will? *Journal of Management and Governance*, 14(1), 1–16.

Lambert, D., and Lester, A. (2004). Geographies of colonial philanthropy. *Progress in Human Geography*, 28(3), 320–341.

Landim, L., and Thompson, A. (1997). Non-governmental organisations and philanthropy in Latin America: An overview. *Voluntas*, 8(4), 337–350.

Leat, D. (2004). What do Australian foundations do – Who knows and who cares? *Australian Journal of Public Administration*, 63(2), 95–104.

Leat, D. (2007a). The infrastructure of global philanthropy, Wings and Wings-CF. In H. K. Anheier, A. Simmons, and D. Winder (eds) *Innovation in Strategic Philanthropy, Global and Local Perspectives* (pp. 199–212), New York, Springer.

Leat, D. (2007b). *Just Change: Strategies for Increasing Philanthropic Impact*, London, Association of Charitable Foundations.

Levy, N. (2002). Against philanthropy, individual and corporate. *Business and Professional Ethics Journal*, 31(3/4), 95–108.

Litz, R. A., and Stewart, A. C. (2000). Charity begins at home: Family firms and patterns of community involvement. *Nonprofit and Voluntary Sector Quarterly*, 29(1), 131–148.

Lyons, M., and Hasan, S. (2002). Researching Asia's third sector. *Voluntas*, 13(2), 107–112.

Ly, P.-E. (2007). The charitable activities of terrorist organizations. *Public Policy*, 131(1), 177–195.

McCarthy, D. (2004). Environmental justice grantmaking: Elites and activists collaborate to transform philanthropy. *Sociological Inquiry*, 74(2), 250–270.

McCarthy, K. D. (1996). Women and philanthropy. *Voluntas*, 7(4), 331–335.

Minstrom, M., and Vergari, S. (2003). Foundation engagement in education policymaking. Research paper 18, The Center on Philanthropy and Public Policy, University of Southern California, Los Angeles, www.usc.edu/schools/sppd/philanthropy/private/docs/RP18.pdf

Monsma, S. (2007). Religion and philanthropic giving and volunteering: Building blocks for civic responsibility. *Interdisciplinary Journal of Research on Religion*, www.religjournal.com/articles/2007.php

Moore, G., Sobieraj, S., Whitt, J. A., Mayorova, O., and Beaulieu, D. (2002). Elite interlocks in three U.S. sectors: Nonprofit, corporate, and government. *Social Science Quarterly*, 83(3), 726–744.

Morris, M. (2007). Foundation officers, evaluation, and ethical problems: A pilot investigation. *Evaluation and Program Planning*, 30(4), 410–415.

Muukkonen, M. (2009). Framing the field: Civil society and related concepts. *Nonprofit and Voluntary Sector Quarterly*, 38(4), 684–700.

Newell, P., and Frynas, J. G. (2007). Beyond CSR? Business, poverty and social justice: An introduction. *Third World Quarterly*, 28(4), 669–681.

Nickel, P. M., and Eikenberry, A. (2009). A critique of the discourse of marketized philanthropy. *American Behavioral Scientist*, 52(7), 974–989.

Oppedisano, J. (2004). Giving back: Women's entrepreneurial philanthropy. *Women in Management Review*, 19(3), 174–177.

Ostrander, S. (2007). The growth of donor control: Revisiting the social relations of philanthropy. *Nonprofit and Voluntary Sector Quarterly*, 36(2), 356–372.

Ostrower, F. (2003). *Trustees of Culture: Power, Wealth and Status on Elite Arts Boards*, Chicago, University of Chicago Press.

Ostrower, F. (2007). The relativity of foundation effectiveness: The case of community foundations. *Nonprofit and Voluntary Sector Quarterly*, 36(3), 521–527.

Payton, R. L., and Moody, M. (2008). *Understanding Philanthropy: Its Meaning and Mission*, Bloomington, Indiana University Press.

Peterson, G. (2005). Overseas Chinese and merchant philanthropy in China: From culturalism to nationalism. *Journal of Chinese Overseas*, 1(1), 87–109.

Petrovits, C. M. (2006). Corporate-sponsored foundations and earnings management. *Journal of Accounting and Economics*, 41(3), 335–362.

Pharoah, C. (2009a). Family foundation philanthropy in an international context: An expression of personal, family and/or the social and cultural values of their time? Researching the Voluntary Sector Conference, Voluntary Sector Studies Network and National Council for Voluntary Organisations, University of Warwick.

Pharoah, C. (2009b). *Family Foundation Philanthropy 2009 – UK, Germany, Italy and US*, London, Alliance Publishing Trust, www.cass.city.ac.uk/philanthropy/Family FoundationsPhilanthropy2009.pdf

Prewitt, K., Dogan, M., Heydemann, S., and Toepler, S. (2006). *The Legitimacy of Philanthropic Foundations: United States and European Perspectives*, New York, Russell Sage Foundation.

Roelofs, J. (2007). Foundations and collaboration. *Critical Sociology*, 33(3), 479–504.

Rudich, I. (2007). Not for love of man alone: An overview of theoretical approaches to philanthropy. The Center for the Study of Philanthropy in Israel, The Hebrew University of Jerusalem, www.sw.huji.ac.il/upload/rudich2006Eng.pdf

Saiia, D. H., Carroll, A. B., and Buchholtz, A. K. (2003). Philanthropy as strategy: When corporate charity "begins at home." *Business and Society*, 42(2), 169–201.

Salamon, L. (1992). *America's Nonprofit Sector: A Primer*, New York, Foundation Center.

Sanchez, C. M. (2000). Motives for corporate philanthropy in El Salvador: Altruism and political legitimacy. *Journal of Business Ethics*, 27(4), 363–375.

Scaife, W. (2006). Challenges in indigenous philanthropy: Reporting Australian grantmakers' perspectives. *Australian Journal of Social Issues*, 41(4), 437–452.

Schuyt, T. (2009). Introduction. In P. Wiepking (ed.) *The State of Giving Research in Europe* (pp. 6–8), European Research Network on Philanthropy, Amsterdam, Amsterdam University Press.

Scott, J. (2009). The politics of venture philanthropy in charter school policy and advocacy. *Educational Policy*, 231, 106–136.

Shaw, E., and Carter, S. (2007). Social entrepreneurship: Theoretical antecedents and empirical analysis of entrepreneurial processes and outcomes. *Journal of Small Business and Enterprise Development*, 14(3), 418–434.

Sidel, M. (2001). Recent research on philanthropy and the nonprofit sector in India and South Asia. *Voluntas*, 12(2), 171–180.

Sidel, M. (2006). The third sector, human security, and anti-terrorism: The United States and beyond. *Voluntas*, 17(3), 119–210.

Silver, I. (2007). Disentangling class from philanthropy: The double-edged sword of alternative giving. *Critical Sociology*, 33(3), 537–549.

Sulek, M. (2009). On the modern meaning of philanthropy. *Nonprofit and Voluntary Sector Quarterly*, published OnlineFirst.

Taylor, M. L., Coates, T., Strom, R., Renz, D., and Holman, R. (2008). The entrepreneur's evolution to philanthropist. *Journal of Leadership & Organizational Studies*, 15(1), 79–95.

Toroman, C., Tuncsiper, B., and Yilmaz, S. (2007). Cash Awqaf in the Ottomans as philanthropic foundations and their accounting practices. Paper presented to the Fifth Accounting History International Conference, Banff, Alberta.

Uhlaner, L. M., Goor-Balk, H. J., and Masurel, E. (2004). Family business and corporate social responsibility in a sample of Dutch firms. *Journal of Small Business and Enterprise Development*, 11(2), 186–194.

Van Slyke, D. M., and Newman, H. K. (2006). Venture philanthropy and social entrepreneurship in community redevelopment. *Nonprofit Management and Leadership*, 16(3), 345–368.

Van Slyke, D., Ashley, S., and Johnson, J. L. (2007). Nonprofit performance, fund-raising effectiveness, and strategies for engaging African Americans in philanthropy. *The American Review of Public Administration*, 37(3), 278–305.

Wadham, H., and Williams, I. (2009). Engaging business in development: The story of the Africa Progress Panel's Business Advisory Group and Concern Universal. Researching the Voluntary Sector Conference, Voluntary Sector Studies Network and National Council for Voluntary Organisations, University of Warwick.

Wang'ombe, J. K. (1995). The "permanent project syndrome": A counter productive consequence of philanthropy. *Social Science & Medicine*, 41(5), 603–604.

Weber, P. C. (2008). Terrorism and philanthropy, counter terrorism financing regimes, international civil society and religious fundamentalism. ISTR Conference working papers, www.istr.org/conferences/barcelona/WPVolume/index.htm

Werbner, P. (2002). The place which is diaspora: Citizenship, religion and gender in the making of chaordic transnationalism. *Journal of Ethnic and Migration Studies*, 28(1), 119–133.

Wiepking, P. (2007). The philanthropic poor: In search of explanations for the relative generosity of lower income households. *Voluntas*, 18(4), 339–358.

Wilkinson-Maposa, S., Fowler, A., Oliver-Evans, C., and Mulenga, C. F .N. (2008). *The Poor Philanthropist: How and Why the Poor Help Each Other*, Cape Town, University of Cape Town Graduate School of Business, www.gsb.uct.ac.za/gsbwebb/BCP_BookDownload.asp

Wood, A., and Martin, M. (2007). Market based solutions for financing philanthropy. Social Science Research Network, http://ssrn.com/abstract=980097

Wright, K. (2001). Generosity vs. Altruism: Philanthropy and charity in the United States and United Kingdom. *Voluntas*, 12(4), 399–416.

Yermack, D. (2009). *Deductio ad absurdum*: CEOs donating their own stock to their own family foundations. *Journal of Financial Economics*, 94(1), 107–123.

Chapter 11
Leadership and Governance

Vicky Lambert and Irvine Lapsley

Introduction

The concept of governance has assumed a central role in the regulation, monitoring, operation, and reporting of the third sector despite a lack of clarity over its exact meaning in the context of nonprofit organizations (Hyndman and McDonnell 2009). In part, this lack of clarity is a function of the inherent complexity of this sector of the economy. It is also a reflection of the state of the art in governance, which has the standing of a facet of modern organization that is both deemed to be an essential attribute and may not have obvious operational features. It has been suggested that the governance of nonprofit organizations necessarily requires a broad approach, given the above subtleties of third sector organizations (Hyndman and McDonnell 2009). The particular dimension of governance addressed in this chapter is that of leadership. This is addressed in the following sections that focus on the role of leadership, particularly in the context of managing third sector organizations, governance in nonprofit organizations, and case study evidence of different models of leadership, from a governance perspective.

Leadership or Management?

The concept of leadership is a major interest in all sectors of the economy. The general focus of leadership thinking has been on the private sector. There are concerns within the third sector literature that this private sector orientation does not capture the subtleties of third sector organizations (Hailey and James 2004). There are also issues, generally, over the meaning of what constitutes "leadership." In particular,

V. Lambert (✉)
University of Edinburgh, Scotland, UK
e-mail: vicky.lambert@ed.ac.uk

I. Lapsley (✉)
University of Edinburgh, Scotland, UK
e-mail: irvine.lapsley@ed.ac.uk

R. Taylor (ed.), *Third Sector Research*, DOI 10.1007/978-1-4419-5707-8_11,
© Springer Science+Business Media, LLC 2010

the notion of "leadership" (as a visionary, inspirational figure) is often conflated with the idea of management, in which management is a problem-solving, results-focused activity. Indeed, even within the third sector literature, there is a mistaken temptation to align "leadership" with "management" (Hailey and James 2004). However, despite these reservations over what constitutes "leadership" specifically in a third sector context, it is suggested here that some parts of the general leadership literature may have relevance to nonprofit organizations.

There are six concepts of "leadership," which are frequently discussed in the literature: democratic leadership, oligarchic leadership, situational leadership, transactional leadership, leadership by default, and transformational leadership. Of these six models, however, it can be shown that two are extremely narrow in their application (democratic leadership and oligarchic leadership), three are forms of management rather than leadership (situational leadership, transactional leadership, and leadership by default), and only one, transformational leadership, is truly within the scope of what constitutes leadership.

Narrow Concepts of Leadership

Within this category we place democratic leadership and oligarchic leadership. The category of democratic leadership is rarely found in practice, according to Markham et al. (2001). One particular kind of nonprofit organization where democratic leadership might be expected is universities. Hardy (1991) elaborates on the pluralist nature of university organization, which traditionally eschewed the unitary, hierarchical model of management favored by private sector corporations. However, the idea of elected leaders in universities has been overtaken by events as universities resort to explicit managerial models and marginalize the role of democratic decision-making (Deem 2004). The oligarchic model is similar to the democratic model of leadership in that this will apply to organizations that have democratic processes of electing leaders, but which will be subverted by the leadership to maintain rule by an entrenched elite (Markham et al. 2001). The idea of oligarchic leadership emanates from an early study by Michels (1962) of unions and political parties in Europe, but as a model of leadership it is rather restricted in terms of its application.

Leadership as Management

Within this category there are models that purport to be "leadership" but that, in practice, are closer to management. This includes the idea of situational leadership, which emanates from Fielder's (1967) analysis of the level of control that the leader can exert in a given situation. Variations on this model have been devised by Hersey and Blanchard (1969), which factor in motivations and actions of the "leader." Subsequent to this early work, there is a continuing preoccupation with a situational approach to leadership (see, e.g., Nicholls 1986). However, fundamentally, these situational models fit within the general schema of contingency models of management action.

As such, these are reactive models of management practice, rather than leadership models per se. Another leadership model of this ilk is transactional leadership. The concept of transactional leadership was depicted by Burns (1978) as an exchange process in which there are reciprocal actions by leaders and followers to their mutual benefit. This perspective is affirmed by Bass (1998), in which the rewards for job performance are seen as an integral element of the leadership function. This particular model is more suited to private sector settings and a culture of performance-related pay that percolates through the organization. For third sector organizations, however, this concept may be seen as a form of management, but not of high-level leadership. A third form of management that has been described as a leadership model is leadership by default. This approach derives from the work of Pearce (1980, 1982, 1993). In essence, this model describes the situation where it is difficult to recruit anyone to assume a leadership role (Markham et al. 2001). This particular situation resonates with the experiences of recruiting academics as managers in universities or hospital doctors as the representative of the medical profession in hospitals who assumes an administrative role. This, however, is administration or management, but not leadership.

Leadership as Transformation

The quest for transformational leadership is most closely associated with the work of Bass (1985). This work and a whole series of subsequent offerings (Bass and Avolio 1993; Bass and Riggio 2006; Bass and Steidlemeier 1999) present the case for the leader of the organization as a visionary and catalyst for change. This concept of the leader as an orchestrator of organizational change has filtered across from the private to the public sector as part of the movement for the reinvention of public administration (Osborne and Gaebler 1993). This extension to the public sector has met resistance over the appropriateness of this leadership model to public services. There are a number of reasons for this: the strength of professional groupings within public services, resistance to change in the face of continuing reforms, and opportunities for isomorphic behavior, which does not require high leadership skills (Lapsley 2008). It is also possible to challenge this particular model as one that requires a heroic figure to discharge this role. However, despite doubts and hesitations, the vigorous advocacy of this model by Bass and colleagues maintains a high profile for a leadership model that has obvious intuitive appeal, particularly for policy makers intent on change.

Despite both the advocacy and the reservations, the transformational leadership model may have a particular promise for third sector organizations. As Denhardt and Campbell (2006) observe, the originator of the concept of transformational leadership was Burns (1978) and not Bass. While the concept of transformation pervades both of these leadership models, the Burns (1978) model also includes an ethical dimension to the leadership model, by focusing on morality and values. This particular interpretation of leadership resonates with the mission of third sector organizations. And, in fact, Bass and Steidlemeier (1999) do argue that to be truly transformational, leadership must be grounded in ethical and moral considerations. While this stance reaffirms the potential relevance of the transformational leadership to the nonprofit sector, this mode of leadership has been advocated most of all for private and even public sector organizations. There are serious issues about the heroic nature of the role envisaged for transformational leaders in whatever context, but there can be little doubt that the moral or ethical dimension would be an essential attribute within the third sector.

Governance

The broader definition of governance referred to above sees the fundamental attributes of charitable organization governance as the distribution of rights and responsibilities within and between stakeholders and their role in the performance of the organization (Hyndman and McDonnell 2009). This includes issues such as the role of the board, the relationship between the board and the management of the organization, and the composition of the board of directors of nonprofit organizations, particularly the introduction of expertise from more business-like organizations – which has been criticized as undermining the ethos of altruism in the third sector (Landsberg 2004). The handling of these issues constitutes a key challenge for leaders of third sector organizations, as elaborated below.

A plethora of literature exists on governance in charities, which considers these issues. In terms of the role of the board, there is a large body of prescriptive literature outlining what the role of the board should be; however, a number of empirical studies find issues surrounding a lack of role clarity and a lack of role fulfilment. The role of the board is widely regarded as being strategic (Axelrod 2005; Houle 1990), but there are studies reporting that these strategic roles are not being fulfilled. Cornforth and Edwards (1999) report variations in the strategic contribution of volunteer boards; only slight strategic contributions were made by the board of a local voluntary organization and local authority school in their study, in contrast to a national voluntary organization and college where the contribution was much larger. Leatherwood and O'Neal (1996) found that members of nonprofits undertook a more operational role, with their boards more responsible for service than for strategy or control. Findings of a study of Australian nonprofits by Steane and Christie (2001) indicate that nonprofit directors engage in day-to-day issues as well as strategic issues. Furthermore, Inglis et al. (1999) found a gap that exists between role importance and role fulfilment in community nonprofit organizations. Lack of clarity of board roles has also been reported, for example, by Widmer (1993) and McAdam and Gies (1985). Issues relating to the role of the board outlined above have been suggested as creating tension between the board and the management (Chait and Taylor 1989; Taylor et al. 1996).

The composition of the board is extremely significant to nonprofit organizations; the organization must make sure that it has the right mix of people on the board to enable it to achieve its mission. A number of studies have been conducted, which consider the impact of board composition on a number of aspects of the organization (Austin and Woolever 1992; O'Regan and Oster 2005; Siciliano 1996); yet one of the most significant issues surrounding board composition is raised by Abzug and Galaskiewicz (2001). They consider the inclusion of a specific group of individuals on the board – the recruitment of trustees with college education and/or professional managerial occupations – and find that trustees with college education, managers, and professionals continue to have significant representation on nonprofit boards.

Despite the universal acknowledgment that the adoption of business practices in charities is a significant issue, there is a considerable lack of research on the impact this has on governance, in particular the impact that business professionals have on charity boards, which, coupled with the increasing emphasis for charities to have these individuals on their boards, is surprising. One study though, by Bowen (1994), has looked into the divergence of performance of business executives on charity boards. Here several factors were identified that may impinge on the success of these individuals in their role as charity trustees. For example, professional staff in charities may be quick to dismiss business professionals as they may feel they will not understand the unique qualities and professional norms of the organization or may be insensitive toward them. Another problem identified was that there may be an amount of hostility directed toward business professionals from those within the organization.

Although in practice Bowen's paper appeared to highlight a clash between business professionals and those from within the charity, Bowen was still supportive of the idea of business people serving on the boards of charities and notes that these organizations have a considerable amount to learn from their for-profit counterparts and the operations of corporate boards, calling for the adoption of certain business practices such as the routine use of benchmarking and monitoring discrepancies between results and planned outcomes. An earlier study that considered the impact of business professionals on charity boards was undertaken by McFarlan (1999), who highlighted the significant differences between nonprofit and for-profit boards; an issue raised here was that business professionals underestimate and are not fully aware of what being a charity trustee actually involves. Consequently, this lack of understanding of the role, and its time-consuming nature, results in high board turnover. The success of business people on charity boards, according to McFarlan, requires that they understand the differences between the nonprofit and private sectors and realize that not all their skills and expertise are appropriate for application in the nonprofit sector.

Dees (1998), in considering ways in which nonprofits can effectively become more business-like, highlighted the import of recognizing that board members from business are a valuable resource. Dees (1998, p. 66) noted that if nonprofits are to become more business-like, managers must be trained in business methods:

One way to gain such training is to reach out for help. Nonprofit managers can begin in their own backyards by finding more effective ways to draw on board members with relevant business experience. The resulting exchange will be a learning experience for both parties. Business board members are often an underutilised source of management expertise, and they need coaching and coaxing to adapt their business frameworks to the context of a social enterprise.

As in the mini-case studies discussed below, this perspective on the exploitation of business expertise can have a significant, positive impact on the leadership of nonprofit organizations. One empirical study of this issue, by Austin (1998), considered the involvement of business-people on charity boards in the United States. In considering the benefits to nonprofits, it was found that nonprofits benefited significantly from the expertise of business people and their distinct managerial and business perspective; in addition, 80% of business people were found to be "as or more effective" and 90% "as or better prepared" than other board members. There was a tendency for them to be viewed differently to their counterparts, due to their skills, knowledge, experience, and the way they enriched board discussions.

The above studies – although highlighting potential issues with the involvement of business people on charity boards – have been largely positive about their involvement and the impact it has. However, there are also studies where this is not the case. An example of this is Landsberg (2004), who conducted a case study on a US mental health center and found that the result of more business people being recruited onto nonprofit boards is a greater emphasis on financial concerns in place of issues related to mission. This point can also be seen in Siciliano's (1996) consideration of the relationship between board member diversity and organizational performance. Here, an example is given where the board is considering a long-standing YMCA program; Siciliano (1996, p. 1318) describes the discussion thus:

The program had not been cost-effective for several years and was beginning to drain on other sources of revenue. Several board members with business backgrounds were strongly opposed to its continuance. However, viewpoints of other board members tended to stress the program's benefit of building family relationships. After hearing both sets of arguments, the board voted to continue the program for another year.

This example emphasizes Landsberg's concern that business people tend to focus on finance; however, it also shows that a variety of knowledge and views can help organizations make difficult decisions. Another study, which questions such business influence, is that by Alexander and Weiner (1998), who move away from the specific focus of business people on charity boards and consider the adoption of a for-profit model of governance for charities, the "corporate governance model," as a potential solution to financial and competitive pressures experienced by the sector. The uptake of the corporate governance model was not found to be a widespread solution to these issues; adoption was concentrated predominantly in nonprofit organizations that were large in size and that were not experiencing financial difficulties, or adverse affects of competition. Those that may have benefited from such a model did not have sufficient resources to support such a change, and in addition, it was put that certain aspects of the model may conflict with the mission and the values of these organizations.

The impact of business practices on nonprofit organizations has been identified as a highly contentious issue; however, in order to offer potential leadership models for third sector organizations, we turn to examine the fusion of influences – external business expertise, management, and leadership – in two case study settings.

Leadership in Action: Case Study Evidence

Here we focus on two mini-case studies of leadership styles that are intimately related to the governance of two third sector organizations. The first leadership style we refer to as "substantive"; the second leadership style we refer to as "aspirational." In both of these case study settings the leadership style is of a shared responsibility and duty rather than the highly individualistic style favored by the proponents of transformational leadership. In both the case study settings, the governance systems were crucial to the emergence of these leadership styles. This opened up the possibility of distinct high-level management expertise working alongside the existing third sector organizations' management. This was a precondition for the fusion of business thinking and fundamental nonprofit organizations into these shared forms of leadership, which proved to be rewarding for both organizations. The two case study settings are in social care and affordable housing.

Social Care Case Study

In this organization, the founding member had started this entity to make a difference to the provision of social care in the Lothian area of Scotland. This organization, henceforth "SocCare," is 20 years old. The founding member is the current chief executive officer (CEO). SocCare has an annual budget of £5 million, and its work has grown to encompass social work, housing, and health care.

This growth in activities has caused management and organizational challenges for SocCare. The initial response to these challenges was the establishment of a management committee of 17, which had two elements: statutory and non-statutory activities. The statutory element had three representatives each from health, social work, and housing. This arrangement persisted for the first 7 years of the organization's life. As the organization grew, the founder member saw the existing management arrangements were cumbersome and not suited to a turbulent environment in which the major services of health social care were undergoing significant structural, managerial, and policy changes. His response was to seek out professional management expertise to contribute at board level.

This receptivity to change on his part led to the appointment of a management consultant as a board member. The management consultant introduced the ideas of "the board cycle," based on the work of Garratt (2003), on the board as part of a learning organization. The CEO and the management consultant worked together on this shared vision of how the board and the organization should function with demonstrable success – and with the willing cooperation of management, after some initial skepticism. This we see as substantive leadership.

Affordable Housing

Our second case study is of an organization that provides housing for poorer members of society. This is an organization, "AffoHous," which was first formed in 1995 in response to the acute need for affordable housing in the Lothian area of Scotland. This is an organization that has found it difficult to recruit external expertise to its board. This difficulty is perpetuated by the particular circumstance of the board for AffoHous in which members of the board may stay in this role without time limit. At least five members of the board were on the initial steering group that established the organization. AffoHous has had success, and its annual budget has risen to £5 million.

The CEO of AffoHous was formerly a member of the initial steering group and then progressed to being the director of finance, before assuming his current position. The particular challenge facing this CEO is the lack of strategic focus at board level. The longstanding members of the board have a preoccupation with the day-to-day practical issues facing the organization and have a reluctance to engage in strategic thinking. The present board is not responsive to forward-looking suggestions such as the inclusion of tenant's representatives on the board. The longstanding board members have a limited regard for the concerns of other stakeholders.

In this stalemate situation, the CEO sought to introduce senior management expertise to the board. One of the newcomers is a senior finance officer from a major public sector body. This person has a view and a vision for the board which is very progressive. This is a shared vision with the present CEO. This shared relationship is, however, based on a tension. While the CEO accedes to the merits of the way forward, he is also reluctant to take this forward in the face of entrenched attitudes and perspectives on how the organization should work. The crystallization of this view based on shared views but underpinned by tension, we describe as aspirational leadership.

Conclusion

The governance of nonprofit organizations is a complex affair. What constitutes governance in nonprofit organizations is contested. This requires a broad perspective on what governance is, or might be. In this chapter, our particular concern has been with leadership in the context of governance. The subject of leadership is, in itself, a highly topical and hotly debated issue. Much of the writing on leadership is directed at the for-profit, rather than the nonprofit sector of the economy. Also, many contributions to the leadership literature are really discussions of management rather than leadership per se, which must incorporate elements of vision and of message. Where there are truly leadership models, the proponents conjure up leaders as heroic figures, which makes them a tenuous prospect for universal adoption.

Also, there is an issue in the nonprofit sector over how ethics and values feature as cornerstones of the nonprofit movement. The fundamental attribute of many non-profit organizations is to make a difference to society. This ethos represents a set of values based on altruism (Gassler 1998). A major concern of the movement for nonprofit organizations is the manner in which concepts of leadership and management practices which emanate from the private sector of economies may attenuate these ethical values which are at the very core of nonprofit activity. This in itself has implications for governance systems, particularly the ways in which and extent to which, external – especially business – expertise is utilized within third sector organizations. This chapter has offered illustrations of two different modes of leadership style – substantive and aspirational – in which shared leadership between external business experts has worked to move forward third sector organizations. The extant literature on leadership tends to focus on the traditional concept of the leader, as a single person, a single voice. Here, we suggest more subtle forms of leadership are more appropriate for this, most complex sector of the economy.

References

Abzug, R., and Galaskiewicz, J. (2001). Nonprofit boards: Crucibles of expertise or symbols of local identities? *Nonprofit and Voluntary Sector Quarterly*, 30(1), 51–73.

Alexander, J. A., and Weiner, B. J. (1998). The adoption of the corporate governance model by nonprofit organizations. *Nonprofit Management and Leadership*, 8(3), 223–242.

Austin, D. M., and Woolever, C. (1992). Voluntary association boards: A reflection of member and community characteristics. *Nonprofit and Voluntary Sector Quarterly*, 21(2), 181–193.

Austin, J. E. (1998). Business leaders and nonprofits. *Nonprofit Management and Leadership*, 9(1), 39–51.

Axelrod, N. R. (2005). Board leadership and development. In R. D. Herman and Associates (eds) *The Jossey-Bass Handbook of Nonprofit Leadership and Management*, 2nd edn (pp. 131–152), San Francisco, Jossey-Bass.

Bass, B. (1985). *Leadership and Performance Beyond Expectations*, New York, Free Press.

Bass, B. M. (1998). *Transformational Leadership: Industrial, Military, and Educational Impact*, Mahwah, NJ, Lawrence Erlbaum Associates.

Bowen, W. G. (1994). When a business leader joins a nonprofit board. *Harvard Business Review*, Sept–Oct, 38–43.

Bass, B. M., and Avolio, B. J. (1993). *Improving Organizational Effectiveness through Transformational Leadership*, Thousand Oaks, CA, Sage.

Bass, B. M., and Steidlmeier, P. (1999). Ethics, character, and authentic transformational leadership behaviour. *Leadership Quarterly*, 10(2), 181–217.

Bass, B. M., and Riggio, R. E. (2006). *Transformational Leadership*, Mahwah, NJ, Lawrence Erlbaum.

Burns, J. M. (1978). *Leadership*, New York, HarperCollins.

Chait, R. P., and Taylor, B. E. (1989). Charting the territory of nonprofit boards. *Harvard Business Review*, Jan–Feb, 44–54.

Cornforth, C., and Edwards, C. (1999). Board roles in the strategic management of non-profit organisations: Theory and practice. *Corporate Governance*, 7(4), 346–362.

Deem, R. (2004). The knowledge worker, the manager-academic and the contemporary UK university: New and old forms of public management? *Financial Accountability and Management*, 20(2), 107–128.

Dees, J. G. (1998). Enterprising nonprofits. *Harvard Business Review*, Jan–Feb, 55–67.

Denhardt, J. V., and Campbell, K. B. (2006). The role of democratic values in transformational leadership. *Administration and Society*, 38(5), 556–572.

Fielder, F. (1967). *A Theory of Leadership Effectiveness*, New York, McGraw Hill.

Gassler, R. S. (1998). Altruism and the economics of non-profit organisations. *Financial Accountability & Management*, 13(3), 173–182.

Garratt, B. (2003). *The Fish Rots from the Head. The Crisis in Our Boardrooms: Developing the Crucial Skills of the Competent Director*, London, Profile Books.

Hailey, J., and James, R. (2004). Trees die from the top: International perspectives on NGO leadership development. *Voluntas*, 15(4), 343–353.

Hardy, C. (1991). Pluralism, power and collegiality in universities. *Financial Accountability and Management*, 7(3), 127–143.

Hersey, P., and Blanchard, P. (1969). The life cycle theory of leadership. *Training and Development Journal*, 23(5), 26–34.

Houle, C. O. (1990). *Governing Boards: Their Nature and Nurture*, San Francisco, Jossey-Bass.

Hyndman, N., and McDonnell, P. (2009). Governance and charities: An exploration of key themes and the development of a research agenda. *Financial Accountability and Management*, 25(1), 5–31.

Inglis, S., Alexander, T., and Weaver, L. (1999). Roles and responsibilities of community nonprofit boards. *Nonprofit Management and Leadership*, 10(2), 153–167.

Landsberg, B. E. (2004). The nonprofit paradox: For-profit business models in the third sector. *The International Journal of Not-for-Profit Law*, 6(2) www.icnl.org/knowledge/ijnl/vol6iss2/index.htm

Lapsley, I. (2008). The NPM agenda: Back to the future. *Financial Accountability & Management*, 24(1), 77–96.

Leatherwood, M., and O'Neal, D. (1996). The transformation of boards in corporate and not-for-profit sectors: Diminishing differences and converging contexts. *Corporate Governance*, 4(3), 180–192.

Markham, W. T., Walters, J., and Bonjean, C. M. (2001). Leadership in voluntary associations: The case of the "International Association of Women," *Voluntas*, 12(2), 103–130.

McAdam, T. W., and Gies, D. L. (1985). Managing expectations: What effective board members ought to expect from nonprofit expectations. *Nonprofit and Voluntary Sector Quarterly*, 14(4), 77–88.

McFarlan, F. W. (1999). Working on nonprofit boards: Don't assume the shoe fits. *Harvard Business Review*, Nov–Dec, 64–80.

Michels, R. (1962). *Political Parties: A Sociological Study of the Oligarchical Tendencies of Modern Democracy*, New York, Free Press.

Nicholls, J. R. (1986). Congruent leadership. *Leadership and Organization Development Journal*, 9(1), 27–31.

O'Regan, K., and Oster, S. M. (2005). Does the structure and composition of the board matter? The case of nonprofit organizations. *The Journal of Law, Economics and Organization*, 21(1), 205–227.

Osborne, D., and Gaebler, T. (1993). *Reinventing Government: How the Entrepreneurial Spirit is Transforming the Public Sector*, New York, Penguin.

Pearce, J. L. (1980). Apathy or self-interest: The volunteer's avoidance of leadership roles. *Journal of Voluntary Action Research*, 9 (January), 85–94.

Pearce, J. L. (1982). Leading and following volunteers: Implications for a changing society. *Journal of Applied Behavioural Science*, 18(3), 385–394.

Pearce, J. L. (1993). *Volunteers: The Organizational Behavioural of Unpaid Workers*, New York, Routledge.

Siciliano, J. I. (1996). The relationship of board member diversity to organizational performance. *Journal of Business Ethics*, 15(12), 1313–1320.

Steane, P. D., and Christie, M. (2001). Nonprofit boards in Australia: A distinctive governance approach. *Corporate Governance*, 9(1), 48–58.

Taylor, B. E., Chait, R. P., and Holland, T. P. (1996). The new work of the nonprofit board. *Harvard Business Review*, Sept–Oct, 36–46.

Widmer, C. (1993). Role conflict, role ambiguity, and role overload on boards of directors of nonprofit human service organizations. *Nonprofit and Voluntary Sector Quarterly*, 22(4), 339–356.

Chapter 12
Nonprofit Marketing

Bernd Helmig and Julia Thaler

Introduction

For years, interdisciplinary researchers have focused on nonprofit organizations, and such multidisciplinarity has created diverse nonprofit research (Helmig et al. 2004). From a managerial point of view, research into nonprofit organizations often focuses on the marketing discipline; the use of marketing by nonprofit organizations began in the late 1960s, has accelerated in recent years, and has been widely accepted and practiced (Kotler and Andreasen 2002). Furthermore, nonprofit marketing has great importance for the ever-increasing number of nonprofit organizations, which have, in the past 25 years, vastly widened their scope. They currently provide and contribute to health, education, and social welfare causes all over the world (Liao et al. 2001). The growth of the nonprofit sector thus has increased competition among organizations that provide similar services, and that competition has heightened as a result of reduced government funding in many countries (Bendapudi et al. 1996). Moreover, commercialization and internationalization enhance the degree of competition. All these aspects may help explain the rising relevance of nonprofit marketing from a practical point of view, as well as the increasing attention that nonprofit managers and researchers pay to marketing issues.

In the context of such growing interest for the marketing discipline in nonprofit management research and practice, this chapter aims to promote understanding of nonprofit marketing. To this end, it first demonstrates the increasing relevance of nonprofit marketing by outlining the evolution of marketing in general and proposing a definition that features key aspects of nonprofit marketing. Then we identify and critically review various strands of research so as to determine some of the most pressing concerns around nonprofit marketing today.

B. Helmig (✉)
University of Mannheim, Germany
e-mail: sekretariat@oebwl.bwl.uni-mannheim.de

J. Thaler (✉)
University of Mannheim, Germany
e-mail: thaler@oebwl.bwl.uni-mannheim.de

R. Taylor (ed.), *Third Sector Research*, DOI 10.1007/978-1-4419-5707-8_12,
© Springer Science+Business Media, LLC 2010

Evolution and Definition of Nonprofit Marketing

The development of the nonprofit marketing discipline, as well as its changing relevance, can best be traced through the evolution of general marketing definitions, as represented by the American Marketing Association's (AMA) published versions. Table 12.1 lists these marketing definitions, which serve as a basis for comparison herein.

Table 12.1 AMA marketing definitions over time

Year	American Association of Marketing (AMA) definition	Focus
1935	Marketing is the performance of business activities that direct the flow of goods and services from producers to consumers	Business activities
1985	Marketing is the process of planning and executing the conception, pricing, promotion, and distribution of ideas, goods, and services to create exchanges that satisfy individual and organizational objectives	Normative approach Exchange paradigm
2004	Marketing is an organizational function and a set of processes for creating, communicating, and delivering value to customers and for managing customer relationships in ways that benefit the organization and its stakeholders	Relationship Value creation paradigm
2007	Marketing is the activity, set of institutions, and processes for creating, communicating, delivering, and exchanging offerings that have value for customers, clients, partners, and society at large	Satisfaction of customer wants Serving a society's needs

The earliest AMA marketing definition did not include nonprofit organizations or, consequently, nonprofit marketing. Instead, the first definition to broaden marketing's field of application was the one offered by Kotler and Levy (1969, p. 15): "[*Marketing*] is the concept of sensitively serving and satisfying human needs." With this definition, Kotler and Levy created considerable controversy about whether marketing should be restricted to pure market transactions (Arbuthnot and Horne 1997). When the *Journal of Marketing* published a special issue devoted to marketing in nonprofit organizations in 1971, the marketing community seemingly came to accept nonprofit marketing as an interesting research topic. Despite the narrowness of existing marketing definitions in the 1970s, research focused on the application of marketing tools to college recruiting, public transportation, health services, and religious and arts organizations, showing that nonprofit managers already had adopted the managerial function of marketing (Kotler 1979). The evolution of the broadened application coincided with newer marketing definitions (e.g., Kotler 1972, 1984; Pride and Ferrel 1977), which made the 1935 AMA definition obsolete.

In a 1985 definition, the AMA took a more normative approach and included the notions of exchange and process, while also considering both organizations and individuals (Ringold and Weitz 2007). Thus, it seemed to correspond better with the ongoing debates and developments, because it included the distribution of ideas in addition to the exchange of both goods and services, which are predominant in the nonprofit sector. However, marketing based on the exchange paradigm cannot apply to the nonprofit sector, with its complicated, multilevel customer relationships, which result in nonmarket-mediated exchanges (Clarke and Mount 2001).

A demanded and relevant shift from an exchange paradigm to a value-creation paradigm appeared in the 2004 AMA definition, as the relevance of intangible goods, such as services, was continuing to grow and perhaps even overwhelm tangible products. Beyond offering the value-creation concept, which better fits the nonprofit context than the exchange paradigm, this definition did not really reflect the increased relevance of nonprofit marketing though. It prompted strong criticism for its potentially restrictive focus on organizational marketing and its failure to consider societal and public policy issues (Gundlach 2007; Wilkie and Moore 2007; Zinkhan and Williams 2007). Sheth and Uslay (2007) also criticized the prevalent and seemingly single-minded focus on the role of customers as buyers, which underlies the 2004 AMA definition of marketing but is adequate only in a business context. These criticisms resulted in a broadened and softened AMA marketing definition in 2007. The acceptance of marketing in the nonprofit sector continues to increase and expand. Marketing no longer can be concerned exclusively with the exchange of goods and services; it must include a focus on the satisfaction of customer wants and needs and on the sensitive effort to serve the needs of a society (Sargeant 2009).

These different approaches to traditional marketing, developed over time and with varying focus (e.g., activities, relationships, and management), have resulted in an integrative definition of marketing, according to which marketing comprises both a company-external and a company-internal facet (Homburg et al. 2009). In line with this modern view, we define nonprofit marketing as follows: *Marketing for nonprofit organizations is a philosophy that includes internal and external activities that aim to contribute to the fulfilment of an organization's overall mission*. In this context, the organization-external aspects include instrumental aspects of nonprofit marketing such as market research, product, price, place, promotion, and politics. The organization-internal aspects of nonprofit marketing entail a leading philosophy that focuses on people to create broader acceptance of external-oriented marketing within the organization. Both the external and internal approaches work to improve relationships with all the customer groups of a nonprofit organization, so that the organizational goals and mission can be achieved. Figure 12.1 depicts these features of an integrative nonprofit marketing definition.

Marketing products and services to a wide range of target groups represents a key feature of nonprofit marketing. The specific focus on both internal and external marketing aspects also emphasizes the nonprofit organization's unique customer groups. Kotler (1982) delineated four constituent categories, which he calls the "publics" of a nonprofit organization: input (e.g., donors), internal (e.g., volunteers), intermediary (e.g., consultants), and consuming publics (e.g., clients). Ten years later,

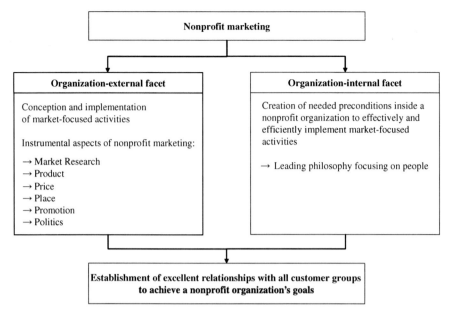

Fig. 12.1 Integrative approach of nonprofit marketing

Gwin (1990) identified three nonprofit customer groups: resource generators, service users, and regulators. In contrast, Álvarez González et al. (2002) mentioned only two target groups: the beneficiaries of the nonprofit action and resource donors. Smith and Friedman (1994) discussed the customer–consumer dichotomy prevalent in the nonprofit sector, and following a marketing logic, Helmig et al. (2009) stuck to the term "customers" instead of using stakeholders or publics to describe the target groups of a nonprofit organization and its marketing activities.

These latter authors identified four categories of customers, similar to those suggested by Kotler: direct customers (e.g., members and patients), indirect customers (e.g., family of a patient), internal customers (e.g., volunteers), and donors (who may give money or objects). These four target groups provide the basis for a broad nonprofit marketing concept that covers internal and external activities; traditional marketing applications (market research, product, promotion, price, place, politics), adapted to the nonprofit context; and special marketing applications, such as promoting volunteerism or fundraising. In the nonprofit sector, the marketing strategies must attract resources (e.g., time from volunteers, money from government and the public) and then allocate those resources (e.g., investing in a campaign to persuade people to stop smoking, helping particular patients) (Shapiro 1974). An elaborated nonprofit marketing concept therefore should focus on all four customer groups using different but sometimes overlapping marketing techniques. Figure 12.2 displays the different customer groups and the resultant primary marketing focus for each group.

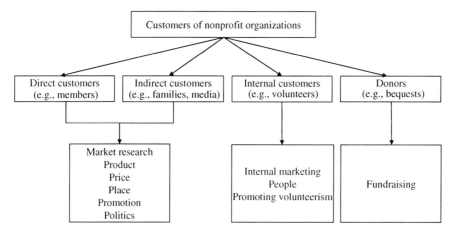

Fig. 12.2   Customers and respective marketing focus of nonprofit organizations

Nonprofit Marketing Research Reviewed

Major scholarly journals in the nonprofit area (*Voluntas*, *Nonprofit Management and Leadership*, and *Nonprofit and Voluntary Sector Quarterly*) rarely publish articles dealing directly with marketing (Helmig et al. 2004). Nevertheless, several articles offer some relevance for nonprofit marketing, including Couto (2001), Gibelman and Gelman (2001), Hermann and Rendina (2001), and Kottasz (2004) which were all published in *Voluntas*. The interdisciplinarity of these general nonprofit journals dictates that they do not primarily target managerial issues (except for *Nonprofit Management and Leadership*). Marketing-related topics, therefore, have been more likely to be published in high-ranked (i.e., impact factors and journal ratings) general marketing journals, such as *Journal of Marketing, Journal of Marketing Research*, and *Marketing Science*, as well as in nonprofit marketing-specific journals such as the *International Journal of Nonprofit and Voluntary Sector Marketing, International Review on Public and Nonprofit Marketing, Journal of Nonprofit and Public Sector Marketing*, and *Journal of Public Policy & Marketing* (Helmig et al. 2004). Published articles in these journals cover a multitude of research fields, such as the core issues of nonprofit marketing oriented toward a particular customer group (e.g., fundraising) and social marketing. In what follows we provide a critical review of the diverse research streams, illustrated chronologically in Fig. 12.3.

Social Marketing

From a marketing perspective, social issues have appeared since the late 1960s, largely as a result of the debate about broadening the concept of marketing. This debate not only caused controversy but also encouraged the development of social

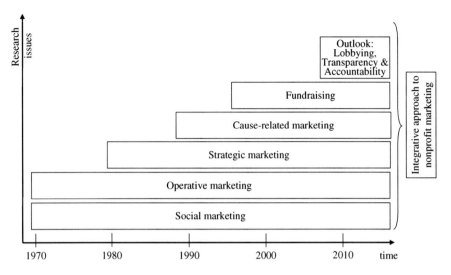

Fig. 12.3 Development of central nonprofit marketing research issues over time

marketing. Social marketing primarily focuses on nonprofit organizations and government in their efforts to deal with social problems, such as health support, equal educational opportunity, or the alleviation of poverty (Wilkie and Moore 2003). Early articles discussed and analyzed planned social change, population problems, recycling, and air pollution. As a field of application for marketing concepts and tools, social marketing thus became broadly accepted and was defined by Kotler and Zaltman (1971, p. 5) as "the design, implementation, and control of programs calculated to influence the acceptability of social ideas and involving considerations of product planning, pricing, communication, distribution, and market research." Social marketing currently reflects "the use of marketing principles and techniques to influence a target audience to voluntarily accept, reject, modify, or abandon a behavior for the benefit of individuals, groups or society as a whole" (Kotler et al. 2002, p. 5). These definitions primarily identify it as a society-oriented field of marketing, yet its close link to nonprofit marketing remains evident.

Shapiro (1974) highlights another function of nonprofit marketing, namely, to persuade people to do something that is desirable for society as a whole but that does not contribute to the nonprofit organization. Social marketing campaigns, such as health support, anti-smoking, or anti-litter campaigns, can be part of a nonprofit organization's marketing, even though these campaigns do not focus on or require interaction with that organization. People can contribute to fulfilling an organization's goals by changing their attitudes and behavior rather than, say, contributing as a donor. Therefore, these nonprofit marketing activities target the entire society as indirect customers.

The current relevance of social marketing becomes evident in the presence of a special issue on social marketing published by the *International Journal of Nonprofit and Voluntary Sector Marketing* (2008). The topics featured in this special issue are mainly experimental, such as how to improve workplace safety for younger workers, improve physical activity campaigns, influence young adults to avoid driving while under the influence of alcohol, and improve social marketing campaigns aimed at smoking cessation and avoidance (Wymer 2008). Social marketing research thus clearly emphasizes the effectiveness of particular campaigns, yet further research, including perhaps a meta-analysis of the effectiveness of social marketing campaigns, still is needed to draw empirically based conclusions from the multitude of diverse study results.

Operative Marketing in Nonprofit Organizations

Research into the application of traditional marketing techniques to the nonprofit sector analyzes, for example, the traditional marketing mix: pricing, product policy, channels of distribution, and communications (Ford and Mottner 2003; Mindak and Bybee 1971; Shapiro 1974; Wenham et al. 2003). Several authors consider advertising, promotion, and public relations in nonprofit organizations (Aldrich 2004; Hooper and Stobart 2003; Peattie 2003; Self 2001; West and Sargeant 2004). The need to optimize applications of commercial marketing tools through adaptation to the nonprofit context makes the marketing situation more complex and marketing success more difficult to assess (Kline Henley 2001; Rothschild 1979; Shapiro 1974). Furthermore, applying marketing techniques to a specific type of nonprofit organization, such as religious or cultural institutions, attracts some research attention (Attaway et al. 1995; Cuadrado et al. 2000; Gainer and Padanyi 2002; Smith and Santandreu 1997). Thus, the application of marketing techniques as a research stream focuses on the operative aspects of nonprofit marketing in its efforts to target direct and indirect customers, strictly separate from nonprofit-specific marketing functions such as volunteer recruitment and fundraising (Gainer and Moyer 2004).

Strategic Marketing in Nonprofit Organizations

Nonprofit researchers examine a wide range of strategic issues, including strategic marketing planning (Arbuthnot and Horne 1997; Cousins 1990; Kotler 1979), the concept of market orientation (Álvarez González et al. 2002; Vázquez et al. 2002), and the relationship of market orientation with organizational performance (Gainer and Padanyi 2002). Against the backdrop of a relevant nonprofit market orientation, Liao et al. (2001) propose a "societal orientation" that might be more adequate in the nonprofit sector (see also Sargeant et al. 2002).

The customer value concept also has great relevance in the nonprofit sector (Knowles and Gomes 1997; Petkus 2001). Strategic nonprofit research efforts focus on examining the relevance of branding, including the concepts of brand personality (Voeth and Herbst 2008), branding dimensions (Stride 2006), and their influence on organizational performance or received donations in the nonprofit context (Hankinson 2001; Heller 2008; Napoli 2006; Reed et al. 2007; Stride and Lee 2007; Venable et al. 2005).

To avoid a departmental view of nonprofit marketing, focusing exclusively on one or two customer groups, the overall concept of relationship marketing should be applied to beneficiaries, which represent the direct customers of the nonprofit action; indirect customers; the internal customers who contribute their time and know-how; and donors of money and objects (Álvarez González et al. 2002; Hayes and Slater 2003). Whereas general research on relationship marketing is broad, managing relationships in a nonprofit context is insufficiently researched (Michalski and Helmig 2008), though recent studies highlight an integrative marketing concept focused on relationships with all different customer groups (Arnett et al. 2003; Conway and Whitelock 2007; Passebois and Aurier 2004; Rentschler et al. 2002).

In the context of a strategic implementation of an integrative marketing concept, several researchers in the nonprofit marketing field consider internal customers, internal marketing, and promoting volunteerism (Bennett and Barkensjo 2005; Callow 2004; Judd 2001; Lindenmeier 2008; Wymer 1999). Internal marketing essentially describes a strategy designed to enhance the customer orientation of (board) members and volunteers, as well as achieve membership tenure through identification with the organization (Bhattacharya et al. 1995). These internal customers become conscious of the organization's philosophy (Judd 2001). The strategic introduction of people, including both volunteers and board members, into the marketing mix of a nonprofit organization represents a further adaptation to existing practices in the for-profit context (Judd 2001).

Cause-Related Marketing

Cause-related marketing, as defined in the late 1980s, is "the process of formulating and implementing marketing activities that are characterized by an offer from the firm to contribute a specified amount to a designated cause when customers engage in revenue-providing exchanges that satisfy organizational and individual objectives" (Varadarajan and Menon 1988, p. 60). Typically, such efforts feature advertising that promises some amount of money will be donated to a charity for every purchase of a product (Helmig et al. 2004). The use of cause-related marketing as a form of business collaboration with nonprofit organizations has been growing steadily since the early 1980s (Wymer and Sargeant 2006), due to nonprofit organizations' increased need for funds and for-profit enterprises' need for greater differentiation from their competitors. From a profit-oriented company's point of view, cause-related marketing can help create a better image of the brand and company and increase profit through higher sales numbers (Sargeant 2001b).

Drumwright (1996) outlines the fundamentals of cause-related marketing campaigns in her discussion of the need for new approaches to successful advertising with a social dimension, based on appropriate quantitative measures that can evaluate the long-term, company-oriented, and noneconomic objectives that constitute key elements of cause-related marketing campaigns. In cause-related marketing research, the consequences of and responses to such marketing represent outcomes of collaborations with profit-oriented companies, as well as the determinants of these collaborations (Webb and Mohr 1998; Wymer and Sargeant 2006). Studies analyze the relationships among a nonprofit organization, the donating organization, and the customers (Nowak and Clarke 2003); several studies also show that consumers' attitudes toward a profit-oriented organization influence their behavior toward the brand, the cause, and, consequently, the nonprofit organization (Basil and Herr 2003; Garcia et al. 2003; Strahilevitz 2003).

On a more operative basis, researchers focus on the structural elements of cause-related marketing campaigns, including the quantification of donations, the amount donated relative to the price of the product, the presence of donation deadlines, and the promotional effort to publicize the campaign (Landreth Grau et al. 2007). Furthermore, several authors assess the role of compatibility between the company and the cause and donation size in creating positive customer reactions to a campaign, including their perceptions of the donating organization and their purchase intentions (Hajjat 2003; Trimble and Rifon 2006).

This overview of relevant issues in cause-related marketing research implies that the focus primarily has been on a nonprofit customers' group of donors. The impact on the target group of indirect customers, such as making the general public aware of a certain cause, also is relevant though. Thus, the link between nonprofit marketing and cause-related marketing is evident. However, cause-related marketing remains a marketing tool of profit-oriented companies as well.

Fundraising

The practical relevance of fundraising derives from the growing importance of encouraging donations in response to shrinking governmental support for both funding and task fulfilment. Nevertheless, raising resources from donations and, consequently, understanding donor behavior remain significant challenges for nonprofit organizations, which must undertake nonprofit marketing to target the customer group of donors (Bendapudi et al. 1996). Donor identification, attraction, and retention are the principal concerns for marketing managers, as well as for researchers in the field of fundraising (Webb et al. 2000). In the past decade, explicitly competitive strategies have emerged in charity fundraising, and fundraising has become even more complex (Abdy and Barclay 2001) and subject to greater attention in nonprofit research (Lee 2003; Marudas and Jacobs 2004, 2007).

In academic research, donation motives, donor behavior and attitudes, and the application of marketing tools to fundraising with a focus on fundraising effectiveness or performance constitute the most important research fields (see Fig. 12.4). Research pertaining to donor behavior, motives, and attitudes includes conceptual

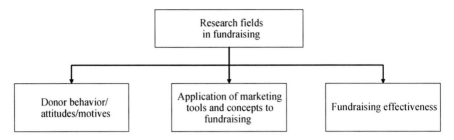

Fig. 12.4 Overview of issues in fundraising research

behavior models that attempt to improve the quality and targeting of fundraising campaigns (Lichtenstein et al. 2004; Sargeant 1999; Webb et al. 2000). Early models focused on donation in general as the primary output; Sargeant (1999) includes more detailed outputs, such as the level of the gift, lifetime value of the donor, and extent to which a donor may support the organization by donating time in addition to money. But research has yet to focus sufficiently on understanding donors rather than merely attempting to transfer marketing techniques and technology to implement successful fundraising (Arbuthnot and Horne 1997; Shang et al. 2008).

In the twenty-first century, academic researchers began to base their research on findings derived from more than 20 years of research on advertising effectiveness in the business context (Diamond and Gooding-Williams 2002). Such research also applies marketing tools to the nonprofit context in the field of fundraising research. A particular focus centers on direct mail-based charitable solicitations (Diamond and Gooding-Williams 2002; Diepen et al. 2009). Moreover, donor-focused approaches and marketing concepts play increasingly important roles in fundraising research and practice. For example, Sargeant (2001a) explains the link between the relatively recent concept of relationship marketing and fundraising. Relationship fundraising, an adaptation of relationship marketing, appeals to donors and maximizes funds per donor in the long term. Accordingly, Burnett (2002, p. 38) defines relationship fundraising as "an approach to the marketing of a cause that centers on unique and special relationships between a nonprofit and each supporter. Its overriding consideration is to care for and develop that bond and to do nothing that might damage or jeopardise it."

The effectiveness of different forms of fundraising, including direct mail, telemarketing, and corporate fundraising, pertain to the potential of major gift fundraising, local fundraising, corporate fundraising, and trust fundraising (Sargeant et al. 2006; Sargeant and Kähler 1999). Fundraising performance as a result of the dimensions of market orientation (Bennett 1998), fundraising events (Higgins and Hodgins 2008; Higgins and Lauzon 2003), and the fundraising effectiveness of particular efforts undertaken by different types of nonprofit organizations (Rooney 1999) further exemplify the focus of this research stream.

Lobbying

Closely related to the idea of influencing society through social marketing campaigns is the conceptualization of persuasion in the form of a nonprofit organization's lobbying activities. Lobbying studies appear in economics, sociology, and political science research, but as a form of marketing communication, it is largely under-researched and rarely mentioned in general marketing literature (Harris and Lock 1996; Lahiri and Raimondos-Møller 2000). As part of the broader field of public relations though, lobbying clearly should be part of marketing (Milbrath 1960). In the 1990s, lobbying gained importance in business contexts through close links to a wide range of business disciplines, including marketing communications and public relations (Andrews 1996). Lobbying represents a special form of marketing communications, engaged with similar concerns, measurements, and promotional campaigns, which contribute directly to business performance (Andrews 1996). Mack (2005) also regards lobbying as an issue for communication management that must be developed as intensely as marketing or advertising campaigns. McGrath (2007) confirms this attitude and focuses on framing lobbying messages.

Lobbying plays roles in the business context and in nonprofit organizations, which usually aim to influence public policy (Nyland 1995). The social marketing and lobbying activities of a nonprofit organization may be very similar, except for their different target groups, and both contribute to a nonprofit organization's ability to fulfil its mission. Consequently, lobbying relates closely to nonprofit marketing, even though it is often regarded as more closely linked to political marketing (Dann et al. 2007). In the nonprofit context, this field holds particular interest, because issues such as conquering cancer, preserving the environment, decreasing famine, or fighting for human rights are directly or indirectly affected by governmental decisions (Smucker 2005). Nevertheless, nonprofit marketing research has not yet targeted lobbying, ignoring legislators as part of a nonprofit organization's indirect customers.

Further research should focus on lobbying from a marketing perspective but also adopt a nonprofit marketing perspective. As a first step, results from academic marketing research on lobbying, such as the importance of framing lobbying messages, should be applied appropriately to the nonprofit context.

Transparency and Accountability through Nonprofit Marketing

Against the backdrop of current scandals in nonprofit organizations, accountability and transparency have gained greater relevance in this sector (Gibelman and Gelman 2004). Transparency in nonprofit organizations helps prove their accountability to donors, which attracts the necessary resources from them, and to the other customer groups, which cements the nonprofit organization's reputation in the external environment (Kearns 1994). Furthermore, transparency and accountability toward all customer groups should increase the trustworthiness of the nonprofit organization, because relationships with customers depend on transparency, which is based on trust and commitment (Lamming et al. 2001; Morgan and Hunt 1994). Nevertheless, academic nonprofit literature has yet to relate transparency and accountability to nonprofit marketing; rather, the link applies only to governance and finance (Andrés-Alonso et al. 2006; McCambridge 2004; McCarthy 2007). The academic relevance of accountability in the nonprofit sector emerges clearly in articles by Pratten (2004) and Ebrahim (2005).

In the business context, transparency and accountability as integral aspects of marketing management have been discussed by Holden (2000). Further contributions to a broader understanding of transparency appear in consumer marketing, communications, relationship marketing, and services marketing (Christensen 2002; Eggert and Helm 2003; Lovelock et al. 1999). Hultman and Axelsson (2007) expand the concept of transparency and propose a transparency typology for marketing management research. In this typology, the relevance of transparency results from its inherent promise of efficiency and effectiveness, which demonstrates the close link with accountability.

Research in the field of marketing management confirms the relevance of transparency and accountability in the marketing context. Therefore, transparency as a nonprofit marketing research issue should expand to reflect the findings in general marketing management research, which must be adopted and adapted to the nonprofit marketing context. Exploratory research into transparency in the context of nonprofit marketing is a critical need.

Conclusion

This chapter provides a review of scholarly research in the broader field of nonprofit marketing, including discussions of current topics in nonprofit marketing, such as social marketing and cause-related marketing. These research fields focus on both direct and indirect customers of nonprofit organizations – as does research into strategic nonprofit branding. Considering the relevance of internal marketing in nonprofit organizations, as well as nonprofit fundraising, oriented toward donors, in combination with the focus on relationship marketing, it appears that all four customer groups of nonprofit marketing are current topics of nonprofit marketing research.

Nonprofit marketing as an applied discipline of traditional marketing must constantly adapt to changes to keep pace. As this chapter reveals, challenges for nonprofit organizations include the adoption and adaptation of traditional marketing techniques and concepts to their own particular context (Dann et al. 2007). For example, the value and applicability of the recently introduced service-dominant logic (Vargo and Lusch 2004, 2008) to nonprofit marketing requires consideration, and nonprofit organizations may need to adopt or adapt the concept of customer cocreation. The cocreation of value in the nonprofit context might include collaborations with all customer groups, because according to the service-dominant logic, marketing entails a process of interactions with customers to create value (Lusch 2007). Abela and Murphy (2008) and Vargo and Lusch (2008) regard the service-dominant logic as particularly accommodating to nonprofit marketing, because it is based on the idea that the exchange of services occurs mutually, an assertion that is absolutely true for the services offered by nonprofit organizations.

In addition to the need to keep pace with recent changes in traditional marketing research, nonprofit marketing should be a key focus of academic researchers because of its increasing practical relevance. Furthermore, researchers in the nonprofit field should emphasize and undertake a broader range of empirical studies, particularly quantitative studies, because nonprofit marketing is no longer an exploratory field, as demonstrated by this chapter's detailed analysis of its current status. Complex research methods and multi-item measures remain recent and underdeveloped in the nonprofit context. The close link between traditional marketing and nonprofit marketing suggests that research questions specific to the latter can be answered through the same elaborated methods adopted by the former.

References

Abdy, M., and Barclay, J. (2001). Marketing collaborations in the voluntary sector. *International Journal of Nonprofit and Voluntary Sector Marketing*, 6(3), 215–230.

Abela, A. V., and Murphy, P. E. (2008). Marketing with integrity: Ethics and the service-dominant logic for marketing. *Journal of the Academy of Marketing Science*, 36(1), 39–53.

Aldrich, T. (2004). Do-it-yourself DRTV: A practical guide to making direct response television advertising work for charities. *International Journal of Nonprofit and Voluntary Sector Marketing*, 9(2), 1465–4520.

Álvarez González, L. I., Santos Vijande, M. L., and Vázquez Casielles, R. (2002). The market orientation concept in the private nonprofit organization domain. *International Journal of Nonprofit and Voluntary Sector Marketing*, 7(1), 55–67.

Andrés-Alonso, P. de, Martín Cruz, N., and Romero-Merino, M. E. (2006). The governance of nonprofit organizations: Empirical evidence from nongovernmental development organisations in Spain. *Nonprofit and Voluntary Sector Quarterly*, 35(4), 588–604.

Andrews, L. (1996). The relationship of political marketing to political lobbying. An examination of the Devonport campaign for the Trident refitting contract. *European Journal of Marketing*, 30(10/11), 76–99.

Arbuthnot, S., and Horne, S. (1997). The marketing activities of UK charities. *Journal of Nonprofit and Public Sector Marketing*, 5(1), 63–79.

Arnett, D. B., German, S. D., and Hunt, S. D. (2003). The identity salience model of relationship marketing success: The case of nonprofit marketing. *Journal of Marketing*, 67(4), 89–105.

Attaway, J. S., Boles, J. S., and Singley, R. B. (1995). Exploring consumers' attitudes toward advertising by religious organisations. *Journal of Marketing Management*, 5(1), 71–83.

Basil, D. Z., and Herr, P. M. (2003). Dangerous donations? The effects of cause-related marketing on charity-attitude. *Journal of Nonprofit and Public Sector Marketing*, 11(1), 59–76.

Bendapudi, N., Singh, S. N., and Bendapudi, V. (1996). Enhancing helping behaviour: An integrative framework for promotion planning. *Journal of Marketing*, 60(3), 33–49.

Bennett, R. (1998). Marketing orientation among small to medium sized UK charitable organisations: Implications for fundraising performance. *Journal of Nonprofit and Public Sector Marketing*, 6(1), 31–45.

Bennett, R., and Barkensjo, A. (2005). Internal marketing, negative experiences, and volunteers' commitment to providing high-quality services in a UK helping and caring charitable organization. *Voluntas*, 16(3), 251–274.

Bhattacharya, C. B., Rao, H., and Glynn, M. A. (1995). Understanding the bond of identification: An investigation of its correlates among art museum members. *Journal of Marketing*, 59(4), 46–57.

Burnett, K. (2002). *Relationship Fundraising: A Donor-Based Approach to the Business of Raising Money*, 2nd edn, San Francisco, Jossey-Bass.

Callow, M. (2004). Identifying promotional appeals for targeting potential volunteers: An exploratory study on volunteering motives among retirees. *International Journal of Nonprofit and Voluntary Sector Marketing*, 9(3), 261–274.

Christensen, L. T. (2002). Corporate communication: The challenge of transparency. *Corporate Communications*, 7(3), 162–168.

Clarke, P., and Mount, P. (2001). Nonprofit marketing: The key to marketing's "mid-life crisis"? *International Journal of Nonprofit and Voluntary Sector Marketing*, 6(1), 78–91.

Conway, T., and Whitelock, J. (2007). Relationship marketing in the subsidised arts: The key to a strategic marketing focus? *European Journal of Marketing*, 41(1/2), 199–222.

Cousins, L. (1990). Marketing planning for the public and nonprofit sectors. *European Journal of Marketing*, 24(7), 15–30.

Couto, R. A. (2001). The third sector and civil society: The case of the "yes" campaign in Northern Ireland. *Voluntas*, 12(3), 221–238.

Cuadrado, M., Gil, I., and Mollá, A. (2000). Empirical evidence of marketing practices in the non-profit sector: The case of performing arts. *Journal of Nonprofit and Public Sector Marketing*, 8(3), 15–24.

Dann, S., Harris, P., Sullivan Mort, G., Fry, M.-L., and Binney, W. (2007). Reigniting the fire: A contemporary research agenda for social, political and nonprofit marketing. *Journal of Public Affairs*, 7(3), 291–304.

Diamond, W. D., and Gooding-Williams, S. (2002). Using advertising constructs and methods to understand direct mail fundraising appeals. *Nonprofit Management and Leadership*, 12(3), 225–242.

Diepen, M. van, Donkers, B., and Franses, P. H. (2009). Dynamic and competitive effects of direct mailings: A charitable giving application. *Journal of Marketing Research*, 46(1), 120–133.

Drumwright, M. E. (1996). Company advertising with a social dimension: The role of noneconomic criteria. *Journal of Marketing*, 60(4), 71–87.

Ebrahim, A. (2005). Accountability myopia: Losing sight of organizational learning. *Nonprofit and Voluntary Sector Quarterly*, 34(1), 56–87.

Eggert, A., and Helm, S. (2003). Exploring the impact of relationship transparency on business relationships. A cross-sectional study among purchasing managers in Germany. *Industrial Marketing Management*, 32(2), 101–108.

Ford, J. B., and Mottner, S. (2003). Retailing in the nonprofit sector: An exploratory analysis of church-connected retailing ventures. *International Journal of Nonprofit and Voluntary Sector Marketing*, 8(4), 337–348.

Gainer, B., and Moyer, M. (2004). Marketing for nonprofit managers. In R. D. Herman and Associates (eds) *The Jossey-Bass Handbook of Nonprofit Leadership and Management* (pp. 277–309), San Francisco, Jossey-Bass.

Gainer, B., and Padanyi, P. (2002). Applying the marketing concept to cultural organizations: An empirical study of the relationship between market orientation and performance. *International Journal of Nonprofit and Voluntary Sector Marketing*, 7(2), 182–193.

Garcia, I., Gibaja, J. J., and Mujika, A. (2003). A study on the effect of cause-related marketing on the attitude towards the brand: The case of Pepsi in Spain. *Journal of Nonprofit and Public Sector Marketing*, 11(1), 111–136.

Gibelman, M., and Gelman, S. R. (2001). Very public scandals: Nongovernmental organizations in trouble. *Voluntas*, 12(1), 49–66.

Gibelman, M., and Gelman S. R. (2004). A loss of credibility: Patterns of wrongdoing among nongovernmental organizations. *Voluntas*, 15(4), 355–381.

Gundlach, G. T. (2007). The American Marketing Association's 2004 definition of marketing: Perspectives on its implications for scholarship and the role and responsibility of marketing in society. *Journal of Public Policy & Marketing*, 26(2), 241–250.

Gwin, J. M. (1990). Constituent analysis: A paradigm for marketing effectiveness in the not-for-profit organisation. *European Journal of Marketing*, 24(7), 43–48.

Hajjat, M. M. (2003). Effect of cause-related marketing on attitudes and purchase intentions: The moderating role of cause involvement and donation size. *Journal of Nonprofit and Public Sector Marketing*, 11(1), 93–110.

Hankinson, P. (2001). Brand orientation in the charity sector: A framework for discussion and research. *International Journal of Nonprofit and Voluntary Sector Marketing*, 6(3), 231–242.

Harris, P., and Lock, A. (1996). Machiavellian marketing: The development of corporate lobbying in the UK. *Journal of Marketing Management*, 12(4), 313–328.

Hayes, D., and Slater, A. (2003). From "social club" to "integrated membership scheme": Developing membership schemes strategically. *International Journal of Nonprofit and Voluntary Sector Marketing*, 8(1), 59–75.

Heller, N. A. (2008). The influence of reputation and sector on perception of brand alliances of nonprofit organization. *International Journal of Nonprofit and Voluntary Sector Marketing*, 20(1), 15–36.

Helmig, B., Jegers, M., and Lapsley, I. (2004). Challenges in managing nonprofit organizations: A research overview. *Voluntas*, 15(2), 101–116.

Helmig, B., Michalski, S., and Thaler, J. (2009). Besonderheiten und Herausforderungen der Kundenintegration in Nonprofit-Organisationen. (Particularities and challenges of customer integration in nonprofit organizations.) In M. Bruhn and B. Stauss (eds) *Forum Dienstleistungsmanagement, Kundenintegration (Forum Services Management, Customer Integration)* (pp. 271–492), Wiesbaden, Gabler.

Herman, R. D., and Rendina, D. (2001). Donor reactions to commercial activities of nonprofit organizations: An American case study. *Voluntas*, 12(2), 157–169.

Higgins, J. W., and Hodgins, A. (2008). The grape escape: A fundraising bike tour for the Multiple Sclerosis Society. *Journal of Nonprofit and Public Sector Marketing*, 19(2), 49–67.

Higgins, J. W., and Lauzon, L. (2003). Finding the funds in fun runs: Exploring physical activity events as fundraising tools in the nonprofit sector. *International Journal of Nonprofit and Voluntary Sector Marketing*, 8(4), 363–380.

Holden, A. C. (2000). Transparency and accountability: An integral part of the marketing plan of the New European Central Bank. *Journal of Nonprofit and Public Sector Marketing*, 8(2), 65–84.

Homburg, C., Kuester, S., and Krohmer, H. (2009). *Marketing Management: A Contemporary Perspective*, Berkshire, UK, McGraw-Hill Education.

Hooper, P., and Stobart, S. (2003). Using third-party services to reduce the development cost and improve the effectiveness of charity websites. *International Journal of Nonprofit and Voluntary Sector Marketing*, 8(4), 328–336.

Hultman, J., and Axelsson, B. (2007). Towards a typology of transparency for marketing management research. *Industrial Marketing Management*, 36(5), 627–635.

Judd, V. C. (2001). Toward a customer-orientation and a differentiated position in a nonprofit organization: Using the 5th P – people. *Journal of Nonprofit and Public Sector Marketing*, 9(1), 5–17.

Kearns, K. P. (1994). The strategic management of accountability in nonprofit organizations: An analytical framework. *Public Administration Review*, 54(2), 185–192.

Kline Henley, T. (2001). Integrated marketing communications for local nonprofit organizations: Communications tools and methods. *Journal of Nonprofit and Public Sector Marketing*, 9(1/2), 157–168.

Knowles, P., and Gomes, R. (1997). Use of the customer value/mission (CV/M) matrix in strategic nonprofit marketing analysis. *Journal of Nonprofit and Public Sector Marketing*, 5(2), 43–63.

Kotler, P. (1972). A generic concept of marketing. *Journal of Marketing*, 36(2), 46–54.

Kotler, P. (1979). Strategies for introducing marketing into nonprofit organizations. *Journal of Marketing*, 43(1), 37–44.

Kotler, P. (1982). *Marketing for Nonprofit Organizations*, 2nd edn, Englewood Cliffs, NJ, Prentice Hall.

Kotler, P. (1984). *Marketing Management: Analysis, Planning, and Control*, 5th edn, Englewood Cliffs, NJ, Prentice Hall.

Kotler, P., and Andreasen, A. R. (2002). *Strategic Marketing for Nonprofit Organizations*, 6th edn, Englewood Cliffs, NJ, Prentice Hall.

Kotler, P., and Levy, S. J. (1969). Broadening the concept of marketing. *Journal of Marketing*, 33(1), 10–15.

Kotler, P., Roberto, N., and Lee, N. (2002). *Social Marketing – Improving the Quality of Life*, Thousand Oaks, CA, Sage.

Kotler, P., and Zaltman, G. (1971). Social marketing: An approach to planned social change. *Journal of Marketing*, 35(3), 3–12.

Kottasz, R. (2004). Differences in the donor behavior characteristics of young affluent males and females: Empirical evidence from Britain. *Voluntas*, 15(2), 181–203.

Lahiri, S., and Raimondos-Møller, P. (2000). Lobbying by ethnic groups and aid allocation. *The Economic Journal*, 110(462), C62–C79.

Lamming, R. C., Caldwell, N. D., Harrison, D. A., and Phillips, W. (2001). Transparency in supply relationships: Concept and practice. *Journal of Supply Chain Management*, 37(4), 4–10.

Landreth Grau, S., Garretson, J. A., and Pirsch, J. (2007). Cause-related marketing: An exploratory study of campaign donation structures issues. *Journal of Nonprofit and Public Sector Marketing*, 18(2), 69–91.

Lee, S. (2003). The regulation of fundraising: In search of the "public good" or an intractable problem of vested interest? *International Journal of Nonprofit and Voluntary Sector Marketing*, 8(4), 307–314.

Liao, M.-N., Foreman, S., and Sargeant, A. (2001). Market versus societal orientation in the nonprofit context. *International Journal of Nonprofit and Voluntary Sector Marketing*, 6(3), 254–268.

Lichtenstein, D. R., Drumwright, M. E., and Braig, B. M. (2004). The effect of corporate social responsibility on customer donations to corporate-supported nonprofits. *Journal of Marketing*, 68(4), 16–32.

Lindenmeier, J. (2008). Promoting volunteerism: Effects of self-efficacy, advertisement-induced emotional arousal, perceived costs of volunteering, and message framing. *Voluntas*, 19(1), 43–65.

Lovelock, C. H., Lewis, B., and Vandermerve, S. (1999). *Services Marketing: A European Perspective*, London, Prentice-Hall.

Lusch, R. F. (2007). Marketing's evolving identity: Defining our future. *Journal of Public Policy & Marketing*, 26(2), 261–268.

Mack, R. (2005). Lobbying effectively in Brussels and Washington: Getting the right result. *Journal of Communication Management*, 9(4), 339–347.

Marudas, N. P., and Jacobs, F. A. (2004). Determinants of charitable donations to large U.S. higher education, hospital, and scientific research nonprofit organizations: New evidence from panel data. *Voluntas*, 15(2), 157–179.

Marudas, N. P., and Jacobs, F. A. (2007). The extent of excessive or insufficient fundraising among US arts organizations and the effect of organizational efficiency on donations to US arts organizations. *International Journal of Nonprofit and Voluntary Sector Marketing*, 12(3), 267–273.

McCambridge, R. (2004). Underestimating the power of nonprofit governance. *Nonprofit and Voluntary Sector Quarterly*, 33(2), 346–354.

McCarthy, J. (2007). The ingredients of financial transparency. *Nonprofit and Voluntary Sector Quarterly*, 36(1), 156–164.

McGrath, C. (2007). Framing lobbying messages: Defining and communicating political issues persuasively. *Journal of Public Affairs*, 7(3), 269–280.

Michalski, S., and Helmig, B. (2008). What do we know about the identity salience model of relationship marketing success? A review of the literature. *Journal of Relationship Marketing*, 7(1), 45–63.

Milbrath, L. W. (1960). Lobbying as a communication process. *The Public Opinion Quarterly*, 24(1), 32–53.

Mindak, W. A., and Bybee, H. M. (1971). Marketing's application to fundraising. *Journal of Marketing*, 35(3), 13–18.

Morgan, R. M., and Hunt, S. D. (1994). The commitment–trust theory of relationship marketing. *Journal of Marketing*, 58(3), 20–38.

Napoli, J. (2006). The impact of nonprofit brand orientation on organizational performance. *Journal of Marketing Management*, 22(7/8), 673–694.

Nowak, L. I., and Clarke, T. K. (2003). Cause-related marketing: Keys to successful relationships with corporate sponsors and their customers. *Journal of Nonprofit and Public Sector Marketing*, 11(1), 137–149.

Nyland, J. (1995). Issue networks and nonprofit organizations. *Policy Studies Review*, 14(1/2), 195–204.

Passebois, J., and Aurier, P. (2004). Building consumer/arts institution relationships: An exploratory study in contemporary art museums. *International Review on Public and Nonprofit Marketing*, 1(2), 75–88.

Peattie, S. (2003). Applying sales promotion competitions to nonprofit contexts. *International Journal of Nonprofit and Voluntary Sector Marketing*, 8(4), 349–362.

Petkus, E., Jr. (2001). A customer value perspective in the nonprofit marketing context: Expanding the means–end chain for multiple stakeholders. *Journal of Nonprofit and Public Sector Marketing*, 8(3), 25–37.

Pratten, B. (2004). Charity law reform: Implementing the strategy unit proposal. *International Journal of Nonprofit and Voluntary Sector Marketing*, 9(3), 191–201.

Pride, W. M., and Farrell, O. C. (1977). *Marketing: Basic Concepts and Decisions*, Boston, Houghton Mifflin.

Reed II, A., Aquino, K., and Levy, E. (2007). Moral identity and judgments of charitable behaviors. *Journal of Marketing*, 71(1), 178–193.

Rentschler, R., Radbourne, J., Carr, R., and Rickard, J. (2002). Relationship marketing, audience retention and performing arts organization viability. *International Journal of Nonprofit and Voluntary Sector Marketing*, 7(2), 118–130.

Ringold, D. J., and Weitz, B. (2007). The American Marketing Association definition of marketing: Moving from lagging to leading indicator. *Journal of Public Policy & Marketing*, 26(2), 251–260.

Rooney, P. M. (1999). A better method for analysing the costs and benefits of fundraising at universities. *Nonprofit Management and Leadership*, 10(1), 39–56.

Rothschild, M. L. (1979). Marketing communications in nonbusiness situations or why it's so hard to sell brotherhood like soap. *Journal of Marketing*, 43(2), 11–20.

Sargeant, A. (1999). Charitable giving: Towards a model of donor behavior. *Journal of Marketing Management*, 15(4), 215–238.

Sargeant, A. (2001a). Relationship fundraising: How to keep donors loyal. *Nonprofit Management and Leadership*, 12(2), 177–192.

Sargeant, A. (2001b). Social and cause-related marketing: The growth of a discipline. *Journal of Nonprofit and Public Sector Marketing*, 9(4), xiii–xv.

Sargeant, A. (2009). *Marketing Management for Nonprofit Organizations*, 3rd edn, Oxford, Oxford University Press.

Sargeant, A., Foreman, S., and Liao, M.-N. (2002). Operationalizing the marketing concept in the nonprofit sector. *Journal of Nonprofit and Public Sector Marketing*, 10(2), 41–65.

Sargeant, A., Jay, E., and Lee, S. (2006). Benchmarking charity performance: Returns from direct marketing in fundraising. *International Journal of Nonprofit and Voluntary Sector Marketing*, 16(1/2), 77–94.

Sargeant, A., and Kähler, J. (1999). Returns on fundraising expenditures in the voluntary sector. *Nonprofit Management and Leadership*, 10(1), 5–19.

Self, D. R. (2001). Promotional products: Adding tangibility to your nonprofit promotions. *Journal of Nonprofit and Public Sector Marketing*, 9(1/2), 205–213.

Shang, J., Reed II, A., and Croson, R. (2008). Identity congruency effects on donations. *Journal of Marketing*, 43(3), 351–361.

Shapiro, B. P. (1974). Marketing in nonprofit organizations. *Nonprofit and Voluntary Sector Quarterly*, 3(1), 1–16.

Sheth, J. N., and Uslay, C. (2007). Implications of the revised definition of marketing: From exchange to value creation. *Journal of Public Policy & Marketing*, 26(2), 302–307.

Smith, L. J., and Friedman, M. L. (1994). Measuring satisfaction with services when the customer is not the consumer: The child care service example. *Journal of Nonprofit and Public Sector Marketing*, 2(1), 9–28.

Smith, S. C., and Santandreu, J. R. (1997). Marketing in the nonprofit sector: The unique case of arts museums. *Journal of Nonprofit and Public Sector Marketing*, 5(2), 77–90.

Smucker, B. (2005). Nonprofit lobbying. In R. D. Herman and Associates (eds) *The Jossey-Bass Handbook of Nonprofit Leadership and Management*, 2nd edn (pp. 230–253), San Francisco, Jossey-Bass.

Strahilevitz, M. (2003). The effects of prior impressions of a firm's ethics on the success of a cause-related marketing campaign: Do the good look better while the bad look worse? *Journal of Nonprofit and Public Sector Marketing*, 11(1), 77–92.

Stride, H. (2006). An investigation into the values dimensions of branding: Implications for the charity sector. *International Journal of Nonprofit and Voluntary Sector Marketing*, 11(2), 115–124.

Stride, H., and Lee, S. (2007). No logo? No way: Branding in the non-profit sector. *Journal of Marketing Management*, 23(1/2), 107–122.

Trimble, C. S., and Rifon, N. J. (2006). Consumer perceptions of compatibility in cause-related marketing messages. *International Journal of Nonprofit and Voluntary Sector Marketing*, 11(1), 29–47.

Varadarajan, P. R., and Menon, A. (1988). Cause-related marketing: A coalignment of marketing-strategy and corporate philanthropy. *Journal of Marketing*, 52(3), 58–74.

Vargo, S. L., and Lusch, R. F. (2004). Evolving to a new dominant logic for marketing. *Journal of Marketing*, 68(1), 1–17.

Vargo, S. L., and Lusch, R. F. (2008). Service-dominant logic: Continuing the evolution. *Journal of the Academy of Marketing Science*, 36(1), 1–10.

Vázquez, R., Álvarez, L. I., and Santos, M. L. (2002). Market orientation and social services in private nonprofit organisations. *European Journal of Marketing*, 36(9/10), 1022–1046.

Venable, B. T., Rose, G. M., Bush, V. D., and Gilbert, F. W. (2005). The role of brand personality in charitable giving: An assessment and validation. *Journal of the Academy of Marketing Science*, 33(3), 295–312.

Voeth, M., and Herbst, U. (2008). The concept of brand personality as an instrument for advanced nonprofit branding – Empirical evidence. *Journal of Nonprofit and Public Sector Marketing*, 19(1), 71–97.

Webb, D. J., Green, C. L., and Brashear, T. G. (2000). Development and validation of scales to measure attitudes influencing monetary donations to charitable organisations. *Journal of the Academy of Marketing Science*, 28(2), 299–309.

Webb, D. J., and Mohr, L. A. (1998). A typology of consumer responses to cause-related marketing: From sceptics to socially concerned. *Journal of Public Policy & Marketing*, 17(2), 226–238.

Wenham, K., Stephens, D., and Hardy, R. (2003). The marketing effectiveness of UK environmental charity websites compared to best practice. *International Journal of Nonprofit and Voluntary Sector Marketing*, 8(3), 213–223.

West, D. C., and Sargeant, A. (2004). Taking risks with advertising: The case of the not-for-profit sector. *Journal of Marketing Management*, 20(9/10), 1027–1045.

Wilkie, W. L., and Moore, E. S. (2003). Scholarly research in marketing: Exploring the "4 eras" of thought development. *Journal of Public Policy & Marketing*, 22(2), 116–146.

Wilkie, W. L., and Moore, E. S. (2007). What does the definition of marketing tell us about ourselves? *Journal of Public Policy & Marketing*, 26(2), 269–276.

Wymer, W. W. (1999). Hospital volunteers as customers: Understanding their motives, how they differ from other volunteers, and correlates of volunteers intensity. *Journal of Nonprofit and Public Sector Marketing*, 6(2/3), 51–76.

Wymer, W. W. (2008). Editorial: Special issue on social marketing. *International Journal of Nonprofit and Voluntary Sector Marketing*, 13(3), 191.

Wymer, W. W., and Sargeant, A. (2006). Insights from a review of the literature on cause marketing. *International Review on Public and Nonprofit Marketing*, 3(1), 9–21.

Zinkhan, G. M., and Williams, B. C. (2007). The new American Marketing Association definition of marketing: An alternative assessment. *Journal of Public Policy & Marketing*, 26(2), 284–288.

Chapter 13
Social Accounting

Laurie Mook

Introduction

Social accounting broadens the range of information presented in an accounting statement to highlight economic, social, and environmental issues and enables the participation of a larger group of stakeholders in its formulation. It is a fairly new field, and social accounting for nonprofits is newer still. This chapter outlines some of the emerging work in this area and gives some real-life examples of social accounting for nonprofits.

The Emergence of Social Accounting

In the 1960s and 1970s, a group of accounting scholars began to systematically question the assumptions underlying traditional accounting and the notion that accounting is objective, neutral, and value-free (Gray 2002; Hines 1988; Morgan 1988; Tinker 1985). For instance, critical accountants argue that, by the very act of counting certain items in the accounting statement and excluding others, accounting shapes a particular interpretation of social reality. This interpretation, which corresponds to particular assumptions about how society functions and should function, has in turn implications for decision-making and policy (Hines 1988; Tinker et al. 1982).

Critical accounting seeks not only to understand the world but also to change it. It urges us to reflect upon the conditions and consequences of accounting and to consider accounting within a broad, societal context (Lodh and Gaffikin 1997; Roslender and Dillard 2003). Critical accounting asserts that organizations have an impact on a wide group of stakeholders and that accountability to these groups is a desirable democratic mechanism (Gray et al. 1997).

L. Mook (✉)
University of Toronto, Canada
e-mail: laurie.mook@utoronto.ca

R. Taylor (ed.), *Third Sector Research*, DOI 10.1007/978-1-4419-5707-8_13,
© Springer Science+Business Media, LLC 2010

Social accounting grew out of these critiques and provides a working framework that considers a broader range of factors and actors in the accounting process than does conventional accounting. This broadening is of particular importance to nonprofit organizations, as the accounting statements they currently use were developed for profit-oriented businesses and not with all the users of nonprofit accounting information in mind.

Critiques of Social Accounting

Social accounting, especially for for-profit organizations, is not without its critiques. The traditional response relates to Friedman's (1970, p. 32) often quoted statement on corporate orientation: "There is one and only one social responsibility of business – to use its resources and engage in activities designed to increase its profits so long as it stays within the rules of the game, which is to say, engages in open and free competition without deception or fraud." From this perspective, social responsibility is narrowly constructed to mean the maximization of profits, and thus any focus outside of this is not in the best interest of the firm.

From a critical accounting standpoint, social accounting has been argued to legitimize the status quo, by not questioning the role that capitalism plays in perpetuating unequal and exploitive social relations and by providing an illusion that progress can be made by corporations (Everett and Neu 2000). Lehman (1999, p. 220) goes even further and states, "The procedural and instrumental tendencies within reform accounting models can stall the construction of more critical and interpretive models." Indeed, it is argued that the current form of capitalism, "based on private property rights, growth and expansion, competition, maximizing consumption of non-essentials, maximizing returns to shareholders and directors and so on," is not sustainable and cannot be sustainable (Gray and Milne 2004, p. 73; see also Gore 2006; Gray 2005).

Nonprofit Accounting

Conventional accounting for nonprofits is, for the most part, similar to that for for-profit organizations and consists of recording, classifying, and reporting revenues and expenditures in order to provide information for a variety of decision-makers who wish to assess the performance of the organization in order to make future decisions. For instance, the typical Statement of Income and Expenditures for a nonprofit social services organization would show that it received monies from individual and corporate donations, grants from foundations and government, and perhaps some earned income from charging a fee for some of its services. It would also show the amount spent on wages and benefits, as well as purchases of materials and supplies, utilities, rent, and other such expenses. The net amount at the end of the fiscal year would be close to zero, or a small balance to carry forward to the subsequent year.

However, as we know, the primary objective of nonprofit organizations is not the same as for-profit organizations. Conventional accounting statements, which are formulated to report the "success" (i.e., profit or loss) of for-profit organizations, miss a critical feature of nonprofits – that their social impact is a vital part of their performance story. In addition, nonprofit organizations rely in varying degrees on volunteers and members, yet the value and impact of this unpaid service is normally excluded from accounting statements.

Social accounting for nonprofits attempts to remedy this (Mook et al. 2003). It reorients accounting to a broader set of variables and social interests. One definition of social accounting is "a systematic analysis of the effects of an organization on its communities of interest or stakeholders, with stakeholder input as part of the data that are analyzed for the accounting statement" (Mook et al. 2007, p. ii). From this perspective, the social accounting statement includes both financial and non-financial information and takes a stakeholder approach both in how stakeholders contribute to the organization and how the organization impacts them. Thus, social accounting expands the range of criteria that are taken into consideration when measuring performance and looks at the organization in relation to its surrounding environment, both social and natural. Additionally, social accounting for nonprofits emphasizes that the audience interested in their performance is broader and may differ from that of for-profit businesses.

Multiple Accountabilities

Nonprofit organizations often have multiple accountabilities to numerous stakeholders, unlike for-profit organizations, which are ultimately accountable to one stakeholder group (return to owners, or shareholders) (Ebrahim 2003). Generally, four issues can be addressed in terms of accountability: effectiveness (achieving mission), efficiency (getting the most out of resources), risk (minimizing), and corruption (guarding against individuals benefiting excessively) (Herzlinger 1996). Accountability for nonprofit organizations in practice, however, is often narrowly gauged by the "proper" use of financial resources; for example, how much of a donor's dollar goes to administrative expenses and how much goes to program expenses, and what an acceptable ratio of this would be. From this view, accountability is seen as a set of controls imposed on the organization by external bodies: "primarily in terms of rule-bound responses by organizations and individuals who report to recognized authorities such as government agencies or donor organizations in order to ensure that the resources they receive are used properly and that the work they undertake is carried out effectively" (Lewis and Madon 2004, p. 120).

This narrow view of accountability is fed and reinforced by conventional accounting, which is limited by the items it includes in the accounting statement. For instance, it excludes volunteer labor; however, for many nonprofit organizations, volunteers provide significant labor resources and should be considered when analyzing the efficient use of resources by the organization. Conventional accounting also excludes many environmental impacts, yet these can have significant risk implications.

Accountability Frameworks

As concerns grew in the mid-1990s over the quality of various approaches emerging for social and ethical accounting, auditing, and reporting, several nonprofit organizations began to work on establishing voluntary international accountability standards. One such accountability framework is AccountAbility 1000 (AA1000), which defines accountability as "acknowledging, assuming responsibility for and being transparent about the impacts of your policies, decisions, actions, products and associated performance" (AccountAbility 2008, p. 6). In this framework, three principles provide guidance for the realization of accountability: inclusivity, materiality, and responsiveness. Inclusivity implies the commitment to be accountable to those the organization has an impact on and to provide structures that enable the participation of these stakeholders in identifying issues and solutions. The materiality principle provides guidance in determining which issues are relevant and of significance to an organization's stakeholders. Finally, the responsiveness principle outlines different mechanisms that guide the organization in how it responds to different stakeholder issues, for instance, through establishing policies and through measuring and monitoring performance.

Another voluntary accountability standards framework is Social Accountability 8000, or SA8000. SA8000 is based on the conventions of the International Labour Organisation (ILO), the Universal Declaration of Human Rights, and the UN Convention on the Rights of the Child (SAI n.d.). In terms of environmental accountability, the series of standards relating to environmental management is ISO 14000, managed by the International Organization for Standardization. ISO 14000 covers environmental management systems, environmental auditing, eco-labeling, life cycle assessment, environmental aspects in product standards, and environmental performance in evaluation (Baxter 2004).

Three Approaches to Social Accounting for Nonprofits

In different parts of the world, organizations are starting to implement social accounting in their daily practices. This chapter focuses on three approaches that have been used by nonprofit organizations: the Global Reporting Initiative (GRI), the Balanced Scorecard, and the Expanded Value Added Statement (EVAS). These approaches integrate financial, social, and environmental information. In other words, the economic, social, and environmental dimensions are not supplemental to the financial accounts; rather, together they are integral. In current practice, the Balanced Scorecard is usually reported to internal audiences, while the GRI and EVAS are reported both internally and externally.

Global Reporting Initiative

The Global Reporting Initiative or GRI is one framework that communicates economic, social, and environmental performance in order to measure, disclose, and discharge accountability (GRI 2006, p. 40). It is used by organizations in the for-profit, public, and nonprofit sectors.

The nonprofit organization that coordinates the networks that came together to develop the Global Reporting Initiative (GRI) framework is Stichting Global Reporting Initiative, based in The Netherlands. The organization was started in 1997 as a partnership between the Coalition for Environmentally Responsible Economies (CERES) in Boston and the United Nations Environment Program (UNEP) and published its first guidelines in 2000. Its mission is "to create conditions for the transparent and reliable exchange of sustainability information through the development and continuous improvement of its Sustainability Reporting Framework" (SGRI 2007).

The Global Reporting Initiative provides protocols for indicators in six dimensions: economic, environment, human rights, labor, product responsibility, and society. Each dimension is then divided into aspects, which are further divided into core and additional indicators. Core indicators are those that have been identified as being of interest to most stakeholders and assumed to be material unless deemed otherwise. Additional indicators are also suggested that may be material to some organizations, but not to the majority.

Today, using a global, multi-stakeholder, consensus-seeking approach, the GRI guidelines are in their third version (G3), and numerous supplements providing specialized guidance have been developed for different industry sectors. More than 1,000 organizations (private, public, and nonprofit) have self-declared the use of the GRI guidelines in their sustainability reports. Many others use the guidelines on a more informal basis.

In 2008, a multi-stakeholder working group was established to research and draft a nonprofit sector supplement that would provide guidelines to report on the sustainability performance of nonprofit organizations specifically. The working group for this supplement includes representatives from nonprofit organizations and from user groups such as labor organizations, government agencies, and donors and uses a consensus-seeking process. The supplement for nonprofits was initiated as a response to an increasing demand for accountability from nonprofit organizations, especially those carrying out functions previously undertaken by the state, and a lack of transparency in discharging that accountability (GRI 2008).

The GRI in Use

The Credit Union Foundation of Australia (CUFA), a nonprofit development agency of the Australian credit union movement, has been using the GRI approach since 2006 (CUFA 2008). Within Australia, CUFA focuses on community advocacy and education, and internationally it focuses on development of access to financial services for disadvantaged communities of the South East Asia and Pacific regions. It has developed a Corporate Social Responsibility Toolkit for its credit union members, to help them position themselves as "a different type of banking" (CUFA 2006). It is a small organization, operating with the labor of just over 14 full-time equivalent positions (including volunteers and interns). Its budget in 2008 for both its domestic and international trust funds amounted to almost $1 million AUD in financial resources and almost $700,000 AUD in non-monetary resources (in-kind contributions of labor, services, and equipment).

In 2009, CUFA was recognized as one of the top-performing Australian NGOs by the Australian Centre for Corporate Social Responsibility (ACCSR 2009). It currently uses the GRI G3 guidelines. The G3 guidelines provide a framework for the report and cover the areas of strategy and analysis, organizational profile, governance, stakeholder engagement, commitments to external initiatives, economic performance, environment, labor practices and decent work, and society. As CUFA states in its 2008 Sustainability Report (p. 21),

> As the development agency of the Australian credit union movement, CUFA seeks to act with responsibility and transparency. How we act and perform in non-financial terms is core to this, and we are now committed to publishing an annual statement detailing our sustainability actions and outcomes. As a small organisation, we are also keen to advocate other smaller organisations to do the same, and hope to provide a good example to our credit union stakeholders by 'walking the talk.'

Particular attention is paid to the section on the environment. Here, CUFA outlines its performance in the areas of consumption, waste, optimization, offsetting, and its environmental footprint. As they now have issued three sustainability reports, they can provide comparative data to show their influence in these areas. Their biggest environmental impact is from air travel of the board, staff, volunteers, and participants, and which they calculated to be 612,021 km for the fiscal period. This amounted to 53% of their greenhouse gas emissions, followed by electricity at 40%, road travel at 6%, and waste at 1%. Through monitoring and minimizing their air travel, and offsetting travel miles through tree planting and land rehabilitation, they seek to minimize their impact on greenhouse gases.

Stakeholder dialogue is also an important component of CUFA's operations. The GRI guidelines emphasize transparency and CUFA achieves this through posting documents, newsletters, and reports on its website. One of its project officers is dedicated to stakeholder relations, and projects are planned and approved by its various stakeholder groups.

For each of its ongoing and newly completed projects, CUFA reports on goals and progress toward those goals during the year. It also reports on goals and progress in the general areas of governance, stakeholder dialogue, people, projects, and environment. In 2008, CUFA approved and launched its Reconciliation Action Plan (RAP), which sets out how it will improve conditions for indigenous Australians around financial literacy and community development. At the end its sustainability report, a full listing of all the GRI indicators, is provided, along with a summary of the results of each area. If for some reason information is not available for an indicator, or it is deemed not to be relevant, that is also stated in the report.

Balanced Scorecard Approach

The Balanced Scorecard was developed in the 1980s to address deficiencies in the financial accounting model, especially the failure to provide for increases in value due to intangible assets such as information technology and employee skills and knowledge (Kaplan 2001; Moore 2003). Although initially developed by a for-profit company, the Balanced Scorecard has subsequently been implemented by nonprofit and other social organizations (Manville 2007; Somers 2004; Speckbacher 2003). The Balanced Scorecard approach is differentiated from the Global Reporting Initiative described in the previous section by a reduced number of metrics and connection to the strategic planning process.

The Balanced Scorecard is used as a performance measurement and management tool as part of the strategic planning process to provide a more "balanced" view of an organization's performance and creation of value. Although the Balanced Scorecard is generally thought of as a for-profit management tool, nonprofit organizations have been drawn to it because of its broader view of value creation and its focus on processes and relationships (Moore 2003). The scorecard includes both financial and non-financial metrics, generally in four areas: financial, customer, internal management processes, and organization learning and growth.

Applying the Balanced Scorecard approach to the nonprofit sector is not without its challenges. Nonprofit users are cautioned when adopting a business model approach to evaluation to consider the assumptions underlying that model (Speckbacher 2003). In its "classic" form, the Balanced Scorecard does not consider the unique features of nonprofits, including value-based programming, volunteer participation, and related distinctive reward and compensation systems (Bozzo 2000). In the nonprofit sector, mission, rather than shareholder objectives, drives strategic planning and guides the Balanced Scorecard process. In addition, the Balanced Scorecard is complex in nature and requires a high level of resources and management time (Bull 2007; Zimmerman 2006). However, the overall concept of the Balanced Scorecard – its holistic nature and its recognition that both financial and non-financial measures related to the processes and outcomes of a strategic plan are important – can be useful in developing a framework relevant for nonprofits (Bull 2007; Harber 1998; Kaplan 2001; Martello et al. 2008; Moore 2003; Speckbacher 2003; Zimmerman 2006).

To be effective for nonprofits, the four perspectives of the Balanced Scorecard should be modified to reflect the needs of the organization. For example, the financial perspective can be broadened to a sustainability perspective or to a multi-bottom line (Bull 2007; Somers 2004). The customer perspective can be amended to a stakeholder perspective (Bull 2007; Somers 2004). Alternate frameworks, such as the public value framework for accountability and performance management, propose different perspectives altogether: expanding support and authorization, creating public value, and building organizational capacity (Moore 2003).

Implementation-wise, one of the main challenges of the Balanced Scorecard approach is selecting key performance indicators linked to the strategic objectives of the organization (Harber 1998; Martello et al. 2008). Once indicators are selected, it is then necessary to set targets, monitor performance, and report at regular intervals. The information generated must be relevant, and there must be a commitment to change as necessary (Harber, 1998). Key implementation success enablers include (Somers 2004; Zimmerman 2006, p. iii):

- mid-level management of the process, with strong support from the CEO and buy-in from staff;
- education that emphasizes the importance of the Balanced Scorecard to the accomplishment of mission;
- an integral relationship to the strategic plan, and embeddedness in practice at all levels of the organization;
- terminology taken from the organization's culture and supporting the mission of the organization;
- a small number of clearly defined measures;
- cross-organizational support;
- readily and immediately available data.

Key benefits of the approach have been reported as increased understanding about the organization by employees, effective engagement of staff and team members, positive performance of priorities and strategic direction, and more clarity on the value added of investments in training and education (Harber 1998; Somers 2004).

Balanced Scorecard in Use

One organization using the Balanced Scorecard approach is The ReHabilitation Center in the United States. The ReHabilitation Center was started as a grassroots organization in the late 1950s by a group of parents with children with disabilities. The parents met initially to share their experiences and frustrations and immediately started to advocate for children with disabilities. Today, 50 years later, the center operates in more than 40 sites and every day serves more than 700 individuals with disabilities. Its mission is to build brighter futures for people with disabilities, and its vision is "to be a leader in providing people with disabilities the opportunities to pursue their dreams and achieve their goals" (The ReHabilitation Center 2008, p. 4). The center provides a myriad of services, including a children's learning center, residential services, employment training opportunities, sports and recreation, clinics, lifeskill programming, and volunteer opportunities. Its annual budget runs around $25 million.

Prior to adapting the Balanced Scorecard approach, the center relied on consultants to work with its top management group to develop strategic plans. However, they were never able to integrate their strategic planning with the day-to-day operations of the center. In the late 1990s, they hired a director of strategic planning, who decided to implement the Balanced Scorecard system throughout the organization. What was important for the success of this approach was that the private-sector scorecard was modified so that it was suitable for the organization. Additionally, top managers had to be persuaded that this was not a "flavor of the month" and that it would lead to more effective strategic planning. As the top managers began to work with the system, they came onboard and were able to persuade others it added value to running their departments.

For a number of areas within the center, it was extremely difficult to develop measures, and this still is a challenge of the system. However, the Balanced Scorecard system was able to bring together the different areas of the center and start to align their day-to-day operations with strategic objectives. It also forced personnel to look at areas and inter-relationships they had not previously thought about. Importantly, it resulted in an equal emphasis on the "consumer" and "financial" perspectives of the organization, helping the organization to manage its efficiency and effectiveness.

The four perspectives focused on by The ReHabilitation Center are consumer, financial, operational, and learning. Each perspective is broken down into strategy, objective, and a small number of core indicators that relate to specific outcomes envisioned by the strategic plan (Tables 13.1 and 13.2).

Table 13.1 The Rehabilitation Center's Balanced Scorecard: Strategies by perspective

Mission	To build brighter futures for people with disabilities
Perspective	**Strategy**
Consumer	Improve quality of life – maximize independence
	Increase consumer satisfaction
Financial	Maintain financial stability
	Grow new revenues
	Improve productivity/efficiency
Operational	Identify and capture new service opportunities
	Achieve operational excellence
	Increase customer service
	Become a good citizen
Learning	Create a motivated, prepared, and satisfied workforce
	Utilize technology
	Improve organizational culture

Martello et al. (2008).

Table 13.2 Examples of selected objectives and measures for Perspective: Consumer; Strategy: Improve quality of life – maximize independence

Objective	Measures
Provide opportunities for consumers to participate in their communities	% of people who participate in integrated community activities
	Number of public educational activities
	Average number of activities per person
Have and sustain relationships	% of people with friends and/or caring relationships (excluding staff/family)
	% of people feeling lonely
Exercise choice over their lives	% of people who make life choices (housing, jobs, staff, routines, etc.)
	% of people that feel their service plan includes things that are important to them
	% of people who control their own spending

Martello et al. (2008).

Expanded Value Added Statement

The Expanded Value Added Statement (EVAS) puts together information from audited financial statements with monetized social and environmental data and focuses on both economic and social impacts. By combining these factors, the EVAS emphasizes the interconnectedness and interdependence of the economy, community, and environment (Mook 2007).

The EVAS uses a value-added approach (Burchell et al. 1985; Suojanen 1954). Value added is a measure of wealth that an organization creates by adding value to raw materials, products, and services through the use of labor and capital. It can be calculated by taking the market value of the goods and services it provides and subtracting the cost of its externally purchased goods and services. In contrast to profit, which is the wealth created for only one group – owners or shareholders – expanded value added represents the wealth created for a larger group of stakeholders including employees, volunteers, society, government, and the organization itself. The EVAS emphasizes the collective effort needed for an organization to achieve its goals, viewing each stakeholder as important to its viability as a socially and economically responsible organization.

One shortcoming of traditional accounting for nonprofits is that it ignores a significant source of inputs, in particular, volunteer labor (MacIntosh 1995; Mook et al. 2007). The EVAS includes volunteer contributions, but in order to do so, it is necessary to be able to estimate a comparative market value for them. There are several approaches to this; two in particular are opportunity cost and replacement cost.

The opportunity costs approach assumes that "the cost of volunteering is time that could have been spent in other ways, including earning money that could, after taxes, be spent on desired goods and services" (Brown 1999, p. 10). Because time might have been spent generating income, the opportunity cost is tied to the hourly compensation that volunteers normally receive from paid jobs that they hold. However, this procedure could be problematic because the skills associated with a volunteer service may differ substantially from those for which a salary is being received (Brown 1999).

The replacement cost method looks at volunteer value from the perspective of the organization. This procedure, which is favored by the accounting profession in cases where estimation for volunteer value is permitted, assumes that volunteers could be replaced by wage earners as substitutes in terms of skills and productivity.

Determining the market value for the outputs of a nonprofit organization in order to calculate expanded value added presents special challenges because some of a nonprofit's goods and services may not involve market transactions. In order to assign a comparative market value to the outputs of nonprofit organizations, the following procedure can be used (Mook et al. 2007; Richmond 1999):

- look to the market to find a comparative market value for similar goods/services produced in the private sector (for example, for a nonprofit organization delivering employment training services, the cost of similar private sector training could be used);

- if there are no equivalents in the private sector, compare with public sector goods (in the case of employment training, the cost of federal employment training programs could be used);
- if that value is not available, use resources received from government and other sources for providing the services. An estimate needs to be made of non-monetized inputs such as volunteer contributions and in-kind donations. The value of non-market items is then added to financial resources received to come up with a proxy for market value.

Estes (1976) also proposed a number of techniques to estimate a market value for non-market items. His examples are largely in relation to profit-oriented businesses, but they are also relevant to nonprofit organizations. One method is to use a surrogate value: "When a desired value cannot be directly determined, we may estimate instead the value of a surrogate – some item or phenomenon that is logically expected to involve approximately the same utility or sacrifice as the item in which we are interested" (Estes 1976, p. 110). Estes gives the example of estimating the value of building facilities loaned to civic groups and suggests as a surrogate the rent that would be paid for commercial facilities of a similar quality. Another example is establishing a surrogate value for the personal growth and development of volunteers from participating in a nonprofit organization. As a surrogate, the cost of a community college course in personal development could be used.

Surveys are also used to determine value by asking participants what a service is worth to them. To assist in establishing an accurate estimate, Estes (1976) suggests using, as a prompt, a list of either prices or consumer items and asking the respondents to situate the service in relation to others on the list. Another valuation technique is estimating restoration or avoidance costs: "Certain social costs may be valued by estimating the monetary outlay necessary to undo or prevent the damage" (Estes 1976, p. 115). Road salt corrodes automobiles, but frequent washings can prevent the damage, something that can be easily priced. Similarly, it is possible to estimate the cost of restoring environmentally damaged land to either industrial or residential use. In the event of a plant closure, many governments require a cleanup of the work site to residential standards, a liability that can be determined.

The EVAS in Use

The Royal Netherlands Sea Rescue Institution (Koninklijke Nederlandse Redding Maatschappij, KNRM) is an independent voluntary institution established in 1824, and operates with almost 1,000 professionally trained volunteers and 47.4 full-time equivalent employees. It responds to over 1,800 distress calls yearly, rescuing more than 3,400 people from the North Sea and Dutch waters. Its costs are met entirely by donations and legacies, and its financial budget for 2007 was over €10,000,000 (KNRM 2008).

As part of their annual report, the KNRM includes an EVAS showing the contribution of its volunteers. In order to do this, it first needed to place a value on those volunteer contributions and chose the replacement cost method to do this.

Tasks were separated into the categories management, operational, and support, and appropriate wage rates assigned to each volunteer position. Overall, the wage rates ranged from €15 to €75, averaging €24.69 overall. The total number of hours contributed by volunteers in 2007 totaled 235,310, and the total value of the volunteer contributions was calculated as €5,809,125.

The importance of including volunteer contributions if they are significant to an organization is apparent when looking at the value of these contributions in relation to the financial resources received by the organization. The following two pie charts illustrate just this. Figure 13.1 shows the financial resources received by KNRM in 2007. This would be what is shown in most annual reports based on conventional accounting. Figure 13.2 presents this same information, but includes volunteer contributions as well.

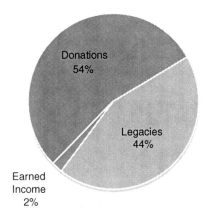

Fig. 13.1 Financial resources received and available for use by KNRM in 2007

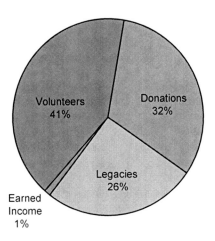

Fig. 13.2 Financial and non-financial resources received and available for use by KNRM in 2007

Table 13.3 Partial EVAS for KNRM (figures in thousands of Euros), 2007

		Financial	Social	Combined
Outputs		€11,219	€5,809	€17,028
Externally purchased goods and services		5,934		5,934
Value added		€5,285	€5,809	€11,094
Employees		€3,280		€3,280
Volunteers	Training	398		398
	Compensation	296		296
Society	Volunteer hours		€5,809	5,809
Organization	Depreciation	1,311		1,311
Value added		€5,285	€5,809	€11,094

A partial EVAS showing the inclusion of volunteer contributions is shown in Table 13.3. The first column shows figures that are available from an organization's conventional financial statements, namely the Statement of Revenues and Expenditures. The second column includes the value calculated for the volunteer hours, and the third column combines the first two columns. Other organizations also include "out-of-pocket" expenses paid by volunteers and not reimbursed and also a value for the skills and development gained by the volunteers through their volunteering activities (Mook et al. 2007).

Conclusion

As can be seen, social accounting includes a broad range of activities in formats such as the Global Reporting Initiative, the Balanced Scorecard, and the Expanded Value Added Statement. Although these approaches differ, they share the common goal of broadening the framework of traditional accounting and attempting to understand the impact that an organization has upon the communities to which it relates and the physical environment. Social accounting, therefore, is useful for nonprofit organizations as they are created to fulfill a social mission. Ignoring their social impact, as traditional accounting does, misses a fundamental feature of their performance story. In an age when so many demands are being made of nonprofit organizations, having tools that assess their accountability and their social impact is essential.

References

AccountAbility. (2008). AA1000 Accountability Principles Standard 2008. www.accountability. com

Australian Centre for Corporate Social Responsibility (ACCSR). (2009). The state of CSR in Australia: 2008 annual review. www.accsr.com.au/ppt/Session-4-Leeora-Black.ppt

Baxter, M. (2004). Taking the first steps in environmental management. *ISO Management Systems*, July/August, 13–18.

Bozzo, S. L. (2000). Evaluation resources for nonprofit organizations: Usefulness and applicability. *Nonprofit Management & Leadership*, 10(4), 463–472.

Brown, E. (1999). Assessing the value of volunteer activity. *Nonprofit and Voluntary Sector Quarterly*, 28(1), 3–17.

Bull, M. (2007). Balance: The development of a social enterprise business performance analysis tool. *Social Enterprise Journal*, 3(1), 49–66.

Burchell, S., Clubb, C., and Hopwood, A. G. (1985). Accounting in its social context: Towards a history of value added in the United Kingdom. *Accounting, Organizations and Society*, 10(4), 381–413.

Credit Union Foundation of Australia (CUFA). (2006). Corporate social responsibility toolkit. www.cufa.com.au/index.jsp?docid=674

Credit Union Foundation of Australia (CUFA). (2008). CUFA Sustainability Report 2008. www.cufa.com.au/introduction/Overview/Reporting/index.jsp

Ebrahim, A. (2003). Accountability in practice: Mechanisms for NGOs. *World Development*, 31(5), 813–829.

Estes, R. (1976). *Corporate Social Accounting*, New York, John Wiley.

Everett, J., and Neu, D. (2000). Ecological modernisation and the limits of environmental accounting. *Accounting Forum*, 24(1), 5–29.

Friedman, M. (1970). Social responsibility of business is to increase its profits. *The New York Times Magazine*, 13 September, pp. 32–33.

Gore, A. (2006). *An Inconvenient Truth*, New York, Rodale Inc.

Gray, R., and Milne, M. (2004). Towards reporting on the triple bottom line: Mirages, methods and myths. In A. Henriques and J. Richardson (eds) *The Triple Bottom Line: Does It All Add Up?* (pp. 70–80), London, Earthscan.

Gray, R. (2002). The social accounting project and accounting organizations and society: Privileging engagement, imaginings, new accountings and pragmatism over critique? *Accounting, Organizations and Society*, 27(7), 687–708.

Gray, R. (2005). Taking a long view on what we now know about social and environmental accountability and reporting. *Electronic Journal of Radical Organisation Theory*, 9(1), www.mngt.waikato.ac.nz/ejrot/Vol9_1/Gray.pdf

Gray, R., Dey, C., Owen, D., Evans, R., and Zadek, S. (1997). Struggling with the praxis of social accounting: Stakeholders, accountability, audits and procedures. *Accounting, Auditing & Accountability Journal*, 10(3), 325–364.

Global Reporting Initiative (GRI). (2006). Sustainability reporting guidelines, version 3.0, Amsterdam, GRI. www.globalreporting.org/NR/rdonlyres/2619F3AD-0166-4C7C-8FB2-D8BB3C5F801F/0/G3_GuidelinesENU.zip

Global Reporting Initiative (GRI). (2008). NGOs. www.globalreporting.org/ReportingFramework/SectorSupplements/NGO/

Harber, B. W. (1998). The Balanced Scorecard: Solution at Peel Memorial Hospital. *Hospital Quarterly*, Summer, 59–63.

Herzlinger, R. E. (1996). Can public trust in nonprofits and government be restored? *Harvard Business Review*, 74(2), 97–107.

Hines, R. D. (1988). Financial accounting: In communicating reality, we construct reality. *Accounting, Organizations and Society*, 13(3), 251–261.

Kaplan, R. S. (2001). Strategic performance measurement and management in nonprofit organizations. *Nonprofit Management & Leadership*, 11(3), 353–370.

KNRM. (2008). Jaarverslag 2007. www.knrm.nl/_images/PDF/jaarverslag2007Trossenlos.pdf

Lehman, G. (1999). Disclosing new worlds: A role for social and environmental accounting and auditing. *Accounting, Organizations and Society*, 24(3), 217–241.

Lewis, D., and Madon, S. (2004). Information systems and nongovernmental development organizations: Advocacy, organizational learning, and accountability. *The Information Society*, 20(2), 117–126.

Lodh, S. C., and Gaffikin, M. J. R. (1997). Critical studies in accounting research, rationality and Habermas: A methodological reflection. *Critical Perspectives on Accounting* 8(5), 433–474.

Macintosh, J. C. C. (1995). Finding the right fit: A call to recognize the special nature of not-for-profit organizations. *CA Magazine*, March, 34–38.

Manville, G. (2007). Implementing a Balanced Scorecard framework in a not for profit SME. *International Journal of Productivity and Performance Management*, 56(2), 162–169.

Martello, M., Watson, J. G., and Fischer, M. J. (2008). Implementing a Balanced Scorecard in a not-for-profit organization. *Journal of Business & Economics Research*, 6(9), 67–80.

Mook, L. (2007). Social and environmental accounting: The Expanded Value Added Statement. Unpublished doctoral dissertation, University of Toronto.

Mook, L., Richmond, B. J., and Quarter, J. (2003). Integrated social accounting for nonprofits: A case from Canada. *Voluntas*, 14(3), 283–297.

Mook, L., Quarter, J., and Richmond, B. J. (2007). *What Counts: Social Accounting for Nonprofits and Cooperatives*, 2nd edn, London, Sigel Press.

Moore, M. H. (2003). The public value scorecard: A rejoinder and an alternative to "Strategic performance measurement and management in non-profit organizations" by Robert Kaplan. Hauser Center for Nonprofit Organizations Working paper 18, Harvard University.

Morgan, G. (1988). Accounting as reality construction: Towards a new epistemology for accounting practice. *Accounting, Organizations and Society*, 13(5), 477–485.

Richmond, B. J. (1999). Counting on each other: A social audit model to assess the impact of nonprofit organizations. Unpublished doctoral dissertation, University of Toronto.

Roslender, R., and Dillard, J. F. (2003). Reflections on the interdisciplinary perspectives on accounting project. *Critical Perspectives on Accounting*, 14(3), 325–351.

SGRI. (2007). The GRI's sustainability report July 2004 – June 2007. www.globalreporting.org/NR/rdonlyres/43127B6A-3816-406C-897F-AC572E0EAB2D/0/GRI_SR_20042007.pdf

Social Accountability International (SAI). (n.d.). Overview of SA 8000. www.sa-intl.org/index.cfm?fuseaction=Page.viewPage&pageId=472

Somers, A. B. (2004). *Shaping the Balanced Scorecard for Use in UK Social Enterprises*, London, Social Enterprises London.

Speckbacher, G. (2003). The economics of performance management in nonprofit organizations. *Nonprofit Management & Leadership*, 13(3), 267–281.

Suojanen, W. W. (1954). Accounting theory and the large corporation. *The Accounting Review*, 29(3), 391–398.

The ReHabilitation Center. (2008). Report to the community 2007. www.rehabcenter.org/images/upload/file/annual%20report.pdf

Tinker, T. (1985). *Paper Prophets: A Social Critique of Accounting*, New York, Praeger.

Tinker, A. M., Merino, B. D., and Neimark, M. D. (1982). The normative origins of positive theories: Ideology and accounting thought. *Accounting, Organizations and Society*, 7(2), 167–200.

Zimmerman, R.A. (2006). Project demonstrating excellence: Issues of development and implementation of a nonprofit Balanced Scorecard. Unpublished doctoral dissertation, Union Institute and University, Cincinnati.

Chapter 14
Corporate Social Responsibility

Brenda Gainer

Introduction

Corporate social responsibility (CSR) is a term that refers to a corporate "movement" – a set of ideas and ideologies about business practice that its advocates hope to see widely adopted across the corporate sector. In terms of contemporary corporate behavior, it is unclear whether this movement has had much impact yet in terms of the number of corporations engaging in meaningful CSR or in terms of social, economic, or environmental outcomes. Nevertheless, the rhetoric of the movement is being widely and enthusiastically adopted by scholars, consultants, politicians, and corporate leaders – and ideas associated with the movement are having an impact on organizations and institutions far beyond the corporate sector.

Although a limited number of corporations have been supporting social initiatives developed and run by third sector organizations for many years, the CSR movement is a relatively new development in two respects: first, it is an attempt to develop a sophisticated, robust, and coordinated set of ideas and principles that have widespread application and will gain general adherence across the corporate sector and in society globally; second, it is focused not only on individual corporate behavior but also on the transformation of the relationship between the whole corporate sector and the state and social sector. In other words, its advocates and those who study the movement see it as a large-scale transformative project with dramatic implications for internal corporate-sector behavior and external inter-sectoral relationships.

The impact of CSR on the third sector has not been theorized to any great extent in the third sector literature. The focus on the unique features of the third sector (if any), the importance of the nonprofit organizational form, the overlapping of spheres of operations, and the diffusion of managerial principles among sectors have all been part of a robust stream of research focusing on the boundaries and integrity

B. Gainer (✉)
York University, Toronto, Canada
e-mail: bgainer@schulich.yorku.ca

R. Taylor (ed.), *Third Sector Research*, DOI 10.1007/978-1-4419-5707-8_14,
© Springer Science+Business Media, LLC 2010

of the third sector that has been well-represented in *Voluntas* in the past two decades (Abzug 1999; Evers 1995; Ferris and Grady 1999; Kramer 2000). The convergence of the sectors in terms of their structure, funding, form, policy environment, and operations appears to be well advanced and now includes many phenomena that span the corporate–third sector divide (Dekker 2009).

The CSR movement may be a contributor to a "blurring" of the boundaries through its engagement in similar economic activities to the third sector, but contemporary CSR is as much ideological as economic. It is at the level of ideology that the potential of the CSR movement not only to change the relations between the corporate and third sectors but also to "reinvent" the third sector itself is great. Of course, part of the impact of CSR on the third sector is that corporations control enormous amounts of money and other resources that could be used to support work focused on social value creation and of course the movement focuses squarely on much of the work traditionally considered to be in the domain of the third sector. The main challenge of CSR to the third sector, however, is that the corporate sector approaches this work with a different set of priorities and values that have the potential not only to cause convergence and "overlap" with the third sector but to displace it entirely as a legitimate institutional force.

The rhetoric of the CSR movement articulates not only a new role for the corporate sector but a major readjustment in the roles and responsibilities of the other sectors. Since the collapse of many governments during the 1990s, no longer capable of delivering the entitlements demanded by their citizens, the superior ability of the corporate sector to deliver both private wealth and public goods has become widely accepted. Major shifts in global political and economic systems and the ideologies associated with them support the idea of an augmented role for corporations not only in the economy but in global governance. As the corporate sector comes to rival governments in terms of global authority, recognition of the third sector as an institutional force, let alone a role for the non-economic activities and responsibilities of the sector, is being dropped from the debate.

In what follows, four key ideas associated with CSR are identified, the first two of which have shaped the evolution of the relationship between the corporate and third sectors over many decades and continue to be important elements of the CSR movement today. Contemporary CSR, however, is distinguished by two additional ideas that are more "revolutionary" than "evolutionary" and have profound implications for the third sector and the organizations that comprise it.

The scope and focus of the CSR movement, in terms of both its rhetoric and its practices, extend well beyond its relationship with the third sector, or even beyond its interest in the traditional social value creation work of the third sector. In fact the third sector is relatively overlooked in the CSR literature except as one of many useful "inputs" to corporate work in the area of social responsibility. Insofar as the CSR literature is focused on shifting roles, responsibilities, and relationships, it concentrates more on an examination of the changing relationship between the corporate sector and the state. Nevertheless, the movement has profound implications for the relationship between the corporate sector and the third sector.

What is CSR?

Although there is a vast literature written by academics and professionals on the CSR movement, it represents only a part of a much larger ideological and strategic development which has been dubbed "philanthrocapitalism" (Bishop 2007). This term was coined to describe a widespread belief among business people, and increasingly among governments, individuals, and third sector leaders, that business models and methods can produce not only economic wealth but social welfare – and, additionally, that business is superior to the public sector and civil society in creating social value and enhancing the public good (Edwards 2008). Trends like social enterprise and venture philanthropy and other market models such as microfinance and fair trade businesses are all manifestations of this wider phenomenon. Corporate social responsibility is the part of this phenomenon that pertains to the particular role of the corporate sector in contributing to this transformative project of capitalism. It is also the most influential component of philanthrocapitalism, partly because the CSR literature and rhetoric often incorporate many of these other models and tend to speak for the general trend toward addressing social issues through market and business models, and partly because ideas advocated by and on behalf of the corporate sector tend to be disproportionately successful in terms of influencing opinion both inside and outside the corporate sector.

Common to all ideological or social movements is the difficulty of enumerating a fixed set of principles that are absolutely definitive of what is a loosely connected composite of ideas and activities held by many diverse individuals and groups and which pertain to many different specific issues and contexts. Below, the focus is on identifying the key ideas which animate the CSR movement and, in particular, on examining the implications of these ideas for the third sector. While this particular relationship is not the focus of CSR rhetoric in general, the approaches to social value creation identified with the CSR movement represent unprecedented opportunities for – and challenges to – the third sector.

The ideas circulating within and about the contemporary CSR movement appear to fall into four conceptually distinct categories with implications for the third sector, namely (1) morality, duty, and responsibility; (2) the strategic "business case" for CSR; (3) the superior efficiency and effectiveness of business; and (4) new governance systems. Of course in scholarly discussions of CSR, let alone in corporate practice, these elements coexist and overlap, but it helps to examine each thread separately in terms of teasing out their meaning for civil society organizations, operations, influence, and legitimacy.

Moral Aspects of CSR

One of the oldest, most powerful, and ongoing approaches of business people to the third sector is based on a moral imperative to "help." At the level of the organization this imperative has been translated, over time, into the construct of corporate philanthropy. In practical terms, the word "philanthropy" is most often associated with the idea of a gift, freely given, from an individual or, in this case, a corporation, to a third sector organization in order to support the mission-based work of that organization. Philanthropy, including in a corporate context, is at least partially motivated by a sense of ethical responsibility for the welfare of others and, additionally, is discretionary or voluntary (Carroll 1979, 1991).

Although current CSR advocacy, especially that directed at practitioners, emphasizes the bottom-line return associated with third sector engagement, it is clear that a desire to do "good" remains an important component of current CSR practices (Steckel et al. 1999; Young 2003), a fact born out in empirical analysis of corporate motivations (Gan 2006). As discussed in the next section on strategic arguments for giving, even contractual buyer–supplier relationships with the third sector continue to include a premium price paid over and above the actual market value of services provided to the corporation. Philanthropic motivations remain an important component of current CSR practices and not just, as Kramer and Kania (2006) have argued, because corporations are fearful and inept in terms of managing risk.

Historically, the primary form of transaction between the corporate and third sectors associated with responsibility was the "donation," a transfer of money (or, on occasion, goods and/or services) to a third sector organization without the expectation of *specific* services being provided to the corporation in exchange for its gift (although certainly reputational and status benefits have come to be offered as reasons for corporate giving over the years as the need to justify corporate philanthropy to shareholders has grown). A corporate donation is considered to be offered primarily for reasons having to do with the creation of the "public good" as opposed to the production of private benefits, which is why, in many areas of the world, governments use tax incentives in order to encourage corporate philanthropy.

What are the implications of the philanthropic model in terms of the relationship between the corporate and third sectors? A donation transaction is technically an exchange transaction, even though the benefits being provided to the corporation are often intangible and abstract. Another implied aspect of a philanthropic relationship is that a donation is an "arms-length" transaction (Moon 2002). Thus, corporations trust the management of the third sector organization to run the operations of the organization (or the specific project, if that is what is funded) independently, based on its experience and knowledge of the issues involved, and do not enter into shared governance arrangements. In a purely philanthropic relationship, the two sides of the relationship retain a great deal of autonomous control over their own operations and management – these gifts are embedded in a context of corporate trust in the management and governance of third sector organizations.

The "Business Case" for CSR

The most common approach to current CSR, as well as to the historical relationship between the corporate and third sectors, is a focus on "bottom line" analysis and motivations. The arguments supporting this strategic approach to the third sector respond to Milton Friedman's famous article in which he states that the only role for business is to focus on shareholder return (Friedman 1970; Lantos 2001). In practice, the basic premise of a strategic business approach to the third sector rests on a cost–benefit analysis which ensures that profits are not being diverted from shareholders but are being invested with the expectation of creating measurable returns on investment for the company (Adler 2006).

Many relationships between the corporate and third sectors based on this classic motivation can be characterized as buyer–seller relationships (Austin 2000), usually specified in legal contracts. Sponsorship offers a concrete "reward" in terms of advertising a corporation's support of a third sector organization, a method of fundraising which exploded in the 1980s as professional fundraisers developed "products" for the corporate sector to buy. In the 1990s, cause-related marketing (CRM) developed as corporations became interested in attaching reputational benefits provided by third sector suppliers to their goods and services, creating a phenomenon recently identified as "consumption philanthropy" (Eikenberry 2009). In both cases the fact that the corporation is community-minded and generous is being advertised, but the source of the messages and the target market at which they are directed differ.

A more recent evolution in the strategic relationships between corporations and third sector organizations is the partnership, which has evolved as corporations engage in the "co-creation" of social value with third sector organizations. These types of social alliances are more akin to a corporate "joint venture" (Austin 2000). This form of corporate–third sector transaction is perhaps the most common relationship advocated and studied in the current CSR literature (Jamali and Keshishian 2009; Loza 2004; O'Regan and Oster 2000; Seitanidi and Crane 2008) although a few prominent authors continue to view the third sector primarily in the role of supplier (Prahalad 2006).

Partnerships are motivated by a desire to gain more control over the outcomes of corporate investments in social value creation. Previous corporate approaches to CSR have been characterized as attempts by "bad" corporations to throw money at "good" NGOs to neutralize negative public opinion about the ethics of business (Kramer and Kania 2006). It has been argued that demonstrable success in social value creation is much more likely to build brand equity and that direct corporate involvement is required to ensure success. When corporations with a strong interest in specific, measurable, and visible results enter into the work of social value creation in conjunction with a third sector organization, the need for control of outcomes has led to the growth of inter-sectoral partnerships.

The belief that business involvement in operations is required for "success" and its implications are discussed more fully below; for the present it is sufficient to note that partnerships are a form of inter-sectoral interaction to which the "business case" approach applies. The difference between the traditional approach, such as sponsorships and CRM, and new partnering approaches is that the former rests on a buyer–seller relationship in which the business of acquiring enhanced reputation is "outsourced" to an independent third sector organization, while the latter rests on a joint venture relationship in which the corporation takes a direct hand in creating its own reputational benefits.

What does a strategic approach to social responsibility and corporate citizenship imply for the third sector? First, as third sector engagement increasingly has come to be sold by both its corporate advocates and third sector fundraisers on the basis of the "business case," it has become clear that the notion of a market exchange, as opposed to pure altruism, is the core of the relationship. Nevertheless, notions of duty and the responsibility of corporations to engage in social issues persist as an important motivation. Second, classic buyer–seller relationships, such as sponsorship and CRM, continue to be "arms-length," and each party retains independent control of its operations, management, governance, and goal-setting. The obligations of both sides to provide value are specified contractually.

Trust in the ability of the other party to manage its business appropriately and to be able to "deliver" is a critical enabling feature of contractual relationships between independent businesses. When trust erodes, we begin to see changes emerge that are often associated with inter-corporate channel management, such as attempts to gain control of the value chain through vertical integration. Thus, while the rhetoric of the CSR movement, including the few examples with an explicit focus on third sector relationships (Austin 2000), suggests that partnership relationships represent an evolution to a superior form of transaction between the sectors, it is possible to view the trend toward third sector partnerships as driven by a corporate need for increased control and even domination of the channel associated with their "reputation suppliers."

The Efficiency and Effectiveness of Business

This is the most overtly ideological of the strands of thought comprising contemporary CSR. The arguments advanced in support of this approach to corporate social responsibility have developed as neoconservative views about the proper role of business in economic, political, and social systems have become dominant. Originating in views about privatization popularized in the Thatcher–Reagan era and advanced in the 1990s as governments around the world either withdrew from or failed in their former role of responsibility for the provision of public entitlements, the private sector has come to be widely viewed as not only the logical but the most efficient and effective creator of social innovation and value.

In its most ambitious form, this approach to CSR is based on market strategies directed at the "bottom of the pyramid" (BOP) whose advocates argue that, if large corporations give up on charitable donations and act only in their own self-interest by entering developing markets, there will be a radical increase in economic development and a decrease in poverty (Prahalad and Hammond 2002). NGOs have a role to play in this scenario as suppliers of information, distribution networks, and so on, if they are able to adapt to the corporate view that developing consumer markets is the chief driver of economic development (Prahalad 2006).

Another variant of this ideological approach to CSR emphasizes the superiority of business management, as opposed to markets, in social value creation. Business methods and models are preferred because of their efficiency and effectiveness, that is to say, their superiority in terms of achieving measurable social impact. In this model, as in the BOP model, there is a genuine interest in solving social problems and a sense of the "moral" responsibility of the corporate sector to take a hand in this work (Young 2003). Unlike the BOP approach, advocates of the power and effectiveness of business methods recognize the need to deploy substantial corporate resources to effect social change and are committed to doing so – as long as the corporation is satisfied that it retains enough management control over operations to ensure that the resources they commit achieve the concrete, measurable, visible, and easily communicated results they expect (Weiser et al. 2006).

Within the contemporary CSR movement, there is a strong sense of disappointment with the results of earlier corporate spends on social value creation, whether through philanthropy or more strategic supplier approaches (Kramer and Kania 2006). As opposed to examining complex, historic, and systemic reasons for the "failure" of their financial support of the third sector in the past to achieve "results," however, advocates of the new CSR have identified the injections of business models and methods as the solution to persistent social and economic issues. This reflects not only disappointment in the third sector but distrust of its traditional management and governance systems.

Some corporations engage in social value creation directly; others may hire experts from the third sector as consultants to these projects. When the third sector holds sufficient supplier power in terms of information, reputation, distribution, or other necessary inputs, a corporate–third sector partnership may develop. CSR-inspired partnerships take many forms; they can be as complex as multi-year, multi-sectoral initiatives to eradicate a disease or as simple as ongoing corporate involvement in an annual fundraising marathon. The key feature of a partnership is that it involves joint management and decision-making and that there is a higher degree of accountability to the corporation and therefore control. It is not an "arms-length" relationship such as a philanthropic or contracted supplier relationship. The type of relationships between the corporate and third sector envisioned by the new CSR is one in which corporations become drawn into "participation in the formulation and enactment, or 'steering' and 'rowing,' of community action" (Moon 2002, p. 391).

The partnership model is a key element of the current CSR approach to third sector relationships. Corporate joint ventures are plagued by conflict stemming from differences in power, values, and culture; the research on third sector partnerships suggests inter-sectoral partnerships are no different. Micromanagement in the traditional independence of third sector operations as a result of power differentials (Berger and Cunningham 2004), ambiguities inhibiting learning (Lewis 1998), and issues with the ethical reputation of partners (Martinez 2003) have all been reported. However, the advantages to third sector organizations are great. NGOs have long been aware of the improvements to efficiency and sustainability that can be derived from the injection of business practices into their operations (Fowler 1997), and partnerships provide not only resources in terms of improved management systems and structures but also the opportunity to receive vastly more money than was previously available for their work. Financial support, of course, is perhaps the major motivation of third sector organizations to engage in corporate partnerships, despite their reluctance to admit this fact publicly (Macdonald and Chrisp 2005).

Resource dependency theory applied to the third sector suggests that goal displacement can be tied to funding sources (Froelich 1999). One of the ways that third sector organizations traditionally have been able to combat this and maintain their focus on the multiple goals associated with their mission is through diversification of revenue streams (Young 2006). A concern with well-funded and jointly managed partnership arrangements is that focus on the explicit goals of the corporate project or program and its implicit values will come to dominate the focus of highly resource-dependent third sector organizations. This may lead to the neglect of traditional priority areas such as advocacy or even more dramatic outcomes such as that described in recent empirical work on NGO–corporation relationships which discusses the strategic use of CSR-inspired partnerships to neutralize opposition and reduce criticism (Yaziji and Doh 2009).

Edwards' critique (2008) of CSR goes beyond the impact of business "hubris" in terms of imposing business models, methods, management, and measurement on individual third sector organizations and thereby limiting the scope of their work to service delivery and away from other traditional areas of responsibility such as organizing and advocacy. He also argues that this ideology – and its adoption by others outside the corporate sector, such as foundations, governments, citizens, and third sector leaders themselves – is not only reducing the scope of the third sector's work but also reframing our collective understanding of and support for the importance of the traditional role and responsibilities of the third sector. The belief that business goals, models, and methods are superior to those of the third sector is not only informing corporate practice and narrowing the focus and scope of third sector organizations to service delivery but also changing public views about what constitutes social value and the creation of the public good.

New Systems of Governance

Recently, the discussion about the immense capacity and superior ability of the corporate sector to create and deliver social value has begun to focus more explicitly on the necessity for it to do so in a world experiencing the institutional failure of government. A new and theoretical CSR literature is emerging, which examines the reconfiguration of the roles and responsibilities of the corporate sector in terms of systems of global governance. The focus of this literature is not simply on the capacity of corporations to take on this role but on the responsibility, no matter how reluctantly assumed, of business to provide entitlements, including social welfare, to citizens as governments weaken and withdraw from their traditional responsibilities. The implication of these developments for CSR and particularly as it applies to the third sector is that it is now considered the responsibility of business to intervene directly in the business of social value creation and to participate in societal governance arrangements (Moon and Vogel 2008). The latter often involve third sector organizations in partnership or network arrangements.

Zadek (2007) advocates a new system of global governance in which politics are reinvented as states fail around the world. His vision is based on the evolution of multi-sectoral partnerships into a new kind of institution focused on *both* the creation of wealth and the stewardship of the public interest. This is a radically different way of thinking about CSR; in fact, Zadek calls it a "paradigm shift" in terms of thinking about the purpose of business as well as in terms of thinking about the multiple actors, their configurations, and their roles in new governance systems. This paradigmatic shift suggests that the primary purpose of business in the future will no longer even be to seek profits. In his view business will have a new place in society which would include production, wealth creation, and governance. Zadek argues that his view is not merely a theoretical model but one that recognizes the "de facto" role that business is already playing in society through current CSR practices. The role that the third sector plays in this model is unclear; although Zadek talks about multiple accountabilities and the evolution of multi-sectoral partnerships, it is not clear whether he considers the third sector to be part of the blended institutions that become part of the "governing" authority or to be part of the "governed."

Crane et al. (2008) argue that the combined effects of the institutional failure of governments, the new political ideologies that since the 1980s have privileged the role of private corporations and market solutions in addressing economic and social issues, and the trend toward globalization, which means that an increasing number of social activities are now taking place beyond the reach of the national state, have led to governments reducing their role in providing the entitlements of citizenship. Their analysis is based on evidence that corporations are increasingly taking on responsibility for many of the former roles of government.

The focus of this analysis is not on the third sector but on the reconfiguration of the relationship between corporations and governments, but it has profound implications for the third sector. The third sector, like corporations, has traditionally been a "citizen" in its relationship with government. However, this analysis shows corporations "migrating" from a position of citizenship to a position equivalent to government in many respects. The impact of this conceptualization of new governance systems for the third sector is that in emerging systems of global governance, as corporations assume more and more of the traditional roles and responsibilities of governments, third sector organizations are no longer being governed by government alone, but also by corporations. (The thrust of the trends outlined above offer support to this idea.)

Traditionally the third sector has seen its role as "outside" both the state and the market. Past research in the tradition of studying the blurring of boundaries has been preoccupied with questions about preserving the core roles and responsibilities of the third sector to society through maintaining a certain amount of independence and distance. However, as corporations and governments become blended into a new type of governing institution or corporations at least begin to play a role more similar to governments in terms of governing relationships with citizens, we have to question whether a preoccupation with maintaining the current institutional form of the third sector or with maintaining the role of independent "outsider" is any longer appropriate – or possible – for the third sector.

The Impact of CSR on the Corporate–Third Sector Relationship

The above review of third sector and CSR literature suggests that the CSR movement is composed of several conceptual strands, some of which have evolved from the attitudes and practice of the past 50 years and others of which are associated with more recent ideological developments with respect to the role of business in economic, political, and social systems. We have seen that as ideas and attitudes about the roles and responsibilities of the corporate sector have changed, so too has the relationship between the corporate sector and the third sector. New forms of interaction have emerged, some related to the explicit rhetoric of the CSR movement and others reflective of more subtle attitudes and assumptions on the part of those who advocate, practice, or study CSR. There are a number of key dimensions to these changes.

The nature of the transactions between the sectors has changed. Traditionally, donations and payments for advertising or marketing benefits were embedded in arms-length exchange relationships characterized by the independence of both parties with regard to their management, governance, and mission. More recently, collaborative relationships have developed on the corporate model of a "joint venture." However, power differentials with respect to resources and organizational capacity, coupled with differences in interests and values, suggest that what appear to be "joint ventures" between equally independent partners may really be more akin to vertical integration of a supply chain in which the most powerful player "governs" the other members of the channel.

A second area in which we have seen changes is in the area of corporate trust in the third sector. As corporations increasingly have come to think of "business management" as superior to that of the third sector, disappointment with the results of previous philanthropic experiences to solve intractable social issues has come to be reframed as failures of third sector management and governance. Joint management of projects funded by corporate revenues has started to be imposed in order to ensure that partnership projects are managed in accordance with corporate goals for social performance and results. It has been argued that this trend increases the likelihood of organizational goal displacement over time and shifts the focus of the third sector as a whole more toward service delivery and market development, reducing the focus on its traditional roles of advocacy, community organization, political opposition, and the creation of social capital.

In terms of governance, while in theory arrangements identified as collaborative mean that both parties become accountable to the other, in practice this has a more severe effect on the weaker partner. Corporations have increasingly raised demands for "accountability" with respect to how the funds they deploy are spent. In practice, accountability initiatives focus on controlling where and how money is spent, and this blocks the ability of third sector organizations to support core operations or cross-subsidize mission-based activities through project funds. This has weakened the ability of third sector organizations to set their own goals and deploy their resources to achieve them.

Over the past three decades, thinking about the balance in the respective roles of governments, the corporate sector, and civil society has changed dramatically. Recent theoretical literature on CSR has become focused on the shifting roles of business and government and suggests that as corporations increasingly become responsible for filling roles formerly held by governments, the role they are playing in systems of global governance is growing. Moreover, it has been suggested that one of the new roles they are playing is a governing role with respect to the third sector.

These changes in corporate–third sector relationships and, more fundamentally, in corporate attitudes toward the third sector are not always explicit. The CSR literature continues to speak of the opportunities that NGOs provide for partnership, but in practice corporate approaches to the third sector seem to be based on increasing control and narrowing definitions of what constitutes social value. These trends raise the specter of decreasing independence and a narrower role for the third sector. The larger project of philanthrocapitalism and, beyond that, the general ideology of privatization and corporate efficiency in which the CSR movement is embedded, has eroded trust in the ability of third sector organizations and management to deliver specific social outcomes that appeal to corporations and consumers. At the same time, increasing comfort with respect to a growing role for the corporate sector in terms of global governance has been accompanied by decreasing interest in identifying a role and unique set of responsibilities for a third sector often seen by the corporate sector as inefficient in its operations and irrelevant in its goals.

Implications for Third Sector Research

As the CSR movement has advanced, it is clear that the relationship between the third and corporate sectors has changed dramatically. Moreover, the fact that corporations are increasingly powerful in terms of creating public opinion means that these changes and their ideological underpinnings have the potential to affect perceptions about the third sector in the minds of those well beyond the corporate sector. The fact that the third sector is becoming not only reconfigured but also "repositioned" in terms of its perceived role and effectiveness points to many avenues for further empirical and theoretical work into the impact of CSR on the third sector.

A major area for further research is whether changes in the relationship between the third and corporate sectors are changing the relationship between the third and household sectors as well. Has eroding corporate trust in the third sector model and its methods also led to eroding trust in the traditional third sector among individuals? The CSR movement argues philanthropy is unnecessary (Prahalad 2006), and there are signs that traditional philanthropic methods of supporting the third sector seem to be considered "old fashioned" or "outmoded" in the CSR literature (Tracey et al. 2005). At the same time, CSR practices communicate that a growing number of social problems can be solved by smart business management, market-based solutions, and consumer action (Eikenberry 2009). Particularly in younger generations brought up in a context of belief in the power of business solutions to solve all problems, organizations that need to ask for help or donations may seem like "poor managers" as opposed to "worthy causes." Is this the message that individuals are internalizing?

A second research area that also pertains to the hegemony of the values associated with CSR is focused on the internal processes and behaviors of third sector organizations. Are values inside third sector organizations themselves changing in response to the values of the CSR movement? We have seen, for example, a dramatic change in the way organizations market themselves – and their clients – to their supporters over the past decade. Common slogans like "people need a hand up, not a hand out" or references to "sweat equity" suggest that the disadvantaged, deprived, and dispossessed are expected to move themselves out of their situation through individual hard work and entrepreneurship. This reinforces the idea that if they are unable to do so, it is the result of the failure of individual effort as opposed to systemic injustice. Changes in public attitudes may also affect more than the way third sector organizations market themselves. At a more fundamental level, there has been a substantial increase in the number of third sector organizations turning to market-based solutions to social and economic injustice, as they encourage the poor to borrow money through microfinance schemes and to start their own businesses to feed their families. The processes through which these phenomena occur represent an important subject for research.

Another area for future research is related to the questions Edwards (2008) raises about the impact of this movement in terms of reducing the scope of activities on which the third sector has traditionally focused. Is it the case that the third sector is in a process of being "repositioned" away from its responsibility for redressing social injustice, inequity, and disadvantage and from its activities associated with convening, organizing, criticism, advocacy, and opposition? Is it shifting away from its role in creating a social space in which citizens can come together to engage in collective endeavors? Even more pressing is research on whether the perceived value of this role and these responsibilities is eroding among new governing institutions as well as among the citizens who accord them authority.

There is a need for empirical examination as well as for theoretical development with respect to the role and responsibilities of the third sector in emerging governance systems. As corporations increasingly join governments in providing what Moon (2002) has called "direction to society," we need to question our assumptions about the viability of a "third" sector "outside" of governments and corporations. Current models identifying a separate third sector are based on assumptions of a balance among the roles and responsibilities of corporations, government, and the third sector – which now appears to be increasingly "unbalanced." An extremely important issue is whether the so-called third sector is actually becoming a second, non-governing, sector – or even ceasing to have any institutional role at all. Future research, then, requires a turn to theorizing the third sector, not in terms of sectoral or organizational survival focused on boundaries or the nonprofit form, but in terms of the survival of its traditional responsibilities and roles in new global systems of power and authority.

The main challenge of CSR to the third sector is in terms of the pressure it brings to bear on the unique role the sector has played and the responsibilities it has assumed for creating "civility." The task for third sector research is to identify and legitimize a new set of responsibilities to ensure that the role of "social space creation" persists within an ideological context that envisions a privileged role for the private sector in emerging economic, political, and social systems. The unique and critical aspects of the third sector's role in contributing to the public good depend on a conceptualization of the third sector as a place of organizing, gathering, and mobilizing citizens freely and consciously. Legitimizing that role and institutionalizing the space where it happens within new systems of global governance is a critical task for the future.

References

Abzug, R. (1999). The nonprofit sector and the informal sector: A theoretical perspective. *Voluntas*, 10(2), 131–150.

Adler, S. (2006). *Cause for Concern: Results-Oriented Cause Marketing*, Ohio, Thompson/South-Western.

Austin, J. (2000). Strategic collaboration between nonprofits and businesses. *Nonprofit and Voluntary Sector Quarterly*, 29(1) supplement, 69–97.

Bishop, M. (2007). What is philanthrocapitalism? *Alliance*, March, p. 30.

Berger, I., and Cunningham, P. (2004). Social alliances: Company/nonprofit collaboration. *California Management Review*, 47(1), 58–90.

Carroll, A. (1979). A three-dimensional conceptual model of corporate social performance. *Academy of Management Review*, 4(4), 497–505.

Carroll, A. (1991). The pyramid of corporate social responsibility: Toward the moral management of organizational stakeholders. *Business Horizons*, July–August, 39–48.

Crane, A., Matten, D., and Moon, J. (2008). *Corporations and Citizenship*, Cambridge, Cambridge University Press.

Dekker, P. (2009). Civil society and business: Crossing borders and keeping distance. Paper presented at the 7th ISTR Regional Conference for Latin America and the Caribbean, Mexico City.

Edwards, M. (2008). *Just Another Emperor? The Myths and Realities of Philanthrocapitalism*, New York, The Young Foundation.

Eikenberry, A. (2009). The hidden costs of cause marketing. *Stanford Social Innovation Review*, 7(3), 50–55.

Evers, A. (1995). Part of the welfare mix: The third sector as an intermediate area. *Voluntas*, 6(2), 159–182.

Ferris, J., and Graddy, E. (1999). The role of the nonprofit sector in a self-governing society: A view from the United States. *Voluntas*, 9(2), 137–154.

Fowler, A. (1997). *Striking a Balance: A Guide to Enhancing the Effectiveness of Non-Governmental Organizations in International Development*, London, Earthscan.

Friedman, M. (1970). The social responsibility of business is to increase its profits. *New York Times*, 13 September, pp. 122–126.

Froelich, K. (1999). Diversification of revenue strategies: Evolving resource dependence in nonprofit organizations. *Nonprofit and Voluntary Sector Quarterly*, 23(3), 246–268.

Gan, A. (2006). The impact of public scrutiny on corporate philanthropy. *Journal of Business Ethics*, 69(3), 217–236.

Jamali, D., and Keshishian, T. (2009). Uneasy alliances: Lessons learned from partnerships between business and NGOs in the context of CSR. *Journal of Business Ethics*, 84(1), 277–295.

Kramer, M., and Kania, J. (2006). Changing the game. *Stanford Social Innovation Review*, 4(1), 20–27.

Kramer, R. (2000). A third sector in the third millennium? *Voluntas*, 11(1), 1–23.

Lantos, G. (2001). The boundaries of strategic corporate social responsibility. *Journal of Consumer Marketing*, 18(7), 595–630.

Lewis, D. (1998). Nongovernmental organizations, business, and the management of ambiguity. *Nonprofit Management and Leadership*, 9(2), 135–151.

Loza, J. (2004). Business–community partnerships: The case for community organization capacity building. *Journal of Business Ethics*, 53(3), 297–311.

Macdonald, S., and Chrisp, T. (2005). Acknowledging the purpose of partnership. *Journal of Business Ethics*, 59(4), 307–317.

Martinez, C. V. (2003). Social alliances for fundraising: How Spanish nonprofits are hedging the risks. *Journal of Business Ethics*, 47(3), 209–223.

Moon, J. (2002). The social responsibility of business and new governance. *Government and Opposition*, 37(3), 385–408.

Moon, J., and Vogel, D. (2008). Corporate social responsibility, government, and civil society. In A. Crane, A. McWilliams, D. Matten, J. Moon, and D. Siegel (eds) *The Oxford Handbook of Corporate Social Responsibility* (pp. 303–326), Oxford, Oxford University Press.

O'Regan, K., and Oster, S. (2000). Nonprofit and for-profit partnerships: Rationale and challenges of cross-sector contracting. *Nonprofit and Voluntary Sector Quarterly*, 29(1) supplement, 120–140.

Prahalad, C. (2006). *The Fortune at the Bottom of the Pyramid: Eradicating Poverty through Profits*, Upper Saddle River, NJ, Wharton School Publishing.

Prahalad, C., and Hammond, A. (2002). Serving the world's poor, profitably. *Harvard Business Review*, September, 48–57.

Seitanidi, M., and Crane, A. (2008). Implementing CSR through partnerships: Understanding the selection, design and institutionalization of nonprofit-business partnerships. *Journal of Business Ethics*, 85(4), 413–429.

Steckel, R., Simons, R., Simons, J., and Tanen, N. (1999). *Making Money While Making a Difference: How to Profit with a Nonprofit Partner*, Homewood, IL, Hightide Press.

Tracey, P., Phillips, N., and Haugh, H. (2005). Beyond philanthropy: Community enterprise as a basis for corporate citizenship. *Journal of Business Ethics*, 58(4), 327–344.

Weiser, J., Rochlin, S., Kahane, M., and Landis, J. (2006). *Untapped: Creating Value in Underserved Markets*, San Francisco, Berrett-Koehler Publishers.

Young, D. R. (ed.) (2006). *Financing Nonprofits: Putting Theory into Practice*, Lanham, MD, AltaMira Press.

Young, S. (2003). *Moral Capitalism: Reconciling Private Interest with the Public Good*, San Francisco, Berrett-Koehler Publishers.

Yaziji, M., and Doh, J. (2009). *NGOs and Corporations: Conflict and Collaboration*, Cambridge, Cambridge University Press.

Zadek, S. (2007). *The Civil Corporation*, 2nd edn, London, Earthscan.

Chapter 15
Third Sector–Government Partnerships

Annette Zimmer

Introduction

The reason the topic of "partnership" is of great importance for third sector research is closely connected with the concept of a "third sector" as such. By definition, the societal spheres or sectors – in particular "market," "state," and "family" – that are based on different logics of operation are necessary in order to make the concept of a third sector work. Inevitably, those organizations (third sector organizations [TSOs], nonprofit organizations [NPOs], nongovernmental organizations [NGOs], or civil society organizations [CSOs]) populating the third sector are thoroughly interrelated with the other sectors. They are embedded (Granovetter 1985) between market, state, and family and, as such, cooperate simultaneously with these very different economic, political, and social environments. As a result, TSOs are significantly interpenetrated by the logics of the state, the market, and the family, which turns the third sector into a fuzzy set of organizations that are open for numerous modes of cooperation.

Focusing specifically on the relationships between the third sector and government, this chapter takes a closer look at why understanding third sector partnerships constitutes a difficult task, at when third sector–government relationships became a prime topic of nonprofit research, at which levels of governance do third sector–government relationships take place, at how these relationships are explained, and at why partnership arrangements with third sector organizations are becoming increasingly popular.

A. Zimmer (✉)
Westfälische Wilhelms-Universität, Münster, Germany
e-mail: a.zimmer@civil-society-network.org

R. Taylor (ed.), *Third Sector Research*, DOI 10.1007/978-1-4419-5707-8_15,
© Springer Science+Business Media, LLC 2010

Partnerships: A Difficult Topic

The Challenge of Multifunctionality

The greatest challenge for understanding third sector partnerships is related to the multifunctional and multidimensional character of third sector organizations. TSOs function simultaneously within very different environments. They are active on both sides of government by being involved in policy development as well as in policy implementation. As service providers, TSOs are working on par with for-profit and public entities. Engaged in interest representation and lobbying activities, they constitute a part of civil society. Moreover, TSOs, at least those that are membership organizations and as such are embedded in local communities, are contributing significantly to social cohesion by providing avenues for societal integration via reciprocity and face-to-face encounters.

How can one come to grips with the complexity and the multidimensional character of TSOs while researching partnership arrangements? Analyzing the partnership dimension of the sector and its organizations, each discipline of the social sciences applies a distinctive perspective by focusing on a specific facet of the activity spectrum of TSOs. Considering the work of TSOs as an important factor for the political economy, economists are mainly interested in the organizations as producers of goods and services. Partnership arrangements including TSOs are perceived as a vital element of coproduction of public goods and services (Osborne 2008; Salamon et al. 1999). Drawing on a wide range of empirical data about membership, volunteering, and giving, sociologists – in particular those active in political sociology – concentrate on the potential of TSOs for promoting participation and integration of citizens into both the community and the realm of politics. Hence in a neo-Tocquevillian tradition, partnership translates into another word for the socializing and democratizing functions of TSOs (Almond and Verba 1963).

A prime focus of political scientific research is to investigate the position of TSOs in the policy process. Referring to David Easton's approach (1957), political scientists examine the activities of TSOs on both sides of government (Bode 2006; Evers 1995; Helfferich and Kolb 2001; Hyman 2005; Lahusen 2004; Pesthoff and Brandsen 2008; Smith and Lipsky 1993). Being engaged in lobbying and advocacy activities, TSOs as part of civil society might be seen to contribute to the input legitimacy of the political system. Since in many countries around the world, TSOs are also heavily involved in the production of social services, the organizations might also substantially add to the output legitimacy of democratically ruled welfare states. Finally, membership in TSOs and support for them in the form of dues, donations, and giving are perceived as an important element of the so-called feedback loop of the policy process, which again adds to the legitimacy of democratic systems. Clearly, from a political science point of view, partnership arrangements with TSOs constitute a complex and again multifaceted topic to address.

The Legal Environment of Partnerships: Terrain to Be Discovered

In order to study the topic of third sector–government partnerships thoroughly and in particular from a comparative perspective, it is necessary to be familiar with the legal environment of TSOs. The legal and organizational framework established by government, including tax regulations for TSOs and tax incentives for donors, constitutes as such a partnership arrangement with government. From a legal point of view, government exercises its legislative capacities to define the frameworks for operation of all the actors of the public sphere, third sector organizations included. In this context, the legal regulations are of a constitutive character, with the state enjoying what is indubitably a privileged position laying down the rules that have to be followed by TSOs.

The role of the state is a privileged one, yet it is limited. A sine qua non for democratic societies is the self-limitation of the state. The democratic state acknowledges and respects human rights, including the right to associate and establish TSOs. Indeed, the concept of partnership in the sense of guaranteeing by law the freedom of association constitutes an integral part of the majority of the constitutions of modern democracies. Moreover, the Universal Declaration of Human Rights stipulates that (1) everyone has the right to freedom of peaceful assembly and association and (2) no one may be compelled to belong to an association (Article 20). Accordingly, democratic governments by law authorize their citizens to convene associations, to establish TSOs, and to pursue charitable activities by way of donations or volunteering. In the same vein, the concept of partnership between civil society and government is thoroughly alien to non-democratic or authoritarian governments that by and large significantly hinder and strictly control the establishment and operations of TSOs.

One of the most important prerequisites for the development of a government–third sector partnership, therefore, is closely related to the existence of legal and organizational forms that are exclusively designed for the nonprofit and civic activities of TSOs. Hence, the analysis of the legal environment of TSOs offers valuable insights with respect to the topic of how the third sector is perceived by government. However, even in the legal sciences, the modes of cooperation between TSOs and government that are backed by the laws of the respective country or region and, hence, the comparative study of the legal regulations, tax incentives, and legal and organizational forms of TSOs have not yet moved into the center of investigation. Particularly from a comparative point of view, there still is much terrain to be covered by third sector researchers (Salamon 1997; Simon 2004; The International Center for Nonprofit Law).

Partnership Arrangements in the Light of Governance

Doubtless, the topic of third sector partnerships has gained momentum especially in light of the increasing importance of governance arrangements. In particular, the shift from "government" to "governance" in political science has given rise to many studies investigating partnership arrangements that include TSOs in various policy fields and at different levels of governance (Kersbergen and van Waarden 2004) – most prominently within the multi-level governance arrangement of the European Union (Kendall 2009; Maloney and van Deth 2008). Our conventional understanding of government was based on the assumption of hierarchical coordination organized and inaugurated by the state. Governance, to the contrary, underlines the horizontal dimension of policy-making and hence draws our attention to complex constellations of actors: on par with government and public entities, private actors are more and more becoming important players and participants in policy arrangements.

Among those private actors, TSOs or civil society organizations count prominently as being promoters of participation and hence democratic legitimacy on the input side of political systems. TSOs, however, are also to be found on the output side of political systems, where they are either in competition or in cooperation with public institutions and for-profit organizations heavily involved in the production of goods and services. This is so primarily in the area of social services, but increasingly so in other welfare domains. Accordingly, governance and in particular the notion of "good governance" is strongly affiliated with the topic of partnership in the sense of nonhierarchical coordination, peaceful conflict resolution, and efficient and effective policy-making. Moreover, TSOs are also perceived as providing avenues for civic participation and hence democratic legitimacy in governance arrangements. Depending on which side of the political system the analysis focuses, either the "advocacy or lobby" or the "public policy" function of TSOs is highlighted when studying the role and importance of TSOs in governance arrangements.

The Advocacy or Lobbying Perspective

Whether, how, and to what extent associations and citizens alike make use of the public sphere by engaging in civic activities constitutes the focal point of the advocacy or lobbying perspective. Democratic states legally guarantee a public space giving room for advocacy work, grassroots campaigning, and lobbying activities of a variety of actors – among them business associations as well as public interest groups. According to political theory, a strong democracy (Barber 1984) is based on an active citizenry organized in public interest groups, associations, and grassroots-based TSOs that balance the power of business associations and other interest groups not working on behalf of the commonweal. The advocacy perspective looks upon the third sector and its organizations "from below," with political participation and social integration of the citizenry constituting key features of analysis and cornerstones of public–private partnerships in governance arrangements. Going back to the classic work of Almond and Verba (1963), the advocacy perspective perceives the third sector and its organizations primarily as a vital part of civil society and as such as an opportunity structure for citizens to become engaged in politics by either criticizing or supporting public activities via membership, donations, and active engagement. From the advocacy perspective, TSOs are important actors in governance arrangements since they are giving voice to the people, thus providing legitimacy to policy-making in governance arrangements.

There is, however, no clear-cut distinction between the lobby and the advocacy perspectives (for an overview with special reference to the United States, see Jenkins 2006). Instead, social sciences witness an increasing blurring of boundaries between the domains of civil society research and the analysis of lobbying activities in which third sector organizations are involved (Freise 2008; Malony and van Deth 2008; van Schendelen 2002).

Despite this caveat, third sector research has significantly benefited from both the "governance turn" in policy analysis and the increased interest in the societal backing of advocacy. Both the social capital approach (see Chapter 16 by Dag Wollebæk and Per Selle, this volume) and the civil society discourse inspired a boom of empirical investigations researching the embeddedness of third sector organizations in local communities (Putnam 1993), as well as the scope and degree of civicness within a region or country. The advocacy perspective highlights an understanding of partnership that perceives cooperation and mutual accommodation between the third sector, or more precisely between civil society and government as the most important prerequisite for the establishment and further development of democracy.

In the past decades, the advocacy perspective has gained prominence in the area of international relations and hence in global governance (Keck and Sikkink 1998; for an overview see Boli 2006) as well as with respect to European governance. Starting in the late 1990s, the European Commission invited TSOs, and specifically their umbrella organizations, to play an increasingly more important role in the multi-level governance arrangement of the European Union (Della Sala and Ruzza 2007a,b; Maloney and van Deth 2008; Zimmer and Freise 2008). In particular with its White Paper on Governance from 2002, the European Commission launched a campaign promoting a partnership arrangement with "organized civil society," and thus with TSOs, that aimed at bridging the "European democratic deficit" by improving European governance with the help of TSOs.

Of late, evidence-based skepticism has replaced the euphoric enthusiasm with respect to the potential of TSOs to develop into a legitimate voice of the people at the European level of governance in Brussels (Kohler-Koch 2008; Kohler-Koch and Rittberger 2007; Papadopoulos 2007). The same holds true for the potential of NGOs involved in global governance arrangements, which has also been met increasingly with scientific skepticism, particularly concerning their potential regarding civicness. Whether TSOs are indeed able to improve legitimacy in governance arrangements has developed into a key issue of research. Or to put it differently, who benefits from partnership arrangements involving TSOs that are supported by specific constituencies, but do not by and large enjoy representativeness, and that very often stand out for a lack of accountability?

The Public Policy Perspective

This public policy perspective highlights the importance of TSOs in governance arrangements that are responsible for the production of social services. Points of departure for the analysis of the partnership between government and TSOs with respect to social service provision are both the welfare mix and the welfare regime approach of Evers (1995) and Esping-Andersen (1990), respectively. The public policy perspective that analyzes governance arrangements, including TSOs, investigates the topics of whether, how, and to what extent TSOs are integrated into welfare state regimes and how and to what extent they are part of a specific welfare mix. Or to put it differently, at the federal, the regional, or the local level of governance, the public policy perspective examines both the scope and the modes of cooperation between government and TSOs as producers of goods and services. Introduced by Lester Salamon's early work on the role and function of TSOs in social service delivery in the United States (Salamon 1981, 1987a,b), this particular topic has developed into a prime domain of third sector research (for an overview see Anheier and Kendall 2001; Smith and Grønbjerg 2006). Currently, a significant body of third sector research focuses on investigating partnership arrangements in Europe (Evers and Laville 2004; Kendall 2009; Osborne 2008).

Interestingly enough, the reason why TSOs have become an important issue of welfare state research is closely affiliated with the rise of "neoliberalism" and "neoconservatism." Currently, we are witnessing the end of an era that was characterized by an almost unrestricted confidence in the competencies of the market. Since the early 1980s, neoliberalism has developed into the hegemonic doctrine worldwide. Margaret Thatcher in the UK and Ronald Reagan in the United States were the first political leaders unrestrictedly supporting the so-called neoliberal revolution. The two had in common a strong dislike of the welfare state as "big government" that stands for heavy public investments in welfare policies. According to Ronald Reagan, the third or "independent" sector had to step in by filling the gap that was left by government, which was no longer willing to finance and administer welfare programs. The neo-conservative rollback of welfare state policies was based on two assumptions: first, not government but society is responsible for the welfare of the citizenry, and second, welfare states are responsible for both the funding and the actual delivery of social services. Accordingly, when government pulls back, society and thus the third sector should take over: the notion of a welfare state as "big government" did not leave any room for partnership arrangements.

When policy research started to investigate how social service provision is regulated, funded, and delivered in modern welfare states, the results did not go along at all with the idea of a welfare state as a coherent and solid entity. In particular, Salamon's work on the funding and provision of welfare services in the United States led to a revision of the concept of the welfare state as an omnipotent bureaucracy, exclusively run by government: Salamon's data showed the importance of TSOs for social service delivery even within the welfare state in the United States (Salamon 1987b, p. 107). But these organizations were not at all fully "independent," receiving their primary support from private contributions (private giving, sponsoring, and foundation grants). On the contrary, the data showed clearly that TSOs active in social service provision are significantly supported by public funding in terms of government grants and other public subsidies regulated by law – such as contributions of insurance funds – and that TSOs furthermore are also heavily dependent on the market because a significant share of their income is based on service charges (Salamon 1992, p. 27).

Besides showing that the third or "independent" sector, a term that still is commonly used in the United States for framing the complexity of nonprofit organizations, was independent far less than previously assumed from both the government and the market, the research also made clear how little, indeed, was known about the sector with respect to its scope, funding structures, and embeddedness in the complex environments of modern society. Without solid knowledge about the scope and structure of the sector, there is no way to make use of the potentials of third sector organizations for policy planning and implementation. Thus, the results of Salamon's investigations clearly illustrated the necessity for further research aimed at the investigation of the size of the sector, its structures, and embeddedness as an intermediary sphere between market, state, and family – a project that was put into practice first in the United States and in the years to follow almost worldwide by The Johns Hopkins Comparative Nonprofit Sector Project (Salamon et al. 1999; see also Chapter 4 by Freda Donoghue, this volume).

As already outlined, the service-providing function of TSOs is just one facet of the organizations' activities in governance arrangements of modern welfare states. Similar to the advocacy perspective that distinguishes between lobbying and civic activities, the public policy perspective also draws our attention to two different facets of the engagement of TSOs in public affairs. Besides being "partners in public service" (Salamon 1995), TSOs are often members of governance arrangements acting on par with other private and public actors that are directly involved in policy formulation at the European, national, or regional level of governance. Indeed, there are many TSOs working in a specific policy field that are "partners of public policy": they are simultaneously engaged in lobbying activities and are also eligible partners of well-established policy arenas or governance arrangements with respect to policy formulation. TSOs such as Greenpeace in the area of environmental policies or the German Welfare Associations in the area of social services provide textbook examples of TSOs being lobbyists on behalf of the common good, highly acknowledged partners of policy networks geared toward policy implementation, and reliable partners of public service production. Depending on the country or region and its welfare regime, there are numerous long-standing traditions of cooperation and partnerships with respect to both policy formulation and implementation in the welfare domains (for European countries, see Evers and Laville 2004; Kendall 2009; Osborne 2008).

A very specific type of third sector–government partnership embracing involvement in both policy formulation and implementation is traditionally labeled neocorporatism (Zimmer et al. 2009). This translates into a situation in which a limited number of so-called umbrella organizations of the third sector – for example, the Welfare Associations in Germany – enjoy a privileged position with respect to access both to the core arenas of policy-making and to public funding. In Germany, this very special partnership arrangement between TSOs and government is laid down in the principle of subsidiarity (Anheier and Seibel 2001; Zimmer 1999), which for decades served as the bedrock for the close cooperation between a limited number of TSOs and government in Germany's core welfare domain. The country hence stands out for a specific pattern of third sector–government partnership that translates into an encompassing integration of TSOs into the German welfare state.

A very different pattern of third sector–government relationships is to be found in the Anglo-Saxon countries, where traditionally TSOs operate at an arm's length principle and therefore stand more apart from government. The relationship is contract based and hence forces TSOs to apply for grants and subsidies in a competitive market. The partnership arrangement is based on the assumption of "nonprofits for hire" (Smith and Lipsky 1993). In the past decades, alongside the introduction of New Public Management techniques, this specific type of third sector–government partnership, based on competition and modeled according to the market, has gained momentum particularly in Central Europe (Anheier and Kendall 2001; Salamon 1995; Zimmer and Priller 2004). Simultaneously, there is a trend toward a closer rapprochement of government and TSOs in the Anglo-Saxon countries. Particularly in the UK, the Labour Government under the guidance of the so-called third way introduced "compacts" at various levels of government (Kendall 2009; Taylor 2004) that codify close cooperation, thus partnership with TSOs. By "emphasizing 'governance' rather than 'government' " (Taylor 2004, p. 135), the notion of partnership has developed in the UK into a central issue of third sector–government relationships. According to Marilyn Taylor (2004, p. 137), the partnership arrangement in the UK constitutes a further step in the direction of an attuned blurring of boundaries, which may lead to the development of institutional arrangements that are neither public nor private but something in-between.

Rationales and Functions of Third Sector Partnership Arrangements

The social sciences not only look at third sector–government partnerships from different perspectives, but also refer to different rationales behind their analysis of partnership arrangements. For economists and scholars of administrative sciences, the topics of effectiveness and efficiency are at the center of interest. After all, the underlying rationale for governments worldwide to seek partnership arrangements with TSOs is closely linked to considerations of efficiency and effectiveness. The aim of best meeting the needs and preferences of clients and consumers also plays an important role, particularly in partnership arrangements affiliated with new public management techniques. Hence, economists and policy advisors keenly search for means of output maximization. By contrast, the key interest of political scientists is linked to questions and topics of how to establish, deepen, improve, and stabilize democracy and – more specifically – democratic governance via partnership arrangements including civil society and third sector organizations. Here the topics of legitimacy and democratic accountability are focal points of analysis.

These two very distinct research foci – the search for legitimacy on the one hand and for effectiveness and efficiency on the other hand – lead to a division of labor among the disciplines when addressing the topic of partnership arrangements between TSOs and government. Economists and scholars of public administration are interested in partnership arrangements involving TSOs that highlight the output dimension of governance, while the key interest of political scientists focuses by and large on the input side of governance. This chapter takes a closer look at two of the best-known heuristic models (Najam 2000; Young 2000) and three of the leading theoretical approaches (Salamon 1987a,b; Seibel 1989, 1991; Salamon and Anheier 1998) developed by third sector researchers to try to make sense of partnership arrangements between TSOs and government.

Najam's Four-C's Model

Adil Najam (2000) developed a typology of interactions between TSOs and government by focusing on both perspectives: that of government toward the sector and, vice versa, the sector's position with respect to government. For analytical purposes, he distinguishes between goals (ends) and strategies (means) that are pursued by government and/or by nonprofit organizations in specific policy fields. Within a certain policy field, each institutional actor – governmental or third sector organization – pursues certain ends (goals) and each has a preference for certain means (strategies). As Najam puts it, "As the organizations float within the policy stream, they bump into each other in one of four possible combinations: (1) seeking similar ends with similar means, (2) seeking dissimilar ends with dissimilar means, (3) seeking similar ends but preferring dissimilar means, or (4) preferring similar means but for dissimilar ends" (Najam 2000, p. 383).

Accordingly, cooperative relationships are based on a convergence of goals and strategies of both government and TSOs. Cooperative relationships are quite often to be found in the policy arenas of human services and relief programs, where government and TSOs not only agree upon the same goals but also prefer the same strategies. Confrontational relationships are "likely when governmental agencies and nongovernmental organizations (nonprofits) consider each other's goals and strategies to be antithetical" (Najam 2000, p. 385); pressure groups and social movements are particularly prone to be involved in confrontational relationships with government. To Najam, complementary relationships are "likely when government and nongovernmental (nonprofit) organizations share similar goals but prefer different strategies" (ibid, p. 387); partnerships based on complementarity are very common in the service provision arena where government provides funding while TSOs are responsible for the delivery of services. Co-optative relationships are "likely when governmental and nongovernmental (nonprofit) organizations share similar strategies but prefer different goals" (ibid, p. 388). This partnership model is often to be found in developing countries where co-optation is the term generally used to describe what governments try to do to TSOs. Najam's model is of particular value because it covers a broad spectrum of partnership arrangements and can be applied in many settings around the world.

Young's Typology of Third Sector–Government Arrangements

Dennis Young's typology (2000) focuses specifically on TSOs as service providers. Furthermore, in accordance with economic thinking, Young's typology is based on the underlying assumption that output improvement, particularly of social service delivery, constitutes the core rationale for third sector–government partnerships. Referring to different strands of economic theory (Steinberg 1987), Young identified three distinct models of third sector–government relationships in which he characterized service provision by TSOs as supplementary, complementary, or adversarial to government supply of social services. According to Young's typology, "in the supplementary model, nonprofits are seen as fulfilling the demand for public goods left unsatisfied by government ... In the complementary view, nonprofits are seen as partners to government, helping to carry out the delivery of public goods largely financed by government ... In the adversarial view, nonprofits prod government to make changes in public policy and to maintain accountability to the public" (Young 2000, pp. 150ff).

Nonetheless, Young makes clear that there are inherent shortcomings in these models. First of all, he draws our attention to the fact that these models are not mutually exclusive. In a given place, TSOs might be in a complementary relationship with government in one policy field, but at the same time in an adversarial position in a different policy field. Furthermore, in some cases, it might be very difficult to distinguish at all between government and the third sector due to longstanding relationships tailored in a complementary fashion, which translate into the emergence of "hybrid organizations" (Young 2000, p. 151). Paving the way for further analyses with a particular focus on the various modes of coproduction (Pestoff and Brandsen 2008), Young's reference to hybridization is of especial import.

Salamon's Interdependence Theory

Why do governments and TSOs work together in welfare states? According to Lester Salamon (1987a,b), the answer is straightforward and simple: in welfare states, government and TSOs are partners because of mutual benefit. Efficiency and effectiveness, therefore, constitute the prime rationales for government–third sector partnerships particularly in social service provision. Salamon developed his argument, first, by drawing on the "government failure" literature (Steinberg 2006) and, second, by pointing for the first time at the deficiencies of third sector service provision. What does not sound revolutionary today was perceived in the 1980s as an affront against the widely shared picture of a sector of "do-gooders" beyond any reproach. Salamon argued that in the area of social service provision, government stepped in particularly in order to counterbalance the "voluntary failures" of the sector.

According to Salamon (1987b, p. 113), the sector is "limited in its ability to generate an adequate level of resources; it is vulnerable to particularism and the favoritism of the wealthy; it is prone to self-defeating paternalism; and it has at times been associated with amateur, as opposed to professional, forms of care." But in welfare state arrangements, the weaknesses and failures of the sector correspond well with government's strengths and vice versa. Here, "Government is in a position to generate a more reliable stream of resources, to set priorities on the basis of a democratic political process … [and] to offset part of the paternalism of the charitable system by making access to care a right instead of a privilege, and to improve the quality of care by instituting quality-control standards" (ibid, p. 113). And, correspondingly, TSOs are closer to the needs of the poor than government bureaucracies; they are more likely to personalize service provision; they operate on a smaller scale; and finally, in contrast to any bureaucratic type of public service, there might be healthy competition among third sector organizations engaged in service competition.

The interdependence theory sparked numerous studies of modes of cooperation in different policy fields and in a number of countries (Anheier and Kendall 2001; James 1989; Smith and Grønbjerg 2006). By taking a closer look at how partnerships are regulated, how they are financed, and which type of organizations are involved in service provision, the theoretical approach received further fine-tuning (Gidron et al. 1992) that significantly improved its applicability in international and comparative studies. Focusing on the modes of cooperation and hence on the question of how partnerships are put into practice on a day-to-day basis revealed significant differences between cooperative relationships established and backed by contracts, and thus organized in a market-based fashion, and those whose modes of cooperation are laid down in the laws and traditions of their respective country or policy field.

A further, even more refined approach, analyzing the composition, and specifically the overlapping of rationales in governance arrangements with TSOs being involved in the production of social services, is the concept of the "welfare mix." Developed by Adalbert Evers (1995), the welfare-mix approach has developed into a valuable analytical tool for investigating the increased "hybridization" of governance arrangements in numerous policy fields and at different levels of social service production (Evers 2008).

Seibel's Theory of Functional Dilettantism

Wolfgang Seibel (1989, 1991) developed his theoretical approach explaining partnership arrangements between the third sector and government by referring explicitly to the work of Salamon and to the economic theories of TSOs (Steinberg 2006).

Similar to the theory of interdependence, Seibel also views the underlying ratio-nale for third sector–government cooperation in terms of mutual benefit. According to Seibel, however, third sector–government partnerships are not at all related to considerations of efficiency and effectiveness. Instead, Seibel's argument is that the legitimacy problems of modern welfare states constitute the key rationale for understanding cooperation and partnerships between government and the third sec-tor. In sharp contrast to Salamon's position that government and the third sector work together because government is in a position to level the deficiencies of the sector and vice versa, Seibel argues that government cooperates with the sector pre-cisely because its organizations stand out for their deficiencies and hence are by nature prone to failure. Why, though, do governments cooperate with organizations that have "deep-seated weaknesses regarding efficiency and control" (Seibel 1989, p. 178)?

Seibel's argument is based in the tradition of neo-Marxist welfare state research (Offe 1984). According to this perspective, democratic governments in welfare capi-talism are confronted sooner or later with significant problems of legitimacy as they find themselves in an increasingly paradoxical situation. Obviously, governments are dependent on the majority of the votes of the citizenry. In order to be elected or re-elected, politicians introduce social policies that not only try to buffer the neg-ative side of highly industrialized societies (such as environmental destruction and the erosion of local communities and networks), but also promise a high standard of living and a good life for everybody. However, financing social policy initiatives and large-scale welfare programs is costly. Hence, governments are highly depen-dent on a smooth running economy that guarantees a steady stream of income that first and foremost is produced by industrial production – a situation that necessitates governments being friendly toward the capitalist interests of firms and companies. Accordingly, modern welfare states end up in a situation in which they are trapped between the aspirations of the voters and the logic of capitalism, which is primarily based on a profit-making incentive. Due to its inherent tendency toward "growth to limits," modern welfare states are faced with problems of legitimacy because they are unable to meet the increasing demands and aspirations of the electorate without endangering their financial bedrock and hence the capitalist economy. To put it dif-ferently, welfare states are unable to live up to their promises, and they are therefore confronted sooner or later with deep-seated problems of legitimacy.

Against this background, Seibel assigns a very important and highly political role to third sector organizations, which are seen to be characterized by amateurism and nonprofessionalism. Basically, Seibel argues (1989, p. 178) that the nonprofit sector serves "as a shunting-yard for social and political problems that, basically, cannot be solved." Hence, governments work with TSOs in partnership arrangements since only these organizations – because of their amateurism and unprofessionalism – are able to disguise that there is a "growth to limits" in modern welfare states. As Seibel (1989, p. 188) puts it, "The nonprofit sector, then, provides an institutional arrange-ment that enables complex societies to cope with social and political problems that cannot be solved. Thus, it discharges government from responsibilities that could lead to unbearable risks for the general legitimacy of the political system." From this perspective then, government welcomes partnerships with TSOs and uses the third sector as a valuable resource for the stabilization of the political system in capitalist economies. With a side blow to Salamon, Seibel underlines that " 'voluntary failure' is necessary for the political functionalism of 'third party government' " (ibid, p. 186). Undoubtedly, Seibel's argument is elegant and convincing. There is, however, no need for any future research to investigate the rationale behind third sector–government relationships if one goes along with Seibel's basic assumption that TSOs are, per se, unprofessional and beyond reform.

Social Origins Theory

A third answer addressing the question as to why the third sector and government are bound together in partnership arrangements is related to historical institutionalism (Pierson and Skocpol 2002). Taking it for granted that the two sectors work together, this line of research is primarily interested in developing a typology of the embeddedness of the sector in governance arrangements by referring to the issue of how and why the partnership originally came into being. Centrally, here the reasons as to why third sector–government partnerships are arranged in a specific form and hence regime-type setting are seen to be closely linked to the historical development of a certain country or region. Again, this line of argument focuses primarily on third sector organizations active in social service delivery.

Drawing on the work of Esping-Andersen (1990) and Barrington Moore (1966), Lester Salamon and Helmut Anheier distinguished four "regimes" of embeddedness of TSOs in welfare state arrangements: the liberal, the statist, the social democratic, and the corporatist model of embeddedness (Salamon and Anheier 1998). They tested each model by referring to the data of The Johns Hopkins Comparative Nonprofit Sector Project (also see Chapter 4 by Freda Donoghue, this volume). According to the social origins theory, the different models of partnership arrangements are the outcome of former societal conflicts; they represent specific solutions to societal crises and cleavage structures of the past, whose resolution was achieved through particular alignments of societal forces – among political parties, trade unions, social movements, and the ruling elites. As such, the identified regimes symbolize different routes to modernity and hence to democratic societies with market economies. In the boundaries of a nation state, the partnership arrangement constitutes a division of labor between the market, the state, and the third sector, which in former times was established in order to either keep the "ruling elite" in power or establish a modernized alignment between new and old elites.

In recent years, social origins theory has moved to considerations as to whether there is a nexus between the "regimes of TSO embeddedness" elaborated by social origins theory and "models of democracy" developed by democratic theory (Held 2006). This is particularly the case with respect to the "liberal regime" of the social origins theory, which clearly overlaps with the concept of a "protective democracy," the key characteristic of which, according to David Held (2006, p. 78), consists of "the separation of state from civil society." The liberal mode of integrating TSOs or civil society organizations into the realm of policy and politics also shows a close connection to the concept of pluralism, as one facet of democratic theory (Schmidt 2008, pp. 226ff).

The same holds true for the "social democratic regime" of social origins theory – where there is a strong articulation with the German political scientist Manfred Schmidt's normative concept of a "social democracy" (Schmidt 2008, pp. 240ff), in which government is responsible for a supportive environment enhancing civic engagement. Similarly, David Held (2006, p. 92) has introduced the term "developmental democracy" to describe the ideal of a democratic state in which TSOs are supposed to flourish under the protection of a benevolent state. There is no close equivalent among models of democracy for the top-down approach toward TSOs described by the "statist model" of embeddedness. However, the "corporatist model" of the social origins theory shows at least some likeness to "consensus democracy" described by Schmidt (2008, pp. 327ff), particularly with respect to Central European countries that tend to give priority to neo-corporatist modes of TSO integration.

Concluding Comments

Third sector organizations have great potential for being integrated into partnership arrangements because they are multifunctional organizations that are not based on just one single rationale or mode of operation. This specific quality makes third sector organizations ideal partners for government in social service provision. In the early 1980s, Salamon was the first third sector researcher who drew attention to the fact that modern welfare states are often based on close cooperation – indeed partnership – with TSOs. From this time onward, researching both the different modes of cooperation and the rationales on which partnerships of TSOs with government in welfare state arrangements are based has developed into a very important branch of third sector research.

The shift from "government" to "governance" in political science further accelerated the growth industry of investigating partnership arrangements, including TSOs in various policy fields and at different levels of governance. Indeed, TSOs are partners of policy formulation and implementation at every level of governance. They are members of advocacy coalitions and policy networks internationally as well as at the European level of governance. In numerous welfare states, TSOs are highly acknowledged service producers in many fields of the core welfare domain. At the local level of governance, they are primarily involved in the coproduction of services; at the regional and national levels of governance, they are active with respect to lobbying and advocacy activities.

The integration of TSOs in governance arrangements has been accompanied by great expectations. Governance and, in particular, the notion of "good governance" are strongly linked to the topic of partnership in the sense of nonhierarchical coordination, peaceful conflict resolution, and efficient and effective policy-making.

In governance arrangements, TSOs are perceived as providing avenues for civic participation. Accordingly, they are supposed to contribute significantly to the legitimacy of democratic regimes. There is, however, an increasing skepticism regarding whether TSOs are indeed able to hold up to their promise. At the global and the European levels of governance, the topics of accountability and representativeness have developed into important strands of third sector research that investigate governance arrangements involving TSOs.

From a theoretical point of view, partnerships between TSOs and government are seen as contributing to either the legitimacy or the effectiveness of the political system. Economists draw our attention to the effectiveness and efficiency of partnerships involving TSOs; the focal point of interest for political scientists is whether the involvement of TSOs in partnership arrangements adds to the legitimacy of the democratic regime. There is no doubt that the multidimensional character of TSOs qualifies these organizations as ideal partners in terms of cooperation and coproduction. At the same time, again due to their multifunctional character, partnerships with TSOs are prone to develop into fuzzy sets of organizational arrangements that stand out for their "blurring of boundaries."

Against this background, "hybridization" has become an important feature of third sector research. In his seminal article of 1973, "The third sector and domestic missions," Amitai Etzioni was the first to refer to the topic of the "blurring of boundaries" by characterizing NPOs as "organizations for the future" or "hybrids" that combine very different rationales, in particular those of private enterprises (i.e., entrepreneurship and efficiency) and those of government with its orientation toward the public good and commonweal. There is then little doubt that in the years ahead the issue of "hybridization" – as well as the difficulties and problems that come along with the blurring of boundaries at each level of governance – will develop into one of the key and most promising issues of third sector research.

References

Almond, G. A., and Verba, S. (1963). *The Civic Culture: Political Attitudes and Democracy in Five Nations*, Princeton, NJ, Princeton University Press.

Anheier, H. K., and Kendall, J. (eds) (2001). *Third Sector Policy at the Crossroads: An International Nonprofit Analysis*, London, Routledge.

Anheier, H. K., and Seibel, W. (2001). *The Nonprofit Sector in Germany: Between State, Economy and Society*, Manchester, Manchester University Press.

Barber, B. R. (1984). *Strong Democracy*, Berkeley, University of California Press.

Bode, I. (2006). Disorganized welfare mixes: Voluntary agencies and new governance regimes in Western Europe. *Journal of Western European Social Policy*, 16(4), 346–359.

Boli, J. (2006). International nongovernmental organizations. In W. W. Powell and R. Steinberg (eds) *The Nonprofit Sector: A Research Handbook*, 2nd edn (pp. 333–350), New Haven, Yale University Press.

Della Sala, V., and Ruzza, C. (eds) (2007a). *Governance and Civil Society in the European Union, Vol. 1: Normative Perspectives*, Manchester, Manchester University Press.

Della Sala, V., and Ruzza, C. (eds) (2007b). *Governance and Civil Society in the European Union, Vol. 2: Exploring Policy Issues*, Manchester, Manchester University Press.

Easton, D. (1957). An approach to the analysis of political systems. *World Politics*, 9(3), 383–400.

Esping-Andersen, G. (1990). *The Three Worlds of Welfare Capitalism*, Princeton, NJ, Princeton University Press.

Etzioni, A. (1973). The third sector and domestic missions. *Public Administration Review*, 33(4), 314–323.

Evers, A. (1995). Part of the welfare mix: The third sector as an intermediate area. *Voluntas*, 6(2), 119–139.

Evers, A. (2008). Hybrid organizations: Background, concepts, challenges. In S. P. Osborne (ed.) *The Third Sector in Europe: Prospects and Challenges* (pp. 279–292), London, Routledge.

Evers, A., and Laville, J.-L. (eds) (2004). *The Third Sector in Europe*, Cheltenham, Edgar Elgar.

Freise, M. (ed.) (2008). *European Civil Society on the Road to Success*, Baden-Baden, Nomos.

Gidron, B., Kramer, R. M., and Salamon, L. M. (eds) (1992). *Government and the Third Sector: Emerging Relationships in Welfare States*, San Francisco, Jossey-Bass.

Granovetter, M. (1985). Economic action and social structure: The problem of embeddedness. *American Journal of Sociology*, 91(3), 481–510.

Held, D. (2006). *Models of Democracy*, Stanford, Stanford University Press.

Helfferich, B., and Kolb, F. (2001). Multilevel action coordination in European contentious politics: The case of the European Women's Lobby. In D. Imig and S. Tarrow (eds) *Contentious Europeans: Protest and Politics in an Emerging Polity* (pp. 143–161), Lanham, Rowman & Littlefield.

Hyman, R. (2005). Trade unions and the politics of the European social model. *Economic and Industrial Democracy*, 26(1), 9–40.

James, E. (ed.) (1989). *The Nonprofit Sector in International Perspective*, Oxford, Oxford University Press.

Jenkins, C. (2006). Nonprofit organizations and political advocacy. In W. W. Powell, and R. Steinberg (eds) *The Nonprofit Sector: A Research Handbook*, 2nd edn (pp. 307–332), New Haven, Yale University Press.

Keck, M. E., and Sikkink, K. (1998). *Activists Beyond Borders: Advocacy Networks in International Politics*, Ithaca, NY, Cornell University Press.

Kendall, J. (ed.) (2009). *Handbook on Third Sector Policy in Europe: Multi-Level Processes and Organised Civil Society*, Aldershot, UK, Edward Elgar.

Kersbergen, K. van, and Waarden, F. van (2004). "Governance" as a bridge between disciplines: Cross-disciplinary inspiration regarding shifts in governance and problems of governability, accountability and legitimacy. *European Journal of Political Research*, 43(2), 143–171.

Kohler-Koch, B. (2008). Civil society in EU governance: A remedy to the democratic accountability deficit? *Concepts & Methods*, 4(1), 3–6.

Kohler-Koch, B., and Rittberger, B. (eds) (2007). *Debating the Democratic Legitimacy of the European Union*, London, Rowman & Littlefield.

Lahusen, C. (2004). Joining the cocktail circuit: Social movement organizations at the European Union. *Mobilization*, 9(1), 55–71.

Maloney, W. A., and Deth, J. W. van (eds) (2008). *Civil Society and Governance in Europe*, Cheltenham, Edgar Elgar.

Moore, Barrington, Jr. (1996). *Social Origins of Dictatorship and Democracy*, Boston, Beacon Press.

Najam, A. (2000). The four-C's of third sector–government relations: Cooperation, confrontation, complementary, and co-optation. *Nonprofit Management and Leadership*, 10(4), 375–396.

Offe, C. (1984). *Contradictions of the Welfare State*, Boston, The MIT Press.

Osborne, S. P. (ed.) (2008). *The Third Sector in Europe: Prospects and Challenges*, London, Routledge.

Papadopoulos, Y. (2007). Problems of democratic accountability in network and multilevel governance. *European Law Journal*, 13(4), 469–486.

Pesthoff, V., and Brandsen, T. (eds) (2008). *Co-Production: The Third Sector and the Delivery of Public Services*, London, Routledge.

Pierson, P., and Skocpol, T. (2002). Historical institutionalism in contemporary political science. In I. Katznelson and H. V. Milner (eds) *Political Science: The State of the Discipline* (pp. 693–721), Washington, DC, American Political Science Association.

Putnam, R. (1993). *Making Democracy Work*, Princeton, NJ, Princeton University Press.
Salamon, L. M. (1981). Rethinking public management: Third-party government and the changing forms of public action. *Public Policy*, 29(3), 255–275.
Salamon, L. M. (1987a). Of market failure, voluntary failure, and third party government: Toward a theory of government–nonprofit relations in the modern welfare state. *Journal of Voluntary Action Research*, 16(1), 29–49.
Salamon, L. M. (1987b). Partners in public services: The scope and theory of government–nonprofit relations. In W. W. Powell (ed.) *The Nonprofit Sector: A Research Handbook* (pp. 99–117), New Haven, Yale University Press.
Salamon, L. M. (1992). *America's Nonprofit Sector*, Washington, DC, Foundation Center.
Salamon, L. M. (1995). *Partners in Public Service: Government–Nonprofit Relations in the Modern Welfare State*, Baltimore, MD, The Johns Hopkins University Press.
Salamon, L. M. (1997). *The International Guide to Nonprofit Law*, New York, Chichester.
Salamon, L. M., and Anheier, H. K. (1998). Social origins of civil society: Explaining the nonprofit sector cross-nationally. *Voluntas*, 9(3), 213–248.
Salamon, L. M., Anheier, H. K., List, R., Toepler, S., and Sokolowski, S. W. (eds) (1999). *Global Civil Society: Dimensions of the Nonprofit Sector*, Baltimore, MD, Center for Civil Society Studies, The Johns Hopkins University.
Schendelen, R. van (2002). *Machiavelli in Brussels*, Amsterdam, Amsterdam University Press.
Schmidt, M. G. (2008). *Demokratietheorien*, Wiesbaden, VS Verlag.
Seibel, W. (1989). The function of the mellow weakness: Nonprofit organizations as problem-non-solvers. In E. James (ed.) *The Nonprofit Sector in International Perspective* (pp. 77–192), Oxford, Oxford University Press.
Seibel, W. (1991). *Der Funktionale Dilettantismus. Zur politischen Soziologie von Steuerungs- und Kontrollversagen im 'Dritten Sektor' zwischen Markt und Staat*, Baden-Baden, Nomos.
Simon, K. W. (2004). Tax laws and tax preferences. In A. Zimmer and E. Priller (eds) *Future of Civil Society* (pp. 147–167), Wiesbaden, VS-Verlag.
Smith, S. R., and Grønbjerg, K. A. (2006). Scope and theory of government–nonprofit relations. In W. W. Powell and R. Steinberg (eds) *The Nonprofit Sector: A Research Handbook*, 2nd edn (pp. 221–242), New Haven, Yale University Press.
Smith, S. R., and Lipsky, M. (1993). *Nonprofits for Hire: The Welfare State in the Age of Contracting*, Cambridge, MA, Harvard University Press.
Steinberg, R. (1987). Nonprofits and the market. In W. W. Powell (ed.) *The Nonprofit Sector: A Research Handbook* (pp. 118–138), New Haven, Yale University Press.
Steinberg, R. (2006). Economic theories of nonprofit organizations. In W. W. Powell and R. Steinberg (eds) *The Nonprofit Sector: A Research Handbook*, 2nd edn (pp. 117–139), New Haven, Yale University Press.
Taylor, M. (2004). The welfare mix in the United Kingdom. In A. Evers and J.-L. Laville (eds) *The Third Sector in Europe* (pp. 122–143), Cheltenham, Edgar Elgar.
The International Center for Not-for-Profit Law. Visit www.icnl.org
Young, D. R. (2000). Alternative models of government–nonprofit sector relations: Theoretical and international perspectives. *Nonprofit and Voluntary Sector Quarterly*, 29(1), 149–172.
Zimmer, A. (1999). Corporatism revisited: The legacy of history and the German nonprofit-sector. *Voluntas*, 10(1), 37–49.
Zimmer, A., and Freise, M. (2008). Bringing society back in. In W. A. Maloney and J. van Deth (eds) *Civil Society and Governance in Europe* (pp. 19–42), London, Edward Elgar.
Zimmer, A., Appel, A., Dittrich, C., Lange, C., Sitterman, B., Stallmann, F., and Kendall, J. (2009). Germany: On the social policy centrality of the Free Welfare Associations socio-political complex. In J. Kendall (ed.) *Handbook on Third Sector Policy in Europe: Multi-Level Processes and Organised Civil Society*, (pp. 21–42), Aldershot, UK, Edward Elgar.
Zimmer, A., and Priller, E. (eds) (2004). *Future of Civil Society: Making Central European Nonprofit Organizations Work*, Wiesbaden, VS-Verlag.

Chapter 16
Social Capital

Dag Wollebæk and Per Selle

Introduction

According to Robert Putnam (2000a), social capital is generated through face-to-face interaction in "horizontal" networks. Voluntary organizations are seen as the most pervasive type of such networks and therefore a main source of social capital. However, empirical support for such claims is scanty. An increasing number of studies report no relationship between the extent of face-to-face interaction in organizations and social capital (Claibourn and Martin 2000; Dekker and van den Broek 1998; Freitag 2003; Hyggen 2006; Mayer 2003; Ødegård 2006; Stolle 2001; von Erlach 2005; Wollebæk and Selle 2002b, 2007; Wollebæk and Strømsnes 2008). This has led some to conclude that the importance of associations in generating trust is exaggerated (Stolle 2003). Instead, it is claimed, we should focus on the role of public policy and how institutions function (Rothstein 2002; Rothstein and Stolle 2003).

We believe this view represents a clear-cut case of throwing the baby out with the bathwater. In our view, the negative findings regarding participation and social capital reflect that the relationship between voluntary associations and social capital is misconceived, but not overstated. Our view is that civil society institutions embed and institutionalize trust.

We argue that this occurs through three processes. First, through *cognitive inference:* experiences of how such associations function – be they personal or mediated – influence our view of the cooperative spirit of others. If organizations are successful and visible in a society, it proves the rationality, normality, and utility of cooperation for the common good. Second, organizations act as *intermediary structures* linking individuals to society and citizens to the political system. Like other

D. Wollebæk (✉)
University of Bergen, Norway
e-mail: dag.wollebak@isp.uib.no

P. Selle (✉)
University of Bergen, Norway
e-mail: per.selle@isp.uib.no

R. Taylor (ed.), *Third Sector Research*, DOI 10.1007/978-1-4419-5707-8_16,
© Springer Science+Business Media, LLC 2010

types of infrastructure, such as roads or telephone lines, they do not need to be used by everyone all the time in order to be useful; as the benefits of roads are not limited to the people who at a given time drive them, nor are the benefits of organizations limited to those who at a given time are active. In a strong organizational society, non-members are aware of the opportunity to get involved in organizational activity or to contact organizations for assistance, should the need arise. Thus, it is acknowledged that institutionalized collective action is not only rational, normal, and useful, but also generally available. Third, dense, overlapping, and interlocking organizational networks create cross-pressures that have a *moderating* effect on tension and conflict (Rokkan 1967). Cross-cutting networks have been found to increase tolerance and understanding for the argument of others (Mutz 2002). If tensions are reduced between those affiliated, it is likely to benefit people on the outside of organizational society. All these arguments presume democracy and de facto freedom of organization and are valid only in societies with these characteristics.[1]

These ideas are closely linked to theories of pluralism and representative democracy. Such influences are definitely present in Putnam's early work (1993) and correspond with his concept of *rainmaker effects* of organizational activity, which appears in one book chapter (Putnam 2000b). Yet it breaks radically with the socialization approach in his later work, which is influenced by theories of participatory democracy (Macpherson 1977; Pateman 1970), the works of Alexis de Tocqueville (1968), some aspects of communitarianism, and social psychological assumptions. Thus, while associations are seen as crucial in both a socialization and an institutional approach, they are so for different reasons. The relative value that they place on different types of associations (i.e., political vs. non-political) and modes of participation (i.e., active vs. passive and singular vs. multiple) varies.

This chapter compares the socialization perspective with an institutionally oriented approach in a cross-national context. While the results further weaken the face-to-face postulate, they do not support downplaying the role of voluntary organizations. Rather, our findings underline that voluntary organizations are crucial to the sustenance of social capital – not mainly as agents of socialization, but as institutions within which social capital is embedded.

Specification of Hypotheses

Table 16.1 summarizes the two perspectives on how organizations foster social capital. Both agree that organizational affiliation impacts individual levels of social capital. In a socialization perspective, however, only active participants develop

---

[1] The conditions for voluntary activity vary greatly among authoritarian and totalitarian states. In many cases, the organizations that are likely to be tolerated by an authoritarian state are either instruments of the state apparatus, pure leisure or cultural activities, or small-scale community projects (Booth and Richard 2001; Juknevičius and Savika 2003). In such situations, it is unlikely that organizations are the main source of social capital, whether through socialization or institutionalization.

Table 16.1 A socialization and an institutional approach to voluntary organizations and social capital: hypotheses for empirical examination

	Socialization perspective	Institutional perspective
Research question		
[1] Effect of organizational affiliation?	Yes	Yes
[2] *Intensity:* Active members higher levels of social capital than passive?	Yes	No
[3] *Intensity vs. scope:* High intensity more important than broad scope of participation?	Yes	No
[4] *Type:* Non-political, horizontal groups more valuable than conflict-oriented, "vertical" groups?	Yes	No
[5] Stronger effects at micro- or macro-level?	Equal	Macro-level
[6] Perception of value of organizations or participation in organizations?	Participation	Both (interplay): the fewer the personal links to organizations, the more important perception becomes

social capital through organizational activity, as passive members are not exposed to face-to-face interaction. In an institutional perspective, members will tend to have somewhat higher levels of social capital than non-members as their linkages to organizations provide them with direct representation by the organization, moderated views resulting from cross-pressures, and more direct knowledge about what the organization does. The main distinction is between the organized and the non-organized, not between those exposed to social contact and those who participate by proxy. Consequently, active and passive affiliations should yield similar levels of social capital (research question [2] in the table).

Rather than the *intensity* of the involvement, an institutional perspective stresses its *scope* ([3] in Table 16.1): the more linkages, the better. Thus, a passive member of two associations should have higher social capital than an active member of one. By contrast, Putnam (2000a, p. 58) asserts that the number of passive memberships does not compensate for the lack of direct involvement. In this perspective, active members of one association should have higher social capital than passive members of several, and societies characterized by numerous passive members should display *lower* levels of social capital than societies with fewer, but more active members.

Putnam also attributes particular importance to non-political, "horizontal" associations (research question [4] in the table), as they provide plenty of opportunities for social interaction and recruit across societal divisions. By contrast, interest groups, unions, and political organizations are seen as divisive and their role for social capital formation is frequently downplayed (Foley and Edwards 1996). Thus, from Putnam's perspective, those affiliated with non-political associations should possess higher levels of social capital than members of other types of groups. Furthermore, societies characterized by many non-political organizations should score highest on social capital in aggregate terms (Putnam 1993).

However, bowling clubs and music choirs are unlikely to counterweigh state dominance or act as intermediary, democratic institutions (Berman 1997; Foley and Edwards 1996; Quigley 1996; Rueschemeyer et al. 1998). Their frequently localist nature – in a sense, their very "horizontality" – makes them less visible and less useful as a civic infrastructure than federated, hierarchical groups (Skocpol 2003). Moreover, pluralists would assert that the supposedly negative effect of memberships in conflict-oriented groups is reduced if memberships are multiple and overlapping. From an institutional perspective, therefore, we would expect that nonpolitical "Putnam groups" (Knack and Keefer 1997) are *less* productive sources of social capital than organizations that are more conflict oriented and outward reaching.

In a socialization perspective, social capital is developed at the individual level and mirrored at the aggregate level (cf. Putnam 1993, 2000a). Consequently, similar effects should emerge at the micro- and macro-levels at comparable magnitudes. In an institutional perspective, by contrast, variations between communities should be much larger than within communities (research question [5] above). As personal experiences are secondary to the prevalence of organizations in a society, non-members in communities with encompassing voluntary sectors should display higher levels of social capital than members in weak organizational societies.

Stronger effects at the macro-level than the micro-level would give support to an institutional perspective. However, such results would not give direct information about the causal link at the micro-level. In order to get at this relationship, we introduce one additional test (research question [6] in Table 16.1): if the main contribution of organizations to social capital lies in demonstrating the value of collective action and providing the infrastructure for such pursuits, it should be *sufficient* for individuals to be *convinced* that organizations fulfil these functions in order to develop the desired values. This implies, first, that belief in the efficacy of organizations is an independent path to generalized trust, which is more important if personal linkages to organizational society are weak. Second, assuming the sufficiency of perceptions, personal participation is not necessary for trust levels among those who do believe in the efficacy of organizations. In statistical terms, we expect interplay between scope of participation and perceptions of the usefulness of organizations on generalized trust. By contrast, from a socialization perspective, if a correlation between perceptions of organizations and social trust exists, this is a spurious effect of the fact that those intensely involved in organizations hold more positive views of their efficacy.

Data and Operationalizations

The main data source of the present study is the European Social Survey (ESS). This is a cross-national individual survey undertaken in 2002/2003 (Jowell 2003).[2]

---

[2]The data has been made available by the Norwegian Social Science Data Services (NSD). Neither NSD nor the central coordinating team of the European Social Survey bears any responsibility for the analyses and the inferences from the analyses made here.

The 19 European countries (the former EU-15 plus Norway, Poland, Slovenia, and Hungary), which included reliable questions about associational activity and qualify as democracies, were selected for the analysis.[3] Face-to-face interviews were the main mode of data collection. Response rates varied from 43.7% (Italy) to 80.0% (Greece), with an average of 62.4% (NSD 2003). For the aggregate analyses, the 19 countries were divided into 141 regions, following the regional classifications made by ESS local associates, which was based on the NUTS taxonomy.[4] Regions with fewer than 100 unweighted responses were merged with adjacent regions.[5] For the final analysis concerning perceptions of the efficacy of organizations, the Norwegian Citizen Involvement Survey (2001) was utilized (Strømsnes 2003). This was conducted as a mailed survey, with a response rate of 46% and a net sample size of 2,297.

The *independent variables* are measurements of the scope, intensity, and type of association involvement. Scope is operationalized as the number of associations with which each individual is affiliated. The scope of involvement includes memberships, volunteering, and participation in activities. If a person has reported several modes of participation for the same type of association, this is only counted once. The intensity of the involvement is measured as active participation or volunteering for the organization over the past 12 months. The type of affiliations is classified into three groups, more or less following Knack and Keefer's (1997) distinction between horizontal, non-political "Putnam groups," and more politically oriented "Olson groups," the latter with reference to Mancur Olson's (1982) work on interest organizations. The Putnam groups include cultural/hobby activities, social clubs, sports and outdoors activities, and humanitarian organizations. Olson groups include science/education/teacher's organizations, trade unions, professional organizations, consumer's organizations, and political parties. Our classification deviates from Knack and Keefer on one point, as they, under doubt, include religious associations among the "Putnam groups." However, while Putnam (2000a, p. 67) sees religiosity as a factor contributing to civic engagement, he also states that religious organizations in some contexts (e.g., Southern Italy) may be counterproductive to social capital (Putnam 1993). Consequently, this group is kept apart as a separate third category.

The main *dependent* variable is a three-item index measuring generalized trust based on saved scores from a factor analysis requesting a one-factor solution. The trust index includes the following three items (measured by 11-point self-placement scales): "Most people can be trusted vs. you cannot be careful enough," "Most people try to be helpful vs. mostly looking out for themselves," and "Most people try to be fair vs. try to take advantage of me" (Cronbach's alpha = 0.77 for 19-country sample, 0.81 for Norwegian sample).

---

[3] The Czech Republic and Switzerland are excluded because of errors in the questionnaire design with regard to questions on organizational participation (NSD 2003).

[4] NUTS, nomenclature of territorial units for statistics; http://europa.eu.int/comm/eurostat/nuts/splash_regions.html

[5] Exceptions were made for Sardinia (Italy), Northern Ireland (UK), the Canary Islands (Spain), and Bornholm (Denmark) to which there are no adjacent regions.

The *control variables* in the micro-level analysis include standard sociodemo-graphic variables (age, education, gender, marital status, and population density). We also control for trust in law and order institutions, which is emphasized as a major explanation of interpersonal trust by scholars in the institutional vein (Rothstein 2002, 2004; Rothstein and Stolle 2003). This is represented by a sim-ple additive two-item index consisting of trust in the police and the legal system, ranging from 0 (no trust) to 10 (very high trust) (Cronbach's alpha = 0.75 for entire 19-country sample, 0.76 for Norwegian data).

For the macro-analysis, we have control for a number of factors that have been found to affect levels of social capital: ethnic diversity (Knack and Keefer 1997; Putnam 2002), socioeconomic inequality (Uslaner 2003), levels of religiosity (Offe and Fuchs 2002; Putnam 2000a), education (Haddad 2004; Putnam 2000a), and urbanization (Putnam 2000a, p. 284).

Empirical Analysis: Individual-Level Data

The regression analysis, undertaken at the regional as well as the European level, shows weak, but statistically significant effects of affiliation. Its explanatory power increases when the analysis is extended to the whole of Europe, thus including the highest (Nordic) and lowest (Southern European) ranking countries on both trust and participation. The face-to-face hypothesis is rejected in Southern Europe, where active members are slightly *less* trusting than their passive counterparts. Only in Western Europe do we find a weak, positive effect of intensity. However, scope and type (Putnam group) do not fare much better. Both show weakly positive effects at the European level, which are significant because of the gigantic sample size. Both are irrelevant in Eastern Europe and the Nordic countries (Table 16.2).

Institutional trust is by far the most important predictor of social trust emanat-ing from the regression analysis. This gives empirical credence to the claims of Rothstein and Stolle (2003). We are not able to resolve here whether it is the impar-tiality of the law that makes us trust other people more. A "Putnamian" response would be that pervasive generalized trust in a society creates well-functioning insti-tutions, which people in turn are more likely to trust. In any case, a crucial part of this argument, namely, the link between face-to-face interaction and social trust, is weakened for every new empirical test.

Delving more deeply into the results for each country reveals that members and volunteers are more trusting than outsiders in 17 of the 19 countries (not shown). Spain and Portugal represent the only exceptions. Comparing only those who are affiliated, the scope has weak, but significant effects in nine of the countries. In only five countries does active involvement play any positive role, while it is *negatively* related to trust levels in Spain and Italy.

Furthermore, variations between countries are much larger than within-country variation. Non-members in Norway, Finland, and Denmark are more trusting than active members of several associations in any country outside Scandinavia. The

Table 16.2 OLS regression analysis of generalized trust, standardized coefficients

	Eastern Europe		Nordic countries		Southern Europe		Western Europe		Central Europe		All	
	Model		Model		Model		Model		Model		Model	
	1	2	1	2	1	2	1	2	1	2	1	2
Affiliated	0.07**		0.05*		0.09**		0.07**		0.07**		0.15**	
Intensity		0.04		0.01		-0.05**		0.06**		0.003		0.001
Scope		0.02		0.04		0.05**		0.01		0.03*		0.06**
Type (P-group)		0.05		0.02		0.02		0.04**		0.04**		0.04**
Institutional trust	0.26**	0.29**	0.34**	0.33**	0.19**	0.22**	0.34**	0.34**	0.29**	0.29**	0.28**	0.31**
Education	0.10**	0.09**	0.09**	0.08**	0.12**	0.13**	0.07**	0.06**	0.10**	0.10**	0.12**	0.10**
Female	0.04**	0.05	0.09**	0.10**	0.01	-0.01	0.01	0.04**	0.03**	0.05**	0.03**	0.04**
Year of birth	0.04*	0.05	-0.08**	-0.09**	-0.01	-0.01	-0.12**	-0.14**	-0.01	0.004	-0.05**	-0.05**
Urban-rural	-0.04*	0.01	0.02	0.02	0.05**	0.01	0.06**	0.04**	0.02*	-0.01	0.03**	0.03**
Married	-0.05**	0.05	0.02	0.01	-0.01	-0.02	0.02	0.02	-0.01	-0.02	-0.03**	-0.02**
R^2 adjusted	0.10	0.11	0.15	0.15	0.07	0.07	0.15	0.15	0.11	0.11	0.14	0.13

Weighted by population size and design weight. Model 1 includes all respondents, model 2 only those affiliated with organizations.
* $p \leq .05$, ** $p \leq .01$.

Southern European countries display the lowest levels of social trust. As the same countries score high on participation as well as trust, the effects of being affiliated are higher when analyzing Europe as a whole than any single country. However, even at the European level, intensity of involvement remains irrelevant.

Aggregate Data

Above, we saw that variations in levels of trust between countries were much larger than the individual variations within each country. To recap, this is in line with our hypothesis, which suggests weak micro-effects of participation and strong institutional effects visible only at the aggregate level. In the following section, we explore the relationship at the aggregate level (141 European regions) in more detail.

The almost perfect correlation between generalized trust and the scope of organizational life is visualized in Fig. 16.1. The Nordic regions rank highest on both measures, followed by Western and Central Europe and finally Eastern and Southern Europe. The main outlier is Alentejo and Algarve in Southern Portugal, where trust

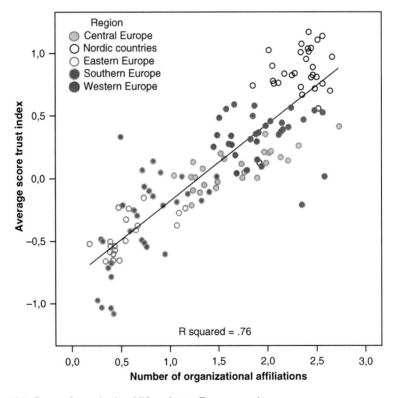

Fig. 16.1 Scope of organizational life and trust, European regions

is much higher than organizational participation should suggest. As an example of the opposite, the two Belgian regions of Wallonia and Brussels display lower-than-average values of trust, while organizational life is strong. One reasonable explanation for this deviation is the strong cultural divide between the Flemish and French-speaking groups in Belgian society, divisions that are reproduced and reinforced through economic disparities and separate organizational societies (Lijphart 1984).

Does this relationship hold in multivariate analysis? Table 16.3 shows regression analyses at the regional level. Model 1 includes only the control variables, which combined explain 56% of the variance. When institutional trust is included in model 2, r^2 increases to 70%, while the introduction of the organizational participation data elevates the explained variance even further, to 82%.

The analysis confirms the existence of an intimate relationship between the strength of organizational society and social capital; even when controlling for a wide array of factors, the proportion of the population holding membership in organizations represents the single most powerful predictor of social trust. The activity

Table 16.3 OLS regression analysis of social capital at the regional level, standardized coefficients

	Trust		
	Model 1	Model 2	Model 3
Percentage of population who are members			0.56***
Scope[a]			0.15*
Intensity[b]			0.008
Type (Putnam)[c]			–0.08*
Institutional trust		0.44***	0.17***
Diversity[d]	–0.14**	–0.08	–0.19***
Educational levels[e]	0.28***	0.27***	0.05
Inequality[f]	–0.43***	–0.15*	–0.02
Urbanization[g]	–0.07	–0.12**	–0.04
Religiosity[h]	–0.22***	–0.36***	–0.19***
R^2 adjusted	0.56	0.70	0.82
N=140 regions[i]			

* $p \leq .10$, ** $p \leq .05$, *** $p \leq .01$.
[a]Percentage of affiliations which are multiple.
[b]Percentage of affiliations which are active.
[c]Percentage of affiliations which are "Putnam group" memberships.
[d]Three-item index: percentage speaking another language than the majority language at home, percentage belonging to other religious denominations than the majority religion, percentage who reported that they or one of their parents were born in another country.
[e]Percentage aged 25–59 with at least upper secondary level education.
[f]Regional Theil's *t*-statistic on pay inequalities between sectors: Galbraith and Garcilazo (2005).
[g]Percentage living in large cities or suburbs.
[h]Self-placement scale (1–10) on which the respondents were asked to assess their own religiosity.
[i]Luxembourg excluded because of lack of inequality data.
All measures except inequality aggregated from survey responses.

level of the sector and the proportion of affiliations that were "Putnam groups" proved once again to be more or less irrelevant, while extensive multiple memberships has a slight positive effect on trust. Thus, the institutional interpretation of the role of organizations in social capital construction is strengthened, while the socialization approach is weakened.

In summary, a broad organizational society emerges as the main explanation for variations in generalized trust across regions, followed by trust in institutions. The effects of pervasive organizational life are much stronger at the aggregate than at the individual level. This indicates that organizations contribute to the formation of social capital, not mainly through socialization of individuals, but as institutions entrenching in a population the value and rationality of cooperation.

Testing the Causal Link at the Micro-level

Establishing this empirical connection at the aggregate level is of course insufficient to identifying underlying causal mechanisms. As mentioned above, the finding that perceptions of the effectiveness of organizations have an independent effect on social trust would strengthen the case for an institutional theory of social capital formation through organizations.

Table 16.4 shows that this is indeed the case: those who believe that one can influence decisions effectively in society by working in voluntary organizations are also more trusting than others, independent of individual participation pattern.

In addition, we find the anticipated interaction effect between personal attachments to organizations and perceptions of the efficacy of organizations, as illustrated in the figure attached to Table 16.4. Among those who are attached to organizational society with several links, perceptions of the utility of organizations hardly matter at all. However, for those who have weaker ties to organizational life, believing that organizations are effective tools of collective action is highly important for levels of social trust. Those who have faith in the available organizational infrastructure are more trusting, irrespective of personal linkages to, or experiences with, organizations. Once again, intensity of involvement, here measured as time spent in the association, proves to be irrelevant to social trust. Thus, the impact of individual behavior is at best secondary to the role organizations play as institutions in the development of social capital.

Discussion and Conclusion

Table 16.5 summarizes the main findings. Except for the overall effect of being affiliated to organizations, a hypothesis shared by the socialization and institutional perspectives, none of the assertions of the socialization perspective were backed by the data. Active members did not display higher levels of social capital than their

Table 16.4 Assessment of organizations as intermediary structures and generalized trust (NSD 2001), OLS regression, standardized coefficients

Intermediary (assessment of organizations as intermediary structures)[a]	0.20**
Scope	0.22**
Scope*intermediary	−0.20**
Intensity[b]	0.004
Type (Putnam group)[c]	0.03
Institutional trust (police, judiciary)	0.25**
Education[d]	0.07**
Female	0.14**
Year of birth	−0.17**
Married/co-habitant	0.09**
Urban–rural[e]	−0.007
R^2 adjusted	0.21
N	1,607

Influence decisions in society effectively by working in voluntary organizations

*$p \leq .05$, **$p \leq .01$.
[a]Agreement with statement "Influence decisions in society effectively by: Working in voluntary organizations" (self-placement scale [0] Not effective at all, [10] Very effective).
[b]Categorized measure of time spent participating in voluntary associations over the past year: (1) 0–1 h, (2) 1–4 h, (3) 5–10 h, (4) 11–20 h, (5) 20 h or more.
[c]Affiliated with "Putnam group" (dummy).
[d]Years of full-time schooling.
[e]Nine-value ordinal measure.

passive counterparts. Activity level was not more important than scope of affiliations, although the effect of the latter at the micro-level was admittedly modest. Members of non-political organizations were no more trusting than members of other types of organizations, and trust in public institutions mattered a great deal to the development of social trust.

As predicted by the institutional perspective, the same effects that were found at the micro-level surfaced at the macro-level as well, but in greater magnitude. Here as well, activity levels and type of associations were unrelated to social capital formation, while the scope of organizational life in a region proved to be a crucial explanatory variable. Finally, perceiving organizations as useful tools of collective action was sufficient to raise levels of social trust, irrespective of organizational behavior. In accordance with expectations, this effect was amplified among those with non-existent or few ties to organizational life.

Table 16.5 Summary of findings

	Socialization perspective	Institutional perspective	Empirical result
Research question			
[1] Effect of organizational affiliation?	Yes	Yes	Yes
[2] *Intensity:* Active members higher levels of social capital than passive?	Yes	No	No
[3] *Intensity vs. scope:* High intensity more important than broad scope of participation?	Yes	No	No
[4] *Type:* Non-political, horizontal groups more valuable than conflict-oriented, "vertical" groups?	Yes	No	No
[5] Stronger effects at micro- or macro-level?	Equal	Macro-level	Macro-level
[6] Perception of value of organizations or participation in organizations?	Participation	Both/interplay	Both/interplay

Thus, there is nothing in the data to suggest that the relationship between organizations and social capital has anything to do with the face-to-face social interaction that takes place within such organizations. As Hooghe (2003) argues, the theoretical basis for this claim was thin to begin with: it is not self-evident that we would generalize from trust in people we know within a group to people in general. The social psychological literature on group interaction does not support the idea that repeated interaction increases general trust in outsiders; rather, experiments point in the opposite direction (Hooghe 2003, p. 92). If repeated interaction in fact *did* generate trust, it would be tough to defend the view that organizations represent a more important sphere than the workplace, schools, neighborhoods, and so forth, where we spend a much larger proportion of our time.

This chapter indicates that the organizational socialization perspective on the formation of trust is a dead-end. However, analysis indicates that the role of organizations is misconstrued rather than exaggerated. We need to reconceptualize a relationship that the present analysis shows is unquestionably present, but insufficiently understood. This is a pressing task, as misapprehensions of how organizations create social capital may lead us to focus on the wrong types of organizations and activities and prescribe wrong or even harmful remedies for civic revitalization (Skocpol 2003). There is nothing in the data to suggest that a revival of locally oriented social clubs offering plenty of face-to-face interaction and social contact will help. They do not seem to make their members more trusting over time. Furthermore, Eliasoph's (2003) account of how localist, non-political volunteering organizations may foster a culture of civic apathy and delegitimize and curtail political discussion is a timely reminder that laying the burden of maintaining democracy on the shoulders of such groups may not be such a good idea.

The present results indicate that if social capital is to be sustained, what a society needs is extrovert, visible organizations that act as real intermediary institutions between citizen and polity, and individual and society. In order to fulfil these functions, associations need to provide translocal links reaching beyond local communities and into the political system (Skocpol 1996, 2003; Wollebæk and Selle 2002a). They would also need to do more than providing arenas for social interaction – and actually get involved in political life. The preoccupation with whether organizational members are meeting face-to-face or not appears increasingly irrelevant. Needless to say, this does not mean that people should be encouraged to be passive. Most organizational societies rely on the time and efforts of activists, without whom organizations would be weakened as institutions. What the above analyses shows is simply that the externalities of the efforts they are putting in are incomparably greater than the effect the activity has on them personally.

A shift from a socialization to an institutional perspective implies changing the focus from looking for catalysts or vehicles of social capital to analyzing how social capital is conserved and strengthened and how it is destructed. The findings above suggest that the prominence of visible institutions in civil society is highly consequential. Such institutions are not shaped by social encounters, but by history, social context, and politics. This is the realm within which the study of social capital in the context of democracy should remain.

References

Berman, S. (1997). Civil society and the collapse of the Weimar Republic. *World Politics*, 49(3), 401–429.

Booth, J. A., and Richard, P. B. (2001). Civil society and political context in Central America. In B. Edwards, M. W. Foley, and M. Diani (eds) *Beyond Tocqueville: Civil Society and the Social Capital Debate in Comparative Perspective* (pp. 43–55), Hanover, NH, University Press of New England.

Claibourn, M., and Martin, P. (2000). Trusting and joining? An empirical test of the reciprocal nature of social capital. *Political Behavior*, 22(4), 269–291.

Dekker, P., and van den Broek, A. (1998). Civil society in comparative perspective: Involvement in voluntary associations in North America and Western Europe. *Voluntas*, 9(1), 11–38.

Eliasoph, N. (2003). Cultivating apathy in voluntary associations. In P. Dekker and L. Halman (eds) *The Values of Volunteering: Cross-Cultural Perspectives* (pp. 199–212), New York, Kluwer Academic/Plenum Publishers.

Foley, M. W., and Edwards, B. (1996). The paradox of civil society. *Journal of Democracy*, 7(3), 38–52.

Freitag, M. (2003). Social capital in (dis)similar democracies: The development of generalised trust in Japan and Switzerland. *Comparative Political Studies*, 36(8), 936–966.

Galbraith, J., and Garcilazo, E. (2005). Pay inequality in Europe 1995–2000: Convergence between countries and stabilities inside. UTIP Working paper 30, http://utip.gov.utexas.edu/papers/utip_30.pdf

Haddad, M. A. (2004). Community determinates of volunteer participation and the promotion of civic health: The case of Japan. *Nonprofit and Voluntary Sector Quarterly*, 33(S3), 8–31.

Hooghe, M. (2003). Voluntary associations and democratic attitudes: Value congruence as a causal mechanism. In M. Hooghe and D. Stolle (eds) *Generating Social Capital* (pp. 89–112), New York, Palgrave Macmillan.

Hyggen, C. (2006). Risk and resources: Social capital among social assistance recipients in Norway. *Social Policy & Administration*, 40(5), 493–508.

Jowell, J. (2003). *European Social Survey 2002–2003: Technical Report*, Centre for Comparative Social Surveys, City University, London.

Juknevičius, S., and Savicka, A. (2003). From restitution to innovation: Volunteering in postcommunist countries. In P. Dekker and L. Halman (eds) *The Values of Volunteering: Cross-Cultural Perspectives* (pp. 127–142), New York, Kluwer Academic/Plenum Publishers.

Knack, S., and Keefer, P. (1997). Does social capital have an economic payoff? A cross-country investigation. *The Quarterly Journal of Economics*, 12(4), 1251–1288.

Lijphart, A. (1984). *Democracies: Patterns of Majoritarian and Consensus Government in Twenty-One Countries,* New Haven, Yale University Press.

Macpherson, C. B. (1977). *The Life and Times of Liberal Democracy*, Oxford, Oxford University Press.

Mayer, N. (2003). Democracy in France: Do associations matter? In M. Hooghe and D. Stolle (eds) *Generating Social Capital: Civil Society and Institutions in Comparative Perspective* (pp. 43–76), New York, Palgrave Macmillan.

Mutz, D. C. (2002). Cross-cutting social networks: Testing democratic theory in practice. *American Political Science Review*, 96(1), 111–126.

NSD. (2003). *ESS Documentation Report 2002/2003,* 5th edn, Bergen, Norwegian Social Sciences Data Services.

Ødegård, G. (2006). *Ungdom og demokratiskolering, Vedlegg 2 i NOU 2006:13*, Oslo, Barne og familiedepartementet.

Offe, C., and Fuchs, S. (2002). A decline in social capital? The German case. In R. D. Putnam and K. Goss (eds) *Democracies in Flux* (pp. 189–244), New York, Oxford University Press.

Olson, M. (1982). *The Rise and Decline of Nations,* New Haven, Yale University Press.

Pateman, C. (1970). *Participation and Democratic Theory*, Cambridge, Cambridge University Press.

Putnam, R. D. (1993). *Making Democracy Work: Civic Traditions in Modern Italy*, Princeton, NJ, Princeton University Press.

Putnam, R. D. (2000a). *Bowling Alone: The Collapse and Revival of American Community*, New York, Simon & Schuster.

Putnam, R. D. (2000b). Introduction: What's troubling the trilateral democracies? In S. Pharr and R. D. Putnam (eds) *Disaffected Democracies* (pp. 3–30), Princeton, NJ, Princeton University Press.

Putnam, R. D. (2002). Conclusion. In R. D. Putnam and K. Goss (eds) *Democracies in Flux* (pp. 393–416), New York, Oxford University Press.

Quigley, K. F. F. (1996). Human bonds and social capital. *Orbis*, 40(2), 333–343.

Rokkan, S. (1967). Geography, religion and social class: Crosscutting cleavages in Norwegian politics. In S. M. Lipset and S. Rokkan (eds) *Party Systems and Voter Alignments* (pp. 367–444), New York, The Free Press.

Rothstein, B. (2002). Social capital in the social democratic state. In R. D. Putnam (ed.) *Democracies in Flux* (pp. 289–332), New York, Oxford University Press.

Rothstein, B. (2004). Social capital and institutional legitimacy: The Corleone connection. In S. Prakash and P. Selle (eds) *Investigating Social Capital: Comparative Perspectives on Civil Society, Participation and Governance* (pp. 113–136), New Delhi, Sage.

Rothstein, B., and Stolle, D. (2003). Social capital, impartiality and the welfare state: An institutional approach. In M. Hooghe and D. Stolle (eds) *Generating Social Capital* (pp. 191–210), New York, Palgrave Macmillan.

Rueschemeyer, D., Rueschemeyer, M., and Wittrock, B. (eds) (1998). *Participation and Democracy East and West: Comparisons and Interpretations*, Armonk, NY, M. E. Sharpe.

Skocpol, T. (1996). Unraveling from above. *The American Prospect*, 25, March–April, 20–25.

Skocpol, T. (2003). *Diminished Democracy*, Norman, University of Oklahoma Press.

Stolle, D. (2001). Clubs and congregations: The benefits of joining an association. In K. Cook (ed.) *Trust in Society* (pp. 202–244), New York, Russell Sage Foundation.

Stolle, D. (2003). The sources of social capital. In M. Hooghe and D. Stolle (eds) *Generating Social Capital* (pp. 19–42), New York, Palgrave Macmillan.

Strømsnes, K. (2003). *Folkets Makt,* Oslo, Gyldendal Akademisk.

Tocqueville, A. de (1968). *Democracy in America*, ed. J. P. Mayer and M. Lerner (a new translation by G. Lawrence), London, Collins.

Uslaner, E. M. (2003). Trust, democracy and governance: Can government policies influence generalised trust? In M. Hooghe and D. Stolle (eds) *Generating Social Capital* (pp. 171–190), New York, Palgrave Macmillan.

von Erlach, E. (2005). Politisierung in Vereinen. Eine empirische Studie zum Zusammenhang zwischen der Vereinsmitgliedschaft und der Teilnahme an politischen Diskussionen. *Swiss Political Science Review*, 11(3), 27–59.

Wollebæk, D., and Selle, P. (2002a). *Det nye organisasjonssamfunnet: demokrati i omforming, (The New Organization Society: Democracy in Transition)*, Fagbokforl, Bergen.

Wollebæk, D., and Selle, P. (2002b). Does participation in voluntary associations contribute to social capital? The impact of intensity, scope, and type. *Nonprofit and Voluntary Sector Quarterly*, 30(1), 32–61.

Wollebæk, D., and Selle, P. (2007). The origins of social capital: Socialisation and institutionalisation approaches compared. *Journal of Civil Society*, 3(1), 1–14.

Wollebæk, D., and Strømsnes, K. (2008). Voluntary associations, trust and civic engagement: A multi-level approach. *Nonprofit and Voluntary Sector Quarterly*, 37(2), 249–263.

Chapter 17
Transforming Democracy?

Marilyn Taylor

Introduction

The 1990s hailed a new dawn for democracy, with the first free elections in the post-Soviet countries and in South Africa. Yet even as television flashed pictures of the long queues of first time voters in South Africa around the world, the quality of democracy in the more established democracies was coming under increasing scrutiny (Putnam 2000; Skocpol 2003). Voting figures in many Western democracies were plummeting, as were levels of trust in government. Governing elites were seen as increasingly professionalized and divorced from their citizens. Meanwhile, globalization was said to be "hollowing out" the nation state with citizens at the mercy of forces beyond their control.

The response of the state in many established democracies has been an expansion of the participatory sphere (Cornwall 2008a), with the growth of new mechanisms for participation and the development of new governance spaces in which nongovernmental actors are invited to participate. As it has become clear in a globalizing world that the state no longer has the resources, knowledge, or legitimacy to govern on its own (Kooiman 2003; Stoker 1998), hierarchical forms of government are said to be giving way to networked forms of governance.

This has been paralleled by a growing interest in "civil society" – a concept with a long and distinguished history but one that had attracted relatively little attention in contemporary debate prior to the 1990s. In part this new interest arose in the aftermath of the struggles against socialism in the Soviet bloc, where civil society was hailed as a major driver of change; in part, it arose from the ideologically quite different struggles against authoritarian regimes in other parts of the world, notably in Latin America. More generally, civil society offered a counterbalance to the forces of global capitalism and the market; it also offered a response to "the crisis of development" (Salamon 1995, pp. 256–258), i.e., the inability of weak states to address the needs of their populations. A further factor in the rediscovery of civil

M. Taylor (✉)
University of West England, Bristol, UK
e-mail: marilyn.taylor@uwe.ac.uk

R. Taylor (ed.), *Third Sector Research*, DOI 10.1007/978-1-4419-5707-8_17,
© Springer Science+Business Media, LLC 2010

society was the growing phenomenon of "globalization from below," as increased use of the Internet facilitated the emergence of the World Social Forum, global social movements, and large-scale popular demonstrations at meetings of world leaders.

Civil society is, of course, a highly contested term. As Zimmer has explained elsewhere (2009), it can be used – following Habermas – to denote a societal arena for discussion, deliberation, and public discourse, which operates beyond any organizational infrastructure and embeddedness. In this sense, attention has also focused on Gramscian ideas of civil society as the arena in which the struggle for hegemony unfolds and where counter-hegemonic groups can gain strength. But the term has alternatively come to be used in both policy and academic circles to describe the world of associations and NGOs – as distinct from the state or the market. In this latter sense, "understood as the realm of private voluntary association, from neighbourhood committees to interest groups to philanthropic enterprises of all sorts," civil society has come to be seen as "an essential ingredient in both democratisation and the health of established democracies" (Foley and Edwards 1996, p. 38), a view endorsed in Zimmer's chapter in this volume.

Drawing on the earlier work of Almond and Verba (1963) and Berger and Neuhaus (1977), scholars have highlighted the potential of the sector to act as a mediating structure between the state and the citizen, while some have even argued for a new "associative" form of democracy (Hirst 1997). In the United States, Lester Salamon hailed the global associational revolution (1995) and Robert Putnam (1993) celebrated the role of associations as a central component in building the social capital that, he argued, made democracy work. Later Putnam was to make a direct link between the crisis of democracy in the United States and the decline in associational activity, building on a long theoretical tradition in that country from the work of Alexis de Tocqueville onward (Putnam 2000).

So to what extent does the third sector have the potential to reinvigorate or even transform democracy? This chapter first reviews different models of democracy and the role of the third sector in each. It then considers the challenges that third sector organizations (TSOs) face if they are to contribute to the transformation of democracy in the twenty-first century.

Models of Democracy

In understanding the role the third sector can play in democracy, we need first to agree what democracy is. Scholte (2002, p. 285) defines it as "a condition where a community of people exercises collective self-determination [*taking*] decisions that shape their destiny jointly, with equal rights and opportunities of participation and without arbitrarily imposed constraints on debate."

Foley and Hodgkinson (2003) have mapped developments in thinking about Western democracy. They start from the Athenian concept of direct democracy whereby all citizens (i.e., free men) were engaged in decision-making in the city state. As the polity expanded, however, this became increasingly impractical. Liberal democracy emerged at national level as a qualified form of representative democracy based on popular elections and individual rights. This form of representative democracy remains a dominant model, although it takes different forms. In its purist neoliberal form – which in contemporary society privileges the role of the market – it advocates a minimal state, but democratic socialist and social democratic forms allow for a more prominent state role and at least a mixed economy of welfare, in the interests of social justice. However, as many critics have pointed out, this form of representative democracy still leaves power in the hands of an elite, with citizens only able to exercise their right to choose between elites every few years. Furthermore, as Saward (2005, p. 181) argues, representation is a blunt medium for the expression of the diverse preferences in society: "Traditional geographical constituencies do not have characteristics, faultlines and policy preferences that can be simply ... read-off by would-be elected representatives."

Pluralist models of democracy by contrast (e.g., Dahl 1989) recognize the diversity of interests within society, allowing equal competition between interest groups with the state acting as neutral arbiter. The overlapping nature of citizen interests, the pluralists argue, helps to ensure cohesion. However, this analysis fails to address the resource imbalances within society or ways in which superior stocks of social, political, and economic capital still privilege the elite. In addition, rather than being a neutral arbiter, critics argue that the state protects dominant economic and elite interests. Corporatism is a particular form of pluralism (see Zimmer, Chapter 15), in which potentially fragmented and conflicting interests are institutionalized along religious or economic lines through peak organizations that are incorporated into the policy-making process (Schmitter 1974). However, this too privileges certain interests over others. In addition, it offers no guarantee against elitism – with peak organizations themselves bureaucratic and undemocratic.

Critics of these various systems have called for new approaches to democracy in the twenty-first century. The state's response, as we have seen, has been a move from government to governance, which, in theory at least, opens up policy communities to a wider spread of actors (Rhodes 1997). As the limitations of the state have become increasingly apparent, new participatory spaces have been established "at a distance from the state" into which a range of new actors have been invited to engage in governing. At one end of the governance spectrum, policy communities may remain quite closed; at the other a range of participatory mechanisms has developed, providing opportunities for citizens to engage at many different levels.

Some have hailed this as "the ultimate in hands-off government" (Rhodes 1997, p. 110); others – following Foucault and Bourdieu – describe how these spaces reinforce existing flows of power (for a summary see Taylor 2007). They argue that new governance spaces remain inscribed with the agendas of the elite who, as we have seen, bring into these spaces stocks of social, economic, political, and symbolic capital that other players cannot match. Thus, their agendas continue to frame operating assumptions and debate. New technologies of governing operate to secure the "willing compliance" of participants, ensuring that policy communities operate according to common norms and assumptions, framing and addressing problems in similar ways (Atkinson 1999). In this way, Carmel and Harlock (2008) argue, the third sector is instituted as a "governable terrain," while Rose describes how, as community has become a new site of governance, the "community discourse" has "hi-jacked a language of resistance and transformed it into an expert discourse and professional vocation" (Rose 1999, p. 175).

An alternative approach has been to argue for "associative" forms of democracy. In the 1990s, Hirst proposed "a new democratic welfare system based on provision through self-governing associations" (1997, p. 16). This system would not replace the state or market exchange but anchor these institutions in self-governing bodies answerable to those who serve and those who participate in them (ibid, p. 17). Drawing on ideas which go back to de Tocqueville, this model resonates with the communitarian ideal of self-governing communities, which would enable all their members to participate in collective processes affecting their lives. However, while it does see a continued role for the state, this model does not adequately address the question of coordination, on the one hand, or the conflicts that are inherent in the associational world, on the other. In addition, as Fung and Wright (2003) point out, associative democracy, like other models, can have its "thin" or "deep" versions. They warn of the risks of elite domination or capture, of "balkanisation," of unrealistically high expectations in relation to popular commitment, and of unsustainability (see also Gaventa 2006, p. 20).

David Held's model of "democratic autonomy" allows a greater role for the state, but argues for the development of self-managed enterprises "which allow their members control of the resources at their disposal without direct interference from the state, political agencies or other third parties" (Held 1996, p. 323). However, Held raises questions about the precise bundle of rights and opportunities that citizens would have to accept in such a system as well as the relationship between associations and direct forms of democracy. He is also concerned that such a model would blur the boundary between the polity on the one hand and the everyday life of citizens on the other, thus risking undue intrusion of public regulation and control into the "life-world" (Habermas 1984).

These models are concerned with the *structures* of policy- and decision-making. There are also a number of streams of thought which address the *processes* of decision-making. In an influential critique of the narrow instrumental rationality that dominates decision-making in liberal democracies, Habermas (1984) promotes instead a "communicative rationality," whereby societal decisions would be based on ongoing dialogue and the development of mutual understanding between different interests in an "ideal speech" situation, i.e., between people who are equal in power and understanding and anchored in civil society. Cohen and Fung (2004, p. 24), in their work on deepening democracy, argue similarly for the "common reason of equal citizens as the dominant force in democratic life."

Some communitarians have adopted a parallel approach, advocating a form of cooperative inquiry as the basis for decision-making (Tam 1998).[1] However, while attractive as an ideal, it is not easy to see how such a dialogue would mediate the

---

[1] At the time of writing, Henry Tam is the UK government's lead civil servant on the English Community Empowerment strategy.

conflicting and fragmented interests in society. Deliberative forums often have the same problems as traditional representative mechanisms (Alonso and Costa 2004, p. 57), with the most affected groups outnumbered and lacking the knowledge, skills, and confidence that would enable them to participate. Citizens are not socialized into their new role in interactive decision-making (Verlet et al. 2007). In these circumstances, as Saward (1998, p. 2) argues, "Democracy is vulnerable to claims about people's knowledge of their own interests; even sympathetic critics argue that often there is a large gulf between citizen's preferences and their real interests."

Others look for a more fundamental transformation in democracy. Drawing on Ellison (1997), Leach and Scoones (2007, pp. 15, 18) maintain that "the multiplication of identities, affiliations and forms of solidarity" in a globalized world "requires the dissolving of more conventional boundaries between the public and private, the political and the social" with a more integrative vision of "practised engagement through emergent social solidarities." Saward (2005, p. 182) similarly argues for a new political imaginary with "new modes of non-electoral citizen engagement and interaction with policy makers and managers," which will "challenge received notions of public and private in terms of who the makers and recipients of policy are." He maintains that, in a post-statist globalized context that has no single center of authority, it is necessary to think in new ways, with mechanisms across boundaries that constitute new political communities. He advocates a form of "stakeholder governance," which would, he believes, enfranchise the previously marginalized, respond to intense interests that are not recognized by one person one vote systems, and also recognize emergent interests.

What role, then, can the third sector play in such a transformation? And can it help to address the criticisms of existing systems outlined above? The next section considers the roles that third sector organizations have played in different models of democracy and the roles it could play now in meeting the challenges of the twenty-first century.

The Third Sector as a Democratic Actor

Zimmer (2009) describes how civil society has been summoned up on a global scale as an antidote to the state and the market, providing complementary forms of representation and an institutional alternative for influencing and building public opinion and thus for policy-making. She goes on to describe how, in the European Union, much criticized for its democratic deficit, overtures to civil society – in the form of the third sector – have been used as a proxy for the transparency and democracy that the EU itself is said to lack. Scholars are, though, skeptical about the way in which civil society has been claimed as the saviour of democracy. Alexander (1998, p. 15), for example, describes the civil society discourse as largely "positive, progressive, emancipating and utopian," a use which may qualify it as a flag of convenience for all those who wish to claim these values, but which significantly reduces its explanatory power. Indeed, much has been written about the conflicts, insularity, and factionalism that characterize this sphere as well as the unequal power relations between its members (Foley and Edwards 1996; Taylor 2003).

While much of the civil society discourse may be seen as utopian, however, TSOs have undoubtedly played a variety of democratic roles across time and space. They may operate in collaboration with the state, working in partnership to formulate, develop, and implement policies. In this respect, they extend the legitimacy, knowledge, and resources available to the state and support both the formulation and the implementation of policy. Alternatively, they inform political debate, framing issues in new ways, bringing new issues onto the political agenda, challenging the existing hegemony, and expressing previously unheard voices. They mobilize citizens, creating an interested, informed, and aware public, which can contribute to society in many ways – as well as holding the state to account. The space for them to carry out these roles has varied over time and according to the dominant model of democracy (as Table 17.1 demonstrates).[2]

In the classic liberal model, TSOs are "outsiders" with a residual function addressing market or state failure (and, in a neoliberal model, reducing reliance on the state). They can, of course, try to influence policy through campaigning and lobbying but, as such, may be viewed at best as irrelevant and at worst as interfering in the policy process. In market liberalism, citizens are constructed as individual consumers and the operating logic is choice. TSOs have a role as competitors in the market, preferably without the advantages of tax benefits, and perhaps in addressing market failure (although this distorts the operation of the market, hence concerns about unfair competition). They may also have a role in providing advice and information to consumers. In a social democracy, they are more likely to function as the "junior partner in the welfare firm" (Owen 1966), complementing and supplementing state provision and contributing to the policy process. They also have a role in advising citizens how to access and negotiate state provision and have developed roles as watchdogs on the state, campaigning for neglected or emergent interests.

In a pluralist model, citizens are organized according to competing and overlapping interests, negotiating with each other and the state to reach an optimal equilibrium. TSOs clearly have a role in expressing, organizing, and advocating for different interests, as well as in making provision to meet the diversity of needs. In the corporatist model, as we have seen, the major interests in society are incorporated into the decision-making process and/or as major providers of welfare. In some countries, TSOs and their peak organizations have been key actors in such models (Salamon and Anheier 1998; Zimmer, Chapter 15). However, corporatism does not necessarily privilege the third sector and, where economic interests are privileged, may instead bypass it.

In the associative model, by contrast, it is the small association that is the dominant societal unit, bringing together its members as active citizens, generating social

---

[2]This bears some similarities to a table developed by Kendall (2009), who grouped third sector roles under three ideological headings, two of which – consumerist (market) and democratic revival (participatory) – are similar to the market and participatory headings here (see also Kendall and Taylor 2010).

Table 17.1 The third sector in democracy

	Model of citizen	Mode of operation	Role of third sector (ascribed; *espoused*)	Roles of the state
Liberal	Voter	Interest aggregation Representation	Residual, reducing reliance on the state *Campaigning; expressing excluded voices; meeting unmet needs*	Upholding the rule of law and citizen rights
Market liberalism	Consumer	Choice	Offering choice as a competitor in the market Informing consumer choices *Campaigning against the injustices of the market*	Minimal; ensuring the free movement of capital
Social democracy	Voter	Representation	Junior partner in the welfare firm *Watchdog; Campaigning; expressing excluded voices, special and emergent interests*	Provider
Pluralism	Interests	Negotiation Competition	Expressing, organizing and advocating for different voices Delivering a variety of responses to need	Mediator between different interests
Corporatism	Institutionalized interest	Bargaining	Corporate partner *Watchdog; Campaigning; expressing excluded voices*	Partner
Associative/ communitarian	Member	Participation	Anchoring democracy in participatory institutions Generating social capital	Minimal
Participatory/ governance	Active and informed citizen	Deliberation Communicative action	A channel for citizen voices Educator/information provider Partner in policy-making and implementation *Critical friends*	Coordinating and steering Arbiter and facilitator

capital, meeting needs, and inculcating and expressing values – in contrast to the overweening and controlling state. TSOs are thus the expression of the associative principle (Putnam 2000), and it is often this ideal that informs normative ideas of civil society and social capital.

The ideal type "governance" model is presented here as a Habermasian model in which policy is generated through deliberation, but deliberation in which the state is an (ideally) equal partner and facilitator. Here, it is possible to argue that the third sector will have a prominent role to play in mobilizing and supporting informed citizens, in small "p" political education, in reaching the disengaged, in framing and facilitating debate, and in contributing as equal partners – and perhaps as critical friends – to the policy process. Such a role, however, will pose significant challenges, and it is to these that I now turn.

Challenges for the Third Sector

Earlier, this chapter identified some of the risks and challenges associated with existing models of democracy. Principal among these were the risks of elitism and of the replication of existing patterns of power in new spaces. A key challenge, meanwhile, was that of representing, coordinating, and mediating the conflicting interests in society. In what follows, therefore, I first consider how far the expansion of the participatory sphere offers genuine opportunities for the engagement of TSOs and citizens more generally or simply maintains existing forms of power. Second, I consider the challenges of representation and ask what legitimacy and accountability third sector actors bring into new forms of participatory democracy. Third, I consider the challenge of coordination and mediation.

The first challenge for third sector organizations is to be heard. Although there is plenty of evidence of the expansion of participatory mechanisms, there is a growing body of research arguing that new opportunities for engagement in governance have not yet significantly shifted the balance of power between the state and the third sector (Atkinson 1999, 2003; Cooke and Kothari 2001; Jones 2003; Raco 2000; Somerville 2005). The quantity of participatory opportunities has certainly increased and the argument for inclusion has been won in many places (though certainly not all), but there are reservations about the quality of these opportunities in terms of the levels of engagement and influence offered (Gaventa 2006). Indeed, a number of scholars in both the North and South have dismissed new governance spaces as sites of cooption, cost-shifting, and continuing centralization (Cooke and Kothari 2001).

Many opportunities offer a low level of engagement. Cornwall (2008b) notes, for example, how the World Bank defines giving information and consultation as forms of participation and empowerment; this is tokenism (Arnstein 1969). But even where there is a commitment to greater participation, many studies show that the rhetoric fails to match the reality (e.g., Grimshaw and Lever 2009). Across the globe, agendas are still set by the state, and research has found that a great deal of the influence TSOs bring to bear is still peripheral – in micropolitics. State actors may feel threatened by the participation agenda or lack the skills to apply participatory methods – Djordjevic (2007) suggests that this is a particular issue in post-Soviet countries. For their part, TSOs often lack the resources or the organizational capacity to get involved in decision-making (Grimshaw and Lever 2009). As Cooke and Kothari (2001, p. 9) argue, unless governance spaces take into account the relative bargaining power of stakeholders, "they are in danger of merely providing opportunities for the more powerful." Partnership working also enshrines a consensual approach which is likely to result in voices that do not "fit" being excluded and suppressed (Taylor et al. 2009), while a managerialist approach to policy risks marginalizing political debate in favor of technical solutions to society's problems.

Meanwhile doors that have opened can close again, which suggests that new opportunities may be a temporary phenomenon and still very much in the gift of the state. Thus, Naidu (2008) describes how, in South Africa, formal mechanisms like ward committees have replaced many vibrant local initiatives. Participatory budgeting in Porto Alegre has taken a different turn with the change in political power, while, in Nicaragua, the election of Daniel Ortega has clientelized participatory spaces, closing down options for those who do not align themselves with the ruling party (Howard and Serra 2008). The institutionalization of participatory approaches to decision-making may have been what many TSOs may have wished for, but Cornwall argues (2008a) that, as these invited spaces expand, more contentious forms of exercising voice – such as demonstrations, strikes, and petitions – have become less acceptable than seeking a seat at the consultation table. Is toeing the line, as Dryzek (2000) argues, to be the "price of inclusion?" De Filippis et al. (2009), writing in the United States, note the shrinking of political goals implicit in the focus on community in and of itself, while Taylor et al. (2009) argue that the disappearance of traditional channels of citizen voice and dissent in the UK leaves those who do not fit the new opportunities for engagement with nowhere to go.

A second challenge relates to legitimacy. If, as Zimmer (2009) argues in relation to the EU, the engagement of TSOs offers legitimacy to a system much criticized for its democratic deficit, what *kind* of legitimacy do TSOs bring? The democratic anchorage of the new governance spaces is open to question, for there are privileged pathways through this new territory (Taylor 2007). Many of these spaces demand considerable knowledge and expertise and thus are dominated by those players who can bring the most resources and strategic knowledge to the table as well as those who can engage in the dominant discourse, speaking the language of power, rather than speaking truth to power. Bang (2005, pp. 160–161) contrasts these "expert citizens" with the "everyday makers" who he sees as more strongly embedded in the day-to-day life of the community, arguing that the new governance is still republican elitism at heart. He is "highly sceptical of those who celebrate the growing influence of non-governmental organisations (NGOs) in governance as the victory of autonomous civil society" (ibid).

There is, however, an inevitable tension between leadership and expertise on the one hand and widespread participation on the other – they are goals that are difficult to reconcile (Taylor 2003). Gaventa (2006) describes this as a tension between depth and breadth. A wide range of innovative mechanisms has been developed to reach the "everyday maker" and tap the views of the "ordinary" or "average" citizen, so that these can be taken into account by decision makers – thus broadening democracy. But when it comes to engaging TSO players in decision-making itself – deepening democracy – the numbers engaged are relatively few and the demands made on third sector participants can be considerable. In these circumstances, it is all too easy for "expert citizens" to lose touch with their constituencies and to adopt instead the cultural referents of their counterparts in the state – ceasing even to recognize the way that power is working and the assumptions that govern such spaces. While much is made of the democratic anchorage of TSOs and their ability to reach out to citizens, legitimacy is accorded to TSOs as much for the knowledge they bring as their "political legitimacy" (Taylor and Warburton 2003), and managerial and professional competence are often preferred to political values; as Häikiö writes (2007, p. 11), "the task of political decision-making is to guarantee the functioning of service markets, instead of creating a public arena for decision-making."

TSOs can be "underdemocratic, or non-democratic, or sometimes even antidemocratic" (Scholte 2002, p. 300). Accountability requires time and resources which are rarely available especially to the most marginalized groups. In post-Soviet countries, for example, many organizations are small and may be run by a charismatic individual or two and a handful of friends (Djordjevic 2007; Taylor et al. 2009). Accountability is not top of their agenda, and they rarely have the resources to exercise it. Even in Latin American countries, with a strong and embedded social movement tradition and where many NGOs elect their leaders, research suggests that there are "perennial leaders" or "community oligarchs" who are rarely challenged or replaced (Howard and Serra 2008; Pearce and Taylor 2009). This is a phenomenon that is frequently observed in the wider third sector literature.

As TSOs scale up beyond the local to higher levels, problems of accountability and legitimacy are intensified. Accountability chains become longer and more tenuous. In addition, Scholte (2002) observes that the nature of the global demos is so multifaceted and fluid that it is not clear *who* should be represented in popular assemblies for transworld governance institutions. He argues that civil society (as he defines it) has a particularly important role to play in an arena where public participation and accountability are weak. It can increase public transparency and increase public accountability, thus bolstering the legitimacy of global governance arrangements. But on the whole, he finds, civil society engagement at this level rests on an overly narrow cultural base, whereby "the privileged claim to speak for the subordinated, often with limited if any direct consultation of the would-be constituents" (Scholte 2002, p. 296).

The third challenge relates to cohesion and diversity. How, Foley and Hodgkinson (2003, p. viii) ask, can citizens of diverse interests and experiences come together in the common project of citizenship? State institutions tend to want uniformity and a single voice, and the consensual culture of many governance spaces discourages dissent and conflict. But Scholte (2002) reminds us that civil society is itself a site of struggles to be heard, while Alexander (1998, pp. 14, 16) has described how appeals to civil society as a "seamless, overarching principle of social integration and coherence" conceals "intense struggles for legitimacy and legitimation."

How then can TSOs overcome their inherent differences and their own exclusive tendencies? While policy has often focused on bonding forms of social capital, Putnam and others increasingly emphasize the importance of bridging capital between communities (Evers 2003; Forrest and Kearns 2000; Portes 1998; Putnam 2000). But there is a long way to go as yet in seeking solutions to the deep divides between communities who define themselves as much by who they are not as who they are.

Addressing the Challenges

Both the opportunities for engagement and third sector responses to the challenges they bring will be shaped by the sociopolitical context in which they emerge. Recent research that I carried out with colleagues (Taylor et al. 2009), for example, contrasted the fragile cultures of participation in a post-Soviet country (Bulgaria) with the strong sense of agency found in a Latin America country (Nicaragua). In the former, a complete absence of any legacy of independent collective action vis-à-vis an authoritarian state had left a sense of powerlessness, with individuals generally preferring to seek advancement through the market; in the latter, a strong movement tradition and a constitutional right to participation combined with the sector's central role in meeting the needs of citizens in the context of a relatively weak state to produce a "radical habitus" (Crossley 2003), which underpinned any engagement with the state. We contrasted that with a Western country (the UK), where the institutionalization of participation has given the sector a central and high-profile role but one that threatens to marginalize traditional forms of dissent. Even in Latin America, research suggests that "there seems to be a lack of space and support for participants to develop autonomous agendas" (NCVO 2008, p. 8). However, Pearce and Taylor (2009) have argued that, there, the vibrant history of autonomous collective action has left a legacy that can be harnessed when opportunities open up, so long as TSOs nurture this history rather than succumbing to professionalization.

In discussing participation, Cornwall (2004) distinguishes between "invited spaces," in the gift of the state and "popular" or "claimed" spaces set up by citizens. A number of authors have suggested that autonomous and firmly grounded third sector voices in "invited spaces" depend on a vibrant local politics and on the existence of "claimed" spaces, in which third sector actors can construct their own narratives in parallel with – and sometimes in opposition to – those of the state or other elite actors (Taylor et al. 2009). De Filippis et al. (2009, p. 49) develop this position, to argue for local action to connect with broader social movements, on the basis that "going beyond the local is a central aspect in the struggle for social and economic justice." They provide examples of organizations that, despite receiving outside funds, have been able to protect their autonomy, connecting service provision with political education, advocacy, and action. Craig et al. (2004) similarly describe how third sector actors have developed ways of working "in and against the state": they may form alliances through which they can campaign at one stage removed from their organization; larger organizations who participate in governance spaces may provide "docking points" for smaller organizations who want to maintain their independence; and key national third sector players may find themselves invited into state-led discussions while their members at the front-line are still engaging in high-profile campaigns. Critical to these strategies – indeed more generally to the workings of democracy in a complex world – are boundary spanners with experience and respect in both sectors (Howard and Taylor 2010).

Others have looked to the Internet as a potential saviour of democracy, as the place where political discourses are increasingly created, structured, and influenced (Vatrapu et al. 2008) and which has fed "globalization from below." Here it is possible to go beyond the local or even national to build solidarity and drive social change. The Internet has also provided opportunities for those who do not engage easily with conventional politics – young people, for example – to develop their political awareness and skills. However, it also creates new forms of digital exclusion and new problems of legitimacy – Navarria (2008), for example, warns of the need to avoid shallow demagoguery. It remains to be seen how these opportunities develop and how they are used by TSOs, particularly in reaching through all strata of society to the most disadvantaged.

What of the other legitimacy issues this chapter has raised? Does the third sector lend the state legitimacy? Or is its legitimacy compromised by the new governance? Rather than striving for some unattainable holy grail of representativeness, Cornwall argues (2008a, p. 276) that "it makes more sense to think in terms of *optimum* participation: getting the balance between depth and inclusion right for the purpose at hand." If it is only likely to be the few that engage at the "deep" end of governance, transparency and accountability are likely to be significant and more attainable goals than "representativeness." Ultimately, therefore, the legitimacy of these few and of the decisions taken in governance spaces will depend on the existence of an informed public, which has the knowledge and motivation to hold both them and their state partners to account. This is likely to require investment in a variety of channels for engagement at different levels. Experiences across the world have shown how it is possible to engage the citizenry more widely (Cornwall 2008b), and there is a strong argument for more sharing these ideas and the learning from them between South and North.

Saward (2005) argues that more multi-polar and participative forms of governance open up spaces for new types of representative claim, characterized by flexibility and looseness of identity. He argues that more attention needs to be given to the role of representation in actually constituting identities and issues within consultative, participative, or implementation processes – identities which relate to networks rather than hierarchies, giving voice to groups who are "not united or cohesive in their political opinions but whose perspectives condition their interests and opinions" (ibid, p. 191). This gives prominence not only to stakeholders but also to marginalized interests, emergent interests, and "intense interests." It allows for the expression of the diversity of claims and interests within the sector, and, like Leach and Scoones' idea of "practised engagement through emergent social solidarities" discussed earlier (2007, p. 18), it encourages us toward new, more fluid ways of grappling with these difficult concepts. But while this frees us up from more conventional accounts of accountability and takes us closer to a new form of politics based on Habermas' ideas of communicative action (Habermas 1984), it is not clear what the implications are for TSOs.

This brings us to our third challenge – of reconciling cohesion with diversity. The research evidence suggests that healing divisions requires painstaking face-to-face work from the very local level, building face-to-face opportunities to build confidence in excluded communities and to combat stereotypes. However, while destructive conflict and forms of exclusion do need to be addressed, it may be neither realistic nor appropriate to seek consensus across the third sector. Powell (2009, p. 52) is dismissive of "Alexis de Tocqueville's bucolic picture of Americans associating in a utopian world," preferring the European vision of "a robust democracy, based on conflict." Pearce and Taylor (2009) remind us too that the participatory world will never be a pristine universe of easy consensus building.

Democracy needs diversity, and it is this feature of the third sector – its ability to release diverse resources, to meet diverse needs, and to give voice to diverse groups of citizens – that is its major contribution to democracy. But its organizations also need to know when it is important to work in harmony and when it is necessary to let a diversity of voices speak. As Gaventa (2006) notes, it remains difficult to reconcile issues of difference and diversity with the more universalizing notions of participation and deliberation. One of the major challenges of the future will be to build the skills that can work creatively with conflict and develop political skills among citizens. Again, the answers to this challenge may be best found by increasing opportunities to learn across different parts of the globe.

Conclusion

So can the third sector contribute to the transformation of democracy? I have argued above that it is the diversity of the sector that is its major contribution to democracy – rather than any particular set of values claimed for it. However, issues remain about the distribution of power within the third sector – in its widest sense. Evers (2003, p. 19) argues that we need to "repair civil society":

> The challenges of civil society do not so much consist in inviting ordinary people to participate and volunteer to a higher degree, but in studying the ways in which the more powerful groups in society make their interests heard.

David Held (1996), too, argues for the break-up of old patterns of power in civil society. Hence his promotion, in an argument that has since become familiar, of experimentation with new forms of self-managed enterprises and social provision, which will challenge old understandings of how society is organized.

Our discussion above suggests that democracy will depend on an untamed and highly diverse third sector, with TSOs operating in and against the state and holding each other to account. But it also suggests that to make its full contribution to democracy the voluntary sector needs the mediating hand of the state. Held and others have argued that civil society and the state are the condition of each other's democratization (Held 1996, p. 322; see also de Filippis et al. 2009; Evers 2003; Keane 1988). Indeed, Held (1996, p. 316) has argued that "for democracy to flourish today, it has to be reconceived as a double-sided phenomenon ... with the *re*-form of state power and, on the other hand, with the restructuring of civil society." It is difficult, however, to conceive of a society where the state would relinquish control to quite the extent envisaged. Even in Porto Alegre, famed for its participatory democracy, a change of administration has dramatically shifted the balance of power.

Gaventa (2006, p. 8), however, usefully reminds us how far democracy progressed in the twentieth century – from a point where there were no states that met the standards of an electoral democracy to one where there were 85 "full" democracies in place in terms of the rule of law and civil and political rights (out of 192 existing states). In looking to the future, he (ibid, p. 27) sees democracy not as a set of institutional designs but as a concept constantly under construction through contestation amongst actors in different settings. He sees potential for new resolutions to the dilemmas identified above in the dialogue between the local and the global and the debates that need to be developed around global citizenship and democratic governance.

Democracy's work in progress will also be influenced by the dissolving of conventional boundaries between the public and the private and the state and the citizen. In work elsewhere, Gaventa (2004, p. 38) has argued that democratic progress is most likely at the interstices between popular or "claimed spaces" and "invited" spaces. "Navigating the intersections of relationships," he argues, may "in turn create new boundaries of possibility for action and engagement" (ibid). This is territory in which the third sector has operated for a long time and the dilemmas that it experiences and that we have charted here will become more common across the sectors. But it will also require new skills that can work creatively with conflict and uncertainty and new understandings of legitimacy. This hybridization – as Zimmer argues elsewhere in this volume – is likely to become one of the key issues not only of third sector but also of political science research in the future.

References

Alexander, J. (1998). *Real Civil Societies: Dilemmas of Institutionalization*, London, Sage.
Arnstein, S. (1969). A ladder of participation in the USA. *Journal of the American Institute of Planners*, 35(4), 216–224.
Almond, G., and Verba, S. (1963). *The Civic Culture: Political Attitudes and Democracy in Five Nations*, Boston, Little Brown.
Alonso, A., and Costa, V. (2004). The dynamics of public hearings for environmental licensing: The case of the Sao Paolo ring road. *IDS Bulletin*, 35(2), 49–57.

Atkinson, R. (1999). Discourses of partnership and empowerment in contemporary British urban regeneration. *Urban Studies*, 36(1), 59–72.

Atkinson, R. (2003). Addressing social exclusion through community involvement in urban regeneration. In R. Imrie and M. Raco (eds) *Urban Renaissance? New Labour, Community and Urban Policy* (pp. 109–119), Bristol, The Policy Press.

Bang, H. (2005). Among everyday makers and expert citizens. In J. Newman (ed.) *Remaking Governance: Peoples, Politics and the Public Sphere* (pp. 159–178), Bristol, The Policy Press.

Berger, P., and Neuhaus, J. (1977). *To Empower People: The Role of Mediating Structures in Public Policy*, Washington, DC, American Enterprise Institute for Public Policy Research.

Carmel, E., and Harlock, J. (2008). Instituting the "third sector" as a governable terrain: Partnership, procurement and performance in the UK. *Policy and Politics*, 36(2), 155–171.

Cohen, J., and Fung, A. (2004). Radical democracy. *Swiss Political Science Review*, 10(4), 23–34.

Cooke, B., and Kothari, U. (2001). *Participation: The New Tyranny?* London, Zed Books.

Cornwall, A. (2004). New democratic spaces? The politics & dynamics of institutionalized participation. *IDS Bulletin*, 35(2), 1–10.

Cornwall, A. (2008a). Unpacking "participation": Models, meanings and practices. *Community Development Journal*, 43(3), 269–283.

Cornwall, A. (2008b). *Democratising Engagement: What the UK can Learn from International Experience*, London, Demos.

Craig, G., Taylor, M., and Parkes, T. (2004). Protest or partnership? The voluntary and community sectors in the policy process. *Social Policy and Administration*, 38(3), 221–239.

Crossley, N. (2003). From reproduction to transformation: Social movement fields and the radical habitus. *Theory, Culture and Society*, 20(6), 43–68.

Dahl, R. (1989). *Democracy and Its Critics*, New Haven, Yale University Press.

De Filippis, J., Fisher, R., and Shragge, E. (2009). What's left in the community: Oppositional politics in contemporary practice. *Community Development Journal*, 44(1), 38–52.

Djordjevic, M. (2007). Citizen participation in strategic planning in large cities: The limited achievements of Budapest and Warsaw city governments since 1990. Paper presented to Citizen Participation in Policy Making, Cinefogo, Bristol.

Dryzek, J. (2000). *Deliberative Democracy and Beyond: Liberals, Critics and Contestations*, Oxford, Oxford University Press.

Ellison, N. (1997). Towards a new social politics: Citizenship and reflexivity in late modernity. *Sociology*, 31(4), 697–717.

Evers, A. (2003). Social capital and civic commitment: On Putnam's way of understanding. *Social Policy and Society*, 2(1), 13–21.

Foley, M., and Edwards, R. (1996). The paradox of civil society. *Journal of Democracy*, 7(3), 38–52.

Foley, M., and Hodgkinson, V. (2003). Introduction. In V. Hodgkinson and M. Foley (eds) *The Civil Society Reader* (pp. 9–24), Lebanon, NH, University Press of New England.

Forrest, R., and Kearns, A. (2000) Social cohesion, social capital and the neighbourhood. *Urban Studies*, 38(12), 2125–2143.

Fung, A., and Wright, E. (2003). *Deepening Democracy: Institutional Innovations in Empowered Participatory Governance*, London, Verso.

Gaventa, J. (2004). Towards participatory governance: Assessing the transformative possibilities. In S. Hickey and G. Mohan (eds) *Participation: From Tyranny to Participation* (pp. 25–41), London, Zed Books.

Gaventa, J. (2006). Triumph, deficit or contestation? Deepening the "deepening democracy" debate. IDS Working paper in conjunction with Logolink and the Citizenship DRC, Institute for Development Studies, University of Sussex.

Grimshaw, L., and Lever, J. (2009). Citizens' participation in policy making. Online: http://cinefogo.cuni.cz/

Habermas, J. (1984). *The Theory of Communicative Action*, Boston, Beacon Press.

Häikiö, L. (2007). Citizenship in the context of local administrative reform. Paper presented to Citizen Participation in Policy Making, Cinefogo, Bristol. Online: http://cinefogo.cuni.cz/

Held, D. (1996). *Models of Democracy*, Cambridge, Polity Press.

Hirst, P. (1997). *From Statism to Pluralism*, London, UCL Press.

Howard, J., and Serra, L. (2008). Non-governmental actors in new governance spaces: The case of Managua – Navigating the gap between rights and implementation? Paper presented to NGPA Latin American Workshop, Bradford.

Howard, J., and Taylor, M. (2010). Hybridity in partnerships: Managing tensions and opportunities. In D. Billis (ed.) *The Erosion of the Third Sector? Hybrid Organisations in a New Welfare Landscape* (pp. 175–196), London, Palgrave Macmillan.

Jones, P. (2003) Urban regeneration's poisoned chalice: Is there an impasse in (community) participation-based policy? *Urban Studies*, 40(3), 581–601.

Keane, J. (1988). *Democracy and Civil Society*, London, Verso.

Kendall, J. (2009). Losing political innocence. TSRC Working paper 13, Third Sector Research Centre, www.tsrc.ac.uk

Kendall, J., and Taylor, M. (2010). On the interdependence between politics and policy in the shaping of English horizontal third sector initiative. In B. Gidron and M. Bar-Ahmog (eds) *Policy Initiatives Towards the Third Sector* (pp. 189–212), New York, Springer.

Kooiman, J. (2003). *Governing as Governance*, London, Sage.

Leach, M., and Scoones, I. (2007). *Mobilising Citizens: Social Movements and the Politics of Knowledge*, Brighton, Institute of Development Studies.

Naidu, R. (2008). Deepening local democracy and governance – An experiential perspective. *The Governance Link*, Issue 4, Action Aid.

Navarria, G. (2008). Transparency, accountability and representativeness in the age of blogging: The complex case of beppogrillo.it/. Paper presented to The Normative Implications of New Forms of Participation for Democratic Policy Processes, Cinefogo, Grythyttan, Sweden.

NCVO. (2008). *Changing Governance: How are Civil Society Organisations in the UK and Overseas Experiencing the Shift from Government to Governance*, London, National Council for Voluntary Organisations.

Owen, D. (1966). *English Philanthropy 1660–1960*, Cambridge, MA, Harvard University Press.

Pearce, J., and Taylor, M. (2009). Comparing cultures of participation across North and South. Presentation at the final conference of the Non-Governmental Public Action Programme: Organizing for Social Justice and Poverty Reduction, London.

Portes, A. (1998). Social capital: Its origins and applications in modern society. *Annual Review of Sociology*, 24(4), 1–24.

Powell, F. (2009). Civil society, social policy and participatory democracy: Past, present and future. *Social Policy and Society*, 8(1), 49–58.

Putnam, R. (1993). *Making Democracy Work*, Princeton, NJ, Princeton University Press.

Putnam, R. (2000). *Bowling Alone: The Collapse and Revival of American Community*, New York, Simon & Schuster.

Raco, M. (2000). Assessing community participation in local economic development – Lessons for the new urban policy, *Political Geography*, 19(5), 573–599.

Rhodes, R. (1997). *Understanding Governance Policy Networks, Governance, Reflexivity and Accountability*, Buckingham, UK, Open University Press.

Rose, N. (1999). *Powers of Freedom: Reframing Political Thought*, Cambridge, Cambridge University Press.

Salamon, L. (1995). The global associational revolution: The rise of the third sector on the world scene. In L. Salamon (ed.) *Partners in Public Service: Government–Nonprofit Relations in the Modern Welfare State* (pp. 243–269), Baltimore, MD, The Johns Hopkins University Press.

Salamon, L., and Anheier, H. (1998). Social origins of civil society: Explaining the nonprofit sector cross-nationally. *Voluntas*, 9(3), 213–248.

Saward, M. (1998). *The Terms of Democracy*, Oxford, Wiley-Blackwell.

Saward, M. (2005). Governance and the transformation of political representation. In J. Newman (ed.) *Remaking Governance: Peoples, Politics and the Public Sphere* (pp. 179–196), Bristol, The Policy Press.

Schmitter, P. (1974). Still the century of corporatism? *The Review of Politics*, 36(1), 85–131.

Scholte, J. (2002). Civil society and democracy in global governance. *Global Governance*, 8(3), 281–304.

Skocpol, T. (2003). *Diminished Democracy: From Membership to Management in American Civic Life*, Norman, University of Oklahoma Press.

Somerville, P. (2005). Community governance and democracy. *Policy and Politics*, 33(1), 117–144.

Stoker, G. (1998). Governance as theory: Five propositions. *International Social Science Journal*, 155, 17–28.

Tam, H. (1998). *Communitarianism*, London, Palgrave Macmillan.

Taylor, M. (2003). *Public Policy in the Community*, London, Palgrave Macmillan.

Taylor, M. (2007). Participation in the real world: Opportunities and pitfalls in new governance spaces. *Urban Studies*, 44(2), 297–317.

Taylor, M., and Warburton, D. (2003). Legitimacy and the role of UK third sector organizations in the policy process. *Voluntas*, 14(3), 321–339.

Taylor, M., Howard, J., Harris, V., Lever, J., Mateeva, A., Miller, C., Petrov, R., and Serra, L. (2009). Dilemmas of engagement: The experience of non-governmental actors in new governance spaces. NGPA Working paper series, no. 31, London School of Economics.

Vatrapu, R., Robertson, S., Dissanayke, W., and Jeedigunta, A. (2008). Are political weblogs public spheres or partisan spheres? A virtual ethnographic study of on-line participations and implications for civic participation in the Internet age. Paper presented to Empowerment and e-Participation in Civil Society: Local, National and International Implications, Örebro, Sweden.

Verlet, D., Steyvers, K., Reynaert, H., and Devos, C. (2007). Attitudes towards citizen involvement: Looking from both sides of the gap. Paper presented to Citizen Participation in Policy Making, Cinefogo, Bristol. Online: http://cinefogo.cuni.cz/

Zimmer, A. (2009). There is no business like show business: Governance revisited. Paper presented to Social Rights, Active Citizenship and Governance in the European Union, Cinefogo, Brussels.

Chapter 18
The Dark Side

Jonathan Murphy

Introduction

The third sector has been remarkably successful in recent years in positioning itself as an unalloyed force for good.[1] However, just as governments and business should be publicly accountable, so too should third sector organizations, especially as the sector grows in economic and political strength (Taylor 2004), and is increasingly represented at the top tables of elite decision-making forums, from informal clubs like the Davos World Business Forum to global governance arenas like the United Nations and the World Bank.

The sector has by no means always had its current overwhelmingly positive image. Indeed the modern welfare state was constructed at least in part as a conscious effort to ensure that those in need would not be subject to the capricious and judgemental approaches of many of the private, and particularly religious, distributors of charity in the pre-welfare state era (Kenny 2002). In contrast with the sector's current claims to represent a force for democratic social change, Gramsci (1971) characterized civil society as a key intermediary in assuring the preservation of the existing hegemonic order. The question arises whether, notwithstanding its liberal use of terms like participation and empowerment, the sector continues to serve as implementing vehicle of Northern business and government interests (Manji and O'Coill 2002).

Third sector leaders regularly make substantial claims about the sector's normative superiority in comparison with government, private business, and even "traditional" democratic institutions. Kumi Naidoo, perhaps the sector's most prominent leader on the global governance circuit, has described the rise of an organized civil society sector as follows: "A global phenomenon in which

J. Murphy (✉)
Cardiff University, Wales, UK
e-mail: murphyj3@cardiff.ac.uk

[1]I will use the terms third sector organizations, civil society organizations, and NGOs somewhat interchangeably, for the sake of simplicity, although I understand these categories are not necessarily synonymous.

R. Taylor (ed.), *Third Sector Research*, DOI 10.1007/978-1-4419-5707-8_18,
© Springer Science+Business Media, LLC 2010

citizen-inspired associations have spread through millions of villages and communities leaving more democratic forms of governance and improved social and economic welfare in their wake" (Naidoo 2003). In this statement Naidoo is making three claims. The first is that the third sector, the "citizen-inspired associations" of which he writes, represents a fundamentally different form of human organization from government and private business. The second claim is that the sector reflects and promotes "more democratic forms of governance." The third claim is that the third sector's impact is to create a more equitable world with "improved social and economic welfare."

In this chapter it is argued that these claims, which appear quite representative of the self-perceptions of third sector leaders, substantially exaggerate the extent to which third sector organizations are different from their private sector and government cousins. This chapter responds to these claims by looking at three case studies of larger third sector organizations in action. These address the government and business ties of large environmental conservation organizations, the moulding of a global anti-poverty agenda into a vehicle for restructuring the post-colonial state, and the framing of anti-corruption action excluding broader normative questions surrounding neoliberal globalization. These cases reveal that (a) the third sector does not always act autonomously from business and government (Hindess 2008); (b) NGO policies may not be authentically driven by their grassroots constituencies but rather by leadership interests (Chandhoke 2005); (c) NGOs may not be democratic in a meaningful sense (Anderson and Rieff 2005); and (d) they may not consistently support greater economic and social equity (Murphy 2008).

This is not to say that the third sector can never epitomize Naidoo's ideals, but rather that it does not necessarily do so, and that the sector is prone to the same tendencies to elite domination and power concentration as other sectors. The cases will demonstrate a pattern of third sector majors building alliances with government and business to impose neoliberal policy solutions. Through these alliances, the third sector – with its claims to represent a superior, participatory form of democracy – may play a key role in extending the technology of governance (Foucault 1991) and legitimizing elite social domination (Lipschutz 2005).

Case Study One: Elite Partnerships for Managing the Planet's Resources?

Large nature conservation NGOs, of which the World Wildlife Fund for Nature (WWF) is the best known, devote considerable efforts to marketing themselves as effective stewards of the world's flora and fauna. According to WWF, its panda logo, designed by the organization's founder Peter Scott in 1961, has a 77% recognition rate in the United Kingdom.[2] Beneath the cuddly exteriors, however, WWF and a number of other international conservancy NGOs have developed into powerful institutions whose support can not only facilitate preservation of the global

---

[2] Visit www.wwf.org.uk/filelibrary/pdf/pandalogo.pdf

environment, but also permit its exploitation against the interests and wishes of affected citizens.

The environmental majors were pioneers in the third sector strategy of building ties with government and business. Chapin (2004) notes that WWF for many years fitted the stereotype of the financially struggling, volunteer-driven NGO, with committed activists crowded into rented office space. This changed suddenly when the organization became "extremely large and wealthy in a short period of time" (Chapin 2004, p. 17). From a small office in Switzerland in 1961, by 2000 WWF had over 4,000 staff and programmes in 90 countries. In 2002 the combined expenditures in developing countries of the three largest US-based environmental NGOs alone – WWF-USA, Conservation International (CI), and The Nature Conservancy (TNC) – were nearly $500 million. This was more than the expenditures in the same year of the intergovernmental Global Environmental Facility (GEF) which consolidates the environmental investments of the United Nations, World Bank, and a number of regional development banks (Bray and Anderson 2005). The exponential growth of the environmental NGO majors coincided with their strategy, beginning in the early 1980s, of building working ties and long-term financial relationships with major transnational corporations, bilateral development agencies such as USAID and Britain's Department for International Development (DFID), and transnational governance institutions such as the World Bank.

Conservation NGO collaboration with corporations can take a variety of different forms. One common approach involves programmes that provide sustainability certification for potentially environmentally damaging commodities such as intensive food crops, biofuels, and wood products. WWF, for example, coordinates an international sustainable soy production roundtable that also involves Brazil's Gruppo Maggi, the world's largest private soy producer that has been blamed for 48% of Amazon rainforest deforestation in 2004 (Sonderegger 2007). Palm oil, touted as a key biofuel replacement for gasoline, has a similar industry–NGO partnership. The Roundtable on Sustainable Palm Oil is chaired by an executive from the consumer products major Unilever and vice-chaired by a WWF representative. However, there is substantial scientific evidence that using palm oil as biofuel both contributes to harmful carbon dioxide emissions and deprives developing country citizens of food crops (Reijnders and Huijbregts 2008; Scharlemann and Laurance 2008).

WWF was also a founding member of the Forest Stewardship Council (FSC), a coalition of forest products companies, environmental and conservancy NGOs, and indigenous groups. FSC provides a certification for wood products that they have been produced using sustainable methods. After some initial resistance, FSC successfully brought onboard the major corporate actors in the forestry industry, but critics argue that sustainability criteria still allow harmful forest practices such as monoculture wood production (Lang 2008) and that FSC domination by the major players effectively freezes out small-scale producers and indigenous communities from benefiting from the sustainability certification (Taylor 2005).

The WWF sought to replicate the FSC model with the Marine Stewardship Council (MSC), established in 1996, which would provide a similar sustainable production certification for marine food products. This time, however, WWF, apparently drawing conclusions from its FSC experience, followed a much more closed process. Whereas FSC is a membership organization with open General Assemblies that allow dissident organizations to put forward critical policy resolutions, MSC was essentially built on an alliance between WWF and (once again) Unilever, a major marine products processor and vendor. MSC is set up on a corporate model, with an appointed rather than elected board of directors (Gale and Haward 2004). Those grassroots organizations representing developing country producer interests and that are seen as having disrupted the smooth working of FSC are explicitly excluded from MSC (Ponte 2008).

Another key strategy of major conservancy NGOs since the 1980s has been the development of Integrated Conservation and Development Programs (ICDPs), in which local (often indigenous) communities supposedly co-manage resources with government and private interests, with the international NGO providing technical support ("animation") for the development of ICDP agreements and processes. Radical critics argue that, in practice, the concerns and needs of indigenous people (in which addressing endemic poverty is usually top priority) are relegated below conservation concerns and even the interests of oil, mining, and logging companies (Whitmore 2006). The political demands of indigenous groups – which above all else usually involve securing land tenure – are kept "off the table" except in rare cases where community leaders are able to seize control of the agenda away from the professional NGO experts (Walker et al. 2007).

The partnership approach of WWF and other conservancy and environmental INGOs has been consistently criticized by more radical environmental groups as well as by indigenous rights organizations who argue that environmental and indigenous peoples' interests are being sacrificed at the altar of such collaborations. It is impossible to prove definitively that the working and financial relationships between the large conservancy NGOs and governments, transnational institutions, and corporations run contrary to the NGOs' founding missions. The WWF strongly rejects such claims, arguing that its corporate and government partnerships benefit both the natural environment and indigenous people (WWF 2005). However, since the WWF and other major environment and conservation NGOs embarked on their partnership approach in the 1980s, critics argue they have become "organisations with annual turnovers in excess of €15 million, hundreds of paid employees, and possessing 'branded' conservation solutions and sophisticated marketing, advocacy and policy departments. . . [that] . . . look and act increasingly like a morph between trans-national corporations and government development agencies" (Jepson 2005, p. 516).

Case Study Two: International Anti-poverty NGOs and the Global Social Policy Consensus

If the activities of WWF and other major conservancy NGOs have been subject to a fairly consistent and wide-ranging radical critique, development NGOs command strong public support in most Western countries (Smillie and Helmich 1998) and are rarely publicly criticized in either developed or developing countries.

Many international development NGOs have gradually shifted their focus away from a charitable service focus towards an activist agenda including policy advocacy. Amongst the more vocal and effective policy advocates is Oxfam, which has expanded far beyond its original British roots to become a decentralized, multinational NGO active in at least 70 developing countries. While Oxfam continues to devote most of its resources to charitable and humanitarian initiatives, an increasing proportion of the agency's energies are devoted to networking with other NGOs and development actors (including bilateral and multilateral development agencies), convening organizations to work together on common development concerns, and advocating for specific development policy changes at the national and international levels (Oxfam 2008). Oxfam and other international NGOs (INGOs) are omnipresent at international governmental meetings including the G8 and G20, as well as annual meetings of transnational institutions such as the World Bank and the IMF. Relationships between INGOs and transnational governance institutions are extremely complex. INGOs find themselves criticizing the same institutions upon which they are dependent for funding, while also seeking to develop policy influence. Effective execution of this three-prong strategy requires strong working relationships, while avoiding being co-opted into the agendas of the much larger, wealthier, and more powerful bilateral and transnational institutions, among whom the World Bank is perhaps preeminent.

In this case study, focus falls on a cross-sectoral partnership between the World Bank and INGOs, including Oxfam as a major player, aimed at implementing universal primary education. This is an internationally sanctioned development goal included as one of the United Nations' Millennium Development Goals (MDGs). The MDGs represent a generally accepted set of development objectives and thus participating in joint initiatives to further those goals might seem an obvious strategy. However, the World Bank has long been widely criticized both for acting in a domineering fashion in collaborations and for subordinating development programming to an overall neoliberal agenda that is inimical to development (Murphy 2008). Under the leadership of the Clinton administration appointee James Wolfensohn between 1995 and 2005, the Bank moved away from an exclusive focus on economic restructuring towards a more inclusive approach that included an explicit focus on poverty reduction and ecological sustainability, along with significant outreach to civil society. At the same time, the rationale for Bank actions remained within a neoliberal framework. A business case needed to be made for environmental action (Marschincki and Berle 2005), and poverty reduction action centred on increasing the economic competitiveness of the developing country poor (Cammack 2004).

It is in this context that the Bank forged a partnership with a number of major INGOs including Oxfam, Save the Children, and Action Aid, as well as the international teaching union Education International, in order to pursue the MDG initiative of universal primary education through the Global Campaign for Education (GCE). In many countries, Oxfam has been the driving force behind GCE lobbying campaigns. The principal thrust of GCE is implementation of the Fast Track Initiative

(FTI), a Bank-coordinated programme in which additional Western donor funding is promised to developing countries in return for what the Bank calls "a credible plan" but is in fact a series of predetermined conditions that replicate the Bank's preoccupation with neoliberal economics (Development Committee 2004; World Bank 2007). Several of these conditions extend far beyond education. For example, countries are expected to restrain overall government spending to between 14% and 18% of GDP – a far smaller proportion than in any Western country. Education-related conditions for FTI participation include the allocation of at least 50% of education expenditures on primary schools and target student–teacher ratios of 40:1 – the World Bank does not believe that higher education expenditure in developing countries is a good use of resources or that teacher–student ratios are a significant factor in education outcomes (Mingat and Tan 1985, 1998).

Despite "Education for All" (EFA), the hiring of teachers is not exempt from the usual World Bank/IMF condition of a public service hiring freeze imposed on countries requiring loans. In fact, the Bank is clear that it wishes to dismantle the teaching profession in developing countries, which it views as "unaffordable," replacing it with a corps of semi-skilled, underpaid, contractuals (Bruns et al. 2003; Mingat 2002), responsible for rolling out a mass literacy programme of dubious quality. In West Africa, contract teachers hired on temporary contracts with no benefits at salaries of $50–$100 per month, compared with $250 plus for professional teachers. The cost-cutting manoeuvre was criticized from both inside and outside the World Bank. Long before FTI was implemented, the Bank's Zymelman and DiStefano (1989, p. 49) had warned that proposals to expand education coverage in developing countries through drastically reducing teacher salaries were "simplistic." UNICEF's Mehrotra and Buckland (1998, p. 18) noted that "expansion of access has involved strategies which could pose a threat to quality. Where the quality of educational provision has deteriorated seriously, enrolment levels have tended to decline, demonstrating the inextricable relationship between quality and access."

The programme went ahead despite these concerns about quality, which have been confirmed in practice (Murphy 2005). The Bank's own evaluation of its programme in Mali found that replacing professional teachers with underpaid contractuals was a fiasco: "The Government of Mali was compelled to recruit contract teachers with little or no pre-service teacher education and struggled, without Bank support, to provide them with short-term courses" (Bender et al. 2007, p. 37). The Government of Niger noted that more than 6,000 schools were headed by contractuals, contrary to programme guidelines, that strikes by contractuals had "drastically reduced the amount of schooling children received," and that there was an endemic problem of the poorly paid contractual teachers abandoning their posts (Gouvernement du Niger 2007).

The casualization of teaching that has been central to implementation of the programme has been the subject of widespread protests in Southern civil society (Ekwè 2007; Pole Dakar 2009). In Niger, contract teachers, prohibited even from joining a union, went on strike for better conditions (L'Ecuyer 2003). Contract teachers also struck in Senegal and complained to the International Labour Office (ILO) about their treatment (Unesco 2005). The ILO itself has criticized the widespread imposition of these drastically worsened working conditions on teachers in developing countries, with minimal or no consultation with teachers' organizations (Fyfe 2007; Ratteree 2004).

In 2006, Education International and Action Aid complained belatedly about the situation of casualized developing country teachers, *after* their support for EFA/FTI had helped dismantle the professional teaching corps across the developing world (Education International 2006). Three years earlier, when the EFA/FTI initiative's fundamental reliance on workforce casualization was already set in stone, both organizations as well as Oxfam and others had published a report demanding speeded-up implementation of EFA/FTI, failing once to mention the term "contract teacher" (Global Campaign for Education 2003). In 2007, Oxfam produced a disingenuous report that simultaneously criticized the IMF for restricting the size of the public service in developing countries, while lauding the success of the EFA/FTI initiative as proof that "aid works" (Oxfam 2007).[3]

Oxfam's close working relationships with official development agencies has drawn criticism from within and outside the sector (Manji and O'Coill 2002). In 2005, Britain's left-of-centre *New Statesman* magazine reported concerns of other development NGOs that Oxfam was becoming "far too cosy" with Britain's New Labour government, giving overly generous credit for its development initiatives; "they go out on a limb to endorse the government." An executive from the mainstream NGO Christian Aid said, "A number of organisations wish Oxfam would be more radical and critical of the government" (Quarmby 2005). Barbara Stocking, Oxfam's CEO, responded to the *New Statesman* article by stating that she was "shocked at the injustice," arguing that the article was a "punch in the stomach" to the struggle against poverty, implying that it would endanger "700,000 people who rely on Oxfam to survive" in Darfur and claiming that in daring to criticize Oxfam, the magazine had discredited itself (Stocking 2005). Her response was somewhat surprising given that Oxfam regularly uses much sharper language than Quarmby's in its own attacks on opposing policy positions.

Notwithstanding Stocking's protestations, there is a significant bilateral flow of senior personnel between Oxfam and Britain's Labour government. Shriti Vadera, a 14-year veteran of investment bank UBS Warburg, was trustee at Oxfam from 2000 to 2005 while acting as senior adviser at the Treasury (Sparrow 2009). During this time she was on hiring panels for senior Oxfam staff. In 2007 she was awarded a life peerage and became a junior minister in an international development portfolio. In 2004, Justin Forsyth, Oxfam's policy director, moved to Tony Blair's Prime Minister's Office as an international development advisor, before being promoted by Blair's successor Gordon Brown to a major communications role in Downing Street as press and policy advisor in 2008 (Sweeney 2008). Prior to coming to Oxfam in

---

[3] The IMF is frequently criticized by NGOs and others for its regressive policies, while criticism of the World Bank tends to be more muted. In fact, the IMF and World Bank, whose headquarters are adjacent to each other in Washington, DC, work together extremely closely and most major development funding requires the approval of both institutions. The "bad cop–good cop" analogy is suitable to explain the relationship of the two organizations.

2001, Stocking had herself headed the Blair government's highly strategic and politically charged National Health Service modernization agenda. In 2008, Brown's government made her a Dame of the British Empire (Russell 2008). Undoubtedly, the close relationship between Oxfam and the government forged through these senior personnel links does permit Oxfam to lobby more effectively within government, but it also reduces the organization's effective autonomy and provides evidence for radical critics' suggestion that third sector organizations may promote a form of social contract polyarchy rather than authentic participatory democracy.

Case Study Three: Fighting Corruption Cautiously

Transparency International (TI) provides another example of the close relationship between INGOs and business, government, and international institutions. In the early 1990s, Peter Eigen, a senior World Bank official, became frustrated by the impact of corruption on World Bank programmes. Eigen agitated for the Bank to take action itself and when he was forbidden from pushing the issue, which Bank orthodoxy considered "political" and thus outside the organization's mandate, he quit and founded TI in 1993 (Polzer 2001). TI recruited leading politicians (including the former presidents of Nigeria and of Costa Rica) as well as senior business people, including the presidents of Coopers & Lybrand and Fairfax Group consulting companies, as members of the advisory board (McKnickle 1993). TI soon started delivering anti-corruption materials and programming, which focused around international corruption perception indices (Transparency International 2008a). From the beginning, TI was an elite-driven NGO.

TI's early years coincided with the arrival at the World Bank of James Wolfensohn, who, as discussed earlier, reoriented the World Bank towards a more populist agenda. Wolfensohn's structural and strategic reform of the Bank included adoption of political (good governance) development objectives. This coincided with the rise within the academic economics establishment of neo-institutionalist economists, among whose most prominent advocates is the Bank's own chief economist from 1997 to 2000, subsequent Nobel Prize winner Joseph Stiglitz. The new thinking in the Bank was that weak institutions lay at the heart of market failure and thus many development problems. Corruption was one of the most obvious and pernicious of these negative institutional factors that would need to be eradicated in order to permit effective markets to operate and development to succeed. The Bank started taking action against blatant corruption, for example, suspending aid to Kenya in 1997 due to a major corruption scandal in that country.

Thus, only a few years after being marginalized by the Bank for his concerns over corruption, Eigen was invited back in the middle of things, helping the Bank to design an anti-corruption strategy which was launched in 1999. Transparency International became a donor darling, receiving large grants from USAID, Britain's DFID, and the World Bank itself, as well as from the plethora of major corporations that sought to associate themselves with the anti-corruption initiatives. The organization developed rapidly and by 2009 had over 90 national chapters around the world; the headquarters organization alone had revenues of nearly €10 million, and TI participated in countless activities, planning and executing national anti-corruption strategies.

Despite TI's overt success, there has been a consistent chorus of criticism about both the quality and the objectivity of TI's research and advocacy. Radical critics have accused TI of supporting a Western, and specifically US agenda of destabilization of radical governments, particularly in Haiti and Venezuela. In Haiti, TI was accused of exaggerating corruption issues faced by the left-wing president Jean-Bertrand Aristide (Pina 2003), who was subsequently toppled by a US-backed coup (Hallward 2004). In regard to Venezuela, in 2008 TI produced a report on the transparency of 42 major oil- and gas-producing companies; Venezuela's state-owned company ranked lowest (Transparency International 2008b). The data underpinning the ranking proved to be inaccurate; however, TI refused to correct the error (Tucker 2008). The national TI branch is led by a number of staff active in the opposition movement against leftist president Hugo Chavez. Several have direct or indirect links with various organizations involved in the US-backed attempted putsch against Chavez in 2002. Mercedes de Freitas, head of TI's Caracas office, who collected the incorrectly damning information about Venezuela's oil sector, went on record defending the 2002 coup, which was thwarted by a popular uprising of Chavez supporters.

Several studies have revealed links between TI national chapters and right-wing political movements. One researcher found that Italy's TI branch is dominated by supporters of the extreme-right political party Lega Nord and claimed that they had helped to "muffle news" about corruption scandals involving the government of Silvio Berlusconi, of which Lega Nord is a member (deSousa 2005, p. 14). Ecuador's national TI chapter, profiled at TI's first international Annual General Meeting in Quito in 1994, was headed by the country's Vice President Alberto Dahik, a former finance minister and leading Conservative Party politician. Dahik's role in TI caused uproar at the meeting, and the Ecuador branch was dissolved (Lindstrom 2002). The next year, Dahik, who had been a poster child of the global neoliberal establishment for pushing through tough market reforms in Ecuador, fled to Costa Rica after secret bank accounts were found; Ecuador's Supreme Court accused him of embezzlement, and a warrant was issued for his arrest (Handelman 1995).

There are broader critiques of TI. The organization's flagship methodology is the Corruption Perceptions Index (CPI), which is itself based on a number of corruption perception measures developed by third party organizations. Some of these organizations, such as Freedom House, are closely associated with the American intelligence community and various prominent US neoconservatives, casting doubt on the objectivity of their data (Herman and Chomsky 2002, p. 28). Methodologically, the index emphasizes bribe-takers over bribe-payers, thus resulting in a corruption profile that strongly endorses the perspective that corruption is mainly a problem for, and the fault of, the people of developing countries (Andersson and Heywood 2008) – a point of view which has already been shown to

be endemic in traditional development discourse (Escobar 1995). TI's 2007 CPI ratings show a close correlation between "underdevelopment" and "corruption," also
corresponding closely with the distribution of wealth and power around the globe
(Transparency International 2007). With only a few outliers, the wealthy countries
are "clean" and the poor "dirty." Anti-tax haven campaigner John Christenson of
Britain's Tax Justice Network criticizes the index for assessing many tax havens as
among the world's least corrupt jurisdictions (Campbell 2006).

Transparency's definition of corruption is itself revelatory. In its *Source Book*
(Pope 2000, p. 2), which remains TI's definitive handbook for designing anti-
corruption programming, corruption is defined narrowly as "behaviour on the part
of officials in the public sector, whether politicians or civil servants, in which they
improperly and unlawfully enrich themselves, or those close to them, by the misuse of the power entrusted to them." To be fair to TI, it has subsequently extended
this definition in practice; it has in recent years paid more attention to the (mainly
corporate) givers of bribes, and indeed its 2009 Global Corruption report addresses
corruption in the private sector. However, the corruption focus remains constrained
both by the organization's blue chip "don't-rock-the-boat" support base and by an
assumption that corruption is defined by the illegal passing of bribes, rather than the
broader misuse of power (Bukovansky 2006).

There is always a problematic relationship between corruption and neoliberal
capitalism, because the market assumes an individualist approach to social relationships that requires regulation; however, regulation is normative and depends on
power relationships in a society. TI would only rank activities that were illegal in a
particular jurisdiction as corrupt, whereas the same activity might be legal in another
jurisdiction, for example, a secretive tax haven, where TI would rate the activity
as not corrupt. In times of economic, political, and social stability, the hegemonic
order is able to achieve general consent for a narrow definition of corruption such
as promoted by TI. However, when the taken-for-granted nature of social and economic relationships comes into question, for example, due to economic crisis, the
line between corrupt and non-corrupt behaviour becomes a point of social debate
and the socially determined foundation of the concept of corruption becomes apparent. Thus, TI finds itself trailing public opinion and even governments as the scope
of defined corruption is expanded.

Similarly, jurisdictions whose economic existence is predicated on the "lawful"
but antisocial evasion ("avoidance") of taxes come under scrutiny at times of crisis as consensus evaporates on definitions of a legitimate hegemonic order. In the
global economic crisis beginning in 2007, tax havens have been clearly indicted
as primary locales for the manoeuvres in which international bankers engaged in
order to construct fantastically complex and systemically dangerous financial instruments from which they pocketed enormous fees, also typically realized in these
"offshore financial centres" (Lim 2008). TI has never called for the closing down of
tax havens.

Brown and Cloke (2007, p. 318) argue that corruption and near-corruption
are fundamental to the normal workings of the capitalist system: "the grey/black
economy is neither an aberration, nor the fault of a few rotten apples, but has a

considerable historical background, is mainstream, and a fundamentally important motor within the European financial system." Black (2009), a US regulator during the 1980s Savings and Loans (S&L) crisis, points out that the fundamental cause of the 2007–2009 sub-prime crisis is the same as in the S&L debacle: the making of bad loans and derivative instruments on those loans, whose primary purpose is to generate fees for financial managers, what he calls "control fraud." Black indicts the US administration for failing to identify the emerging pattern of fraud, stop these activities, and take action against its perpetrators. A similar indictment could be laid against Transparency International, whose comprehensive website, as of mid-2009, managed only a single reference to the sub-prime crisis in a German-language press release of 30 October 2008, long after the crisis had wreaked economic havoc.[4]

TI's failure to define financial legerdemain as corruption or to campaign for such antisocial behaviour to be outlawed raises real doubts about whether it can properly be described as an autonomous civil society organization, rather than a quasi-state rule-maker (Dahl 2007; Hindess 2005). By placing a narrow range of corrupt actions outside the bounds of acceptability, TI effectively authorizes those activities that are not categorized as corrupt. Hindess (2008, p. 270) puts it more sharply: the "international anti-corruption movement, of which TI is a prominent member, should be seen as a stalking horse for the neo-liberal reform of non-Western states."

Discussion and Conclusion

The three examples explored in this chapter involve different policy domains. However, the case findings show several common characteristics. In all three cases, policy directions were clearly driven from Northern country headquarters. There was minimal if any consultation with grassroots, developing country citizens, the people in whose interests all three of the INGOs claim to speak. Many of the policy initiatives being promoted were contrary to the interests of substantial constituencies in developing countries.

WWF's sustainability certification initiatives have consistently marginalized small-scale producers in favour of large, Northern multinationals; the trend in its multi-stakeholder sustainability initiatives seems to be towards less, rather than more involvement of impacted indigenous communities. The impact of the universal primary education campaign on the teachers' profession in developing countries has been catastrophic, but Oxfam insists its work on this project shows that "aid works." Transparency International's anti-corruption agenda has been shown to be particularly questionable. Its critique of corruption singles out Southern countries, downplaying the role of Western-based multinational corporations in fostering corruption. Meanwhile, TI ignored overwhelming evidence of unethical – but possible technically legal – business practices in the United States and other Northern

---

[4]Visit www.transparency.org/news_room/latest_news/press_releases_nc/2008/2008_10_30_germany_financial

countries that led directly to the global economic crisis. This crisis, which was widely predicted and was founded on blatantly unethical behaviour (Crotty 2009), is causing misery for citizens in developed and developing countries alike.

In democratic society, organizations, third sector or otherwise, should be perfectly entitled to promote social, political, and economic agendas as they see fit. However, the peculiar feature of much contemporary third sector discourse is the claim of a privileged voice based on a combination of normative superiority and inherent representation of the interests of their chosen constituencies. While the former claim – demonstrated above in Oxfam's response to criticism – is perhaps an inevitable outcome of single-minded commitment to a legitimate cause, it is the latter claim that can have widespread and potentially devastating consequences for the developing country poor.

The belief in the superior legitimacy of the third sector over developing country states has become a taken-for-granted assumption within many Northern INGOs, justifying the examples documented in this chapter of policies imposed on developing country citizens by multi-sector partnerships. Thus, Anne Hudock, a prominent US-based third sector theorist, supports the "impetus" the World Bank provides "for governments to support a more enabling environment for NGO work" (Hudock 1999, p. 49) and proposes NGOs as an alternative to "failed" developing country governments: "NGOs are uniquely positioned to facilitate the development of a global civil society in which state behaviour becomes less central to collective choice. Most bilateral donors have realized that their development assistance has in some cases been thwarted by an inefficient and corrupt state, one which was overly involved in its economy" (ibid, p. 58).

Anne-Marie Goetz, another social movement theorist, writes, "there is increasing recognition of the 'comparative advantage' exercised by NGOs over state bureaucracies in delivering development resources to the poor" (O'Brien et al. 2000, p. 28). Marc Williams, an environmental activist, supports NGO campaigns to impose environmental standards in development and trade even when, "in opposition to the interests of Third World governments," which can be justifiable because "it is a moot point whether the governments are truly representative of their peoples" (O'Brien et al. 2000, p. 157). Naidoo (2003) explicitly prefers the participatory techniques of the third sector over traditional democracy of which he notes "the meaningful interface between citizens and the elected is minimal between election periods" and that citizens are turning "away from traditional engagement in favour of new forms of participation." Consistent with these claims, there are increasingly widespread and explicit calls for a global governance system to be established on the basis of tripartite, expert-driven committees including NGO, private sector, and government representatives (Benner et al. 2004; Rischard 2002; Slaughter 2004).

Despite these assertions about the superior representativity of the third sector, in the cases discussed in this chapter, third sector organizations' partnerships with business and the state were centrally driven and frequently seem to run roughshod over the very constituents that the sector claims to represent. These findings coincide with Chandhoke's (2005, p. 362) assertion that "INGOs hardly ever come face to face with the people whose interests and problems they represent." They also align with critical development management theorists who argue that participatory discourse in development often represents a "new tyranny" in which aid recipients are called upon to enact a ceremonial endorsement of predetermined development strategies (Cooke and Kothari 2001).

As underlined at the beginning of the chapter, the aim is not to dismiss the third sector or denigrate the work that it does. Rather, it has been to deflate some of the more exaggerated propositions of some in the sector about its inherent rectitude. Third sector organizations' claims about their representativity, the value of their programmes, and the correctness of their policy positions should not be accepted ipso facto, but judged on their merits, acknowledging the extraordinary diversity of the third sector and its state of constant flux (Munck 2007). The third sector organization is prone to elite capture as is any form of human organization. Thus, it should not be surprising that large, internationally institutionalized NGOs might play a similar role in embedding and normalizing a hegemonic order to that of the church in Gramsci's writings. At the same time, as Gramsci (1971) also underlined, non-state, non-business organizations can be irreplaceable drivers of social change. This will only occur, however, when third sector organizations are driven from below and rigorously self-critical.

References

Anderson, K., and Rieff, D. (2005). "Global civil society": A sceptical view. In H. Anheier, M. Glasius, and M. Kaldor (eds) *Global Civil Society: 2004/5* (pp. 26–39), London, Sage.

Andersson, S., and Heywood, P. (2008). The politics of perception: Use and abuse of Transparency International's approach to measuring corruption. *Political Studies*, 45(3), 417–435.

Bender, P., Diarra, A., Edoh, K., and Ziegler, M. (2007). *Evaluation of the World Bank Assistance to Primary Education in Mali: A Country Case Study*, Washington, DC, World Bank.

Benner, T., Reinicke, W., and Witte, J. (2004). Multisectoral networks in global governance: Towards a pluralistic system of accountability. *Government and Opposition*, 39(2), 191–210.

Black, W. (2009). Those who forget past regulatory successes... *Economic and Political Weekly*, 44(13), 80–87.

Bray, D., and Anderson, A. (2005). Global conservation non-governmental organizations and local communities. Working paper 1, Conservation and Development Series, Institute for Sustainability Science in Latin America and the Caribbean, Florida International University.

Brown, E., and Cloke, J. (2007). Shadow Europe: Alternative European financial geographies. *Growth and Change*, 38(2), 304–327.

Bruns, B., Mingat, A., and Rakotomalala, R. (2003). *Achieving Universal Primary Education by 2015: A Chance for Every Child*, Washington, DC, World Bank.

Bukovansky, M. (2006). The hollowness of anti-corruption discourse. *Review of International Political Economy*, 13(2), 181–209.

Cammack, P. (2004). What the World Bank means by poverty reduction and why it matters. *New Political Economy*, 9(2), 189–211.

Campbell, D. (2006). Britain is "as corrupt as worst African states." *The Guardian*, 4 September, p. 25.

Chandhoke, N. (2005). How global is global civil society? *Journal of World Systems Research*, 11(2), 355–371.

Chapin, M. (2004). A challenge to conservationists. *WorldWatch*, November–December, pp. 17–31.

Cooke, B., and Kothari, U. (eds) (2001). *Participation: The New Tyranny?* London, Zed.

Crotty, J. (2009). Structural flaws in the US financial system. *Economic and Political Weekly*, 44(13), 127–136.

Dahl, M. (2007). States under scrutiny: International organizations, transformation and the construction of progress. Ph.D. dissertation, School of Business, Stockholm University.

de Sousa, L. (2005). Transparency International: In search of a constituency. Asia Pacific School of Economics and Government Working paper 05–14, Australian National University.

Development Committee. (2004). Education for All (EFA—Fast Track Initiative Progress Report). Washington, DC, World Bank/IMF.

Education International. (2006). *Annual Report, 2006*, www.eiie.org/annualreport2006/ start.html

Ekwè, D. (2007). Vincent Bikono: Contract worker and not proud of it. *UNESCO Courier*, 10, http://portal.unesco.org/en/ev.php-URL_ID=41199&URL_DO=DO_TOPIC&URL_SECTION=201.html

Escobar, A. (1995). *Encountering Development: The Making and Unmaking of the Third World*, Princeton, NJ, Princeton University Press.

Foucault, M. (1991). Governmentality. In G. Burchell, C. Gordon, and P. Miller (eds) *The Foucault Effect: Studies in Governmentality* (pp. 87–104), Chicago, University of Chicago Press.

Fyfe, A. (2007). The use of contract teachers in developing countries: Trends and impact. Working paper 252, Geneva, ILO.

Gale, F., and Haward, M. (2004). Public accountability in private regulation: Contrasting models of the Forest Stewardship Council (FSC) and Marine Stewardship Council (MSC). Paper presented at the Australasian Political Studies Association Conference, University of Adelaide.

Global Campaign for Education. (2003). Education for All Fast Track: The No-Progress Report (that they didn't want you to see). http://siteresources.worldbank.org/CSO/Resources/OxfamEFA.pdf

Gouvernement du Niger. (2007). Programme Décennal de Développement de l'Education au Niger (PDDE): 2ème PHASE: 2008–2010. Ministry of National Education, Niamey.

Gramsci, A. (1971). State and civil society. In *Selections from The Prison Notebooks of Antonio Gramsci* (pp. 210–276), New York, International Publishers.

Hallward, P. (2004). Option zero in Haiti. *New Left Review*, 27, 23–47.

Handelman, S. (1995). Two sorts of power failure weaken Ecuadorian stability. *The Toronto Star*, 23 November, p. A29.

Herman, E. S., and Chomsky, N. (2002). *Manufacturing Consent: The Political Economy of the Mass Media*, New York, Pantheon Books.

Hindess, B. (2005). Investigating international anti-corruption. *Third World Quarterly*, 26(8), 1389–1398.

Hindess, B. (2008). Government and discipline. *International Political Sociology*, 2(3), 268–270.

Hudock, A. (1999). *NGOs and Civil Society: Democracy by Proxy*, London, Polity.

Jepson, P. (2005). Governance and accountability of environmental NGOs. *Environmental Science & Policy*, 8(5), 515–524.

Kenny, S. (2002). Tensions and dilemmas in community development: New discourses, new Trojans? *Community Development Journal*, 37(4), 284–299.

Lang, C. (2008). FSC: Stop certifying monoculture tree plantations! *World Rainforest Movement Bulletin*, 134, www.wrm.org.uy/bulletin/134/viewpoint.html

L'Ecuyer, P. (2003). Education conflict reaches new depths in Niger. *Alternatives*, 8(3), www.alternatives.ca/article957.html

Lim, M. (2008). Old wine in new bottles: Subprime mortgage crisis – Causes and consequences. *Journal of Applied Research in Accounting and Finance*, 3(1), 1–13.

Lindstrom, K. (2002). High road or low? Transparency International and the Corruption Perceptions Index. Kennedy School of Government Case KSG1658.0, Harvard University.

Lipschutz, R. (2005). Power, politics and global civil society. *Millennium*, 33(3), 747–769.

Manji, F., and O'Coill, C. (2002). The missionary position: NGOs and development in Africa. *International Affairs*, 78(3), 567–583.

Marschinski, R., and Behrle, S. (2005). *The World Bank: Making the Business Case for Environment*, Potsdam, Potsdam Institute for Climate Impact Research.

McNickle, M. (1993). Group set to combat third-world graft. *International Herald Tribune*, 2 October, www.nytimes.com/1993/10/02/your-money/02iht-mrtrans.html

Mehrotra, S., and Buckland, P. (1998). *Managing Teacher Costs for Access and Quality*, UNICEF Staff working paper, New York, UNICEF.

Mingat, A. (2002). Deux études pour la scolarisation primaire universelle dans les pays du Sahel en 2015. World Bank, Dakar.

Mingat, A., and Tan, J. (1998). The mechanics of progress in education: Evidence from cross-country data. World Bank Policy research paper 2015, World Bank, Washington, DC.

Mingat, A., and Tan, J. (1985). On equity in education again. *Journal of Human Resources*, 20(2), 298–308.

Munck, R. (2007). Global civil society: Royal road or slippery path. *Voluntas*, 17(4), 325–332.

Murphy, J. (2005). The World Bank, INGOs, and civil society: Converging agendas? The case of universal basic education in Niger. *Voluntas*, 16(4), 353–374.

Murphy, J. (2008). *The World Bank and Global Managerialism*, London, Routledge.

Naidoo, K. (2003). Civil society, governance, and globalization. Presidential Fellows Lecture, World Bank, Washington, DC, http://info.worldbank.org/etools/bspan/PresentationView. asp?EID=63&PID=133

O'Brien, R., Goetz, A.-M., Scholtze, J., and Williams, M. (2000). *Contesting Global Governance*, Cambridge University Press, Cambridge.

Oxfam. (2007). Paying for people: Financing the skilled workers needed to deliver health and education services for all. Oxfam Briefing paper 98, www.oxfam.org.nz/imgs/about/070314payingforpeople.pdf

Oxfam GB. (2008). *Annual Report 2007–2008*, Oxford, Oxfam.

Pina, K. (2003). Propaganda war intensifies against Haiti. *The Black Commentator*, 62, 30 October, www.blackcommentator.com/62/62_haiti_1.html

Pole Dakar. (2009). *La scolarisation primaire universelle en Afrique: le defi enseignant*, Unesco, Dakar.

Polzer, T. (2001). Corruption: Deconstructing the World Bank discourse. DESTIN Working paper 01-18, London School of Economics.

Ponte, S. (2008). Greener than thou: The political economy of fish ecolabeling and its local manifestations in South Africa. *World Development*, 36(1), 159–175.

Pope, J. (2000). *The Transparency International Sourcebook: Confronting Corruption: The Elements of a National Integrity System*, Berlin, Transparency International.

Quarmby, K. (2005). Why Oxfam is failing Africa: Inside the Make Poverty History movement. *New Statesman*, 30 May, www.globalpolicy.org/component/content/article/176-general/32064.pdf

Ratteree, B. (2004). Teachers, their unions and the Education for All campaign. Report 2005/ED/EFA/MRT/PI/41, Unesco, Paris.

Reijnders, L., and Huijbregts, M. (2008). Palm oil and the emission of carbon-based greenhouse gases. *Journal of Cleaner Production*, 16(4), 477–482.

Rischard, J. (2002). *High Noon: Twenty Global Problems, Twenty Years to Solve Them*, New York, Basic Books.

Russell, B. (2008). Charitable works are deemed to be the most deserving cause: The Queen's Birthday Honours. *The Independent*, June 14, p. 32.

Scharlemann, J., and Laurance, W. (2008). How green are biofuels? *Science*, 4 January, pp. 43–44.

Slaughter, A. (2004). *A New World Order*, Princeton, NJ, Princeton University Press.

Smillie, I., and Helmich, H. (eds.) (1998). *Public Attitudes and International Development Co-operation*, Paris, OECD.

Sonderegger, R. (2007). Caution: Greenwash! www.aseed.net

Sparrow, A. (2009). Profile: Shriti Vadera. *The Guardian*, January 15.

Stocking, B. (2005). Oxfam bites back. *New Statesman*, June 6, p. 35.

Sweeney, M. (2008). Stephen Carter gets communications post in cabinet reshuffle. *The Guardian*, 3 October, www.guardian.co.uk/media/2008/oct/03/television_digitalmedia

Taylor, P. (2005). In the market but not of it: Fair Trade Coffee and Forest Stewardship Council Certification as market-based social change. *World Development*, 33(1), 129–147.

Taylor, R. (ed.) (2004). *Creating a Better World: Interpreting Global Civil Society*, Bloomfield, CT, Kumarian Press.

Transparency International. (2007). *Corruption Perceptions Index, 2007*, www.transparency.org/policy_research/surveys_indicies/cpi/2007

Transparency International. (2008a). *Global Corruption Report, 2008*, Cambridge, Cambridge University Press.

Transparency International (2008b). *Promoting Revenue Transparency: 2008 Report on Revenue Transparency of Oil and Gas Companies*, Berlin, Transparency International.

Tucker, C. (2008). Seeing through Transparency International. *The Guardian*, 22 May, www.guardian.co.uk/commentisfree/2008/may/22/seeingthroughtransparencyin

Unesco. (2005). Wanted! Teachers. *Education Today*, 12, January–March, 4–7

Walker, D., Jones III, J., Roberts, S., and Fröhling, O. (2007). When participation meets empowerment: The WWF and the politics of invitation in the Chimalapas, Mexico. *Annals of the Association of American Geographers*, 97(2), 423–444.

Whitmore, A. (2006). The emperor's new clothes: Sustainable mining? *Journal of Cleaner Production*, 14(3/4), 309–314.

World Bank. (2007). *Fast Track Initiative 2007 Annual Report*, Washington, DC, World Bank.

WWF. (2005). Setting the record straight, www.panda.org/about_wwf/what_we_do/policy/indigenous_people/worldwatch/point_by_point.cfm

Zymelman, M., and DeStefano, J. (1989). Primary school teachers' salaries in sub-Saharan Africa. World Bank Discussion paper 45, Washington DC, World Bank.

Chapter 19
Philanthropy in an Era of Global Governance

Patricia Mooney Nickel and Angela M. Eikenberry

Introduction

Recent scholarship has observed a shift in political systems around the world from hierarchically organized, unitary systems of *government* to horizontally organized and relatively fragmented systems of *governance* (Pierre 2000; Rhodes 1994; Sørensen 2002; Sørensen and Torfing 2005). It is now nearly taken for granted that, globally, governments play a less central role in dictating the terms of well-being and its associated administrative arrangements. This shift is variously described as good governance (Bang and Esmark 2009), associational democracy (Hirst 2000), the hollow state (Milward and Provan 2000), government by proxy (Kettl 1988), third party government (Salamon 1987), and the shadow state (Wolch 1990). Concurrently, social policy scholars have observed the globalization of social policy and a resultant variation in social welfare actors beyond the nation state (Deacon 2007). Together, the shift from government to governance and the globalization of social policy represent a significant shift in our understanding of the locus of responsibility for social action, which now takes place within the framework of global governance.

The emphasis on *global* and *nongovernmental* responsibility for human well-being has resulted in an increased emphasis on philanthropy, which transcends national boundaries and citizenship, to serve in the role previously dominated by the welfare state and its associated national policies (Villadsen 2007).[1] In this

---

P.M. Nickel (✉)
Victoria University of Wellington, New Zealand
e-mail: patricia.nickel@vuw.ac.nz

A.M. Eikenberry (✉)
University of Nebraska at Omaha, USA
e-mail: aeikenberry@mail.unomaha.edu

[1] Philanthropy's meaning and manifestations have changed throughout history (Curti 1973; McCully 2008). In recent years it has come to be defined as the act of giving money and other resources, including time, to aid individuals, causes, and charitable organizations (Philanthropy 2000).

R. Taylor (ed.), *Third Sector Research*, DOI 10.1007/978-1-4419-5707-8_19,
© Springer Science+Business Media, LLC 2010

environment, philanthropists increasingly take on roles previously reserved for governments as they redistribute resources via philanthropic organizations, which then embed themselves in governance, directly through volunteer organizations and indirectly through grant funding. Simultaneously, the state now often recognizes and even encourages philanthropists as partners in delivering state policy, leading to widespread acceptance of extra-state institutions in the governing process (Anheier 2005; Chandoke 2003).

With this convergence of trends, human well-being, once regarded as the province of national governments acting to reduce, through social policy, citizens' vulnerability to the market, is increasingly regarded as the legitimate enterprise of non-state philanthropic actors. These nongovernmental actors govern through the pursuit of profit, which is subsequently redistributed as philanthropic monies at the discretion of individuals outside of the realm of the nation state. We call the possession of enough wealth to impact human well-being on a global scale *philanthropic governing capacity*. We contend in this chapter that global governance has created space for the emergence of philanthropic governors who *make* social policy through the accumulation and discretionary redistribution of wealth, thus depoliticizing discourse about global governance by reducing the visibility of the market and the negative impacts that it has on human well-being.[2] First, we demonstrate how philanthropy and social policy are related as the politics of well-being under the umbrella of global governance. Second, we explore how philanthropic governing capacity as the redistribution of wealth becomes depoliticized and subsequently ends vital discourse about the relationship between the market and well-being. Finally, we conclude that philanthropic governing capacity raises serious questions about who is responsible for human well-being in an era of global governance.

Philanthropy and Social Policy as the Politics of Well-Being

In the face of rapidly shifting vocabularies, actors, and practices, it may be easy to forget that the factor common to governance, social policy, and philanthropy is the politics of *human well-being*. Together, global governance and philanthropic governing capacity have serious implications for how we think about and talk about human well-being and governing. If social policy is the improvement of human well-being through the redistribution of wealth or other resources, then both governments and philanthropists make social policy. However, philanthropic social policy – social policy made by individuals with governing capacity – and governmental social policy differ significantly in what they *seem* to represent. Governmental

---

[2] Although there has been much discussion of the impacts of governance on democracy and social equity (see, for example, Boyte 2005; O'Toole 1997; O'Toole and Meier 2004; Sørensen and Torfing 2003; Wälti et al. 2004), the issues that result in the need for social policy in governance are almost entirely neglected, preventing large-scale critique of their impact on the everyday lives of citizens.

social policy seems to represent the actions of an elected government or inter-governmental organization, collecting and redistributing taxes or fees, according to *collective understandings* of well-being.[3] Philanthropic social policy, on the other hand, seems to represent a benevolent individual *giving* out of concern for human welfare.

In reality, social policy made via philanthropic governors represents the actions of an individual who has *accumulated* enough surplus wealth – philanthropic governing capacity – to extend his or her *individual understanding* of well-being to others. Paul Schervish (2003, p. 2) describes this as hyperagency:

> the array of dispositions and capacities that enable [wealthy] individuals to relatively single-handedly produce the social outcomes they desire, as well as the conditions within which they and others exercise their agency. If agency is the capacity to make choices largely within the rules and resources that are socially given, hyperagency is the capacity to be a creator or producer of those rules and resources. If agents are *finders* of the most desirable or fitting place for themselves within a limited range of possibilities, hyperagents are *founders* of those possibilities for themselves, as well as for others.

The important distinction between philanthropic and governmental social policy is that we tend to take for granted that the social policy of governments ought to be contested, yet we rarely contest the social policy made by philanthropists because we mistakenly identify government wealth as being political and individual wealth as being apolitical.[4] Whether they are the result of government action or philanthropic action, the accumulation of wealth, the redistribution of wealth, and the relationship between wealth and well-being are always political. These politics are disguised when philanthropic social policy, unlike government social policy, is divorced from the circumstances by which redistribution is possible; redistribution is always the result of accumulation. In turn, global philanthropists, legitimated by nothing other than their accumulation of wealth, are able to bypass the state and dictate social policy through the reallocation of profit according to their individual preferences.

As a result of the emphasis on philanthropic social policy, philanthropists and the organizations that they fund have become key actors on the global stage in the shift from the national welfare state to global governance. Mega-wealthy individuals such as Bill and Melinda Gates and George Soros have, *via their wealth*, the capacity to bypass the nation state and visibly impact social policy issues on a global scale (Bishop and Green 2008; Byrne 2002; *The Economist* 2004, 2006). The exercise of this capacity is virtually unchecked. With a larger annual global health budget than the United Nations' World Health Organization, the Bill and Melinda Gates Foundation has privately legislated and administered public health-care policy

---

[3]Critical theorists of the state understand that while social policy may appear to function according to the rules of pluralism, in reality this often is not so. Our focus in this chapter, however, is on the appearance of philanthropy.

[4]Though some have warned against a heavy reliance on philanthropy to improve social conditions, few have questioned its basic goodness or acknowledged its political nature (for exceptions, see Arnove 1980; King 2006; Moyo 2009; Roelofs 1995; Wagner 2000).

by funding research and health-care provision in disease-specific areas around the world. While the Gates Foundation's focus on improving world health may be commendable, it has also been criticized, along with other philanthropists, for focusing too narrowly on specific health-care problems (Bishop and Green 2008, p. 67; King 2006). Wealthy individuals like Bill and Melinda Gates have the governing capacity to decide which diseases are eradicated – who lives and who dies – not because they represent the public and collective will, but because they have accumulated massive profits.

Philanthropic governance has a long history of managing the public's perception of wealth in order to make gross inequity appear as though it is a benevolent relationship. Andrew Carnegie observed in 1889 that the "problem of our age is the administration of wealth, so that the ties of brotherhood may still bind together the rich and poor in harmonious relationship" (Carnegie 1992, p. 1). Carnegie called on philanthropists to be what Slavoj Žižek (2006, p. 42) describes as guardians of "frictionless capitalism." Like Carnegie, modern-day philanthropists such as Bill Gates strive to achieve widespread internalization of a story of reality that allows for gross disparities in wealth not only to be taken for granted as a *necessary and natural* condition, but also as a basis for the wealthy governing the poor. Carnegie (1889) idealized the exercise of philanthropic governing capacity as the "ideal State, in which the surplus wealth of the few will become, in the best sense, the property of the many, because administered for the common good; and this wealth, passing through the hands of the few, can be made a much more potent force for the elevation of our race than if distributed in small sums to the people themselves. Even the poorest can be made to see this" (Carnegie 1992, p. 8). Carnegie's recommendation is literally for a world dominated by those who possess the most wealth.

In *World on Fire*, Amy Chua (2003) extends Carnegie's industrial-era scheme to globalization. Given the widespread devastation that results from exporting "free market democracy," Chua suggests that foreign investors engage in philanthropic activity as a means to place a screen between the impact of global capitalism and its effects, which she identifies as breeding ethnic hatred and global instability. Chua concludes (2003, p. 283) that an "honorable way" to balance (not eliminate the cause of) such devastation is "voluntary generosity by market-dominant minorities." Chua describes market-dominant minorities as "ethnic minorities who, for widely varying reasons, tend under market conditions to dominate economically, often to a startling extent, the 'indigenous' majorities around them" (ibid, p. 6). "Market-dominant minority" is in fact a depoliticized phrase for colonization. Chua's suggestion (2003, p. 285) is not that the conditions that sustain market dominance be eliminated, but rather that the conditions that create market-dominant minorities (or investors who dominate the majority) be disguised by funding basketball teams, presumably accompanied with t-shirts bearing market logos: "Ideally, voluntary contributions by market-dominant minorities would be highly visible and directed at large numbers of ordinary members of the disadvantaged majority." Here, philanthropy is unabashedly exposed as being "part of a long-term profit-maximization strategy" (ibid, p. 284). The global philanthropic governance scheme recommended by Chua has taken hold, as demonstrated in Matthew Bishop and Michael Green's (2008) recent *Philanthrocapitalism: How the Rich Can Save the World*, in which today's mega philanthropists seek ways "of harnessing the profit motive to achieve social good" (p. 7).

This convergence of wealth and profit in the name of benevolence has resulted in the widespread assumption that well-being is best achieved not through national social policy, but through the pursuit of profit (Nickel and Eikenberry 2009). As a result, it is increasingly difficult for the average individual, and even for scholars of social policy, to discern *who is governing well-being*. Celebrity philanthropists such as Bono or Angelina Jolie are given status equivalent to that of government officials, and ex-US President Bill Clinton's Global Philanthropy Forum attracts as much or more attention in the media than some official government gatherings. Yet unless album sales (or software sales in the case of Bill Gates) or movie ratings are the equivalent of tax collection and elections, it is unclear at what point Bono, Angelina Jolie, or the Gates achieved legitimacy as public representatives and, more importantly, at what point we are able to hold them accountable for their actions *which govern our lives*. The decreasing visibility of the forces governing our lives coupled with the increasing visibility of wealthy philanthropists as legitimate governance actors raises serious questions about philanthropy and social policy.

Philanthropic Governing Capacity's Depolitization of Well-Being

Philanthropic governing capacity emerges in accord with what we have previously designated the "voluntary state" (Eikenberry 2009; Nickel and Eikenberry 2007). This way of governing, which we critically oppose as a means of disguising how marginalization takes place, is based on two mutually reinforcing factors. First, the voluntary state generates the conditions for the creation of wealth and poverty and then lets the wealthy decide where to volunteer assistance according to their individual preferences. Second, once the state's responsibility for well-being is reframed as a matter of voluntary action, it is further embedded by falsely framing the inhumane conditions imposed on the most impoverished within this system as somehow resulting from their voluntary choice as though the wealthy "choose to do good" and those who benefit least from this system "choose not to." The voluntary state thus provides the illusion of welfare as being a matter of *voluntary choice*. The result is philanthropic governance functioning to de-signify the politics of well-being as it renders well-being voluntary.

When we fail to question the seeming benevolence of modern-day philanthropy and the authority by which philanthropists govern through capacity derived from wealth, the *social significance of philanthropy* ceases to be a political issue. When we focus on the act of giving money as though money has no history, we fail to recognize that modern-day philanthropy is first a failure; an increase in philanthropy represents the failure for an increasing number of people of the current system to result in well-being. Philanthropic governance is not a politically insignificant act of generosity; it is political issue because modern-day philanthropy, the recent rise of "philanthrocapitalism" in particular, does not signify a rise in benevolence – it signifies the accumulation of massive amounts of wealth and with it massive amounts of poverty. We should be focused not on the supposed generosity of philanthropic governors, but instead on the circumstances that have resulted in the denial of well-being for so many people that we are willing to accept a privatized form of governance imposed by the unelected wealthy.

A clear exception to the trend toward the depolitization of well-being is Nancy Fraser's (1989) contention that "reprivatization" is in fact depolitization – an attempt to depoliticize the issues that the government was once responsible for addressing, opening up space for the emergence of philanthropic governors. Fraser demonstrates how "thin" discussions of needs do little to expose the politics that underlie needs discourses or "needs interpretation" (Fraser 1989, pp. 163–164). Especially important to our discussion of the increasing centrality of philanthropy as a means to "meet needs" in an era of governance is Fraser's (1989, p. 164) analysis of how discussion of delivery (what she calls networks of in-order-to relations) serves to blind us from the politics of need:

> Assume that the politics of need concerns only whether various predefined needs will or will not be provided for. As a result, they deflect attention from a number of important political questions … they take the *interpretation* of people's needs as simply given and unproblematic … they assume that it doesn't matter who interprets the needs in question and from what perspective and in the light of what interests; they thus overlook the fact that *who* gets to establish authoritative thick definitions of people's needs is itself a political stake.

Who gets to establish authoritative thick definitions of people's needs is precisely what is at stake in the current emphasis on philanthropy in global governance, which often delegates such authority to philanthropists who have already benefited from a definition of needs that allowed them to amass enough wealth that they are able to establish their own means of delivering social policy independent of the state. As Fraser points out, this is a distinctly political issue. It matters that those who have benefited from the poverty of others then have the power to decide how their poverty will be dealt with. Building on Fraser, we understand the discussion of the role of philanthropy in an era of global governance to be a "thin theory" of needs in that it focuses on who will *deliver* social policy (most efficiently or in the most market-like manner) rather than on what the need for social policy *represents*.

The politics of philanthropy is disguised when philanthropy is divorced from the fact that it can only exist through profit, exploitation, and their result: alienation and poverty. We honor the generosity of mega-wealthy donors for their contributions to the alleviation of social problems (*The Economist* 2004) with little or no discussion of the system that allows them to own most of the wealth while billions of people unnecessarily live in poverty around the world. Žižek (2006, pp. 42–43) describes this disconnect:

> This is what makes a figure like [philanthropist] Soros ethically so problematic. His daily routine is a lie embodied: Half of his working time is devoted to financial speculations and the other half to humanitarian activities … that ultimately fight the effects of his own speculations. Likewise the two faces of Bill Gates: a cruel businessman, destroying or buying

out competitors, aiming at virtual monopoly, employing all the dirty tricks to achieve his
goals . . . and the greatest philanthropist in the history of mankind.

This practice of philanthropy maintains the conditions necessary for the capitalist
mode of production while also disguising its negative impact on human well-being
as benevolence. Philanthropists contend the system that generated their philanthropic governing capacity – wealth – is natural and cannot be remedied except
by those who have excelled within it as a matter of merit. Yet merit is itself a myth
so far as the circumstances into which we are born are not a matter of choice, but of
chance.

Philanthropy in an era of global governance acts to stabilize the *deprivation of
well-being* as philanthropists, who have come to be regarded uncritically as legitimate governors, accumulate the power to make social policy. The assumption
underlying philanthropy today is that its aim is to benevolently end the marginality that results in the denial of well-being for some. Yet, in practice, philanthropy
is frequently constructed and supported by the very thing that it claims to end –
marginality. Philanthropy is dependent on the existence of marginal groups in need
of assistance and a more powerful group in a position to offer this assistance. Thus,
when we discuss philanthropy as a permanent form of governance we assume that
some level of inequity exists and that this inequity is natural. In other words, discussions of how philanthropy might be encouraged and sustained are simultaneously
discussions about how the system, whatever it is and wherever it is, cannot be
changed such that the need for philanthropy would be eliminated. Philanthropy is
not a call for change, but for the stabilization of the circumstances that result in
philanthropic governing capacity. Philanthropy, Carnegie (1889) wrote, would be
the "true antidote for the temporary unequal distribution of wealth, the reconciliation of the rich and the poor – a reign of harmony, another ideal, differing, indeed
from that of the Communist in *requiring only the further evolution of existing conditions,* not the total overthrow of our civilization" (Carnegie 1992, p. 8, emphasis
added).

Philanthropy as a coping strategy for dealing with the problems of marginality is representative of what Michael Ryan (1982, p. 126) has called "the social
theory of marginality." As Ryan recognized, marginality functioning as affirmative social theory is based in "the setting up of norms which are given out to be
self-evident (because derived from such unquestionable truths are consciousness,
presence, nature, life, and ownership) and the marginalization of anything that puts
the norm in question" (ibid). Building on Janice Perelman's *The Myth of Marginality*
(1976), Ryan argues that the branding of marginals acts as a justification of repres-
sion and that such affirmative "social theories, in the hands of the ruling classes,
become social policy" (Ryan 1982, p. 127). Philanthropy as an affirmative social
theory of marginality "preserves the purity of the social system by making a decisive opposition between the good inside and the bad outside" (ibid). Philanthropists
treat poverty as somehow external to their fortunes as the image of their benevolent wealth is "reinforced by the negative image of the marginals who are excluded
from it" (ibid). Philanthropy portrays poverty as somehow existing outside of wealth

when in fact the wealthy and the impoverished exist within the same economic and political system.

Those who are able to accumulate philanthropic governing capacity are already implicated by the system that resulted in the need for philanthropic assistance – "the marginals are in fact internal to the bourgeois system ... the purity of society is already contaminated by a blight it would prefer, for its own protection, to consider as external" (Ryan 1982, p. 127). For example, emergency food clients used to attract donors are often portrayed as patient sufferers, humbly waiting for help (Poppendieck 1998, p. 303). If marginalized groups were to organize and make demands – exercise their rights as citizens – they would lose appeal as a charitable cause (Katz 1989). Thus, philanthropy as it is understood and practiced today often acts as affirmative social theory as it stabilizes the myth of the necessity of marginality through the assumption that the distinction between the haves and have-nots is pre-given or natural and that our efforts are limited to social policies and actors created by the very system that caused this distinction in the first place.

The key point made by Ryan is that blights on the system, such as those addressed by philanthropy, are not external. Much of the suffering that philanthropy aims to alleviate is not the result of a lack of philanthropy, but that of a system that makes philanthropy possible and necessary. Philanthropy is able to act as the social policy of the ruling classes in its distribution of resources, allowing wealthy elites to not only get to decide social policy because of their wealth but also to cover up the hegemonic control they have in society, which perpetuates their wealth and powerful positions (Arnove 1980; Roelofs 1995). This is particularly true in an era of global governance, in which the responsibility for alleviating social problems is devolved to those with the financial, organizational, or political resources to gain access.

When we treat philanthropy and poverty as individual successes and failures rather than as the outcomes of one social system that facilitates both, we forget that philanthropic governing capacity is the result of the accumulation of massive amounts of money. In the case of Bill Gates, it is the accumulation of *billions* of dollars. Why do we not discuss it as such, preferring to discuss his philanthropic governing capacity as an act of benevolence? How does this fact – that today philanthropic governing capacity is possible only through the circumstances that allow for a few to pursue massive amounts of profit – become transformed from a *political issue* into what Ben Agger (1989) calls a "de-signified fact" that we mistakenly interpret as fate instead of a political choice? Agger's (1989, p. 52) answer in his theory of fast capitalism is that we have reached a stage of capitalism in which money and its uneven distribution are now taken as pre-given facts and we fail to recognize that money and the power relations it sustains tells us a lot about the social structure in which we live:

> Money's falsehood lies in the truth it conceals about capital/labor relations, namely that money is possible only if workers are robbed of surplus value. But money is not simply a text to be read against an external standard of validity, namely that of critique ... Money has utility. It also tells the truth in its reified social relation dispersed into the exterior environment.

Philanthropy disguises money as benevolence and thus disguises that it is possible only through capital–labor relations. This understanding, which disguises how philanthropic governing capacity is derived, is then dispersed uncritically into the exterior environment, inhibiting social action on well-being through its insistence on *change through* the pursuit of profit, or money. Philanthropy's capacity to act, money, is particularly difficult to criticize because money is just as easily associated with the achievement of well-being (wealth) rather than the denial of well-being (poverty). Hence, profit derived from marginality appears to be the only means by which to facilitate social action. As global philanthropists exercise philanthropic governing capacity, they further their own capacity to profit through the stabilization of the myth that money is benevolent.

Our awareness of how philanthropic governing capacity is achieved, most often through labor relations that result in the denial of well-being for some and extreme wealth for others, is lost in the seemingly natural medium of money. The social relationship embedded in money proceeds to make social policy via philanthropic governing capacity. When money is used to control the distribution of resources, resources are distributed as social policy according to those who have managed to accumulate it. This is distinctly exclusionary because social policy comes to be dictated by profit in the hands of the few who are able to amass wealth, further marginalizing those who already have been denied well-being. Social policy that is dependent on philanthropists' discretionary exercise of governing capacity legitimates the very system that it is assumed to oppose. It legitimates profit's creation of philanthropic governing capacity by appearing to be benevolence rather than profit. Philanthropists depend on the social system remaining the same if they are to continue to govern.

Conclusion

Global governance and the associated emphasis on granting philanthropic governing capacity to those who are most able to accumulate wealth divorce the public, whether it is national or global, from the politics of the social policy according to which they live. It is the most basic of democratic principles that the individuals whose well-being philanthropic governors seek to impact through their wealth ought to have a voice in how their lives are governed. Yet the undeniable founding principle of philanthropic governing capacity is that those with the most wealth and the most to gain from poverty will have the most impact on poverty. The result of such a scheme for managing well-being is that the poorest among us will have the least voice.

If there is any hope of achieving well-being for most of the world's inhabitants, a goal that must be at least as possible as accumulating billions of dollars, then we must stop portraying the denial of well-being as being unrelated to the pursuit of wealth. When public problems become private publicity crusades, we fail to see the struggle that social problems represent and fail to question the governing capacity that philanthropic actors achieve *at the expense of human well-being*. It is worrisome not only that the capacity to impact governance is now achieved through massive amounts of wealth, but also that this situation is *celebrated* as though it represents what is best about humanity. Genuine generosity would stand apart from wealth and be focused on the systemic conditions that result in the denial of human well-being for some and philanthropic governing capacity for others.

References

Agger, B. (1989). *Fast Capitalism: A Critical Theory of Significance*, Urbana, IL, University of Illinois Press.

Anheier, H. (2005). *Nonprofit Organizations: Theory, Management, Policy*, New York, Routledge.

Arnove, R. F. (1980). Introduction. In R. F. Arnove (ed.) *Philanthropy and Cultural Imperialism: The Foundations at Home and Abroad* (pp. 1–24), Bloomington, Indiana University Press.

Bang, H., and Esmark, A. (2009). Good governance in network society: Reconfiguring the political from politics to policy. *Administrative Theory & Praxis*, 31(1), 7–38.

Bishop, M., and Green, M. (2008). *Philanthrocapitalism: How the Rich can save the World*, New York, Bloomsbury Press.

Boyte, H. C. (2005). Reframing democracy: Governance, civic agency, and politics. *Public Administration Review*, 65(5), 536–546.

Byrne, J. A. (2002). The new face of philanthropy. *Business Week*, 2 December, pp. 82–94.

Carnegie, A. ([1889] 1992). The gospel of wealth. In D. F. Burlingame (ed.) *The Responsibilities of Wealth* (pp. 1–31), Bloomington, Indiana University Press.

Chandoke, N. (2003). *The Conceits of Civil Society*, New Delhi, Oxford University Press.

Chua, A. (2003). *World on Fire: How Exporting Free Market Democracy Breeds Ethnic Hatred and Global Instability*, New York, Doubleday.

Curti, M. (1973). Philanthropy. In P. P. Wiener (ed.) *Dictionary of the History of Ideas: Studies of Selected Pivotal Ideas, Vol. III* (pp. 486–493), New York, Charles Scribner's Sons.

Deacon, B. (2007). *Global Social Policy and Governance*, London, Sage.

The Economist. (2004). Doing well and doing good. 29 July, www.economist.com

The Economist. (2006). Survey: Wealth and philanthropy: The business of giving. 23 February, www.economist.com

Eikenberry, A. M. (2009). *Giving Circles: Philanthropy, Voluntary Association, and Democracy*, Bloomington, Indiana University Press.

Fraser, N. (1989). *Unruly Practices: Power, Discourse, and Gender in Contemporary Social Theory*, Minneapolis, University of Minnesota Press.

Hirst, P. (2000). Democracy and governance. In J. Pierre (ed.) *Debating Governance: Authority, Steering, and Democracy* (pp. 13–35), New York, Oxford University Press.

Katz, M. B. (1989). *The Undeserving Poor: From the War on Poverty to the War on Welfare*, New York, Pantheon Books.

Kettl, D. (1988). *Government by Proxy*, Washington, DC, Congressional Quarterly Press.

King, S. (2006). *Pink Ribbons, Inc.: Breast Cancer and the Politics of Philanthropy*, Minneapolis, University of Minnesota Press.

McCully, G. (2008). *Philanthropy Reconsidered: Private Initiatives–Public Good–Quality of Life*, Bloomington, IN, AuthorHouse.

Milward, H. B., and Provan, K. (2000). Governing the hollow state. *Journal of Public Administration Research and Theory*, 10(2), 359–379.

Moyo, D. (2009). *Dead Aid: Why Aid is Not Working and How There is a Better Way for Africa*, New York, Farrar, Straus, and Giroux.

Nickel, P. M., and Eikenberry, A. M. (2007). Responding to "natural" disasters: The ethical implications of the voluntary state. *Administrative Theory & Praxis*, 29(4), 534–545.

Nickel, P. M., and Eikenberry, A. M. (2009). The discourse of marketized philanthropy: A critique of consumption, profit, and media celebration as the basis for benevolence. *American Behavioral Scientist*, 57(2), 974–989.

O'Toole, L. J. (1997). The implications for democracy in a networked bureaucratic world. *Journal of Public Administration Research and Theory*, 7(3), 443–459.

O'Toole, L. J., and Meier, K. J. (2004). Desperately seeking Selznick: Cooptation and the dark side of public management in networks. *Public Administration Review*, 64(6), 681–693.

Perelman, J. (1976). *The Myth of Marginality: Urban Poverty and Politics in Rio de Janeiro*, Berkeley, University of California Press.

Philanthropy. (2000). *The American Heritage Dictionary of the English Language*, 4th edn, http://dictionary.reference.com/browse/philanthropy

Pierre, J. (2000). *Debating Governance: Authority, Steering, and Democracy*, New York, Oxford University Press.

Poppendieck, J. (1998). *Sweet Charity? Emergency Food and the End of Entitlement*, New York, Penguin.

Rhodes, R. A. W. (1994). The hollowing out of the state: The changing nature of the public service in Britain. *Political Quarterly*, 65(2), 138–151.

Roelofs, J. (1995). The third sector as a protective layer for capitalism. *Monthly Review*, 47(4), 16–25.

Ryan, M. (1982). *Marxism and Deconstruction: A Critical Articulation*, Baltimore, MD, The Johns Hopkins University Press.

Salamon, L. M. (1987). Of market failure, voluntary failure, and third-party government: The theory of government–nonprofit relations in the modern welfare sate. *Journal of Voluntary Action & Research*, 16(1/2), 29–49.

Schervish, P. G. (2003). Hyperagency and high-tech donors: A new theory of the new philanthropists. Paper presented at the Annual Conference of the Association for Research on Nonprofit Organizations and Voluntary Action, www.bc.edu/research/cwp/meta-elements/pdf/haf.pdf

Sørensen, E. (2002). Democratic theory and network governance. *Administrative Theory & Praxis*, 24(4), 693–720.

Sørensen, E., and Torfing, J. (2003). Network politics, political capital, and democracy. *International Journal of Public Administration*, 26(6), 609–634.

Sørensen, E., and Torfing, J. (2005). Network governance and post-liberal democracy. *Administrative Theory & Praxis*, 27(2), 197–237.

Villadsen, K. (2007). The emergence of "neo-philanthropy." *Acta Sociologica*, 50(3), 309–323.

Wagner, D. (2000). *What's Love Got to Do With It? A Critical Look at American Charity*, New York, New York Press.

Wälti, S., Kubler, D., and Papadopoulos, Y. (2004). How democratic is "governance"? Lessons from Swiss drug policy. *Governance*, 17(1), 83–113.

Wolch, J. R. (1990). *The Shadow State: Government and Voluntary Sector in Transition*, New York, The Foundation Center.

Žižek, S. (2006). The liberal communists of Porto Davos. *In These Times*, 11 April, www.inthesetimes.com/site/main/article/2574

Chapter 20
The Question of the Poor

Ashwani Kumar

Introduction

Rejecting the neutral, managerial, donor-driven, and client-oriented developmentalism of the "third sector," this chapter argues for reinventing the meaning and location of the third sector as a normatively and theoretically new paradigm that is centered on the emancipatory political project of transforming dominant structures of power, protecting human rights, and increasing the sphere of democratic life for the poor. Based on an interpretive analysis of two popular pro-poor urban and rural civil society struggles in India, this chapter argues that the notion of the poor requires re-conceptualization of their agency and rights in general. Although the voices of the poor have become more pronounced and effective in the electoral space in India, NGOs and civil society organizations continue to create new modes of mobilizing the poor into a cohesive and robust political force and so redefine governance and democracy. In short, this chapter advocates and endorses a more citizen-centric and agency-oriented activist approach to defining the voluntary sector and abolishing poverty.

Often conceptualized in terms of dichotomies, contrasts, or dangerously seductive hybridity, the idea of a third sector is one of the most used, abused, and also contested concepts in current political thinking on people-led autonomous spheres of collective action for development and democracy. The third sector – often understood as being synonymous with civil society or conceptualized as nonprofit associationalism or "plain-vanilla" volunteering – not only has become a "fad" in social science literature but has also increasingly been embraced by many postmodernist skeptics, anarcho-communitarians, and policymakers of various hues and colors around the world. The continuously growing third sector, especially against the backdrop of the ever-increasing globalization of unpredictable misery and imagined prosperity, has indeed created spaces for a radical politics of "community," but it has also paradoxically led to the valorization of a universal "politics of voluntary

A. Kumar (✉)
Tata Institute of Social Sciences, Mumbai, India
e-mail: ashwanitiss@gmail.com

R. Taylor (ed.), *Third Sector Research*, DOI 10.1007/978-1-4419-5707-8_20,
© Springer Science+Business Media, LLC 2010

action" to maintain dominant hierarchies of power and exploitation in the global order. In other words, the third sector is a site of citizens' initiatives as well as the "emergence of new asymmetrical power relations" (Berdahl et al. 2000, p. 1).

Fueled by the twin processes of associational and informational revolutions and sustained by rising waves of demand for "good governance" in the 1980s, the third sector has slowly and sturdily emerged as an independent sphere of social and political participation outside the state and market for a vast majority of people who have not had the opportunity in the past to be heard by the hegemonic structures of development and democracy. It is not surprising that the third sector theoretically claims to mediate in the "actualization and preservation of the universal which is contained within the particularity of civil society" (Hegel 1991, p. 265). Therefore, the third sector not only refers to an "imaginary repertoire" of public-spirited activists but also normatively seeks to transcend the public/private distinction in the form of a community-centric democratic life and voluntarist conception of social action. It is in this sense that the third sector has the potential to produce "tectonic shifts" in the way the state and market have conducted their relations in the past.

The third sector's inchoate, polymorphous, and presumed neutral character in terms of civil society has been recognized and debated upon by many observers of civil society (Chandhoke 2004; Cohen and Arato 1992; Comaroff and Comaroff 1999; Edwards 2004). Though it remains differentiated from the state and market, the so-called voluntary space in the third sector is constituted and informed by power relations in the state and market. In his book *Third-Sector Development*, Christopher Gunn (2004, p. 2) identifies the third sector as a hybrid sector denoting "a mix of nonprofit and cooperative economic organizations and their activities." In general, the third sector has been defined spatially in terms of sectoral representations that illustrate the interactional relations between major sectors of society such as state/government, market/business, and associational/voluntary (Evers and Laville 2004; see Chapter 3, this volume). In the consolidated American and European democracies, third sector organizations have brought more resources for public policy, participated in policy making, and facilitated collective action for the advancement of the "target community." For many in postsocialist states, the term third sector has also become a "countermodel" of public action to the "dirty realms of politics and business" (Hemment 2004). In the new democracies in Central and Eastern Europe, the third sector does though also represent a "structural and symbolic framework for the reproduction of former elites" of the communist regime (DeHoog and Racanska 2003). It is not, therefore, always genuinely participatory or emancipatory.

Evidence from the United States and Europe suggests that the realm of the third sector has grown beyond initial expectation of galvanizing the famed de Tocquevillian spirit of volunteering. Taking advantage of the "revolution in charitable fundraising," entrepreneurial culture, and innovation in the branding techniques in the venture market, it has successfully marketed itself, accessed public funds, and developed a sturdy "nonprofit infrastructure" (Salamon 2003; Van Til 1988). The language of "sector brokerage" or "partnership" rather than contestation seems to guide the policy and political interactions between government and nongovernmental organizations in many places (Lewis 2008). Writing on the complex relationship between government and third sector, Wolfgang Dorner (2008) argues that "From a more critical perspective, the 'instrumentalization' of third sector organizations is perceived as a cost-cutting exercise following a neo-liberal agenda, aiming at down-sizing the state, or it is seen as a means to increase control over the non-state actors, partly through contractual arrangements and through blurring the boundaries between the state and organized civil society." Due to this process of instrumentalization, the third sector has increasingly become a government-regulated and sanctioned community service provider resulting in the depoliticization of spaces of public action in which poor and marginalized groups neither participate nor are perceived as self-governing agents of change. This has led to a sense of identity crisis and also raised questions as to the democratic credentials of the third sector.

In contrast to the Western experience, in India the third sector has indeed found popular and contradictory resonance among diverse institutional and mobilizational forms of the "nonprofit sector," "voluntary sector," or more precisely "civil society" space populated by development-centric NGOs, community-based organizations (CBOs), cooperatives, self-help groups, philanthropic organizations, and the "rainbow coalition" of social movements of various shapes and scales. In their study of the voluntary sector in India, Priya Viswanath and Noshir Dadrawala (2004) observed that:

> The formal voluntary sector in contemporary India is fairly vibrant. While there is no definitive study on the size of the sector, there are several estimates and projections. According to a recent CAF [*Charities Aid Foundation*] study, it is estimated that there are between two million and three million registered organizations. The factors that have contributed to this astronomical increase in the number of NPOs in the last few decades include weakening government delivery systems, widespread poverty and deprivation and increasing inequity, rising awareness and social concern about under-development and inequity, and the influx of increased funding – both indigenous and foreign – for development purposes. (p. 13)

The booming voluntary space in India has also been attributed to the alleged failure of the Nehruvian model of development and the growing anti-people policies of the government in the 1970s. The importance of the voluntary sector acquired salience in the 1990s when India made the transition from a social-welfare state to an entrepreneurial state. In other words, the third sector in India has been driven more by political processes than by cultural processes (Kumar 2000; Sen 1999; Society for Participatory Research in Asia 2003).

In India, the nonprofit sector and state relations illustrate four trends: (1) some NGOs or civil society organizations – especially those operating in the mode of social movements such as Medha Patkar led NBA (Narmada Bachao Andolan) – act as an "independent opposition" to state power; (2) most development-oriented NGOs prefer to act as an "agent of the state" and deliver services on behalf of the government; (3) many NGOs and civil society organizations, such as Tarun Bharat Sangh (TBS), Parivartan, and Mazdoor Kisan Shakti Sangathan, prefer a dual mode of opposition and collaboration with government in making and implementing public policy for community development and empowerment of poor people; and

(4) most philanthropic organizations, such as Sir Dorabji Tata Trust, shun politics and engage only in target areas such as education, healthcare, population, natural resource management, and enterprise development. Barring anti-state social movements, the relationship between the voluntary sector and the government is more one of collaboration than competition.

Though the third sector has grown exponentially as part of the rapidly expanding civil society of the 1990s, it still remains out of bounds to a vast segment of poor lower castes, tribals, and women in India. Theoretically, the term "civil society" in India has paradoxically come to represent a "small section of citizens" or "an exclusive domain of the elite," whereas most of the popular mobilizations and livelihood struggles of the poor and marginalized people take place in what political theorist Partha Chatterjee (2001, pp. 172–173) has termed "political society" – a distinct space lying between civil society and the state. Following Chatterjee's idiosyncratic but influential formulation of "political society," one may argue that in India "civic activism" generally encompasses an exclusive domain of upper caste, upper-class, English-speaking individuals. This space has, however, incidentally coincided with increasing popular participation of lower caste, tribals, and women in the process of deepening democracy. It is in this sense that the historical development of the Indian third sector is tied to the gradual democratization of state and society in the post-independence era.

The Question of the Poor in Theory and Practice

Though poor and impoverished classes and castes have played a vanguard role in mobilizing struggle against hierarchies of power and social exclusion in both developed and developing countries, they are not often recognized as being capable of exercising independent influence in determining the contours of relations between state and civil society. Most anti-poverty initiatives of government or nongovernmental organizations view the poor as "deviant," "deprived," and "destitute" – in contrast to viewing the poor as having "voice," "agency," and "capability" to change the world. Traditionally, poor people have been understood as people afflicted with hunger, malnutrition, ill-health, unsanitary housing, and lack of medical and educational facilities. This list can be stretched even further to portray poor people as leading subhuman lives. In short, the poor have been perceived as lacking the capabilities to lead a life with dignity and decency. It is rarely acknowledged in the public policy literature that the poor possess positive attributes of humanity and are often fully capable of realizing and relishing "human flourishing." In fact, evidence of the surge of the self-help-group movement and social audit campaigns from India and elsewhere suggests that the poor neither are always resource deficient nor lack agency in devising livelihood strategies and leading social resistance.

Undaunted by the evidence of the poor as successful entrepreneurs in India and elsewhere, the dominant civil society literature inspired by fashionable strands of utilitarianism and libertarianism has often portrayed the poor as merely an "empirical person" or member of a population characterized by the absence of a certain minimal amount of income, wealth, skills, and capacity to support oneself biologically and socially. Following theoretical trajectories of what Ulrich Beck (2003) calls "methodological nationalism" or Thomas Pogge (2002) describes "explanatory nationalism," poverty is defined as a nationally measurable condition of absence of "minimum, nutritionally adequate diet plus essential non-food requirements" (UNDP 1996, p. 222). Though this definition addresses a critical material aspect of poverty, it fails to see poverty as powerlessness and "unfreedom of various sorts: the lack of freedom to achieve even minimally satisfactory living conditions" (Sen 2008, p. xiii).

Typically in welfare policy literature, the poor appear as statistically defined and mechanically identified "end-users" of governmental welfare programs; they often signify a regime dominated not by structures of sovereignty and rights but by techniques of government. In this way, the governmental practices of the modern welfare state create a distinction between "citizen" and "population." As citizens, people are rights-bearing subjects who must govern themselves on their self-determined, sanctioned principles of social justice. In contrast, populations are measured and evaluated according to the target and outcomes of policy designed and implemented from above by a group of experts and policymakers. It is on this plain of "governmentality" (Foucault 2006) that the poor are erased from the purview of popular sovereignty and the realm of civil society. This explains why many development NGOs end up reproducing the interests of the dominant elite in civil society rather than promoting democratic political participation of the poor and marginalized (Ulvila and Hossain 2002).

In other words, "governmentalization" takes the poor to be a passive, inert, non-demanding, and non-self-determining mass of the population. These socially excluded populations are also "stigmatized" and "ostracized" as dirty, filthy, violent, polluted, and non-members of the general civil society. More importantly, the poor are often portrayed as fragmented, partitioned, and parceled out in terms of the traditional territorial boundaries of the "imagined nation-state." This theoretical and discursive bias against the poor has been popularized by Hegel's meta-language of the "theatre of history" in which the poor lead a particularistic and apolitical existence. Lacking the element of universality, Hegel famously characterized the poor as *die Standeslosen*, "those unfortunate of no estate" and without explicit "political functions in relation to the state" (Hegel 1991, pp. 241–246). Since they do not belong to any legally recognized and constituted "estate," the poor actually do not exist in civil society. According to Hegel, in reality the poor lead an irrational, contingent, and negative social existence and deserve the designation *Pubel* (translated as "rabble"). Anticipating the serious political and social consequences of the rise of "non-members" of civil society, Hegel, however, prophetically announced, "The important question of how poverty is to be abolished is one of the most disturbing questions which agitate modern society" (ibid, p. 244).

Following Hegel's cautionary remark about the growing social significance of the poor, Marx came to view the poor as "the elemental class of human society," "those whose property consists of life, freedom, humanity and citizenship of the state, who own nothing except themselves" (Marx and Engels 1975, p. 231). Though Marx retained the original Hegelian meaning of the poor, he accorded the poor agency and envisaged them as harbingers of a revolution that would uproot "petty, wooden, mean and selfish" bourgeoisie civil society (ibid, p. 234). In Marx's hands, poverty is not seen as a barrier to the development of revolutionary proletarian consciousness but he also failed to see that the poor are not "one vast homogenous" mass of the population, for they are in truth internally differentiated by race, class, caste, religion, gender, language, region, and place of origin – a heterogeneity that has been seen by neo-Marxists as an insurmountable impediment to forming a "historic bloc" of the poor (Gramsci 1971, p, 366).

Following a Hegelian bias, conventional liberal democratic theory has also erroneously and scandalously popularized the idea either that poor people lack the necessary agency for "making democracy" or that "poor people make poor democracy." Mainstream social science suggests that the existence of the poor poses a serious challenge to democracy. From Marx's *Eighteenth Brumaire of Louis Bonaparte* (1963) to Lipset's analysis of democracy in *Political Man* (1960), many political scientists and liberal democrats have argued that "poor people are unprepared for democracy or ill-disposed to obey democratic norms: the poor are more likely to succumb to appeals of irresponsible demagogues; they are rigid and intolerant, authoritarian; easily attracted to extremist movements. Political participation by the poor in the realm of civil society is thus a threat to democracy" (Przeworski 2008, p. 125).

The general skepticism and distrust in the capability of the poor to alter prevailing hierarchies of power stems from a deeply flawed understanding of the secularization of poverty and the nature of "civic duty" in Western political theory. This has not only resulted in confining the poor to new secular spaces such as workhouses, prisons, mental asylums, night-shelters, and more recently credit and thrift societies, but also "showed the poor and destitute to be both a consequence of disorder and an obstacle to order" (Foucault 2006, p. 57). This is why in analytical thinking on poverty and democracy the poor are presented as alienated and apart from civil society.

Invisible or Insurgent Citizens: The Engagement of the Poor in India

The evidence from pro-poor mobilizations from India, however, challenges the standard view of the poor as "passive recipient of welfare doles" or a disorderly mass of population. In fact, the so-called illegal poor slum dwellers, in *"Jhuggi-Jhopri"* (small roughly built houses or shelters usually made of mud, wood, or metal with thatch or tin sheet roof covering), are relatively more "active problem-solvers" than other citizens in India (Harris 2006). In contrast to the Western experience of poverty, the poor in India are disproportionately from lower castes and marginalized ethnic communities. The poor not only suffer from various forms of social exclusion and structural inequalities, but also experience disadvantage in their inter-actions with government officials who are commonly from higher castes and classes. This does not, however, prevent the poor from challenging the corrupt and ineffi-cient state officials and their cohorts who monopolize most resources in formal civil society.

It is in this connection that Chatterjee's distinction between "civil society" and "political society" makes sense. Reflecting on the forgotten and disenfranchised poor in the realm of civil society, he writes, "Most of the inhabitants of India are only tenuously . . . rights-bearing citizens in the sense imagined by the constitution. They are not, therefore, proper members of civil society and are not regarded as such by the institutions of the state" (Chatterjee 2004, p. 38). The poor especially landless laborers, rural migrants, slum dwellers, casual construction workers, pave-ment dwellers, project-affected persons, and sex workers are considered easy and soft targets of state-centric modern social policy. Their chronic poverty drives the government to devise "welfare" strategies and schemes that end up simply confining the poor to socially excluded spaces without any constitutionally guaranteed supply of social goods.

In contrast, poor people who are thus defined indulge in actions that are quite often technically illegal – such as squatting on public land or stealing electricity and water – to make claims upon the state for the realization of what they believe to be their rights to welfare. Commenting on the poor's complicated and politically strategic location in civil society, Chatterjee (2001, p. 177) writes,

> The agencies of the state and of non-governmental organizations deal with these people not as bodies of citizens belonging to a lawfully constituted civil society, but as popula-tion groups deserving welfare. The degree to which they will be so recognized depends entirely on the pressure they are able to exert on those state and non-state agencies through their strategic maneuvers in political society – by making connections with other marginal groups, with more dominant groups, with political parties, and leaders, etc.

These "destitutes" and "outsiders" – through their independent initiatives, actions, and struggles – form "political society" as a space of everyday contesta-tion and negotiation that lies between civil society and the state to realize "historical possibilities" of social justice. In other words, the poor constitute a "disturbing ele-ment", a disturbance, a "rupture," and resist assimilation into bourgeois civil society – "the realm of difference" in the modern world. A good case in point is found in Arvind Rajagopal's (2001) study of hawkers that focuses on "poor *Pheriwalas* (lit-erally, those who move around) who roam the streets of Indian cities bearing baskets on their heads or pushing a handcart and offer customers goods and produce cheaper than that found in stores; they form part of the economy that spurs consumption, yet they are seen as a vagrant and legally discomforting population requiring disci-pline," surveillance, and control by the state (p. 91). In other words, a large number of productive, resource-efficient people get banished from the formal civil society.

Ironically, the moral economy between the poor and those state authorities – such as the police officials, civil servants, and politicians – rests on patronage, protection, and money. It is quite well known in India that the poor pay a regular bribe, *hafta*, to local police and municipal authorities. As a consequence of this "infrapolitics" of the poor (Scott 1990), local authorities ignore or selectively enforce the rule of law as defined by court rulings and government statutes. In short, those living on the so-called wrong side of the law in India, such as pavement dwellers, street hawkers, garbage collectors, beggars, and sex workers, often engage in quotidian negotiations with formal, legal bureaucratic doctrine of rationality and subvert a liberal and literal interpretation of civil society. This popular recourse to "paralegal" or quasi-legal processes of social existence by the poor in India symbolizes their attempt to be treated as self-governing people rather than disempowered individual elements of population. Hence, the poor's struggle over welfare or distribution of resources is not one dimensional; it is also connected to the struggle for recognition and discursive power. The poor belonging to various disadvantaged groups – women, the lower caste (*dalits*), impoverished tribals, and various socially excluded ethnic minorities – often organize themselves as collective subjects with the power to solve their own problems.

In short, the politics of welfare and the politics of recognition are embedded in each other. Narratives of popular struggles of the poor in places like Mumbai reveal that much despised and ostracized slum dwellers often build direct and indirect supranational solidarities, collaborations, and exchanges among poor communities based on a "will to federate" and a "spirit to resist." It is quite well known in India that slum dwellers are able to organize a multi-class, caste alliance of "everyday resistance" with support from community-based civil society organizations. Though slum dwellers continue to remain "invisible" to state planners and civil authorities, they rely on their "perpetual social visibility" to articulate their rights. Calling the poor's innovative livelihood struggles in slums as "governmentality from below," Arjun Appadurai (2002, pp. 21–27) concludes that "here, perpetual social visibility within the community (an invisibility in the eyes of the state) becomes an asset that enables the mechanisms of self-monitoring, self-enumerating, and self-regulation to operate at the nexus of family, land, and dwelling that is the central site of material negotiations in slum life."

Case Studies of the Livelihood Struggles of the Poor in India

It is this "governmentality from below" or emergence of "political society" that has become the driving force of the robustness and responsiveness of voluntary or non-profit space in India. In contrast to Western third sector experience, voluntarism of the poor in India has flourished largely in the form of a "political project" – a project in which the poor themselves have played a leading role against the growing twin deficits of democracy and development. Lacking the typical resources and advocacy skills of Western donor-driven third sector organizations, the poor and marginalized in India have frequently violated the law and organized collective action against dominant interests and an unresponsive state. This has led to the rise of a popular politics of the subaltern and also a violent backlash by the elite. To a great extent, this popular upsurge of civil society is both a cause and a consequence of the crisis of "governability" and the increasing number of human rights violations (Khilnani 2003; Kohli 1987, 2002; Kothari 1988; Mendelsohn and Vicziany 1998; Rudolph and Rudolph 1987).

Documented accounts of some of the popular livelihood struggles of the poor clearly demonstrate that the poor have played a historic role in reconfiguring the contours of voluntary action and in deepening democracy. The interesting aspect of the poor's struggle in the realm of the civil society is that they do not generally organize through typical donor-driven development NGOs. Most pro-poor civil society organizations spring up from the conditions of "everyday resistance" and gradually acquire the skills, resources, social capital, and infrastructure of typical third sector organizations. The livelihood struggles waged by civil society organizations such as SPARC (Society for the Promotion of Area Resource Centers) in Mumbai and MKKS (Mazdoor Kisan Shakti Sangathan) in Rajasthan are instructive in this regard as they both developed their innovative mobilization strategy and institutional capacity in the wake of poor people's struggles against discrimination and exclusion from civil society spaces. SPARC in Mumbai was formed as an NGO by a group of social workers to organize pavement dwellers, especially women pavement dwellers, against the policy and political bias of state authorities to deny the poor the right to housing – the most contentious site of livelihood and citizenship struggles in Mumbai. Similarly, MKSS in Rajasthan is a grassroots NGO that grew out of attempts to organize the rural poor against corruption on famine-relief work sites in the late 1980s. The organization slowly realized that getting access to information was the main barrier in the struggle for people's livelihood – and this resulted in the rise of the historic movement for the right to information in India.

The Case of SPARC: Poor Pavement Dwellers

Largely invisible and forgotten on the cognitive map of civil society action, and often considered as "non-citizens" by the state, pavement dwellers in Mumbai have often challenged the prevailing paradigms of justice, citizenship, and state-led governance in India. As pavement dwellers build their houses on pavements rather than on vacant land, they are the most visible yet most forgotten members of urban civil society in Mumbai. Since pavements lie in the domain of public property, any encroachment on free public space is viewed seriously by the dominant middle class and resisted by local civic authorities. In other words, the relationship between the spatial visibility of the urban poor and public policy is a very complicated one, triggering the upsurge of "governmentality from below."

As noted earlier, housing is a most critical site for the politics of citizenship in Mumbai and the urban poor – especially slum and pavement dwellers. And it was the frequent raids by official civic authorities to remove pavement dwellers from the so-called public property or open public spaces that resulted in the formation of SPARC in 1984. In the specific context of the livelihood struggles of the poor,

SPARC organizes slum dwellers and pavement dwellers in Mumbai and also sup-ports two people's movement – the National Slum Dwellers Federation (NSDF) and Mahila Milan (MM) (www.sparcindia.org). Although treated as an "invisi-ble" population without any formal civil rights in official public policy, the slum dwellers' presence on the pavements makes them the most visible part of Mumbai's vast urban population; according to a rough estimate by SPARC, at least 6 million people live in Mumbai slums (Burra 2000). From the point of view of the State Municipal Corporation, pavement dwellers are "illegal occupants" or encroachers of public space. Instead of addressing the housing problem of poor people, the dominant response of the state has been to evict them and demolish their dwelling places. From the perspective of pavement dwellers, the state resembles a "demoli-tion squad" – a predatory roving band. From the point of view of the city's elite, slum dwellers are "unworthy" citizens as they illegally occupy the pavements, clog the free space, steal electricity, and put the infrastructure of the city under severe stress. Politicians and underworld strongmen routinely abuse them for partisan purposes and then abandon them to their "manifest destiny."

Pavement dwellers have routinely and arbitrarily been denied a right to vote – as their names have been kept off the official electoral rolls in Mumbai. As a result of this political invisibility, pavement dwellers are not considered for the "right to com-pensation" if state authorities recover or recapture public land from these so-called encroachers on public property. As Bishnu Mohapatra (2003) argues, pavement dwellers have been sacrificed for political and "policy reasons," because the poor were officially not only forgotten but also denied citizenship rights. SPARC which addresses the case of pavement dwellers in Mumbai is actually an intermediary civil society association that has also emerged as a nodal point on advocacy and networking for the actualization of pavement and slum dwellers' rights.

The persistent demolition of slums including the pavement hutment in Mumbai in the 1980s witnessed sporadic but intense mobilization among pavement dwellers in the city. The litigation at various levels of the legal system also gave fresh opportunity on the part of civil society organizations to intervene in the pro-cess. In this context the judgment of the Supreme Court in *Olga Tellis & Ors vs. Bombay Municipal Case*, July 1985, was significant. This case concerning pave-ment dwellers was brought before the Supreme Court of India by a diverse group of Bombay residents, human rights organizations (such as the Peoples Union for Civil Liberties and the Committee for the Protection of Democratic Rights), and two journalists – one of whom was Olga Tellis. The judgment maintained the pri-macy of the "protection of public property" but it also highlighted the continuing social exclusion of slum dwellers from the hegemonic order of civil society. The judgment upheld the pavement dweller's right to livelihood within the ambit of the right to life in the Constitution but ironically allowed the civic authorities to evict pavement dwellers from public spaces. Reflecting on the contradictory nature of the judgment, Olga Tellis (2003) insightfully commented, "Ironically, [the case] helped the propertied classes; lawyers often cite the case to justify eviction of tenants and slum dwellers. But it also helps the slum dwellers; the Government can't evict them summarily. The case also spawned a lot of interest in fighting for housing as a fundamental right . . . but if you were a pavement dweller, it is not enough."

It is here that the role of a nongovernmental organization like SPARC was of crucial importance. The census of pavement dwellers in Mumbai that was carried out by SPARC in 1985 made the pavement dwellers "visible" and also for the first time portrayed them as "citizens." And this was a great achievement. The census showed that many of these pavement dwellers were born in Mumbai with some 60% having been in the city for over a decade, and some had actually lived in Mumbai for more than four decades (Burra 2000). One ethnographic study of the struggle of pavement dwellers led by SPARC found that:

> The census created a sense of agency among the pavement dwellers, changing how the city they occupy was perceived and conceived, thereby changing power relations. The sense of agency created in the pavement dwellers eventually changed their living conditions; for example, they negotiated the delivery of electricity to their housing. The strategic action eventually led to the first group of pavement dwellers being moved to permanent housing elsewhere in the city. This case of the pavement dwellers showed that the right to the city could be asserted through their lived spaces. Citizenship is not a static category. It needs to and can successfully be challenged. (Knudsen 2007, p. 16)

Buoyed with the success of a participatory census that galvanized the latent agency of poor pavement dwellers, SPARC organized – in association with MM and NSDF – a housing exhibition in 1986; this was again an innovative strategy as it showcased an ideal house for pavement dwellers. The same governmentalizing strategies of enumeration and exhibition were used with great effect in articulating an "insurgent citizenship." The evolving solidarity forged through MM and NSDF played a major role in the gradual empowerment of pavement dwellers in Mumbai.

Mahila Milan is an outcome of the interventions of SPARC and is an association of women pavement dwellers. According to SPARC, "Mahila Milan means 'Women Together' in Hindi and is a decentralized network of poor women's collectives that manage credit and savings activities in their communities. Mahila Milan was initiated in 1986 when 500 women who lived on Mumbai's pavements organized themselves to successfully prevent the demolitions of their homes. Today, Mahila Milan has given out tens of thousands of loans to poor women all across the country and has collected savings worth several crores of rupees" (www.sparcindia.org). SPARC played the role in the initial empowerment of Mahila Milan both in terms of building their awareness and in terms of enabling them to engage with the Municipal Corporation and other government agencies in Mumbai. This coalition was able to put pressure on the government and the municipal authorities not only through demonstrations and *dharna* (public protests) but also through sustained meetings and dialogues structured to articulate the interests and needs of pavement dwellers.

As this case study points out, one of the outcomes of this sustained endeavor was not only the recognition of pavement dwellers in the formal policies of urban development and rehabilitation of the poor in Mumbai but also recognition of poor pavement dwellers as part of civil society in Mumbai. Bowing to the pressures of slum dwellers, the government of Maharashtra agreed in the early 1990s that all people living on slums and pavements are fully eligible for housing schemes and for relocation on nearby vacant land. It is worth noting here that SPARC achieved the success by using a mix of innovative nonviolent mobilization strategies such as dialogue, documentation, meetings, petitioning, participatory people's census, and picketing. At no stage did SPARC follow violent confrontation with the government. Slowly, SPARC formed a coalition with the National Slum Dwellers' Federation which begun as a membership association to represent the aspirations and interests of slum dwellers, not only in Mumbai but in different parts of the country.

By leading the struggles of poor pavement dwellers, the coalition of SPARC, Mahila Milan, and National Slum Dwellers Federation in Mumbai has emerged as an instrument for deepening democracy; it has served to radicalize the notion of the third sector as it has successfully demonstrated that urban civil society space is far from being a "neutral container" but is actually an active political space in which the meaning of citizenship is perpetually contested, negotiated, and reinvented.

The Case of MKSS: The Right to Information for the Rural Poor

The right to information movement led by Mazdoor Kisan Shakti Sangathan in Rajasthan is also a powerful example of the mobilization of the poor. In this case, the struggles of poor rural people for a better livelihood resulted in the enactment – in October 2005 – of a new national law on the right to information.[1] Reflecting on the aims, objectives, and historic success of MKKS, Aruna Roy, Nikhil Dey, and Shankar Singh – three prominent founding leaders of MKSS – write:

> The Mazdoor Kisan Shakti Sangathan (MKSS) is a peoples' organisation that has used processes of collective analysis and political action as a means of empowerment. For those concerned with people living on the edge of poverty and sustenance, development priorities have become linked to the issue of survival. In the face of increasing unemployment and retrenchment, the diminishing role of the state and its withdrawal from social responsibilities, the poor can now see the development strategy as a systematic effort to paralyse their access to power through a variety of methods. Their exploration led to the identification of the *jan sumwai* or public hearing as an effective mode where they could speak and be heard. The public hearings on development expenditure at the panchayat level have led to a crystallization of issues and given a tangible quality to the abstract notion of transparency and the right to information. (2001, p. 36)

The genesis of MKKS is often traced to the actions of a disparate group of middle-class educated social activists supported by local poor people in a land struggle against a feudal landowner in the village of Sohangarh in Deogarh Tehsil of Rajsamand District, central Rajasthan, where, in 1990, a protest rally of around 1,000 people gathered from 27 villages within the Pali, Rajsamand, Bhilwara, and Ajmer districts (Mishra 2003). Aruna Roy, a former officer of the elite Indian Administrative Service, Nikhil Dey, a US-educated social activist, and Shankar

---

[1] The narrative on MKSS is based on personal experience and postings on the MKSS website, as well as several published monographs on MKSS: Aakella and Kidambi (2007), Mander (2000), Mishra (2003), Roy (1996), and Tandon and Mohanty (2003).

Singh, a local barefoot-communicator, were instrumental in organizing this struggle against local landlords taking illegal possession of land, the non-payment of minimum wages, and ghost entries in the muster rolls of poor laborers at famine relief sites.

Through "struggle and constructive action," MKSS slowly began as a nongovernmental organization comprised of the rural landless and poor who were ignored by both government and various development-centric NGOs in the region. The struggle for ensuring fair working conditions and wages in rural Rajasthan led MKSS activists to recognize widespread corruption in the various developmental works of the government as a denial of the "livelihood rights" of the rural poor. Given the specific ecology of Rajasthan and frequency of droughts in the region, famine work relief sites are major sources of public employment for poor people; yet these worksites are notorious for not paying minimum wages and also embezzling public money by faking entries in the muster rolls. Corruption at the worksites had spillover effects on the livelihood of poor people – such as entitlements under the public distribution system and public health centers in the villages of Rajasthan. And the vicious cycle of development deficit was further compounded by criminal collusion among powerful landlords, local politicians, construction contractors, engineers, and police in the region.

After their initial protracted struggle against the local landlord's illegal possession of public land in Sohangarh village and the Dadi Rapat worksite struggle for payment of wages in the late 1980s, leading activists of MKSS realized that ensuring transparency and accountability was integral to securing the poor's livelihood rights. To this end, MKSS focused on asserting people's inalienable right to information. In order to fight corruption and strengthen participatory democracy at grassroots level, MKKS famously advanced the new method of a social audit through the Jan Sunwai (public hearing) to raise poor people's voice. Relying on such mobilizing strategies as sit-ins, rallies, street theater, puppet shows, and lobbying, while also promoting slogans such as "our money, our account" (*Hamara Paisa, Hamara Hisab*) and "the right to know, the right to live" (*Hum Janenge, Hum Jiyenge*), MKSS popularized the public hearing as a powerful civil society tool for public accountability.

In late 1994, in their well-known "entitlement struggle" of the poor in Kot Kirana Panchayat of Raipur Block in Pali district, Rajasthan, MKSS used the public hearing as a "tactical forum" for the holding of a people's court – but without any formal process for pronouncing judgment. People deprived of their entitlements at the worksites spoke out against the corrupt practices in the implementation of development works and identified the guilty culprits. Describing the nature of a public hearing, Aruna Roy and Nikhil Dey (2003) write that it is "conducted in a comfortable, informal idiom of conversation and exchange. Yet it has all the seriousness and impartiality of court proceedings." The public hearing as conceptualized and practiced by MKSS is primarily a community-sponsored mechanism of vigilance and grievance redressal at grassroots level.

Reflecting on the truth-revealing, justice-adjudicating, and conflict-reconciliatory nature of public hearings, MKSS activists write:

Usually, in a public hearing the MKSS first obtains the records pertaining to the public works carried out by the Village Council in the last five years. Once the documents are accessed, the Sangathan then takes the records to each village where the work is said to have been executed and then testimonies are sought from the villagers and the laborers who were employed on the site. The MKSS also does site verifications with the laborers and villagers, and then on the day of the public hearing in front of the general assembly of the villagers the details are read out and testimonies sought. There is also the concept of having a panel of people who are invited to the public hearings, including lawyers, journalists, academicians and government officials. The panel is also allowed to cross-examine and ask for clarifications, and with the administration present attempts are made to try and bring about corrective measures for the irregularities identified. The malpractices usually uncovered are purchase overbilling, sale overbilling, fake labor rolls, under payment of wages and in some cases ghost works (works that are there on record but do not exist). (www.mkssindia.org/node/1)

The first five public hearings in the four Central Rajasthan districts of Pali, Rajsamand, Ajmer, and Bhilwara that were held between December 1994 and January 1995 had the effect of establishing the "social audit" as an integral principle of participatory rights for the poor in India. One of the highlights of the public hearing has been the increasing participation of women in matters of development and livelihood rights. The public hearing campaigns of MKSS also united the poor with the rural middle class who saw added opportunity to demand development of infrastructural works. The legitimacy of the public hearing lay more in the mobilization of the rural poor than in the nature of the auditing panel. Interestingly, the social audit campaigns of MKSS received support from a wide range of civil society groups, eminent citizens, journalists, teachers, lawyers, and sympathetic civil servants in India. Initially, government officials did not participate, but the increasing popularity of public hearings forced them to take part and acknowledge it as a valid tool of participatory development. Slowly, public hearings of rural poor people started changing the dominant statist discourses of public accountability; the victims of development became defenders of development.

In 1994, the growing success of MKSS in organizing poor people through sustained and protected campaigns – especially the Bewar and Jaipur sit-ins – forced the Rajasthan government to concede that people possessed the right to information and the right to conduct social audits of development works. Buoyed with the success in Rajasthan, MKSS also launched the National Campaign for People's Right to Information in 1996. This initiative received enthusiastic support not only from civil society but also from the political class who found the right to information a novel means to restore their declining legitimacy and dwindling fortunes. MKKS also went beyond usual civil society activism and demanded the institutionalization of people's audits or public hearings in the institutions of decentralization known as Panchayati Raj. In 1999, faced with an increasingly vibrant, assertive, and vociferous civil society, the government of Rajasthan committed itself to the passing of a powerful bill for the right to information; it invited MKSS and the National Campaign for People's Right to Information to prepare the draft. The Rajasthan State Legislature passed the Right to Information Law in May 2000. Though Tamil Nadu and Goa had by that time already passed a similar law, the Rajasthan Act cemented the efforts of MKKS in mobilizing the rural poor for more transparent and accountable governance.

The MKSS-led right to information movement received a major fillip when the United Progressive Alliance (UPA) government in Delhi passed a national law on the right to information in October 2005. It is worth noting here that members from MKKS had participated in the national advisory council of the UPA government and provided valuable advocacy and networking support to the institutionalization of the right to information as well as pro-poor welfare programs such as the National Rural Employment Guarantee Act (NREGA) in February 2006. In fact, NREGA's success or failure depends on activating social audit mechanisms as envisaged in the act. Interestingly, MKKS is not an anti-state civil society organization; it often collaborates with the government as it is currently busy facilitating the success of NREGA as a revolutionary pro-poor employment scheme. It is in this sense that MKSS not only has emerged as the torchbearer of civil society activism in India but has also worked to advance the democratic ideals enshrined in the Constitution of India.

Conclusion: Toward Participatory Democracy and Inclusive Development

Characterized by greater mobility urges, participatory leanings, and entrepreneurial moorings, lower castes, tribals, slum dwellers, fishermen, forest dwellers, construction workers, domestic workers, project-affected persons, sex workers, squatters, landless labor, and poor peasants have placed enormous faith in decentralized democratic institutions, redefined the right to development, and learnt to organize, agitate, and protest more frequently in order to widen and equalize civic space in India. Therefore, it comes as no surprise that pavement dwellers in Mumbai became mobilized to help redefine citizenship rights and that MKKS's advocacy of public hearings became a powerful method of reinstituting the livelihood rights of poor people in India. All of this shows the remarkable resilience of what Chatterjee calls "political society" – an essential condition for the success of democracy in India.

Dispelling myths about the poor's role in invigorating civil society and sustaining democracy, Anirudha Krishna (2008, p. 5) writes: "Evidence from India shows that poor people do not value democracy any less than their richer counterparts. Their faith in democracy is as high as that of other citizens, and they participate in democratic activities as much as their richer counterparts. Democracy is not likely to be unstable or unwelcome simply because poverty is widespread." The interpretive analysis of some of the major livelihood struggles waged by innovative civil society organizations in this chapter clearly demonstrates that the poor in India have reframed the meaning of the "third sector" and made it a more popular and emancipatory political project. In contrast, most development-centric and donor-driven NGOs follow a neoliberal agenda and prefer partnership or cooperative relationships with the Indian government. It is in this sense that the third sector is caught in a paradoxical position between political society and civil society in India; the typical middle-class-centered voluntary space continues to remain the monopoly of professional activists and "policy entrepreneurs," whereas the poor organize themselves outside of civil society. In other words, ameliorating the conditions of the poor must first rest on raising marginalized groups and socially excluded classes/castes to a position of "collective equality" before civil society can begin the process of what Habermas calls "rational communication" between free, equal, and sovereign citizens (Calhoun 1993).

Civil society organizations such as SPARC and MKSS contribute to making this "collective equality" possible. Rather than just noting the "neutral" character and managerial disposition of the third sector, this chapter has treated voluntary exchanges between citizens as an open-ended process whereby inegalitarian structures of power, discrimination, and exclusion are interrogated, criticized, challenged, and ultimately reversed. If the notion of the third sector evokes a typical de Tocquevillian associational space where "social capital" is generated and deployed to maintain the uneasy balance between capital and labor, it also refers to a deeply contested "political project" that essentially means resisting dominant structures of power, enhancing the hold of popular sovereignty in decision-making, and also, more importantly, re-conceptualizing the agency and rights of the poor in general. In the midst of the political chaos, economic anarchy, and emotional mayhem caused by the global economic meltdown, pro-poor civil society struggles in India offer the prospect of a post-liberal world.

References

Aakella, K. V., and Sowmya Kidambi, S. (2007). Challenging corruption with social audits. *Economic and Political Weekly*, 42(47), www.epw.org.in/epw/uploads/articles/10222.pdf

Appadurai, A. (2002). Deep democracy: Urban governmentality and horizon of politics. *Public Culture*, 14(1), 21–47.

Beck, U. (2003). The analysis of global inequality: From national to cosmopolitan perspective. In M. Kaldor, H. Anheier, and M. Glassius (eds) *Global Civil Society 2003* (pp. 45–55), Oxford, Oxford University Press.

Berdahl, D., Bunzl, M., and Lampland, M. (eds) (2000). *Altered States: Ethnographies of Transition in Eastern Europe and the Former Soviet Union*, Ann Arbor, University of Michigan Press.

Burra, S. (2000). A journey towards citizenship: The Byculla area resource center Mumbai. DPU Working paper no. 109, Development Planning Unit, University College London, www.ucl.ac.uk/dpu

Calhoun, C. (1993). *Habermas and the Public Sphere*, Cambridge, MA, The MIT Press.

Chandhoke, N. (2004). *The Conceits of Civil Society*, New Delhi, Oxford University Press.

Chatterjee, P. (2004). *The Politics of the Governed: Reflections on Popular Politics in Most of the World*, New York, Columbia University Press.

Chatterjee, P. (2001). On civil and political society in postcolonial democracies. In S. Kaviraj and S. Khilnani (eds) *Civil Society: History and Possibilities* (pp. 165–178), Cambridge, Cambridge University Press.

Cohen, J., and Arato, A. (1992). *Civil Society and Political Theory*, Cambridge, MA, The MIT Press.

Comaroff, J. L., and Comaroff, J. (eds) (1999). *Civil Society and the Political Imagination in Africa: Critical Perspectives*, Chicago, University of Chicago Press.

DeHoog, R. H., and Racanska, L. (2003). The role of the nonprofit sector amid political change: Contrasting approaches to Slovakian civil society. *Voluntas*, 14(3), 263–282.

Dorner, W. (2008). A tool for charting out the relationships between government and third sector organizations in various national settings: Applying social network analysis to national action plans to fight poverty. Paper presented at the ISTR/EMES/Cinefogo Conference, University of Barcelona, Spain.

Edwards, M. (2004). *Civil Society*, Cambridge, Polity Press.

Evers, A., and Laville, J.-L. (eds) (2004). *The Third Sector in Europe*, Cheltenham, Edward Elgar.

Foucault, M. (2006). *History of Madness*, London, Routledge.

Gramsci, A. (1971). *Selections from The Prison Notebooks of Antonio Gramsci*, trans. Q. Hoare and G. Nowell Smith, London, Lawrence and Wishart.

Gunn, C. (2004). *Third-Sector Development: Making Up for the Market*, Ithaca, NY, Cornell University Press.

Harris, J. (2006). Middle class activism and the politics of the informal working class: A perspective on class relations and civil society in India cities. *Critical Asian Studies*, 38(4), 445–465.

Hegel, G. W. F. (1991). *Elements of the Philosophy of Right*, ed. A. Wood, trans. H. B. Nisbet, Cambridge, Cambridge University Press.

Hemment, J. (2004). The riddle of the third sector: Civil society, international aid, and NGOs in Russia. *Anthropological Quarterly*, 77(2), 215–241.

Khilnani, S. (2003). *The Idea of India*, Delhi, Penguin.

Knudsen, A.-M. S. (2007). The right to the city: Spaces of insurgent citizenship among pavement dwellers in Mumbai, India. DPU Working paper no. 132, Development Planning Unit, University College London, www.ucl.ac.uk/dpu

Kohli, A. (1987). *The State and Poverty in India*, Cambridge, Cambridge University Press.

Kohli, A. (ed.) (2002). *Success of Indian Democracy*, Cambridge, Cambridge University Press.

Kothari, R. (1988). *State against Democracy*, Delhi, Ajanta Publications.

Krishna, A. (2008). Introduction: Poor people and democracy. In A. Krishna (ed.) *Poverty, Participation, and Democracy* (pp. 1–27), Cambridge, Cambridge University Press.

Kumar, G. (ed.) (2000). *Dimensions of Voluntary Sector in India*, New Delhi, Charities Aid Foundation India.

Lewis, D. (2008). Crossing the boundaries between "third sector" and state: Life-work histories from the Philippines, Bangladesh and the UK. *Third World Quarterly*, 29(1), 125–141.

Lipset, S. M. (1960). *Political Man*, New York, Doubleday.

Mander, H. (2000). *The Movement for Right to Information*, Delhi, National Center for Advocacy Studies.

Marx, K. (1963). *The Eighteenth Brumaire of Louis Bonaparte*, New York, Lawrence & Wishart.

Marx, K., and Engels, F. (1975). *Collected Works – Vol. 1*, New York, Lawrence & Wishart.

Mendelsohn, O., and Vicziany, M. (1998). *The Untouchables: Subordination, Poverty, and the State in Modern India*, New York, Cambridge University Press.

Mishra, N. (2003). People's right to information movement: Lessons from Rajasthan. Discussion paper series 4, UNDP, www.newtactics.org/sites/newtactics.org/files/resources/Sowmya_notebook_BW_4-2-08.pdf

Mohapatra, B. N. (2003). A view from the subalterns: The pavement dwellers of Mumbai. In R. Tandon and R. Mohanty (eds) *Does Civil Society Matter: Governance in Contemporary India* (pp. 285–314), New Delhi, Sage.

Pogge, T. (2002). *World Hunger and Human Rights: Cosmopolitan Responsibilities and Reforms*, Cambridge, Polity Press.

Przeworski, A. (2008). The poor and the viability of democracy. In A. Krishna (ed.) *Poverty, Participation and Democracy* (pp. 125–146), Cambridge, Cambridge University Press.

Rajagopal, A. (2001). The violence of commodity aesthetics: Hawkers, demolition raids, and a new regime of consumption. *Social Text*, 19(3), 91–113.

Roy, A., and Dey, N. (2003). The right to information: Facilitating people's participation and state accountability. www.10iacc.org/download/workshops/cs54b.pdf

Roy, A., Dey, N., and Singh, S. (2001). Demanding accountability. Seminar, no. 500, www.india-seminar.com/2001/500/500%20aruna%20roy%20et%20al.htm

Roy, B. (1996). Right to information: Profile of a grass roots struggle. *Economic and Political Weekly*, 31(19), 1120–1121.

Rudolph, L. I., and Rudolph, S. H. (1987). *In Pursuit of Lakshmi: The Political Economy of the Indian State*, Chicago, University of Chicago Press.

Salamon, L. M. (2003). *The Resilient Sector: The State of Nonprofit America*, Washington, DC, The Brookings Institution.

Scott, J. C. (1990). *Domination and the Arts of Resistance: Hidden Transcripts*, New Haven, Yale University Press.

Sen, A. (2008). Foreword. To D. Green, *From Poverty to Power: How Active Citizens and Effective States can Change the World*, Oxford, Oxfam International.

Sen, S. (1999). Globalization and the status of current research on the Indian nonprofit sector. *Voluntas*, 10(2), 113–130.

PRIA (Participatory Research in Asia) and The Johns Hopkins University. (2003). *Invisible, Yet Widespread: The Non-Profit Sector in India*, Delhi, PRIA.

Tandon, R., and Mohanty, R. (2003). *Does Civil Society Matter: Governance in Contemporary India*, New Delhi, Sage.

Tellis, O. (2003). Litigating economic, social and cultural rights: Achievements, challenges, and strategies, featuring 21 case studies. Center for Housing Rights and Evictions, Geneva, Switzerland, www.cohre.org/store/attachments/COHRE%20Litigating%20ESC%20Rights%202003.pdf

Ulvila, M., and Hossain, F. (2002). Development NGOs and political participation of the poor in Bangladesh and Nepal. *Voluntas*, 13(2), 149–163.

United Nations Development Program (UNDP). (1996). *Human Development Report*, New York, Oxford University Press.

Van Til, J. (1988). *Mapping the Third Sector*, New York, Foundation Center.

Viswanath, P., and Dadrawala, N. (2004). Philanthropy and equity: The case of India. Global Equity Initiative, Harvard University, www.fas.harvard.edu/~acgei/PDFs/PhilanthropyPDFs/Phil_India_Case.pdf

Chapter 21
Global Environmental Engagement

Vanessa Timmer

Introduction

The failure of national governments to adequately address global environmental problems, such as climate change and biological diversity loss, has stimulated the emergence of third sector actors as new prominent and critical players at the transnational political level (Clark 2003a; Florini 2000; Keck and Sikkink 1998; Smith et al. 1997). This is a relatively recent occurrence as understanding of the human impact on the global environment and the political response to this challenge can be traced to the mid-twentieth century (Clark et al. 2001, p. 3). Scholarly analysis of this phenomenon has also expanded significantly in the past few decades. Third sector engagement in global environmental politics has become a topic of interest to scholars from a wide range of disciplinary fields including international relations, political science, geography, economics, history, anthropology, and biology.

There remains considerable scholarly debate as to the legitimacy of third sector actors in contributing to problem-solving in the global political arena or the actual impact that the third sector has on key actors in this arena including government, international organizations, and corporate decisions and behavior (Florini 2000; Edwards 2000); however, there is little doubt that third sector actors have organized across national borders in order to engage in international advocacy work on environmental issues (Clark 2003b).

In this chapter, I review some of the scholarly analysis of third sector involvement in global environmental politics. I explore the academic debate on the role which a specific third sector actor – the scientific community – has played in defining the nature and scale of global environmental change. I then investigate third sector interactions within the political arena both with nation-states and with non-state actors including international organizations and corporations. Scholars have also studied the internal challenges facing third sector actors seeking to influence global environmental politics, particularly concerns about their legitimacy and accountability;

V. Timmer (✉)
University of British Columbia, Vancouver, Canada
e-mail: vtimmer@interchange.ubc.ca

R. Taylor (ed.), *Third Sector Research*, DOI 10.1007/978-1-4419-5707-8_21,
© Springer Science+Business Media, LLC 2010

this is the focus of the fourth section. The chapter concludes with an exploration of the challenges facing both third sector actors and scholars analyzing these actors in supporting the creation of sustainable futures.

Global Environmental Change and Epistemic Communities

Over the past hundreds of thousands of years, human beings as a species have altered their environment in significant ways. In some cases, this has led to environmental problems at the local, regional, and national levels such as water pollution or soil erosion (Clark et al. 2001, p. 3). It has only been during the past few thousands of years that human beings have altered the environment on a continental and global scale akin to the influence of such processes as erosion, volcanism, and natural selection. In the past century, this human transformation of ecological systems has increased greatly in intensity, scale, scope, and influence (Ruddiman 2003). For some scholars, this era of global environmental change can be called the "anthropocene" – "a new geologic epoch in which humankind has emerged as a globally significant – and potentially intelligent – force capable of reshaping the face of the planet" (Clark et al. 2005, p. 1; see also Crutzen 2002).

Environmental problems that occur or are tackled at a global scale are a relatively new phenomenon (Turner et al. 1990). Currently, environmental changes across scales are happening in complex ways, with unexpected dynamics and at an unprecedented pace (Berkes et al. 1998; Clark et al. 2001; Kates et al. 2005; Turner et al. 2003). Some environmental problems "reach a global magnitude in character … by affecting a realm of the environment that operates as a fluid global system" including climate change and the depletion of the ozone layer, whereas other environmental problems stem from "globally cumulative changes … that reach a global magnitude by either occurring so widely across the Earth's surface as to attain a worldwide character or by significantly affecting the total stock of some resources, however spatially concentrated it may be" (Meyer 2001, p. 608). Examples of globally cumulative changes include habitat and species loss that accumulates into a global biodiversity crisis and rapid and widespread deforestation that accumulates into a problem of global forest destruction and degradation.

Humans are not unique as a species in altering their environment, but have become undeniably successful in competing with other species due in large part to our capacity for language and creation of technology. In fact, human "population size, energy use, carbon dioxide emissions, biomass consumption and geographical range exceed those of similar species by orders of magnitude" (Rees 2009, p. 689). This ability of humans to exploit available natural resources and to expand into available geographical space has been a highly adaptive trait for human survival; however, there is increasing evidence that this evolutionary success is leading to degradation at the global level of the ecosystems that support human survival. The mass extraction of resources such as forests and fish, the depletion of the planet's protective ozone layer, and climate change due to industrial chemicals and greenhouse gas emissions are some examples of the global environmental concerns that have emerged on the agenda in the past few decades.

Scholars have noted the role of the scientific community, as third sector actors, in the growing awareness of the impact of human activity on global environmental change, particularly since the International Geophysical Year in 1957 and since the mid-twentieth century with increased collaboration among scientists to analyze the state of the Earth (Clark et al. 2005; Steffen et al. 2004; Turner et al. 1990). Academic analyses have noted the role that scientists play in creating new knowledge to highlight important issues and in communicating this knowledge to policymakers in order to shape the international policy agenda, standards, and regulations (Clark et al. 2005; Haas 1992; NRC 1999). Individual scientists play a role in raising awareness and understanding through their personal visits to policymakers (Schreurs et al. 2001, p. 361), and scientists have also formed networks, which some scholars have labeled "epistemic communities." Epistemic communities are networks of individuals and organizations, such as scientific and expert networks, that gain their authority and legitimacy in decision-making processes through their professional ties and claims to consensual knowledge and shared causal ideas (Haas 1992). These networks of scientists can vary in their cooperative nature, the length and strength of their engagement, and the degree to which they hold mutual beliefs about causation and a definition of the problem area. The Intergovernmental Panel on Climate Change and the network of scientists engaged in the United Nations Millennium Ecosystem Assessment are two examples of epistemic communities.

Epistemic communities and other knowledge holders "frame" issues (Jasanoff 2005). Framing is a process in which actors denote a "schema of interpretation" in order "to locate, perceive, identify, and label occurrences within their life space and the world at large" (Goffman 1974, p. 21). The process of framing involves discussions on ethics and social values combined with deliberations about what counts as valid knowledge and information for decision-making (Jasanoff 2005). In light of this, Van der Heijden (1997, p. 212) notes that "there is no coherent ecological crisis as such: there are only story lines, problematizing various aspects of a changing physical and social reality." This does not deny that "of course, 'real' disruptive events happen all the time" such as the collapse of the fisheries stock off the east coast of Canada or the Chernobyl nuclear plant accident; however, "framing allows us to see that events ... have to be set within an interpretive context that allows them to function as a starting point for deliberation or concerted action" (Jasanoff 2005, p. 24). Global environmental change is not only a bio-geophysical phenomenon – for example, physical characteristics that can be counted such as species loss, water pollution – but also a *social* phenomenon (Wapner 2002). It is "the particular structure and features of our political, social and economic institutions that lead us to abuse our environment, and this argues for a reconfiguration of institutions rather than more conceptually-simple and simplistic notions such as changes in 'numbers'" (Lipschutz 1996, p. 4).

Framing becomes important not only in identifying problems and their causes – prognostic framing – but also in specifying viable courses of action to address these problems: diagnostic framing (Benford and Snow 2000; McCarthy et al. 1996). With the awareness of human transformation of the global environment and of the resultant problems, there has been a growing recognition of humanity's role in shaping the Earth's and humanity's future (Clark et al. 2005, p. 2). The term "nöosphere" was coined by Vladimir Vernadsky (1998) along with mystic Teilhard de Chardin and philosopher Édouard Le Roy, to describe the collective consciousness, thought, and reflection that is emerging on the consequences of human activities on the global environment (Oldfield and Shaw 2006). This is the sphere of emerging ideas and responses to global environmental change, including the management of human impact and the structuring of power relations to reduce negative consequences of human activity. This is also the realm of global environmental politics. Humanity is attempting not only to understand, monitor, and assess global environmental issues but also to find policy approaches, institutional arrangements, instruments, and effective practices to respond to these challenges.

Global Environmental Politics and the Third Sector

Historical analyses of global environmental politics describe international negotiations on global environmental problems as originating in the nineteenth century; however, the time period after the International Geological Year in 1957 has seen a dramatic increase in collective action to deal with international environmental problems (Porter et al. 2000; Torrance and Torrance 2006). The vast majority of international environmental treaties have been crafted in the later half of the twentieth century. It is for this reason that many political science scholars trace the advent of a *global* environmental politics to the 1980s, even though nation-state deliberations and understanding of cross-border environmental issues pre-date this time period (Porter et al. 2000). Attention to global environmental issues grew in the 1980s in large part as a result of the 1972 United Nations Conference on the Human Environment in Stockholm. The international gathering of national governments, international representatives, and third sector actors led to the development of a plan of action on the environment and the formation of the United Nations Environment Program (UNEP), with the parallel creation of environmental ministries or agencies in many national governments around the world (Torrance and Torrance 2006).

The 1972 UN conference highlighted global ecological interdependence. Along with global geopolitical and economic ties, this interdependence is shaping the way that national governments function. There is a rapid rise in the number of international, regional, and bilateral agreements and treaties on such issues as international trade in endangered species, transboundary air pollution, and the movement of hazardous waste as a response among national governments to transnational environmental problems (Young 1997). These "international decision-making webs" (Smith et al. 1997, p. 67) on different issues have also been defined as international regimes – the legal and political "social institutions composed of agreed-upon principles, norms, rules and decision-making procedures that govern the interaction of actors in specific issue areas" (Levy et al. 1995, p. 274). The vast scholarship on international regimes has traced the emergence and evolution of these regimes across different issue areas (e.g., climate change, deforestation, and whaling) and chronicled how regimes place constraints on national decision-making as domestic and international interests of nation-states are defined in relationship to each other (Keck and Sikkink 1998; Putnam 1988; Risse 2003).

Global environmental politics scholars document the concern by developing or Southern countries about the implications of these international environmental regimes on constraining their right to development (Najam 2005; Selin and Linnér 2005). This concern was central to the discussion at the 1992 United Nations Conference on Environment Development in Rio de Janeiro. This conference – referred to as the Earth Summit – drew representatives of 150 countries and a historically unprecedented number of Heads of State who set an international agenda that tied economic and social development to a sustained environmental resource base and healthy global life support system. The concept of "sustainable development" that "meets the needs of the present without compromising the ability of future generations to meet their own needs" became a meta-frame for discussion among nation-states (WCED 1987). The "sustainable development" frame was "explicitly formulated as a 'bridging' concept – as an idea that could draw together apparently distinct policy domains, and unite very different interests, hopes and aspirations onto the banner of sustainable development" (Meadowcroft 2000, p. 371; see also Clark 2000; Najam 2005).

Scholars of global environmental politics emphasize the role of framing in the political realm as what becomes labeled as an environmental problem worthy of political consideration is often deeply contentious. Environmental problems may be global in magnitude but can have different impacts in different regions and places (Yearley 1996). There are also important distinctions in the extent to which countries are a source of global environmental problems, such as industrialized countries contributing the largest percentage of greenhouse gases that lead to climate change. The Rio Declaration and Agenda 21 negotiated by governments at the Earth Summit reflected these injustices within guiding principles by including the principle of "common but differentiated responsibility," which places the onus of action on the largest perpetrators of environmental harm; however, this remains a point of contention within international debate.

It is within this realm of agenda-setting and framing environmental problems that third sector actors play one of their most prominent roles in global environmental politics. Organizations such as Greenpeace, Friends of the Earth, and World Wildlife Fund and networks such as the Third World Network and the Climate Action Network are active in influencing the issues and agendas of global political debate through pressuring and lobbying governments (Wapner 2002). The strength of these actors lies in their ability to persuade power holders with credible, relevant, and timely information and normative arguments (Bloodgood 2002). As Khagram et al. (2002, p. 4) argue, "one of the primary goals of transnational advocacy is to create, strengthen, implement and monitor international norms" – the shared principles and ethics that coordinate values and expectations among actors and guide and constrain their behavior (Finnemore 1996; Goertz and Diehl 1992; Harrison and Sundstrom 2007; Hurrell 2003).

Scholars note the diversity of interpretive frames which third sector actors bring into global environmental politics, which some attribute to variations in beliefs about the relationships of humans to nature, and their environmental philosophy (Brulle 2000; Carmin and Balser 2002; Dalton 1994). McAdam (1996, p. 340) describes framing as the "principle weapon" available to a third sector actor in managing the demands of the shifting political environment. In analyzing the framing process, scholars have conceived of the transnational organization field as a "political space" in which different actors negotiate and struggle to make sense of complex issues and to define what is "real" in the world around them (Jasanoff 2005, p. 24). The result of the framing process is the construction of frames that define representations of the world, and these frames are powerful in shaping social behavior and can become durable over time. Wapner (2002) notes that over time these frames can shift broad ideational frameworks and cultural politics and change "environmental sensibilities" that, for example, make ocean dumping, transboundary polluting, and whaling morally questionable activities and change the context of political discussion.

McAdam (1996, pp. 340–341) notes that third sector actors also "frame" through their choices of repertoires of actions, the routine forms of activities and clusters of tactics that third sector actors use in a given historical period (Tilly 1978). In recent years, theorists have analyzed the diversity of action repertoires adopted by third sector actors operating at the transnational level in order to analyze the tactics employed and the effectiveness of transnational contention (Arts et al. 2001; Clark 2003b; Corell and Betsill 2001; Florini 2000; Fox and Brown 1998; Keck and Sikkink 1998; Khagram et al. 2002; Princen and Finger 1994; Yanacopulos 2005). Keck and Sikkink (1998, p. 16) identify four key political tools and tactics that third sector actors adopt in order to influence frames at the international level:

(1) *information politics*, or the ability to quickly and credibly generate politically usable information and move it to where it will have the most impact; (2) *symbolic politics*, or the ability to call upon symbols, actions or stories that make sense of a situation for an audience that is frequently far away; (3) *leverage politics*, or the ability to call upon powerful actors to affect a situation where weaker members of a network are unlikely to have influence; and (4) *accountability politics*, or the effort to hold powerful actors to their previously stated policies or principles.

Some scholars adopt a management and problem-solving lens to analyze third sector engagement (Batliwala and Brown 2006a; Brown and Timmer 2006; Social Learning Group 2001) and note that environmental problem-solving consists of phases including problem definition, direction setting, implementation, and performance monitoring. Third sector actors appear to take five roles in these processes: "(1) identifying issues, (2) facilitating voice of marginalized stakeholders, (3) amplifying the importance of issues, (4) building bridges among diverse stakeholders, and (5) monitoring and assessing solutions" (Brown and Timmer 2006, p. 1). Studies document how third sector actors influence initial framing of a problem and the evaluation of the solutions, whereas implementation of solutions predominately remains in the domain of other actors such as governments and the private sector. Even in regimes in which third sector actors were "largely absent from the early history of problem recognition and solution development," one study of the atmospheric regimes notes that they "played – jointly with other actors – a crucial amplifying role in the agenda-setting stage and a predominately monitoring role once implementation of serious management actions were underway" (van Eijndhoven et al. 2001, p. 187).

Academic studies chronicle the diverse range of perspectives and diversity of tactics and strategies which third sector actors employ. One distinction which scholars have identified is the degree to which the third sector actors are driven to seek the *reform* of existing institutions or distributions of power and wealth in society, or to pursue social change that is *radical*, transformative, and revolutionary (McAdam 1996, p. 341; Rees 1995). John Dryzek (1997) argues that reformist actors are predominately structuralists in that they focus their attention on changing sociopolitical structures, in contrast to radical actors that are focused on altering the ideas and belief systems that underlie these structures (see also Mercier 1997). Scholars also categorize the type of tactics employed by third sector actors, including the degree to which their tactics are conventional (e.g., lobbying) or unconventional (e.g., blockades), the violence and/or legality of their tactics, and their engagement in direct democracy (engager, insider) or confrontation with governments (confronter, outsider) (Dalton 1994; Diani and Donati 1999; Grant 2000; McAdam 1996; McCarthy and Zald 2001; Richards and Heard 2005; Van der Heijden 1997; Winston 2002).

In analyzing the diversity of tactics across third sector actors engaged in a global environmental arena, scholars have noted that the diversity of action repertoires can be both a strength and a weakness to their effectiveness. This diversity can lead to a fragmented approach that undermines political power (Caldwell 1990), to inefficiency, to duplication of efforts that can result in a weaker impact, particularly if actors are operating at cross-purposes (Gerlach and Hine 1970), and to a "negative radical flank effect" in which radical actors undermine the activities of the environmental movement (Lofland 1996, p. 294). Strength can come from a "positive radical flank effect" in which "the bargaining position of moderates is strengthened by the presence of more radical groups" (Haines 1984, p. 32), an increased capacity of third sector actors to attract a broad base of supporters from different sectors of society, and an increased chance of political efficacy through the employment of diverse tactics (Dalton 1994, p. 248). Diversity of tactics can also be an advantage in reacting to changes over time in the framing of issues and solutions, in political opportunity structures, in the behavior of other third sector actors, and in the behavior of target actors. Scholars note that the effectiveness of third sector actors is in large part determined by the degree to which they can adjust their organizations, goals, and action repertoires over time in response to these changes (McAdam and Scott 2005; Tarrow 1995, 1998; Zald and Ash 1966), for example, the change in approach of third sector actors engaged in the climate change debates with the election of an engaged US President Barack Obama.

The strategies and tactics which a third sector actor can employ varies not only over time but from country to country, particularly given variations in levels of inclusiveness of third sector actors into decision-making processes of nation-states (Dryzek et al. 2003; Harrison and Sundstorm 2007; Rootes 2002; Van der Heijden 2006). For example, third sector actors seeking to influence authoritarian regimes are not able to use the same tactics as third sector actors operating within democratic regimes (e.g., lobbying, petitioning, and influencing voters). There has also been a significant change in the degree to which developing countries have become engaged in global environmental politics, which has opened opportunities in those countries for the creation and influence of third sector organizations and networks (Najam 2005). Scholars have chronicled how third sector actors either target a specific country directly or, if the government is unyielding, publicize national violations in international forums as a way of encouraging international pressure by other non-violating nation-states on these intransigent countries, a process defined by some scholars as a "boomerang effect" (Risse et al. 1999; see also Hochstetler 2002). Third sector actors have also used UN conferences, such as the Earth Summit, and other international gatherings to influence national governments and their environmental policies through organizing parallel conferences, serving on delegations, protesting, and engaging in advocacy to influence the negotiations and outcomes (Batliwala and Brown 2006b; Torrance and Torrance 2006; Wapner 2002).

Non-State Actors and Third Sector

Recently, scholars have turned their attention to other actors in the global political arena. Increasingly, studies analyze how third sector actors are not only targeting nation-state governments with their activities, but also focusing their efforts on influencing the international agencies that national governments have established, including international organizations (such as the World Trade Organizations and UN agencies), economic institutions (the World Bank and International Monetary Fund, for example), and regional bodies (like the European Union and the Organization of African Unions). Studies show that for each campaign, third sector actors are strategically selecting the level of engagement within the layered organizational field of global environmental politics that "provides them with the greatest opportunities and imposes the weakest constraints" (Tarrow 1996, p. 12). As Klandermans (1997, p. 173) notes, "with the increasing number of political layers involved in the definition and implementation of a policy, the choice of one's adversaries [and the choice of one's allies] becomes less obvious and therefore more a matter of construction."

The international bodies and networks with whom third sector actors interact have expanded rapidly over the past decades to include bilateral and international treaties and conventions along with their secretariats, regional bodies (e.g., European Union and Union of African States), United Nations and other international organizations (e.g., Organization for Economic Co-operation and Development), regional and international financial institutions (e.g., World Bank and Asian Development Bank), trade regimes, networks such as the International Judges Association, and many others (Biermann et al. 2009; Smith et al. 1994). Just as there are clear differences in terms of the inclusiveness of national governments, there are also variations in the degree to which international organizations and networks have established avenues for third sector influence. Formal opportunities for third sector engagement through accreditation and observer status exist for UN bodies (Wapner 2002). In contrast, the World Bank and other international financial institutions traditionally have been more exclusive in their engagement on environmental issues, although this has evolved in large part due to third sector pressure (Nelson 1997; Park 2005; Van der Heijden 2006). In a study of third sector influence on the World Bank, Fox and Brown (1998) noted that in more exclusive contexts, third sector actors' creative tactics include working alongside insider staff who are sympathetic to their demands for more ecologically and socially just development.

There is an active scholarly debate within studies of global environmental politics as to whether the failure of nation-states to adequately address environmental problems is most effectively addressed through a supra-state solution, such as the creation of a robust environmental governance system at the international level (Biermann et al. 2009; Wapner 1996), or whether this governance gap is more effectively addressed through a decentralized and local approach to solutions at the community level (Hawken 2007; Lipschutz 1996). Some third sector actors who have traditionally operated at a local or national scale have become international in scope as they form transnational grassroots networks and movements, such as Slum Dwellers International, supported by communications and information technology (Batliwala 2002; Batliwala and Brown 2006b). Historically, third sector actors engaged in global environmental politics were created and led from Northern, developed countries; however, recently, third sector actors from the South have organized across transnational boundaries to bring their perspective and interests into the global environmental arena (Batliwala and Brown 2006b; Ru and Ortolano 2009; Torrance and Torrance 2006).

Global environmental politics also extends into the realm of changing patterns of economic activity (Wapner 2002). Third sector actors are responding to the increased capacity of multinational corporations "to mix and match flows of mineral, raw materials, manufactured goods, information and services from many sites worldwide [which] has outstripped the capacity of local or national social movements to contest their plans" (Cohen and Rai 2000, p. 8). For example, Hoffman (2001) chronicles the evolution of the response of oil and chemical industries to environmental demands in interaction with third sector actors. In this area, third sector actors seek institutional solutions through market-based approaches, internalization of environmental and social costs into price signals, adjustments of taxes and incentives toward sustainable ends, and certification and tradable permit schemes (Alcock 2005; O'Rourke 2005; Wapner 1996).

Scholars are revealing new third sector strategies and tactics in this realm, including influencing private sector actors along a value chain of a product and insider tactics in which third sector actors purchase shares within a corporation in order to shape the corporate agenda through shareholder meetings (Guay et al. 2004; O'Rourke 2005). Campaigns of collective action against the behavior of corporations often adopt a transnational character as local and national third sector actors in countries impacted by corporate activity gain from making claims alongside activists in the country where a corporation is headquartered (Tarrow 1996, p. 22). There are also possibilities of Northern activists assisting third sector activists in places negatively affected by corporate activities by lending their voice, votes, consumer power, ability to demonstrate, and access to privileged information about the countries and companies in a campaign (Clark 2003a, p. 182).

There is an active debate as to the effectiveness of these third sector tactics on the private sector as different companies and industries require different strategies and tactics depending on their visibility as a target (e.g., many small- to medium-sized businesses as compared to a multinational corporation), their vulnerability to disruptive protest (e.g., susceptibility of a business to boycotts and damage to their brand), and their interest in being perceived as proactive in social and environmental corporate citizenship (Guay et al. 2004). Third sector actors that embrace market-based mechanisms or that partner with private sector actors are vulnerable to criticism of being co-opted or supporting "greenwashing" by corporations (Gereffi et al. 2001). Clark (2003a, p. 119) notes that partnerships among third sector actors and the private sector "require leaps of vision, can be fraught with ethical dilemmas, and can be readily misconstrued by rivals or supporters." Covey and Brown (2001) propose one approach by third sector actors to engage in "critical cooperation" with private sector actors in order to collaborate but maintain their capacity for critique. Increasingly, there is a backlash toward third sector actors by the non-state and state actors whom third sector actors target. They are posing questions about third sector accountability and legitimacy in engaging in global environmental politics as they become more prominent players. As discussed below, scholars have similarly turned their attention to document this legitimacy and accountability debate (Newell 2008).

Legitimacy, Accountability, and Organizational Form

Who does the third sector represent? What is their legitimacy in being engaged in global environmental politics? To whom are they accountable? Scholars have identified different types of legitimacy which third sector actors can have in engaging actively in global environmental politics. Legitimacy has been defined as the right to exist, operate, and influence other actors (Edwards 2000) and can be based on the third sector actor's value claims (moral legitimacy), its expertise in a topic area (technical or performance legitimacy), its compliance with legal requirements (legal legitimacy), and its internal democracy, transparency, and accountability (political legitimacy) (Brown and Moore 2001). The accountability of an organization is the extent to which the third sector actor can be held to its promises. Accountability can usefully be conceived of as a relationship between the third sector actor and its stakeholders wherein duties, responsibilities, and obligations are owed to particular actors (Brown and Moore 2001; Brown et al. 2003; Ebrahim 2003; Kearns 1996; Lloyd 2005; Scholte 2004). The private sector is primarily accountable to shareholders, and democratic public agencies are answerable to their elected representatives and voters; unlike these actors, third sector actors typically do not have one primary stakeholder to whom they are accountable. They usually have multiple stakeholders that offer different forms of support and place various, and often conflicting, expectations on third sector actors (Brown and Moore 2001).

A third sector actor's stakeholders can include donors and supporters that provide funding; regulators that process certification; clients or beneficiaries that receive and use third sector services; partners that cooperate on programs and campaigns; targets of their campaigns that can question the legitimacy of their claims; the third sector staff, volunteers, and board that dedicate themselves to the organization; and members who have joined the third sector organization or network in order to participate in its activities (Brown et al. 2003). For institutional theorists within organizational studies, this accountability system (Brown and Moore 2001) or accountability environment (Kearns 1996) is the organizational field within which an organization operates. The concept of an organizational field leads scholars to analyze the context within which an organization operates by defining the "arena – system of actors, actions and relations – whose participants take one another into account as they carry out interrelated activities" (McAdam and Scott 2005, p. 10). Within the environmental field, this accountability system can be extended to include accountability to other species and to future generations, which further complicates the demands on third sector actors to address accountability challenges. Scholars are also documenting the internal debates about accountability that are happening within the third sector itself. For example, Southern and marginalized players are posing questions about the accountability of Northern third sector activists in representing their interests on the global stage (Batliwala 2002).

Third sector actors are also challenged in terms of determining the most effective organizational structure for advancing their goals over time within a transnational political environment. There has been a recent surge in interest in specifying the various forms that transnational actors and partnerships adopt in order to support their long-term effectiveness (Anheier and Themudo 2001; Batliwala and Brown 2006a,b; Clark 2003a,b; Keck and Sikkink 1998; Khagram et al. 2002; Lindenberg and Bryant 2001; Lindenberg and Dobel 1999; Risse 2003; Rucht 1999; Selle and Strømsnes 1998; Taylor 2002). A common distinction has been made between third sector actors that have adopted a *formal organizational structure* as opposed to *looser "network" configurations*, which can be defined as "forms of organization characterized by voluntary, reciprocal, and horizontal patterns of communication" (Keck and Sikkink 1998, p. 8, see also Risse 2003; Rucht 1999; Smith 2002). Khagram et al. (2002, pp. 6–8) further differentiate network structures by distinguishing between *transnational networks* that are characterized by information sharing, common analyses, and shared discourses; *transnational coalitions* that share strategies and coordinate tactics on a specific transnational campaign in addition to building network capacities; and *transnational social movements* that have a stronger sense of common identity, threaten established social order, and add the capacity to mobilize collective action in multiple countries (see also Clark 2003b, pp. 4–5; Gordenker and Weiss 1995).

Although some scholars have identified network structures as being relatively more effective for third sector actors operating in dynamic and complex transnational political environments (Anheier and Themudo 2001; Clark 2003a; Smith

2005), other scholars and I have made the case that there is not one best generic organizational form for third sector actors but that their structure needs to match the strategies and goals of the actor (Freeman 1979; Timmer 2009). Third sector actors are also hybrid structures as they often contain multiple internal networks and coalitions which complicate their analysis (Anheier 2000). The choice of organizational form stems from a variety of factors including the diversity of members, degree of mission and strategy focus, intensity of member commitment, and prevalence of existing models of organizing (Batliwala and Brown 2006b, p. 209). The desire by third sector actors to design global governance structures to address transnational environmental problems demands that these actors work with a diversity of players including governments, international organizations, and the private sector (Batliwala and Brown 2006b, p. 213; see also Clark 2003a). Creating effective and flexible global governance networks is increasingly important as the scale and urgency of transnational environmental problems becomes apparent. As outlined below, scholars analyzing third sector actors engaged in this field have a role to play in supporting humanity's response to this unprecedented challenge.

The Earth System and a Sustainable Future

Earth systems science highlights the dynamic complexity of the atmosphere, ocean, soil, biota, energy, hydrology, and major chemical components such as nitrogen, carbon, and phosphorous (Clark 2000, p. 87). The increasing numbers of people, consumption patterns, and political and economic interdependence has led to a thickening and heightened interactivity of connections. A report commissioned by the US National Research Council (1999) indicates that the growing interconnectedness of human and natural systems will result, in the medium term, in "environmental threats [that arise] from multiple, cumulative, and interactive stresses, and driven by a variety of human activities" and these threats will become "difficult to untangle from one another and complex to manage" (p. 276). This is an "era of global environmental change and interdependence" and there are complex interactions among ecological, social, political, and economic systems across scales and time (Clark et al. 2001, p. 3). The challenge for scholars is to capture the inherent uncertainties and surprises that are part of both social and physical systems and to support the design of transnational governance structures and political institutions that can proactively respond and adapt to these challenges.

Some scholars argue that political concern about global environmental problems peaked with the Earth Summit in 1992 (Torrance and Torrance 2006); however, others argue that responses to these problems are evolving to become a central concern for humanity and a race to ensure a progressive, ecologically sustainable, and just future based on a notion of collective self-interest and global citizenship (Anheier 2007; Armstrong 2006; Batliwala and Brown 2006a,b; Clark 2003a; Munck 2006; Rees 2009). Hawken (2007) argues that the proliferation of third sector actors is akin to an "immune response" by humanity to respond to issues including large-scale ecological degradation and inequitable distribution of resources. Third sector actors are moving beyond traditional lobbying and activities targeted at the nation-state and other non-state actors, to address the deep cultural and biological origins of the ecological crisis (Rees 2009; Wapner 2002), while recognizing the need for more knowledge about the drivers of human behavior (O'Rourke 2005) and the capacity for learning at a societal and global level (Brown and Timmer 2006; Social Learning Group 2001). Third sector actors are also partnering with other actors in new arrangements of transnational governance that "authoritative[ly] steer network constituents to achieve public goals" (Andonova et al. 2009, p. 53). There is no doubt that scholars have a critical role to play in documenting third sector influence in these cultural and governance shifts, while analyzing the degree to which these result in real changes on the ground to reverse environmental degradation (Dauvergne 1997, 2008).

References

Alcock, F. (2005). Conflicts and coalitions within and across the ENGO community. Paper presented to Berlin Conference on the Human Dimensions of Global Environmental Change, Potsdam, Germany.

Andonova, L. B., Betsill, M. M., and Bulkeley, H. (2009). Transnational climate governance. *Global Environmental Politics*, 9(2), 52–73.

Anheier, H. K. (2000). Managing non-profit organisations: Towards a new approach. Civil Society Working paper, Centre for Civil Society, London School of Economics.

Anheier, H. K. (2007). Reflections on the concept and measurement of global civil society. *Voluntas*, 18(1), 1–15.

Anheier, H. K., and Themudo, N. (2001). Organisational forms of global civil society: Implications of going global. In H. K. Anheier, M. Glasius, and M. Kaldor (eds) *Global Civil Society 2002* (pp. 191–216), London, London School of Economics.

Armstrong, C. (2006). Global civil society and the question of global citizenship. *Voluntas*, 17(4), 349–357.

Arts, B., Noortmann, M., and Reinalda, B. (eds) (2001). *Non-State Actors in International Relations*, Aldershot, UK, Ashgate.

Batliwala, S. (2002). Grassroots movements as transnational actors: Implications for global civil society. *Voluntas*, 13(4), 393–410.

Batliwala, S., and Brown, L. D. (2006a). Introduction: Why transnational civil society matters. In S. Batliwala and L. D. Brown (eds) *Transnational Civil Society: An Introduction* (pp. 1–14), Bloomfield, CT, Kumarian Press.

Batliwala, S., and Brown, L. D. (2006b). Shaping the global human project: The nature and impact of transnational civil activism. In S. Batliwala and L. D. Brown (eds) *Transnational Civil Society: An Introduction* (pp. 204–227), Bloomfield, CT, Kumarian Press.

Benford, R. D., and Snow, D. A. (2000). Framing processes and social movements: An overview and assessment. *Annual Review of Sociology*, 26, 611–639.

Biermann, F., Siebenhüner, B., and Schreyögg, A. (eds) (2009). *International Organizations in Global Environmental Governance*, London, Routledge.

Bloodgood, E. A. (2002). Influential information: Non-governmental organizations' role in foreign policy-making and international regime formation. Unpublished paper, Department of Politics, Princeton University.

Brown, L. D., and Moore, M. H. (2001). Accountability, strategy, and international non-governmental organizations. *Nonprofit and Voluntary Sector Quarterly*, 30(3), 569–587.

Brown, L. D., Moore, M. H., and Honan, J. (2003). Building strategic accountability systems for International NGOs. *AccountAbility Forum*, 2, Summer, 31–43.

Brown, L. D., and Timmer, V. J. (2006). Civil society actors as catalysts for transnational social learning. *Voluntas*, 17(1), 1–16.

Brulle, R. J. (2000). *Agency, Democracy and Nature: The US Environmental Movement from a Critical Theory Perspective*, Cambridge, MA, The MIT Press.

Caldwell, L. K. (1990). *Between Two Worlds: Science, the Environmental Movement, and Policy Choice*, Cambridge, Cambridge University Press.

Carmin, J., and Balser, D. B. (2002). Selecting repertoires of action in environmental movement organizations. *Organization and Environment*, 15(4), 365–388.

Clark, J. (2003a). *Worlds Apart: Civil Society and the Battle for Ethical Globalization*, Bloomfield, CT, Kumarian Press.

Clark, J. D. (ed.) (2003b). *Globalizing Civic Engagement: Civil Society and Transnational Action*, London, Earthscan.

Clark, W. C. (2000). Environmental globalization. In J. S. Nye, Jr., and J. D. Donahue (eds) *Governance in a Globalizing World* (pp. 86–108), Washington, DC, Brookings Institution.

Clark, W. C., Cruzten, P. J., and Schellnhuber, H. J. (2005). Science for global sustainability: Toward a new paradigm. CID Working paper no. 120, Science, Environment and Development Group, Center for International Development, Harvard University.

Clark, W. C., Jäger, J., and van Eijndhoven, J. (2001). Managing global environmental change: An introduction to the volume. In The Social Learning Group (eds) *Learning to Manage Global Environmental Risks* (pp. 1–19), Cambridge, MA, The MIT Press.

Cohen, R., and Rai, S. M. (2000). *Global Social Movements*, London, The Athlone Press.

Berkes, F., Folke, C., and Colding, J. (eds) (1998). *Linking Social and Ecological Systems: Management Practices and Social Mechanisms for Building Resilience*, Cambridge, Cambridge University Press.

Corell, E., and Betsill, M. M. (2001). A comparative look at NGO influence in international environmental negotiations: Desertification and climate change. *Global Environmental Politics*, 1(4), 86–107.

Covey, J., and Brown, L. D. (2001). Critical cooperation: An alternative form of civil society–business engagement. IDR Reports 17(1) [Boston, Institute for Development Research].

Crutzen, P. J. (2002). Geology of mankind. *Nature*, 415(3), 23.

Dalton, R. J. (1994). *The Green Rainbow: Environmental Groups in Western Europe*, New Haven, Yale University Press.

Dauvergne, P. (1997). *Shadows in the Forest: Japan and the Politics of Timber in Southeast Asia*, Cambridge, MA, The MIT Press.

Dauvergne, P. (2008). *The Shadows of Consumption: Consequences for the Global Environment*, Cambridge, MA, The MIT Press.

Diani, M., and Donati, P. R. (1999). Organizational change in Western European environmental groups: A framework for analysis. *Environmental Politics*, 8(1), 13–34.

Dryzek, J. S. (1997). *The Politics of the Earth: Environmental Discourses*, Oxford, Oxford University Press.

Dryzek, J. S., Downs, D., Hernes, H.-K., and Schlosberg, D. (2003). *Green States and Social Movements: Environmentalism in the United States, United Kingdom, Germany and Norway*, Oxford, Oxford University Press.

Ebrahim, A. (2003). *NGOs and Organizational Change: Discourse, Reporting and Learning*, Cambridge, Cambridge University Press.

Edwards, M. (2000). *NGO Rights and Responsibilities: A New Deal for Global Governance*, London, The Foreign Policy Centre.

Finnemore, M. (1996). Constructing norms of humanitarian intervention. In P. J. Katzenstein (ed.) *The Culture of National Security: Norms and Identity* (pp. 153–185), New York, Columbia University Press.

Florini, A. (ed.) (2000). *The Third Force: The Rise of Transnational Civil Society*, Washington, DC, Brookings Institution.

Fox, J. A., and Brown, L. D. (1998). *The Struggle for Accountability: The World Bank, NGOs, and Grassroots Movements*, Cambridge, MA, The MIT Press.

Freeman, J. H. (1979). Resource mobilization and strategy: A model for analyzing social movement organization actions. In M. N. Zald and J. D. McCarthy (eds) *The Dynamics of Social Movements* (pp. 172–175), Cambridge, MA, Winthrop.

Gerlach, L. P., and Hine, V. H. (1970). *People, Power, Change: Movements of Social Transformation*, Indianapolis, IN, Bobbs-Merrill.

Gereffi, G., Garcia-Johnson, R., and Sasser, E. (2001). The NGO–industrial complex, *Foreign Policy*, July/August, 56–65.

Goertz, G., and Diehl, P. F. (1992). Toward a theory of international norms: Some conceptual and measurement issues. *Journal of Conflict Resolution*, 36(4), 634–664.

Goffman, I. (1974). *Frame Analysis*, New York, Harper Colophon.

Gordenker, L., and Weiss, T. G. (1995). NGO participation in the international policy process. *Third World Quarterly*, 16(3), 543–555.

Grant, W. (2000). *Pressure Groups in British Politics*, Basingstoke, Macmillan.

Guay, T., Doh, J. P., and Sinclair, G. (2004). Non-governmental organizations, shareholder activism, and socially responsible investments: Ethical, strategic, and governance implications. *Journal of Business Ethics*, 52(1), 125–139.

Haas, P. M. (1992). Introduction: Epistemic communities and international policy coordination. *International Organization*, 46(1), 1–36.

Haines, H. H. (1984). Black radicalism and the funding of civil rights: 1957–1970. *Social Problems*, 32(1), 31–43.

Harrison, K., and Sundstrom, L. M. (2007). The comparative politics of climate change. *Global Environmental Politics*, 7(4), 1–18.

Hawken, P. (2007). *Blessed Unrest: How the Largest Movement in the World Came into Being and Why No One Saw It Coming*, New York, Viking.

Hochstetler, K. (2002). After the boomerang: Environmental movements and politics in the La Plata River basin. *Global Environmental Politics*, 2(4), 35–57.

Hoffman, A. J. (2001). *From Heresy to Dogma: An Institutional History of Corporate Environmentalism*, Stanford, CA, Stanford University Press.

Hurrell, A. (2003). Norms and ethics in international relations. In W. Carlsnaes, T. Risse, and B. A. Simmons (eds) *Handbook of International Relations* (pp. 137–154), London, Sage.

Jasanoff, S. (2005). *Designs on Nature: Science and Democracy in Europe and the United States*, Princeton, NJ, Princeton University Press.

Kates, R. W., Parris, T. M., and Leiserowitz, A. A. (2005). What is sustainable development? Goals, indicators, values and practice. *Environment*, 47(3), 9–21.

Kearns, K. P. (1996). *Managing for Accountability: Preserving the Public Trust in Public and Nonprofit Organizations*, San Francisco, Jossey-Bass.

Keck, M., and Sikkink, K. (1998). *Activists Beyond Borders: Advocacy Networks in International Politics*, Ithaca, NY, Cornell University Press.

Khagram, S., Sikkink, K., and Riker, J. V. (eds) (2002). *Restructuring World Politics: Transnational Social Movements, Networks, and Norms*, Minneapolis, University of Minnesota Press.

Klandermans, B. (1997). *The Social Psychology of Protest*, Cambridge, Blackwell.

Levy, M. A., Young, O. R., and Zürn, M. (1995). The study of international regimes. *European Journal of International Relations*, 1(3), 267–330.

Lindenberg, M., and Bryant, C. (2001). *Going Global: Transforming Relief and Development NGOs*, Bloomfield, CT, Kumarian Press.

Lindenberg, M., and Dobel, P. (1999). The challenges of globalization for northern international relief and developments NGOs. *Nonprofit and Voluntary Sector Quarterly*, 28(4), 4–24.

Lipschutz, R. D. (1996). *Global Civil Society and Global Environmental Governance*, Albany, State University of New York Press.

Lloyd, R. (2005). *The Role of NGO Self-Regulation in Increasing Stakeholder Accountability,* London, One World Trust.

Lofland, J. (1996). *Social Movement Organizations: Guide to Research on Insurgent Realities,* New York, Aldine de Gruyter.

McAdam, D. (1996). The framing function of movement tactics: Strategic dramaturgy in the American civil rights movement. In D. McAdam, J. D. McCarthy, and M. N. Zald (eds) *Comparative Perspectives on Social Movements* (pp. 339–340), Cambridge, Cambridge University Press.

McAdam, D., and Scott, R. W. (2005). Organizations and movements. In G. F. Davis, D. McAdam, R. W. Scott, and M. N. Zald (eds) *Social Movements and Organization Theory* (pp. 4–40), Cambridge, Cambridge University Press.

Meyer, W. B. (2001). Human impacts on Earth. In A. S. Goudie and D. J. Cuff (eds) *Encyclopedia of Global Change: Environmental Change and Human Society* (pp. 607–613), Oxford, Oxford University Press.

Meadowcroft, J. (2000). Sustainable development: A new(ish) idea for a new century? *Political Studies,* 48(2), 370–387.

Mercier, J. (1997). *Downstream and Upstream Ecologists: The People, Organizations, and Ideas behind the Movement,* Westport, CT, Praeger Publishers.

McCarthy, J. D., Smith, J., and Zald, M. N. (1996). Media discourse, movement publicity, and the generation of collective action frames: Theoretical and empirical exercises in meaning construction. In D. McAdam, J. D. McCarthy, and M. N. Zald (eds) *Comparative Perspectives on Social Movements* (pp. 312–337), Cambridge, Cambridge University Press.

McCarthy, J. D., and Zald, M. N. (2001). Resource mobilization theory: Vigorous or outmoded? In J. H. Turner (ed.) *Handbook of Sociological Theory* (pp. 533–565), New York, Kluwer Academic/Plenum Publishers.

Munck, R. (2006). Global civil society: Royal road or slippery path? *Voluntas,* 17(4), 325–332.

Najam, A. (2005). Developing countries and global environmental governance: From contestation to participation to engagement. *International Environmental Agreements,* 5(3), 303–321.

National Research Council. (1999). *Our Common Journey: A Transition towards Sustainability,* Washington, DC, National Academy Press.

Nelson, P. J. (1997). Deliberation, leverage or coercion? The World Bank, NGOs, and global environmental politics. *Journal of Peace Research,* 34(4), 467–472.

Newell, P. (2008). Civil society, corporate accountability and the politics of climate change. *Global Environmental Politics,* 8(3), 122–153.

Oldfield, J. D., and Shaw, D. J. B. (2006). V. I. Vernadsky and the nöosphere concept: Russian understandings of society–nature interaction. *Geoforum,* 37(1), 145–154.

O'Rourke, D. (2005). Market movements: Nongovernmental organization strategies to influence global production and consumption. *Journal of Industrial Ecology,* 9(1/2), 115–128.

Park, S. (2005). How transnational environmental advocacy networks socialize international financial institutions: A case study of the International Finance Corporation. *Global Environmental Politics,* 5(4), 95–119.

Porter, G., Brown, J. W., and Chasek, P. S. (2000). *Global Environmental Politics,* 3rd edn, Boulder, CO, Westview Press.

Princen, T., and Finger, M. (1994). *Environmental NGOs in World Politics: Linking the Local and the Global,* London, Routledge.

Putnam, R. (1988). Diplomacy and domestic politics: The logic of two-level games. *International Organization,* 42, Summer, 427–460.

Rees, W. E. (1995). Achieving sustainability: Reform or transformation? *Journal of Planning Literature,* 9(4), 343–361.

Rees, W. E. (2009). Human nature, eco-footprints and environmental injustice. *Local Environments,* 13(8), 685–701.

Richards, J. P., and Heard, J. (2005). European environmental NGOs: Issues, resources and strategies in marine campaigns. *Environmental Politics,* 14(1), 23–41.

Risse, T. (2003). Transnational actors and world politics. In W. Carlsnaes, T. Risse, and B. A. Simmons (eds) *Handbook of International Relations* (pp. 255–274), London, Sage.

Risse, T., Ropp, C., and Sikkink, K. (eds) (1999). *The Power of Human Rights: International Norms and Domestic Change*, Cambridge, Cambridge University Press.

Rootes, C. (2002). Global visions: Global civil society and the lessons of European environmentalism. *Voluntas*, 13(4), 411–429.

Ru, J., and Ortolano, L. (2009). Development of citizen-organized environmental NGOs in China. *Voluntas*, 20(2), 141–168.

Ruddiman, W. F. (2003). The anthropogenic greenhouse era began thousands of years ago. *Climatic Change*, 61(33), 261–293.

Rucht, D. (1999). The transnationalization of social movements: Trends, causes, problems. In D. della Porta, H. Kriesi, and D. Rucht (eds) *Social Movements in a Globalizing World* (pp. 206–222), London, Macmillan.

Schreurs, M. A., Clark, W. C., Dickson, N. M., and Jäger, J. (2001). Issue attention, framing and actors: An analysis of patterns across arenas. In The Social Learning Group (eds) *Learning to Manage Global Environmental Risks* (pp. 349–364), Cambridge, MA, The MIT Press.

Scholte, J. A. (2004). Democratizing the global economy: The role of civil society. Centre for the Study of Globalisation and Regionalisation, University of Warwick.

Selin, H., and Linnér, B. (2005). The quest for global sustainability: International efforts on linking environment and development. Center for International Development, Kennedy School of Government, Harvard University.

Selle, P., and Strømsnes, K. (1998). Organized environmentalists: Democracy as a key value? *Voluntas*, 9(4), 319–343.

Smith, J. (2002). Bridging global divides. *International Sociology*, 17(4), 505–528.

Smith, J. (2005). Globalization and transnational social movement organizations. In G. F. Davis, D. McAdam, R. W. Scott, and M. N. Zald (eds) *Social Movements and Organization Theory* (pp. 226–248), Cambridge, Cambridge University Press.

Smith, J., Chatfield, C., and Pagnucco, R. (eds) (1997). *Transnational Social Movements and Global Politics: Solidarity Beyond the State*, Syracuse, NY, Syracuse University Press.

Smith, J., Pagnucco, R., and Romeril, W. (1994). Transnational social movement organizations in the global political arena, *Voluntas*, 5(2), 121–154.

Social Learning Group (eds) (2001). *Learning to Manage Global Environmental Risks: A Comparative History of Social Responses to Climate Change, Ozone Depletion and Acid Rain* (2 volumes), Cambridge, MA, The MIT Press.

Steffen, W. L., Sanderson, A., Tyson, P. D., Jäger, J., Matson, P., Moore III, B., Oldfield, F., Richardson, K., Schellnhuber, H. J., Turner II, B. L., and Wasson, R. J. (2004). *Global Change and the Earth System: A Planet under Pressure*, Heidelberg, Springer.

Tarrow, S. (1995). Cycles of collective action: Between moments of madness and the repertoires of contention. In M. Traugott (ed.) *Repertoires and Cycles of Collective Action* (pp. 89–116), Durham, NC, Duke University Press.

Tarrow, S. (1996). Fishnets, Internets, and Catnets: Globalization and transnational collective action. Estudio working paper 1996/78, Cornell University.

Tarrow, S. (1998). *Power in Movement: Social Movements, Collective Action and Politics*, Cambridge, Cambridge University Press.

Taylor, R. (2002). Interpreting global civil society. *Voluntas*, 13(4), 339–347.

Tilly, C. (1978). *From Mobilization to Revolution*, Reading, MA, Addison-Wesley.

Timmer, V. (2009). Agility and resilience: Adaptive capacity in Friends of the Earth International and Greenpeace. In F. Biermann, B. Siebenhüner, and A. Schreyögg (eds) *International Organizations in Global Environmental Governance* (pp. 244–263), London, Routledge.

Torrance, W. E. F., and Torrance, A. W. (2006). Spinning the green web: Transnational environmentalism. In S. Batliwala and L. D. Brown (eds) *Transnational Civil Society: An Introduction* (pp. 101–123), Bloomfield, CT, Kumarian Press.

Turner II, B. L., Clark, W. C., Kates, R. W., Richards, J. F., Mathews, J. T., and Meyer, W. B. (eds) (1990). *The Earth as Transformed by Human Action: Global and Regional Changes in the Biosphere over the Past 300 Years*, Cambridge, Cambridge University Press.

Turner II, B. L., Kasperson, R. E., Matson, P. A., McCarthy, J. J., Corell, R. W., Christensen, L., Eckley, N., Kasperson, J. X., Luers, A., Martello, M. L., Polsky, C., Pulsipher, A., and Schiller, A. (2003). A framework for vulnerability analysis in sustainability science. *PNAS: Proceedings of the National Academy of Sciences of the United States of America*, 100(14), 8074–8079.

Van der Heijden, H. A. (1997). Political opportunity structures and the institutionalization of the environmental movement. *Environmental Politics*, 6(4), 25–50.

Van der Heijden, H. A. (2006). Globalization, environmental movements and international political opportunity structures. *Organization and Environment*, 19(1), 28–45.

Van Eijndhoven, J., Clark, W. C., and Jäger, J. (2001). The long-term development of global environmental risk management: Conclusions and implications for the future. In Social Learning Group (eds) *Learning to Manage Global Environmental Risks, Vol. 2* (pp. 181–197), Cambridge, MA, The MIT Press.

Vernadsky, V. I. (1998). *The Biosphere*, New York, Copernicus.

Wapner, P. (1996). *Environmental Activism and World Civic Politics*, Albany, State University of New York.

Wapner, P. (2002). Horizontal politics: Transnational environmental activism and global cultural change. *Global Environmental Politics*, 2(2), 37–62.

WCED. (1987). *Our Common Future: Report of the World Commission on Environment and Development*, Oxford, Oxford University Press.

Winston, M. (2002). NGO strategies for promoting corporate social responsibility. *Ethics and International Affairs*, 16(1), 71–87.

Yanacopulos, H. (2005). The strategies that bind: NGO coalitions and their influence. *Global Networks*, 5(1), 93–109.

Yearley, S. (1996). *Sociology, Environmentalism, Globalization: Reinventing the Globe*, London, Sage.

Young, O. R. (ed.) (1997). *Global Governance: Drawing Insights from the Environmental Experience*, Cambridge, MA, The MIT Press.

Zald, M. N., and Ash, R. (1966). Social movement organizations: Growth, decay and change. *Social Forces*, 44, March, 327–341.

Chapter 22
Global Civil Society

Ronaldo Munck

Introduction

Twenty years ago as communism collapsed and globalization "took off," it seemed that the era of global civil society had arrived. Today we live in a much harsher – dare we say uncivil? – world where there are few illusions in this regard. We examine here the discourse and the practice of global civil society and explore its contradictory meanings with a view to discerning its possible futures. In particular, we ask whether its essentially Western liberal usage can be adapted to become an adequate tool for social transformation in the era of globalization. In the never-ending quest for human security, a reconstructed global civil society project may yet prove to be effective in a period of economic meltdown and of great political turbulence. But first it is necessary to take stock around the seemingly simplistic question, "Does civil society exist?"

While in 1989, civil society was seen as the bright shining hope for a better life for all, in 2009 it was "monitored, demonized and repressed" (Howell et al. 2006, p. 17) as part of the "long war on terror" declared after the attacks on the Pentagon and Wall Street in 2001. As Mark Sidel (2006) has argued, at the very least we need much more comparative analysis of the role of the third sector which underpins the project of a global civil society. To contribute to that task, and as a necessary prelude, we need some conceptual clarification about the political categories we are deploying. The argument will proceed from the case that global civil society certainly does exist to then consider the skeptical voices questioning this premise. I then move on to argue that one way forward for the debate is to understand the inherently contradictory nature of civil society and the way in which it is discursively constructed in different ways and for different purposes. Finally, I sketch out a possible research agenda for global civil society studies based on a Polanyi-inspired understanding of a continuously unfolding "double movement" between market and society.

R. Munck (✉)
Dublin City University, Ireland
e-mail: ronnie.munck@dcu.ie

R. Taylor (ed.), *Third Sector Research*, DOI 10.1007/978-1-4419-5707-8_22,

An Emancipatory Concept

The term "global civil society" is quite inseparable from the mood, or *Weltanschauung*, of the late 1980s and early 1990s. In Eastern Europe the "spring of peoples" was coming to fruition and then the Berlin Wall came down in 1989. Throughout the 1980s, dissident intellectuals in Eastern and Central Europe were articulating the notion that "civil society" could promote autonomy and self-organization outside of and against the bureaucratic state. The term "anti-politics" was sometimes used to express this new politics of contestation. In Latin America the mobilization of civil society was seen as a peaceful way to contest the military dictatorships which had come to power from the mid-1970s onward. In this case the inspiration was more post-Marxist rather than the post-politics of the East. On the broader canvas of world politics, Francis Fukuyama (1992) proclaimed the "end of history" and thus the historical contest between capitalism and communism. Civil society, as the 1990s wore on, became less a mode of contesting state power and more a way in which the populations (especially in developing countries) could be incorporated into the anti-statist agenda of the new neoliberal development economics.

The concept of "global civil society" (GCS) gradually emerged to codify, express, and promote the hopeful mood that "the people" could prevail over the state and lead to a new "global citizenship" (Armstrong 2006). A major source of inspiration was the work of the jailed Italian communist leader Antonio Gramsci in the 1920s. While the Western capitalist state was too strong to challenge directly, progressive inroads could be made within "civil society" (that terrain lying between the state and the family), thus moving toward "hegemony" without seizing state power. Yet in Gramsci (1970) there was always a counter-reading of civil society – the trade unions, churches, education system, etc. – which he saw as buttressing the rule of capitalism through popular consent. Thus, from Gramsci we can take a complex and contradictory reading of civil society as at once the arena in which capitalist hegemony is secured and at the same time the terrain on which counter-hegemonic alliances and alternative social projects are articulated. With the rise of globalization in the 1990s – as increased economic integration on a global scale – it seemed that we might be able to "scale up" the notion of civil society to a "global civil society" contesting global capitalist hegemony (Katz 2006).

It would be fair to say that Mary Kaldor perhaps captured best of all the "optimistic" rendering of global civil society as concept and aspiration. This was a view shaped strongly by the transition out of communism and the rise of the new liberal globalism in the late 1980s. As Kaldor puts it, "The new understanding of civil society represented both a withdrawal from the state and a move towards global rules and institutions" (Kaldor 2003, p. 588). Despite a minority radical rendering of civil society by the emerging counter-globalization movement (the World Social Forum, for example), the dominant version tied in very neatly with the new policy agenda set by the World Bank and others set on pushing back the role of the state on behalf of an unregulated market. Kaldor's own reading of global civil society seemed to focus most on what she calls "a growing body of cosmopolitan law, by which I

mean the combination of humanitarian law (the laws of war) and human right law"
(Kaldor 2003, p. 590). In the late 1990s – with the break-up of Yugoslavia – Kaldor
and others found themselves supporting "humanitarian wars," for example, against
the Serbs. They thus ignored the powerful warning by Iris Marion Young that "it is
dangerous to assume ... that stronger institutions of international law themselves
can and should authorise the use of violence" (Young 2007, p. 103).

Many writers then subsequently began to engage with global civil society in a
bid to refine and operationalize the concept. For John Keane, "global civil society is
a vast interconnected, and multi-layered social space that comprises many hundreds
of thousands of self-directing or non-governmental institutions and ways of life"
(Keane 2001, p. 23). Compared to a vast dynamic biosphere, global civil society
is thus seen in its full complexity rather than a normative concept as seemed to be
the case with earlier writers. Since the late 1990s and especially after the "Battle
of Seattle" in 1999 pitting myriad protesters against the World Trade Organization
(WTO), local, national, and transnational civil society organizations have contested
global neoliberal hegemony (Munck 2007). We can thus agree with Keane in seeing global civil society as "overdetermined" by the new global capitalism and not
reducible to a Western vision of the "good life." Global civil society thus comes of
age as global capitalism enters its most dynamic "turbo-charged" period from 2000
onward and, at the same time, we can say that in its turn is dependent on a thriving
civil society at a household, community, regional, and especially transnational level.

Most recently, Helmut Anheier (2007) seeks to clarify the status of global civil
society 10–15 years on from the perspective of the *Global Civil Society Yearbooks*.
He would appear to be somewhat skeptical about the role of conceptual clarification insofar as it "does little to produce new knowledge and understanding as such"
(Anheier 2007, p. 3). Focusing instead, as in his view, on studying contemporary
patterns and developments in global civil society is certainly useful – but surely this
cannot occur without a conceptual framework. Certainly "measurement" of global
civil society is based on a very precise (if limited) understanding of what empirical elements are being examined as "indicators" of global civil society. The issue
of whether global civil society as concept and reality is irredeemably marked by
its Western liberal origins and usage is both a conceptual and an empirical one.
Contrary to Anheier's suggestion, I am not seeking a definition of global civil society with "a high level of purity in terms of value-free social science" (Anheier 2007,
p. 4). Rather, I think we need to foreground the politics of global civil society as
a social reality and as a political aspiration rather than assume that it is a shining
beacon of civility in a very uncivil world.

An Anti-Democratic Concept

The romance around the concept of civil society in Latin America and then in
Eastern/Central Europe had been intense, but it was waning by the mid-1990s. The
concept was becoming more fluid, contradictory, and promiscuous to put it that way

(Taylor 2002, 2004). In its mainstreaming it was inevitably domesticated to some extent and lost some of its radical edge. It was now far less about contesting authoritarian communist or militarist regimes. Civil society was rapidly becoming a major plank in the World Bank's development strategy to promote "good governance" by holding the state to account. In its 1995 annual report, the World Bank then went as far as to reverse its previous implicit opposition to trade unions (as not market-friendly combinations) to laud them as major bulwarks against state dominance and watchdogs over government corruption (World Bank 1996). As for actually existing global civil society in the shape of the international nongovernmental organizations (INGOs), they turned increasingly toward "professionalization" as a way to be heard at the top table of global governance, especially after the confrontations in Seattle and the accommodations which followed whereby "responsible" elements of civil society were brought into negotiations.

Of the various critiques of global civil society, the most far reaching from a critical globalization perspective is the accusation that, in essence, it reflects a narrow Western ethnocentric view of the world. Thus Neera Chandhoke points out that "the domination of global civil society by organised and well-funded NGOs hailing from the West poses some very vexing questions for issues of political representation, political agency and politics in general" (Chandhoke 2002, p. 49). The temptation to "speak for" the poor and the downtrodden has a long tradition in Western liberal politics. Yet to what extent does an international campaign against "global debt," for example, reflect the views of the people and community organizations ("civil society" in short) in the non-Western developing or post-colonial world? Anderson and Rieff (2004, p. 30) take this problematic dimension one step further and argue for a direct analogy between the missionaries of the colonial era and "crusading and do-gooding organisations that see themselves as bearers of universal values." Certainly we can quote counter-examples of best practice in North–South relations, but they cannot invalidate the general case against some nongovernmental or civil society organizations.

We could also argue that global civil society is rather ahistorical and downplays conflict in the making of history. It is sometimes seen in stylized accounts of global civil society that international civil society only burst onto the scene in 1989. There is, for example, a long history of internationalism in the labor movement, in the women's movement, and around ecological issues. The theory and practice of internationalism going back at least 100 years has real historical roots. Internationalism arose in the mid-nineteenth century at least in part as a response to the broad socio-economic and political transformations of the period. During that era, as Alejandro Colás notes, internationalism became "both cause and consequence of the expansion of civil society" (Colás 2002, p. 57). We can certainly argue that a more historically grounded perspective would allow us to understand that international civil society as a domain long predates what we now call globalization. Nor should we conflate the INGOs with international civil society, which is a much broader and disparate family embracing much more radical movements on both the right and the left of the political spectrum.

If the INGOs which flourished in the 1990s are seen as the backbone of global civil society then we must also consider the growing critique of them as agents of social transformation. A nongovernmental organization (NGO) is not necessarily a civil society organization (CSO) if by that we are referring to social movements carrying out a root-and-branch critique of the existing order. It seems understandable that the dominant order will seek to co-opt reasonable interlocutors from among those ranged against its policies. Thus, for example, in Latin America, following acute confrontations over the stabilization plans called for in the Washington Consensus, many governments sought to involve NGOs in the 1990s to manage this discontent. For the critics of this process (Petras 1997, for example), the NGOs then adopt an "apolitical" stance focused on "exclusion" and "empowerment" but failing to address the national and international power structures that perpetuate the present order. That is not to say that all NGOs are colluding with the powers that be – this is certainly not the case – but it serves us to be more aware of the ambiguities inherent in the global civil society discourse and practice.

Finally, and in many ways as a summation of the critique of global civil society, we could argue that it does not in fact promote democracy. For Kaldor, global civil society holds a "potential for emancipation" in that it opens up closed societies and "it offers the possibility to participate in debates about global issues" (Kaldor 2003, p. 591). Yet we need to ask what precisely does that "debate" consist of and how it is conducted. Critics of global civil society as a rather Eurocentric liberal discourse, such as David Chandler, quite rightly point out that debate is meant to be a purposive human activity which needs specific channels and norms if it is to be meaningful (Chandler 2004). Where exactly is this public ethical debate in global space taking place? Websites and electronic discussion forums have their role, but they cannot replace the well-established norms of political parties in deriving a democratic mandate for social change. Reflecting its origins in the Eastern European anti-politics of the 1980s, the global civil society theorists put forward what is actually an anti-democratic elitist politics of those who are "living the truth." In short, as Chandler warns, we must beware of taking up "the fiction of global civil society as an ethical alternative approach to the problems of the political" (Chandler 2004, p. 330).

A Contested Terrain

We could probably find fault quite easily with both the strong case for global civil society and the strong case against it. There is a certain purist strain running through both, and the debate can become rather theological at times, for example, in regard to different readings of Antonio Gramsci. I would thus agree with Olaf Corry for whom rethinking the relationship between democracy, the state, and civil society in the era of globalization is essential and "it is a mistake to give up on 'global civil society' as irreparably statist or inherently undemocratic" (Corry 2006, p. 314). Certainly global civil society should be seen neither as the royal road to the Promised Land (Munck 2006) nor as a project which is inherently inimical to democracy. Even the fiercest critics of the "new" NGO discourse such as James Petras who goes as far as to see them as a vanguard for the neoliberal project recognize that there are, of course, many radical democratic civil society organizations and NGOs promoting a social transformation project. The point is not, though, to say that the "truth" about global civil society lies somewhere between these two poles but, rather, to understand why such polar opposite views have emerged in recent years.

We can then probably all agree that global civil society is a contested term, is quite fluid, and is open to different usages. It is also a contested terrain subject to very different interpretations. If global civil society is conceived of as a terrain – understood in complex spatial, political, social, and cultural terms – then it becomes a site for political intervention and cannot be taken as a pre-given. In the same way that social classes or the global North and South can only be fully understood in relation to each other so global civil society needs to be understood as being constantly under construction by diverse social and political forces. It is not only the Western INGOs who proclaim their commitment to global civil society who form part of this equation. Other non-Western social forces, deemed "fundamentalist" by the INGOs, also have a commitment to grassroots civil society and a democratization of the global economy. What is probably at stake in this debate is the need to move beyond the studiously apolitical stance of many global civil society theorists to bring politics back in. The dominant normative conception of global civil society based on Habermasian communicative rationality is, at the end of the day, profoundly inimical to actually existing politics.

In terms of the politics of global civil society, we can probably argue safely that it is neither wholly progressive nor wholly reactionary. Thus, for example, the dominant discourse of global civil society takes the sanctity of "universal human rights" as a given. The concept of human rights appeals to a transcendent principle that can, ultimately, only apply universally. Human beings are deemed to have universal rights regardless of where they live, their ethnicity, gender, or any other particularizing factor. Universal human rights as inalienable are at the heart of global civil society as liberal cosmopolitan discourse. Yet today, as in the past, the Western powers stand accused of using human rights as rhetoric to impose their worldview and material interests on the non-Western world. The notion of "humanitarian imperialism" (Bricmont 2006) has been coined to expose the close relationship between Western imperialism and a supposedly universal good such as human rights (Woodiwiss 2005). I would argue that if we are to avoid the concept of "global civil society" being similarly compromised, we need to very carefully deconstruct it so as to clearly articulate its diversity of meaning in different world regions, for diverse cultures, and ultimately those with access to the corridors of power and those who do not.

To take the debate forward I would argue that we need to do two things: first, civil society needs to be conceived of not in isolation but in terms of its relationships with the market and the state, and second, we must better understand how civil society is a constructed concept. The economic system became much more internationally integrated in the 1990s. Today the emerging global recession shows to what an extent this internationalization has become consolidated. There is no "decoupling" from the world economy, not even for China. The moves toward a transnational – to not say global – state to govern the global economy have been much more partial. Certainly the IMF, the World Bank, and the WTO do act to set the rules for global competition, but they are far from being a global governance mechanism. Global civil society interacts in myriad ways with the economic processes of development across the globe. Global civil society also interacts with those bodies – such as the United Nations – seeking to construct a stable global governance structure. Thus the trio of global economy, polity, and society can only be conceived dynamically and in their constant interaction both cooperative and conflictual.

Since 1989 the dominant neoliberal reading of how markets, society, and politics interact has acquired the status of unassailable truth (Smart 2003). The logic of market efficiency would ensure the effectiveness of resource allocation and would also promote democracy. Now for the past 5 years or more, that "one right thought" approach has been hotly contested both in theory and in practice, not least through the global recession unleashed in 2008. We now understand the world to be more complex and our futures as much more uncertain. The same could be said, I would argue, about global civil society as a liberal cosmopolitan political alternative. We could usefully consider the approach to capitalism pioneered by Michael Callon (1998), which argues that capitalism does not "exist" as such but is rather constructed by economists. Economics, according to this argument, "at best provides highly abstracted and sociologically impoverished accounts of real economic relations and at worst legitimises inequalities in power and resources" (Barry and Slater 2002, p. 175). This is certainly the case for neoliberal globalization discourse, but we do need to consider that at least in part it is also true of liberal cosmopolitan civil society discourse.

Theoretical Renewal

To argue for a stronger conceptual framework for global civil society is not an argument against more empirical work. On the contrary, there is considerable need to add to our already complex picture of global civil society. In the interests of "grounded theory" (Strauss 1987), it is precisely through such exhaustive close-up studies that we will get a fuller picture and maybe clarify some of the theoretical conundrums. I would agree with Helmut Anheier that this empirical focus might help us move beyond the "increasingly conceptual self-referential nature of the debate [*around global civil society*]" (Anheier 2007, p. 7). What I do not agree with is that we can simply separate our theoretical/normative stance from our empirical work. What we look at in terms of global civil society and how we "measure" or evaluate it are all shaped by our theoretical/political lens. The "facts" do not speak for themselves; they are rather constructed according to our epistemological and conceptual frameworks.

What is required then is a twin track approach whereby empirical and conceptual clarification advance hand in hand. The research agenda confronting global third sector studies is huge and growing in complexity. Anheier has recently summarized the issues as seen from the *Global Civil Society Yearbooks*, which have been a land-mark in the close empirical examination of global civil society. This project has now come of age, and its longitudinal approach has contributed greatly to an opera-tionalization of global civil society as social reality. The approach has become more global and now explicitly confronts its Other, that is, "uncivil society." Conflict is still a weak point in this tradition, and I would agree with Delanty's observa-tion that "if the cosmopolitan vision is to have any real impact in the world it will have to address the problem of violence" (Delanty 2001, p. 41). The John Hopkins Comparative Nonprofit Sector Project has taken a different but parallel approach to the structural-operational definition of the sector which it deems of universal appli-cability. It is certainly the most comprehensive attempt to define and map the third sector lying outside of both the market and the state (see Chapter 4). However, one exhaustive re-consideration of this project by Susanna Morris has found that while the definition used has been useful in mapping the sector, "it is not truly universal in its applicability" (Morris 2000, p. 26). What is interesting about this critique is that it is not so much focused on cultural variation but the lack of historical fit of current third sector definitions with earlier experiences of, for example, the friendly soci-eties or mutual-aid societies which so often preceded the emergence of the modern labor movement.

To argue for a stronger social theory is not, either, an argument for "a singular true and value-free definition," as Anheier suggests in his critique of the critics of global civil society as Western discourse (Anheier 2007, p. 4). It does mean, how-ever, that we should be reflective on the theoretical and political implications of how we deploy global civil society. As with any other concept, it is neither politically nor epistemologically "innocent" to put it that way, insofar as it is constructed on a con-tested political terrain. By assuming as unproblematic a rights-based perspective in democracy, global civil society theorists tend to ignore alternative perspectives. There is also within global civil society discourse an unproblematized political vol-untarism. As Gideon Baker, who articulates many of the problems in the theorization of global civil society, argues, "such voluntarism involves wholesale retreat from questions about the political level itself at a global level" (Baker 2002, p. 932). Maybe there are other paths to global democracy than those implicit in the ethical stance of global civil society? Is global civil society robust enough to compete with other perspectives in the political marketplace? Is global civil society discourse open to other perspectives coming from what it might prefer to dub uncivil society?

My own view of where global civil society fits in with current economic and political upheavals is in terms of the Polanyian double movement. Put most simply, what Karl Polanyi articulated at another global transition period (1943–1946) was that capitalism's "attempt to set up one big self-regulating market" (Polanyi 2000, p. 70) would activate a social counter-movement from within society to protect itself from the anarchy of the market. Powerful social movements and institutions would emerge in a veritable counter-movement to check the actions of the market and reinstate the priority of human interests. What Polanyi posited for the national level in 1945 – in terms of a separation of the economy from the social and political domains of human life – was realized at a global level 50 years on through the phenomenon of globalization. Global civil society can – in terms of the unfolding Polanyian counter-movement in the decade since 1995 – play a role in re-embedding the economy within social relations. This would be very much in the tradition of the third sector and would contribute to the reconstruction of social relations based on trust after the current global recession.

If global civil society is seen as one of the terrains on which the current involvement of a social counter-movement to the unregulated market is occurring then we might conceive of it in different ways. Twenty years ago a rather naïve optimism around global civil society was understandable, but today we need to be much more precise. There is nothing automatic about global civil society becoming a social counterpart to global hegemonic power. In fact, on the evidence of the years since the "long war on terror" began, it is unlikely to become a counterpart. What global civil society is in fact is a terrain of struggle between different social, political, and cultural forces. In other words, global civil society is not pre-given but constructed through political and discursive struggles. Polanyi's counter-movement, it is well remembered, included Roosevelt's New Deal but also Stalin's Russia and Hitler's Germany as possible reactions to the crises of free-market liberalism. With politics back in command we can concentrate on a political mapping of global civil society in all its complex and contradictory glory and not as a vehicle for nostalgic reconstructions of the spirit of 1989. The challenges for social transformation in an era of global economic depression and increased political turbulence are extremely serious, and only a theoretically grounded and focused understanding of global civil society will be fit for the purpose.

References

Anderson, K., and Rieff, D. (2004). "Global civil society": A sceptical view. In M. Glasius, M. Kaldor, and H. Anheier (eds) *Global Civil Society Yearbook, 2004–05* (pp. 26–39), Oxford, Oxford University Press.

Anheier, H. (2007). Reflections on the concept and measurement of global civil society. *Voluntas*, 18(1), 1–15.

Armstrong, C. (2006). Global civil society and the question of global citizenship. *Voluntas*, 17(4), 349–357.

Baker, G. (2002). Problems in the theorisation of global civil society. *Political Studies*, 50(5), 928–943.

Barry, A., and Slater, D. (2002). Introduction: The technological economy. *Economy and Society*, 31(2), 175–193.

Bricmont, J. (2006). *Humanitarian Imperialism: Using Human Rights to Sell War*, New York, Monthly Review Press.

Callon, M. (ed.) (1998). *The Laws of the Market*, Oxford, Blackwell.

Chandhoke, N. (2002). The limits of global civil society. In M. Glasius, M. Kaldor, and H. Anheier (eds) *Global Civil Society Yearbook, 2002* (pp. 35–53), Oxford, Oxford University Press.

Chandler, D. (2004). Building global civil society "from below?" *Millennium*, 33(2), 313–339.

Colás, A. (2002). *International Civil Society: Social Movements in World Politics*, Cambridge, Polity Press.

Corry, O. T. (2006). Global civil society and its discontents. *Voluntas*, 17(4), 303–324.

Delanty, G. (2001). Cosmopolitanism and violence: The limits of global civil society. *European Journal of Social Theory*, 40(1), 41–52.

Fukuyama, F. (1992) *The End of History and the Last Man*, London, Penguin.

Gramsci, A. (1970). *Selections from The Prison Notebooks*, London, Lawrence and Wishart.

Howell, J., Ishkanian, A., Obadare, E., Seckinelgin, H., and Blasius, M. (2006). The backlash against civil society in the wake of the long war on terror. Civil society working paper series, no. 26, The Centre for Civil Society, London School of Economics.

Kaldor, M. (2003). The idea of global civil society. *International Affairs*, 79(3), 583–593.

Katz, H. (2006). Gramsci, hegemony and global civil society networks. *Voluntas*, 17(4) 333–348.

Keane, J. (2001). Global civil society? In M. Glasius, M. Kaldor, and H. Anheier (eds) *Global Civil Society Yearbook, 2001* (pp. 23–47), Oxford, Oxford University Press.

Morris, J. (2000). Defining the nonprofit sector: Some lessons from history. *Voluntas*, 11(1), 25–43.

Munck, R. (2006). Global civil society: Royal road or slippery path? *Voluntas*, 17(4), 325–332.

Munck, R. (2007). *Globalization and Contestation: The New Great Counter-Movement*, London, Routledge.

Petras, J. (1997). Imperialism and NGOs in Latin America. *Monthly Review*, 49(7), 10–18.

Polanyi, K. (2000). *The Great Transformation*, Boston, Beacon Press.

Sidel, M. (2006). The third sector, human security, and anti-terrorism: The United States and beyond. *Voluntas*, 17(3), 199–210.

Smart, B. (2003). *Economy, Culture and Society*, Buckingham, UK, Open University Press.

Strauss, A. (1987). *Qualitative Analysis for Social Scientists*, Cambridge, Cambridge University Press.

Taylor, R. (2002). Interpreting global civil society. *Voluntas*, 13(4), 339–347.

Taylor, R. (ed.) (2004). *Creating a Better World: Interpreting Global Civil Society*, Bloomfield, CT, Kumarian Press.

Woodiwiss, A. (2005). *Human Rights*, London, Routledge.

World Bank. (1996). *Workers in an Integrating World: World Development Report*, Oxford, Oxford University Press.

Young, I. M. (2007). *Global Challenges: War, Self-Determination, and Responsibility for Justice*, Cambridge, Polity Press.

Chapter 23
The World Social Forum

Patrick Bond

Introduction

As a 5-day celebration of workshops and political/cultural events devoted to the idea that "Another World is Possible," not only the periodic global meetings of the World Social Forum (WSF) are a crucial vehicle for building a more coherent progressive civil society, but also the WSF has become the venue for national regroupment of progressives in many countries, and some regions – especially Europe – have generated sustained interest in Social Forum organizing. However, notwithstanding the attractiveness of the transnational network form behind the civil society movements that make up the WSF, major contradictions continue to hamper its growth and sustainability. Ideological convergence has not proceeded at the pace many participants had hoped for, and the future of the world event and many local processes associated with it remain unclear.

In 2001, the WSF was founded as an alternative to the World Economic Forum – the elite Davos, Switzerland, annual gathering – by social democrats associated with the Brazilian Workers Party, the French periodical *Le Monde Diplomatique*, and the Association for the Taxation of Financial Transactions for the Aid of Citizens (ATTAC). The main site in which it is hosted, Porto Alegre, Brazil, was run by a friendly government until 2003, and for the first event some 12,000 people attended. The subsequent events there – in 2002, 2003, and 2005 – attracted progressively more attendees (estimated at 60,000; 100,000; and 150,000, respectively), followed by a return to Brazil – the Amazonian capital Belém – in 2009. In 2004 and 2007, the WSF was moved to Mumbai and Nairobi, where tens of thousands gathered. In between, in 2006 and 2008, the WSF was held first in several cities (Caracas, Bamako, and Karachi) and then in hundreds of locales. After a smaller-scale 2010 event back in Porto Alegre, Dakar, Senegal, was chosen to host the 2011 WSF.

Meanwhile, the innumerable municipal-scale, national, and regional social forums ebb and flow, at the initiative of local organizing committees. In addition

P. Bond (✉)
Centre for Civil Society, University of KwaZulu-Natal, Durban, South Africa
e-mail: bondp@ukzn.ac.za

R. Taylor (ed.), *Third Sector Research*, DOI 10.1007/978-1-4419-5707-8_23,
© Springer Science+Business Media, LLC 2010

to its role in catalyzing the world's largest ever anti-war protest in February 2003, when reportedly more than 15 million people took part as the Bush and Blair governments prepared to invade Iraq – the WSF's main claim to effectiveness is in setting up an alternative pole of world opinion to the dominant neoliberal (market-oriented) ideology associated with Davos (see, e.g., Anand et al. 2003; Blau and Karides 2008; de Sousa Santos 2004; Fisher and Ponniah 2003; Sen 2004; Sen et al. 2007).

Criticisms of the WSF have come from activists who argue that in its origins the WSF merely mirrored Davos with a top-down call for an expensive gathering in a symbolic site. At many of the events, the preponderance of international NGOs (with their sponsored Southern partners) makes the WSF an example more of "globalization from the middle" than "globalization from below." Explicit politics within the WSF can sometimes be intensely contested, such as the periodic debate about permitting entrance to political parties and politicians, or to those who have not renounced violence. In 2009, a WSF International Council meeting was held in Morocco in spite of Western Saharan organizations' objections that this undermined their liberation strategy (the Congress of South African Trade Unions led a boycott call, which was not well heeded). Or as another example, at the 2003 Porto Alegre WSF, organizers were accused of systematically sidelining more radical forces such as Indymedia, the youth network Intergalactica, and the ZNet network. After this event, the anarchist writer Andrej Grubacic asked: "Do we really want to create a movement that will resemble a cocktail party in the lounge of the Plaza São Rafael Hotel in Porto Alegre? Do we want a movement dominated by middle-aged bureaucrats wearing Palestinian scarves" (Grubacic 2003, p. 1; see also Klein 2003).

In other words, there is a natural class critique of the WSF, given that the political stance of many activists is more radical than that of the NGOs, progressive professionals, academics, funders, and other civil society representatives who wield more weight at the event and in its planning. Many, however, would rebut that at least, to its credit, the WSF is not imposing a political "line" or litmus tests on the various ideological groupings. Yet others object that this too is a fatal weakness, leading to an overall inability of a global progressive community to cohere behind a common political perspective and platform (hence the Porto Alegre Manifesto and Bamako Appeal were generated by leading leftist intellectuals including Samir Amin).

Following discussion of the WSF-style network and its application to transnational eco-social justice issues and constituencies, an interrogation of ideological orientations within and around the WSF – as was evident at the 2007 global meeting in Nairobi – allows us to consider whether the Social Forum politics has a future at a time when there is an urgent need for countervailing power and ideology from the left, to take advantage of opportunities offered by the crisis of capitalism.

The WSF as Network Form

What is surely the main accomplishment of the WSF is the construction of dialogical spaces. These spaces might ultimately support ideological, analytical, strategic, and even tactical convergence between far-flung movements that span the globe.

Indeed, the Social Forum network is potentially a means by which the "globaliza-tion of people" can become real, a genuine counterpoint to the "globalization of capital." In the process, Michael Hardt and Antonio Negri (2004, pp. xii–xiii) insist that their new category, "the *multitude*" of oppressed people (as distinct from the "masses"), might also "be conceived as a network: an open expansive network in which all differences can be expressed freely and equally, a network that provides the means of encounter so that we can work and live in common." Again, ideally, the network form provides "the model for an absolutely democratic organization that corresponds to the dominant forms of economic and social production, and is also the most powerful weapon against the ruling power structure" (ibid, p. 85).

As Helmut Anheier and Hagai Katz (2004, pp. 207–208) put it, "global civil soci-ety is a very relational, 'networky' phenomenon" drawing upon "interconnected and multilayered social space," "chains of interaction," and "horizontal relations" and harking back to Manuel Castells' analysis, providing new opportunities for "decen-tralised concentration where a multiplicity of interconnected tasks take place in different sites" (see also Taylor 2004). According to Hardt and Negri (2004, p. 135), the challenge is "to communicate and act in common while remaining internally dif-ferent." Whereas previously, dissenters were divided along sectoral, geographical, and other lines, "today network movements are able to address all of [the grievances] simultaneously," in part because many "target neoliberal globalisation as the source of their poverty" (ibid).

In that sense, internationalist progressive networking traditions that some WSF strategists and allied intellectuals draw upon took their modern form with the rise of Zapatismo solidarity from 1994 (when Mayan Indians from Chiapas, Mexico, revolted against local oppression and the World Trade Organization), and in the North, the Seattle WTO protest of 1999. Others would go to earlier periods, such as slavery-abolition campaigning (albeit with emotional paternalism and indeed powered by British capital's competitive drive), which continued into the twentieth century with pressure against King Leopold's plunder of the then Belgian Congo. Often while exiled in the capitals of the colonial powers, the African continent's nationalist movements forged ties during the twentieth century, in the process estab-lishing newly empowered relations with Northern critics of colonialism, apartheid, and racism. Victorious mass African movements against colonialism and imperial adventurism, stretching from the 1950s Kenyan Mau Mau and Nkrumah's Ghanaian visions to the liberation of South Africa in 1994, inspired leftists and anti-racists – as did a variety of 1960s and 1970s anti-colonial and anti-imperial solidarity movements ranging from Vietnam to Chile to Mozambique.

In reestablishing these connections, the WSF does not represent a brand new mode of politics, although it did provide an opportunity for grassroots militants to break from a sometimes ossified 1980s–1990s mold of nongovernmental, "devel-opmental" activism and to turn their gaze to global norms and processes. Indeed, the network form of organizing has allowed profound critiques and strategies aimed at overthrowing existing power relations to emanate from cross-border coalitions of activists working sector by sector. International solidarity carefully pursued with respect and understanding is a crucial component of this process, as suggested by experiences in various progressive transnational sectoral networks, such as land (Via

Campesino), health care (International People's Health Movement), free schooling (Global Campaign for Education), water (the People's World Water Forum), climate change (Climate Justice Now!), debt (Jubilee South), democratic development finance (World Bank Bonds Boycott), and trade (Our World is Not for Sale!).

The WSF is a site where a variety of such networks can run events and draw in new organizations. There are roughly three dozen categories into which these networks fit, divided into three types: political movements (a very broad category); traditional and cross-sectoral civil society movements; and issue-based civil society movements (see Table 23.1).

Table 23.1 Typology of World Social Forum movements

Political movements for social change
    Political movements/parties representing values/ideas of social democracy, nationalism, socialism, autonomism, and anarchism

Traditional and cross-sectoral civil society movements
    Labor (including unemployed movements, migration, and workplace health/safety)
    Women (including a variety of gender issues)
    Youth (including children)
    Anti-war (including arms sales, nuclear weapons, and land mines)
    Anti-racism (dating to abolition)
    Minority rights and ethnic
    Civil rights
    Democracy (including transparency/corruption)
    Consumer
    Indigenous rights
    Human rights
    Sexual identity
    Disability rights
    Cultural (art/music/literature/crafts/video)
    Religious
    Solidarity
    Elder rights

Issue-based civil society movements
    Finance/debt/aid/investment
    Trade
    Economic subsectors (including recuperated factories)
    Corporate disempowerment and anti-consumerism
    Land/agriculture/forestry/fisheries
    Housing/urban access rights
    Water (including irrigation, groundwater, dams and rivers, household access, and sanitation)
    Energy (including global warming, pollution, and household access)
    Health (including treatment)
    Food/nutrition
    Social security
    Education
    Other environmental movements (including toxics, nuclear, mining, marine)
    Media
    Policing/prisons
    Information/ICT

What, though, are the core characteristics that make these transnational networking opportunities so appropriate to the current conjuncture? As James Ferguson (2006, p. 108) asks:

> Can we learn to conceive, theoretically and politically, of a 'grassroots' that would be not local, communal, and authentic, but worldly, well-connected, and opportunistic? Are we ready for social movements that fight not 'from below' but 'across,' using their 'foreign policy' to fight struggles not against 'the state' but against that hydra-headed transnational apparatus of banks, international agencies, and market institutions through which contemporary capitalist domination functions?

To answer this question requires assessing whether coherence is growing within the WSF movement, toward social movements "fighting across" national borders and against transnational capital and multilateral institutions. A debate precisely along this line took place at the WSF in Nairobi, among other indicators of logistical and political difficulties that seemed to be debilitating.

The World Social Forum "at the Crossroads"

The divergent ways forward for global justice movement political strategy were evident at the 2007 WSF in Nairobi. One of the most influential commentators and activists, Walden Bello (2007, p. 1), found the Nairobi WSF to be:

> Disappointing, since its politics was so diluted and big business interests linked to the Kenyan ruling elite were so brazen in commercializing it ... The WSF is at a crossroads ... many long-standing participants in the Forum are [now] asking themselves: Is the WSF still the most appropriate vehicle for the new stage in the struggle of the global justice and peace movement? Or, having fulfilled its historic function of aggregating and linking the diverse counter-movements spawned by global capitalism, is it time for the WSF to fold up its tent and give way to new modes of global organization of resistance and transformation?

From January 20–25, 2007, the 60,000 registered participants heard triumphalist radical rhetoric and yet, too, witnessed persistent defeats for social justice causes – especially within the WSF's own processes. Many of these were aired at the leading African political webzine, www.pambazuka.org (2007). They included local grievances of activists that remained unaddressed: colonial-era land edicts and policies that dispossessed their communities, the impact of mining and extraction activities on the environment and human livelihoods, discriminatory policies by successive governments that have guaranteed the stubborn survival of pre-colonial conditions of poverty and underdevelopment among many pastoralist and minority communities, the arrogant disregard for the concerns raised by Samburu women raped over the years by British soldiers dispatched on military exercises in those Kenyan communities, and tensions persisting with neocolonial-era settler farmers and indigenous Kenyan comprador businessmen in hiving off thousands of hectares of land while the pastoralists and minority communities are targets of state terror, evictions, and denunciations.

Firoze Manji, the Kenyan director of *Pambazuka* (2007), argued: "This event had all the features of a trade fair – those with greater wealth had more events in the calendar, larger (and more comfortable) spaces, more propaganda – and therefore a larger voice." Such sobering observations were also reflected in a statement by the Social Movements Assembly at a January 24, 2007, rally of more than 2,000 people: "We denounce tendencies towards commercialization, privatization and militarization of the WSF space. Hundreds of our sisters and brothers who welcomed us to Nairobi have been excluded because of high costs of participation" (*Pambazuka* 2007). Conflict areas included the arrest of a dozen low-income people who wanted to get into the event, protests to forcibly open the gates, and the destruction of the notoriously repressive Kenyan interior minister's makeshift restaurant that had monopolized key space within the Kasarani Stadium's grounds. Moreover, the Kenya Airports Authority systematically diverted incoming visitors to hotels, away from home stays (2,000 of which were arranged but only 18 actually materialized due to diversions). Setting these flaws aside, consider a deeper political tension: for Onyang Oloo, "These social movements, including dozens in Kenya, want to see the WSF being transformed into a space for organizing and mobilizing against the nefarious forces of international finance capital, neoliberalism and all its local neo-colonial and comprador collaborators" (*Pambazuka* 2007).

Wither WSF Politics?

Is there a political orientation within the WSF that would prove capable of meeting such expectations? WSF networking has tended toward a strategic formula that aims, first, to build durable and relatively democratic mass movements informed by internationalism yet perhaps paradoxically often aiming – in concrete campaigning terms – at what Walden Bello (2002) has called "deglobalization" (of capital), which in turn permits a "decommodification" of essential goods and services and a "destratification" of society such that access is based on "rights" or even a "commons" approach.

To illustrate, South Africans and other activists have had dramatic victories in deglobalizing the Trade Related Intellectual Property Rights regime, by demanding that decommodified generic anti-retroviral medicines to fight HIV/Aids – instead of branded monopoly-patented drugs (which in the late 1990s had cost $15,000 per person per year) – be provided to all who access public clinics in a destratified manner, not dependent on means testing or other social divisions. The victories that by 2009 permitted 750,000 South Africans access to HIV/Aids medicines would not have been possible without the kind of international networking and solidarity that is exemplified in WSF processes. In South Africa and elsewhere, similar struggles are underway to deglobalize food (especially given the genetically modified organisms threat from transnational corporations), to halt biopiracy, and to send water and energy privatizers back to France and the United States.

More than this, the South African decommodification agenda entails struggles to turn basic needs into genuine human rights including free anti-retroviral medicines to fight HIV/Aids (hence disempowering "Big Pharma"); 50 litres of free water per person per day (hence ridding Africa of Suez and other water privatizers); 1 kWh of free electricity for each individual every day (hence reorienting energy resources from export-oriented mining and smelting to basic-needs consumption); extensive land reform (hence deemphasizing cash cropping and export-oriented plantations); prohibitions on service disconnections and evictions; free education (hence halting the General Agreement on Trade in Services); and the like. A free Basic Income Grant allowance of $15 per month is even advocated by churches, NGOs, and trade unions. All such services should be universal (open to all, no matter the income levels) and, to the extent feasible, financed through higher prices that penalize luxury consumption.

The broader goals in this case and most others are to link movements, enhance consciousness, develop the issues, and build democratic organizational forms and momentum. This potentially unifying agenda could serve as a basis for wide-scale social change, in the manner that Gosta Esping-Andersen (1991) has discussed with respect to Scandinavian social policy. Beyond the issue-by-issue strategies that stress deglobalization of capital, decommodification, and destratification arrived at through internationalist solidarity, these networks are also sites for debates over broader political programs.

Global justice movements at the heart of the WSF have not, though, found it that easy to establish any consensus, given the divergent tendencies between socialism and autonomism. For example, in early 2005 at the WSF in Porto Alegre, 19 well-known movement intellectuals and activists gathered to produce a draft of "Twelve proposals for another possible world" (abridged in Table 23.2).

It can well be argued that these proposals risk the "top-down" danger of imposing programmatic ideas on fluid movements and campaigns (Bond 2005). Reflecting the same tendency, a much longer effort along these lines was made by Samir Amin and Francois Houtart at the January 2006 WSF: the Bamako Appeal. An alternative approach to this would have been to permit the programs to emerge from struggle, as they always have. In any case, the ideological diversity of the WSF has not permitted sufficient clarity on such matters.

In South Africa, the Centre for Civil Society has hosted several debates on this question, with at least four varying points of view emerging (CCS 2006). While the Bamako Appeal combined the traditions of socialism, anti-racism/colonialism, and national development – and the leader of the Organization of African Trade Union Unity, Hassan Sunmonu (also a WSF International Council member), found "a lot of merit in that Bamako Appeal that we can use to transform the lives of ourselves, our organizations and our peoples" (CCS 2006) – it has been contested by Franco Barchiesi, Heinrich Bohmke, Prishani Naidoo, and Ahmed Veriava (2006) on the grounds that it is too "last century" in tone and content and overly reflects the mutation of the WSF from an arena of encounter for local social movements into an organized network of experts, academics, and NGO practitioners. To Barchiesi and others, the Bamako Appeal is seen to be part of "the WSF elite's cold institutional and technicist soup, occasionally warmed up by some hints of tired poeticism ... [providing] little nourishment for local subjectivities whose daily responses to neoliberalism face more urgent needs to turn everyday survival into sustained

Table 23.2 Twelve proposals for another possible world[a]

1	Cancel the external debt of Southern countries
2	Implement international taxes on financial transactions (most notably the Tobin tax on speculative capital), on direct foreign investments, on consolidated profit from multinationals, on weapon trade, and on activities accompanied by large greenhouse effect gas emissions
3	Progressively dismantle all forms of fiscal, juridical, and banking paradises
4	All inhabitants of this planet must have the right to be employed, to social protection and retirement/pension, respecting equal rights between men and women
5	Promote all forms of equitable trade, reject all free-trade agreements and laws proposed by the WTO, and put in motion mechanisms allowing a progressive upward equalization of social and environmental norms
6	Guarantee the right for all countries to alimentary sovereignty and security by promoting peasant, rural agriculture
7	Forbid all type of patenting of knowledge on living beings (human, animal, or vegetal) as well as any privatization of common goods for humanity, particularly water
8	Fight by means of public policies against all kinds of discrimination, sexism, xenophobia, anti-Semitism, and racism. Fully recognize the political, cultural, and economic rights of indigenous populations
9	Take urgent steps to end the destruction of the environment and the threat of severe climate changes due to the greenhouse effect, resulting from the proliferation of individual transportation and the excessive use of non-renewable energy sources
10	Demand the dismantling of all foreign military bases and the removal of troops on all countries, except when operating under explicit mandate of the United Nations, especially for Iraq and Palestine
11	Guarantee the right to access information and the right to inform, for/by all citizens
12	Reform and deeply democratize international institutions by making sure human, economic, social, and cultural rights prevail

[a]The 19 signatories – regrettably 18 men and just 1 woman – were Aminata Traoré, Adolfo Pérez Esquivel, Eduardo Galeano, José Saramago, François Houtart, Boaventura de Sousa Santos, Armand Mattelart, Roberto Savio, Riccardo Petrella, Ignacio Ramonet, Bernard Cassen, Samir Amin, Atilio Boron, Samuel Ruiz Garcia, Tariq Ali, Frei Betto, Emir Sader, Walden Bello, and Immanuel Wallerstein.

confrontations with an increasingly repressive state" (ibid, p. 1). Barchiesi et al. prefer to praise the "powerful undercurrent of informality in the WSF's proceedings [which] reveals the persistence of horizontal communication between movements ... based ... in the life strategies of their participants" (ibid, p. 5).

A third position on WSF politics is the classical socialist, party-building approach favored by Soweto Electricity Crisis Committee founder Trevor Ngwane and other revolutionary organizers. Replying to both Amin and the autonomist critique at the July workshop, Ngwane was concerned about reformist projects that "make us blind to recognize the struggles of ordinary people," but recognized that "militancy alone at the local level and community level will not in itself answer questions of class and questions of power" (CCS 2006). For that a self-conscious socialist cadre is needed, and in this regard the WSF is taken to represent a critical site to transcend localist political upsurges.

A fourth position seeks the twenty-first century's anti-capitalist "manifesto" in the existing social, labor, and environmental movements that are already engaged in the transnational social justice struggle. The WSF's greatest potential – so far unrealized – is the possibility of linking dozens of radical movements in various sectors. At present, though, at each WSF the activists seem to disappear into their own workshops: silos with few or no interconnections. Hence, before a Bamako Appeal or any other manifesto is parachuted into the WSF, it is necessary for activists to compile their existing grievances, analyses, strategies, and tactics. Sometimes these are simple demands, but often they are also articulated as sectoral manifestos.

Lest too much energy is spent on these political scuffles at the expense of ongoing struggle, consider, in closing, the spirit articulated by Ngwane in a Nairobi debate with WSF founder Chico Whitaker:

> Ordinary working class and poor people need and create and have a movement of resistance and struggle. They also need and create and have spaces for that movement to breathe and develop. The real question is what place will the WSF have in that reality. What space will there be for ordinary working class and poor people? Who will shape and drive and control the movement? Will it be a movement of NGO's and individual luminaries creating space for themselves to speak of their concern for the poor? Will it be undermined by collaboration with capitalist forces? I think what some of us saw happening in Nairobi posed some of these questions sharply and challenged some of the answers coming from many (but not all) of the prominent NGOs and luminaries in the WSF. (*Pambazuka* 2007)

References

Anand, A., Escobar, A., Sen, J., and Waterman, P. (eds) (2003). *Are Other Worlds Possible? The Past, Present, and Futures of the World Social Forum*, New Delhi, Viveka.

Anheier, H., and Katz, H. (2004). Network approaches to global civil society. In H. Anheier, M. Glasius, and M. Kaldor (eds) *Global Civil Society 2004/05* (pp. 206–221), London, Sage.

Barchiesi, F., Bohmke, H., Naidoo, P., and Veriava, A. (2006). Does Bamako appeal? The World Social Forum versus the life strategies of the subaltern. Unpublished paper, Workshop on the World Social Forum, Centre for Civil Society, University of KwaZulu-Natal, Durban.

Bello, W. (2002). *Deglobalization*, London, Zed Books.

Bello, W. (2007). The Forum at the crossroads. Foreign Policy in Focus commentary, www.fpif.org/fpiftxt/4196

Blau, J., and Karides, M. (eds) (2008). *The World and US Social Forums: A Better World is Possible and Necessary*, Amsterdam, Brill.

Bond, P. (2005). Discussing the Porto Alegre Manifesto. *ZNet Commentary*, www.zmag.org/sustainers/content/2005-02/22bond.cfm

Centre for Civil Society (CCS). (2006). *CCS WIRED*. University of KwaZulu-Natal, Durban.

de Sousa Santos, B. (2004). *Globalizing Resistance: The State of Struggle*, London, Pluto Press.

Esping-Andersen, G. (1991). *The Three Worlds of Welfare Capitalism*, Princeton, NJ, Princeton University Press.

Ferguson, J. (2006). *Global Shadows*, Durham, NC, Duke University Press.

Fisher, W., and Ponniah, T. (eds) (2003). *Another World is Possible: Popular Alternatives to Globalization at the World Social Forum*, London, Zed.

Grubacic, A. (2003). Life after Social Forums: New radicalism and the questions of attitude towards Social Forums. www.nadir.org/nadir/initiativ/agp/free/wsf/life-after-sf.htm

Hardt, M., and Negri, A. (2004). *Multitude*, New York, Penguin.

Klein, N. (2003). The hijacking of the World Social Forum. www.nologo.org

Pambazuka. (2007). Reports on the World Social Forum. www.pambazuka.org/blogs/wsf2007/

Sen, J. (2004). *World Social Forum: Challenging Empires*, New Delhi, Viveka Foundation.

Sen, J., Kumar, M., Bond, P., and Waterman, P. (eds) (2007). *A Political Programme for the World Social Forum? Democracy, Substance and Debate in the Bamako Appeal and the Global Justice Movements*, New Delhi/Durban, CACIM/CCS.

Taylor, R. (ed.) (2004). *Creating a Better World: Interpreting Global Civil Society*, Bloomfield, CT, Kumarian Press.

Index

Breinigsville, PA USA
21 May 2010
238396BV00005B/108/P